Civil Jury
Trials

Civil Jury Trials

Second Edition

Andrew M Hajducki QC

Avizandum Publishing Ltd
Edinburgh
2006

Published by
Avizandum Publishing Ltd
58 Candlemaker Row
Edinburgh EH1 2QE

First published 1998
2nd edition   2006

ISBN 1-904968-00-7
       978-1-904968-00-9

British Library Cataloguing in Publication Data
A catalogue record for this book is available from the British Library

Typeset by AFS Image Setters Ltd, Glasgow
Printed and bound in Great Britain by The Bath Press

Contents

6   Special cause   45

General considerations – Difficult questions of fact – Difficult questions of law – Difficult questions of fact and law – Difficulties in assessing damages – Claims lacking in specification – Averments of doubtful relevancy – Criminal convictions relied upon – Unusual onus of proof – Several grounds of action – Two different forms of inquiry upon same facts – A third party is brought in – Interest is claimed – Delay in raising or prosecuting action – Defender insured – Miscellaneous factors which might constitute special cause – Miscellaneous factors held not to constitute special cause – Defamation actions – Actions of reduction

7   Tactical and practical considerations   73

Introduction – Liability – Quantum of damages – Reasons why defender might opt for jury trial – Defamation actions

Part Three: Initial Procedure

8   To the closing of the record   83

Raising the action – Principles of pleading – Defences – Subsequent procedure – Remits from sheriff court – Remits to sheriff court

9   The allowance of issues   93

Deciding further procedure – The pleadings – Form of hearing – Grant or refusal of issues – Expenses – Trial without issues

10   Issues   99

Generally – General and particular issues – Where multiple issues required – Where there are several parties – Issues in particular types of action – The schedule of damages

11   Counter-issues   108

Generally – Where counter-issues appropriate – Where counter-issues not appropriate

12   Lodging and approval of issues   112

Lodging of issues – Lodging of counter-issues – Approval of issues and counter-issues – Subsequent amendment of issues

13   Altering the mode of inquiry   117

After amendment of the record – On a material change of circumstances – Where Inner House has laid down the mode of proof

14   Preparing for the trial diet   120

Allocation of a diet – Place of diet – Citation of jurors – Qualification and eligibility of jurors – Excusal of jurors – Offences by jurors – Assessors – Productions – Witnesses – Skilled witnesses – Demonstrative evidence – Evidence on commission – Evidence via live television link – Agreeing the evidence – Other preparations for trial – Late settlement of actions

Part Four: The Trial

Part Five: Appeal and Review

24   Review of the verdict   213

Grounds of review – Misdirection by the presiding judge – Undue admission of evidence – Undue rejection of evidence – Verdict contrary to the evidence – Excess of damages – Inadequacy of damages – Res noviter venians ad notitiam – Other grounds essential to the justice of the cause – Third trials

25   Motions for a new trial   236

Enrolling a motion – Effect of enrolling for new trial – Objections to competency of application – Procedure where no objection to competency – Hearing of application – Disposal of application – Expenses – Alteration of mode of inquiry

26   Applications to enter verdicts on points reserved   243

Verdict on points reserved – Procedure – Hearing of application – Disposal of application

27   Appeals from the Inner House   245

Appendices

Foreword

It is a pleasure to welcome the second edition of Andrew Hajducki's valuable book on civil jury trials.

Until well into the 1970s civil jury trials were an everyday feature of life in Parliament House. Much of the time of the courts was taken up by debates in which defenders tried to prevent the allowance of issues for reasons such as the dimming of the memory of witnesses by the passage of time, the presence of difficult questions of mixed fact and law and, often, alleged problems of relevancy. By the 1980s the institution of civil jury trial, which had been moribund in the sheriff court, had been abolished in that court and had become almost unheard of in the Court of Session. By then there was a general feeling in the profession that judicial awards of damages had increased to realistic levels and were not subject to the uncertainties that attended the decisions of juries. The resurgence of interest in civil jury trial over the last ten years may reflect a changed perception on the part of the profession on that point.

Whatever the reason, the resurgence of civil jury trial has required the current generation of practitioners to master some of the forgotten arts of former times. That is why this textbook is both timely and necessary. It is an excellent work of reference. The author informs his readers as to the law and practice of jury trials, with extensive citation of authority, and sets the institution of jury trial in its historic context and in the context of practice in other jurisdictions. He also discusses all of the main controversies that have attended civil jury trial through the years and gives the reader excellent guidance on detailed practice points that are not, so far as I am aware, to be found in any other source.

This is a splendid example of a practitioners' textbook and I wish the author every success.

The Rt Hon Lord Gill
Parliament House

Preface

The strength of any legal institution can be assessed in the way in which it delivers justice to the public. In this respect the civil jury trial forms a valuable bridge between the way in which lawyers view the world and the needs and aspirations of those whom the system purports to serve, the ordinary man and woman on the mythical omnibus heading for Clapham, Morningside or whatever other destination one might choose. It is, therefore, perhaps not surprising that, in the eight years or so since the first edition of this work appeared, the renaissance of the Scottish civil jury has continued, much of the controversy and perceived hostility towards this venerable but still essential part of the machinery of civil justice in this country have largely evaporated, and it seems likely that a jury of twelve will continue to try issues in appropriate cases well into the reasonably foreseeable future. Since 1998 there have been many changes, both in practice and procedure, some of which have been reported, but much has not, leaving the modern law on the subject often undocumented and obscure. Robert Macfarlane, in his seminal book on the same subject published at the very beginning of Victoria's reign, stated that "to supply this deficiency is the object of the present volume. How far this has been accomplished is for others, not for me, to determine." The author would, in relation to this work, adopt the same sentiments.

In undertaking a book devoted to the subject of the civil jury in Scotland, it is inevitable that an author will rely heavily on the advice, knowledge and assistance of his friends and colleagues who practise in this area of the law. Although it is invidious to single out any particular individuals, particular thanks are given to Craig Allardyce, Roddy Dunlop, Nick Gardiner, Gerry Hanretty QC, Fiona Lake, Preston Lloyd, Robert Milligan, Andrew Smith QC and Gillian Wade, all of whom made contributions and, in the case of some, were unwise enough to volunteer to read over an earlier draft of the manuscript. The author also proffers sincere thanks to the Hon Lord Gill, Lord Justice-Clerk, who answered many questions and advised on many practical matters, to Neil Crighton WS who, in his capacity as Auditor of the Court of Session, discussed jury trial expenses with the author, to the librarian and staff of the Advocates' Library for their invariably cheerful requests for help in tracing arcane information and sources. It almost needs not saying that the author is indebted to Margaret Cherry of Avizandum for her enthusiasm in making this book materialise and for her unfailing forbearance in the face of an author who kept on wanting to add to the text. Finally, the author would like to dedicate this work to his children, Catherine, Kenneth and David, and to his wife Kate who, within the allotted time, answered the single question in the issue in the affirmative.

The author has attempted to state the law, practice and procedure of the civil jury trial in Scotland as at 1 March 2006, but more recent material has been added wherever possible. All errors and omissions remain his. There is the possibility that, as with any legal text, the book may quickly go out of date, and the author cannot anticipate what changes may occur in the future. Accordingly, a free open access online noter-up with details of all new case law, awards and changes in procedure or practice and articles on related topics of interest will be found on a dedicated website, appropriately named **civil-jurytrials.com**. Readers are invited to contribute to or comment on that site through the e-mail address given there.

Parliament House   *AMH*
Edinburgh
St David's Day, 2006

Table of statutes

Table of orders, rules and regulations

Table of cases

Chapter 1

The civil jury in Scotland: an overview

INTRODUCTION

1.01 This book is designed to cover the law and practice of the civil jury trial in Scotland. Those parts of our civil procedure which are common to all actions heard in the Court of Session and present no particular features peculiar to jury trial are either omitted or dealt with only briefly in passing. Echoing the words of the author of a previous book devoted to the subject[1], the present writer has not sought to revisit the ground covered by other more general works[2] and it has been his desire "to avoid, as inconsistent with the object of the work, all theoretical and speculative views and opinions . . . which have not yet received the sanction of practice, or the authority of the court".

1.02 Each year about two thousand reparation causes are set down for a hearing in the Court of Session and of this number a sizeable minority of personal injury actions[3] are allocated a diet for trial by jury rather than a proof before a Lord Ordinary. The vast majority of all personal injuries actions are settled prior to a court hearing and, in the case of actions in which issues have been allowed, only a handful actually run and require the jury to reach a verdict on liability or on the quantum of damages or both. Jury trials in actions involving defamation, false imprisonment and malicious prosecution are rarer and, in actions of reduction, unheard of in modern times. Nevertheless the influence of the civil jury in modern practice is far greater than mere statistics would suggest, even if that influence is not always welcomed, and the long-

---

1 Robert Macfarlane, *The Practice of the Court of Session in Jury Causes* (1837).
2 The best modern guides to the practice of the Court of Session are *Green's Annotated Rules of the Court of Session* (ed Sheriff Nigel Morrison QC) (1996) and published as part of the Parliament House Book, and *Court of Session Practice* (ed Lord Macfadyen) (2005); other general works are Mackay, *Manual of Practice in the Court of Session* (2nd edn, 1893); Maclaren, *Court of Session Practice* (1916); Thompson and Middleton, *Manual of Court of Session Procedure* (1937); and Maxwell, *The Practice of the Court of Session* (1980) but, to a greater or lesser extent, all of these latter works are now seriously dated.
3 In a typical month (February 2004) 25 per cent of these actions involved an accident at work, 15 per cent a road traffic accident, 9 per cent medical negligence and the remainder were miscellaneous actions including those involving an industrial disease. In about 10 to 15 per cent of all personal injury actions issues were being allowed.

held view that a single judge is in some way better equipped to deal with liability and the quantification of damages is no longer as prevalent as it once was. Only a decade or so ago the civil jury in Scotland appeared to be facing inexorable decline and eventual extinction, but there would now appear to be a new-found faith in the value of the involvement of lay persons in the administration of justice and, increasingly, a perception that juries are in touch with the values of the common man and woman. For better or for worse, the civil jury system is now seen as an integral part of the Scots legal system and likely to remain with us, whether in its present or a modified form, well into the twenty-first century.

SCOPE OF THIS WORK

1.03 In this chapter an overview is given of the law, practice and procedure of the jury trial, its sources, general principles, perceived strengths and weaknesses, while subsequent chapters deal with the history of the institution in Scotland, the arguments for and against the civil jury, the impact of human rights legislation, and an outline of the experience of the civil jury in other jurisdictions. Other parts of the book deal with the question of whether or not an action should be tried by a jury, the procedure to be adopted before the trial, the conduct of the trial from the empanelling of the jury to the application of the verdict and the appeal and review procedures that can be used to challenge the verdict. Appendices deal with styles for the various documents peculiar to civil jury trials in Scotland, a model opening speech and some recent jury awards. Throughout the book it should be emphasised that all references to "he" should be construed to cover both sexes unless the context dictates otherwise, and that references to "counsel" include members of the Faculty of Advocates, solicitor advocates having a right of audience in the Court of Session, and (although the situation has rarely arisen in a civil trial) party litigants.

SOURCES OF PRESENT-DAY LAW AND PRACTICE

1.04 The main sources of the present-day practice and procedure relating to the civil jury in Scotland are the Court of Session Act 1988, the Rules of the Court of Session 1994, and a substantial body of case law and practice built up over the two centuries that have elapsed since the return of the institution to this country.

Statutory sources

1.05 The 1988 Act deals principally with substantive matters such as the availability of jury trial, the summoning, selection and management of the jury, the return of the verdict (sections 9–17) and the way in which the verdict can be reviewed (sections 29–31). Although mainly a consolidating measure, the Act followed on from a Scottish Law Commission report on the reform of the procedure and administration of the Court of Session[4], and its provisions in relation to jury trials were intended to reflect and clarify existing practice by placing all the statutory provisions together and by repealing virtually all of the previous legislation applicable to civil juries. The exception to this is found in the limited number of other statutory provisions which deal with miscellaneous points concerning trials, such as the limitation of actions, contempt of court and the composition of the jury, and these statutes, which in the main apply throughout the United Kingdom, are referred to in the text as appropriate.

The Rules of Court

1.06 The main procedural matters relating to civil jury trials are now to be found in the present Rules of the Court of Session[5], a consolidating and tidying-up measure made under the powers granted to the court[6]. These Rules have subsequently been extensively amended on a piecemeal basis and form the backbone of present practice. The Rules are divided into Chapters, two of which are specifically relevant to the subject-matter of this work, namely Chapters 37 and 39 which deal, respectively, with jury trials and applications for a new trial. The power of the court to relieve a party from the failure to comply with any of these rules is dealt with in **1.14** below. A number of prescribed forms are appended to the Rules and these include forms for pleadings and other parts of the process and for summoning witnesses and jurors to attend court. In addition to these are the Practice Notes (sometimes erroneously referred to as "Notices") which are, in effect, administrative directions relating to the manner in which the Rules are to be applied or how an administrative requirement may be dealt with; they are not intended to amend or supplant any rule.

Case law

1.07 There exists a considerable body of reported case law dating back to the very first jury trial heard in 1816 and which reflects contemporary judicial interpretation of both the statutory provisions and the Rules of Court and the practice of the courts in relation to jury trial as it developed over two cen-

---

4 Scottish Law Commission Report No 111 (March 1988).
5 Act of Sederunt (Rules of the Court of Session) 1994 (SI 1994/1443) as amended; these are individually referred to in the present text as "rule 1.0" etc.
6 Court of Session Act 1988, ss 5, 6.

turies. Cases are found in the main series of reports[7] and in the specialist reports such as Murray's Jury Court Reports[8] and the Reparation Law Reports, the latter now including notes of jury decisions and awards. Care should be taken when some of the earlier cases are being considered since many of them dealt with matters which depended on peculiar and specific provisions which are no longer effectual, or to practice which is no longer followed, and, where it is felt that such case law has been superseded or is of little contemporary relevance, it is not referred to in this work. Some cases are referred to in note form only, whether in the Notes section of the Scots Law Times or, more recently, in Green's Weekly Digest and, where such cases are not otherwise reported, citations to these Notes are given. From 1 January 2005, unified neutral citation of all Court of Session cases in which written opinions have been issued has been introduced and all cases from that date onwards are referred to as, e.g. *McFarlane v Thain* [2005] CSOH 22, 2005 SLT 221, the report appearing after the neutral citation which must always be given[9]. All cases in which a written judgment was issued since 1998 are now to be found online at www.scotcourts.gov.uk and a full printout from this source should be tendered as an authority rather than the Green's Weekly Digest note. Where no written judgment was issued and the only reference (if any) to a decision appears in the minute of proceedings, the symbol ★ appears after the date of the judgment or interlocutor. Jury awards tend to be reported on a somewhat haphazard basis, particularly before 1997, and thereafter most, but not all, appear in note form in the Reparation Law Reports, whose editor is dependent on contributors, including counsel and agents who were involved in those cases. To a limited extent contemporary Scottish criminal law cases have been cited in this work when appropriate but only insofar as they have any relevance to specific matters concerning jurors or trial procedures and where they are not based on specific provisions of criminal procedure or law which have no parallel in civil causes.

Practice of the courts

1.08   Since the earliest days of civil jury trials in Scotland contemporary practice has been noted and reported either in case law or in textbooks dealing with Court of Session procedure, and in the omnibus codifying Act of Sederunt of 1913 several lengthy sections were devoted to contemporary practice.

---

7 With precedence being given to reports in Session Cases: see *McGowan v Summit at Lloyds* 2002 SC 636 at 660G and Practice Note No 5 of 2004; similar precedence is to be given to the Scots Law Times reports over those in the Reparation Law Reports: *Wells v Stenhouse* 2000 GWD 21-828.
8 Referred to as "1 Mur 1" etc and found in five volumes dated from 1815 to 1830.
9 Practice Notes Nos 2 and 5 of 2004.

The codifying Act (which is mirrored in the texts of Maclaren and Thompson and Middleton) is no longer in force but many of its provisions are, to a greater or lesser extent, still of practical use where neither supplanted nor modified by later practice, statute or the current Rules. There has, however, been something of a dearth of information available to practitioners as to the actual practice of the courts when faced with the day-to-day administration of justice as it concerns civil jury causes and so, to this end, a number of contemporary examples of practice sanctioned and followed by the courts have been included in this work. Where such examples are the result of rulings by the presiding judge, which were not given in writing, they are given in the form of, for example, *Livingstone v Hardie*, Lord Nimmo Smith, 15 January 2003★ (the date referring to the day on which the ruling was given or, if not known, the date on which the jury delivered its verdict), and the invaluable source of such information has been the counsel or agents involved in these cases. In addition to these sources, articles in legal journals have, from time to time, discussed individual cases and procedural matters which have arisen in them and these are referred to in this work with an appropriate citation.

BRIEF OUTLINE OF PROCEDURE

1.09 In Scotland trial by jury in civil causes is now available only in the Court of Session and is limited to actions which fall within certain defined categories. These categories are actions of damages for personal injuries including those resulting in death, actions of defamation, actions arising out of delinquency and quasi-delinquency (i.e. delict or negligence) or actions of reduction on specified grounds. Section 11 of the 1988 Act provides that there is a *statutory right* to a jury trial in all of the above actions and a decision as to whether or not to exercise this right has to be taken at the time that the action is raised or within a short period of time thereafter, whether or not the action is one to which the new Chapter 43 procedure for personal injury actions applies.

1.10 Unless the parties agree to a proof or proof before answer, the right to a jury trial can only be attacked if one of the parties (usually, but not necessarily, the defender) can persuade the court at a motion roll or procedure roll hearing that there is special cause for a proof or proof before answer based on the individual circumstances of that case and that, accordingly, trial by jury would not be appropriate. Once the court has determined that the case will be tried by a jury issues have to be lodged. These are formal documents in which the pursuer puts the question of liability to the jury as well as a blank schedule for the calculation of his damages. If appropriate the defender can put a question or questions to the jury in the similar form of a counter-issue and these questions can relate to liability, whether sole or apportioned, between the pursuer and defender or any third party, or defences such as *volenti* in a personal injury action or *veritas* in a defamation action. Once the issues have been approved (and, if necessary, adjusted) by the court a diet of trial is fixed, a jury precept issued and a panel of 36 potential jurors resident in Edinburgh and the Lothians, is summoned to hear the action.

1.11 At the trial diet a jury of 12 members (as opposed to the 15 members of a Scottish criminal jury) is duly balloted and empanelled and proceedings then commence with an opening speech from counsel for the pursuer in the English fashion followed by the leading of his evidence. At the close of the pursuer's case the defender's counsel has the opportunity to make an opening speech and to lead his evidence in the same manner. After this the parties make their closing speeches, in which they summarise their respective cases and invite the jury to find for their client. A motion can be made to have the case (or the defence contained in the counter-issue) taken away from the jury in a procedure analogous to the "no case to answer" at a criminal trial. Following the closing speeches the presiding judge then charges the jury and directs it in law but neither he, nor counsel, is permitted to give the jury any detailed guidance on what sums it may award by way of solatium or other non-patrimonial loss. After the judge's charge the jury retires to consider the questions posed in the issues and counter-issues and after its deliberations it returns to deliver its verdict in open court. The verdict can be unanimous or by a bare majority, and will include, where appropriate, a quantification of the damages to be awarded, any deduction to be made in respect of contributory negligence and any apportionment of blame between two or more defenders. The verdict then has to be formally given effect so that diligence can be done upon it. This is done at a subsequent diet by the presiding judge pronouncing an appropriate decree which will include other matters such as expenses, the certification of witnesses and the application of interest to the sums awarded by the jury.

1.12 Any party dissatisfied with any interlocutor of the court, such as the allowance of issues or the form in which they are approved, amendments to the pleadings and the application of the verdict, can appeal such interlocutors to the Inner House in the usual manner. However, any attack on the procedural propriety of the trial or ruling by the presiding judge or any challenge to the decision of the jury on the basis of the verdict being contrary to the evidence or any other specified ground is made by the lodging of a motion for a new trial. If this motion is granted by the Inner House after a hearing on the summar roll a new trial is ordered at which all matters in contention are again aired before a new jury whose verdict can then be challenged in the same manner theoretically *ad infinitum*. Where the challenge to the verdict is on the basis of an excess or inadequacy of damages, however, the new trial is restricted to quantum of damages only but there is no power to allow the Inner House to substitute its own quantification for that of a jury. A further right of appeal against a decision to grant or refuse a new trial lies from the Inner House to the House of Lords.

Necessity to obey procedural codes

1.13 The basis of all civil litigation is that it should be conducted in such a manner as to be consistent with justice between the parties and the right to a fair trial in terms of Article 6 of the European Convention on Human Rights[10]. In the past it was often remarked that jury trial is a formal mode of litigation and, since no laxity should be allowed to enter into the procedure, any divergence from the established rules must usually result in prejudice to one party or another because the peculiar characteristics of jury trials make it difficult where prejudice occurs to do anything to redress the balance[11]. It could, however, be equally strongly suggested that since the purpose of jury trial (and indeed all forms of civil litigation) is to ensure that justice is both done and seen to be done (whether in terms of Article 6 or at common law) then the mere fact that there is a certain formality about the procedure should not obscure this fundamental principle and that the essential test which should be applied is that of whether or not the procedure to be followed, particularly if any irregularity has occurred, is fair and would achieve justice between the parties.

Equitable relief from failure to comply with Rules

1.14 Within this context, there is a general equitable power contained in the present rule 2.1 which provides that the court may relieve a party from the consequences of a failure to comply with the provisions of the Rules when it can be shown that such a failure was due to mistake, oversight or such other excusable cause and will be subject to such conditions, if any, as the court thinks fit[12], and that the court may accordingly pronounce such interlocutor as it thinks fit to enable the cause to proceed as if the failure to comply had not occurred[13]. It is a matter for the discretion of the court, but it should be borne in mind that "procedural rules, being the machinery of the law, should facilitate rather than obstruct legal rights"[14]. The equitable power can be invoked where a party has, for instance, overlooked the significance of a rule, forgotten that it might be applicable in the circumstances of a case or even acted in com-

---

10 Human Rights Act 1998, s 6; for a fuller discussion see chapter 3 below.
11 *Lawrie v Glasgow Corporation* 1952 SC 361 at 366; *Muir v London & North Eastern Railway Co* 1946 SC 216.
12 Rule 2.1(1).
13 Rule 2.1(2).
14 Temporary Judge J G Reid QC in *Jackson v McDougall* 16 June 2004, para [17], 2004 GWD 21-450.

plete ignorance of a specific rule[15], but cannot be invoked in a situation where the failure to comply was deliberate[16]. Rule 2.1 can be used in all situations where there would otherwise be no specific provision for relief, for example where there is a provision allowing for the late lodging of issues[17], but it can be applied only where a breach of the Rules of Court has occurred and not to circumvent any specific statutory provision, for example, a provision contained in the Court of Session Act 1988. Likewise rule 2.1 cannot be used in a situation where the instance has fallen[18] or where parties have agreed to a particular course involving a departure from the Rules since they would then be personally barred from challenging the same[19].

SOME ARGUMENTS FOR AND AGAINST JURY TRIALS

1.15   Finally in this introductory chapter, it is worth considering some of the arguments which are frequently put forward in favour of and against the civil jury in Scotland. Few other institutions in the Scottish legal system appear to have engendered such sustained criticism, comment or enthusiasm as the civil jury trial and this is reflected both in the pamphlets issued by its detractors and proponents in the early days and in the writings and submissions of later writers. The matter has been examined by several commissions and committees and has been subject to repeated scrutiny by the legislature, the Inner House and the House of Lords and, at the end of the day, the arguments put forward both for the retention and the abolition of the institution have been remarkably similar to those advanced in other jurisdictions which use civil juries. The specific arguments connected with the European Convention on Human Rights are dealt with elsewhere and the remaining arguments applicable within the Scottish context are considered in the remaining paragraphs of this chapter.

Arguments against jury trials

(a) The jury is not a suitable body to decide matters of fact

1.16   The main argument deployed against the civil jury in Scotland is that the jury is not a suitable body to decide matters of fact because its members are untrained in the weighing up of evidence and are incapable of analysing evidence which is in some way complex, lengthy or technical. Perhaps, more colourfully, it is a question of "whether men consider that the work of

---

15 *Sutherland v Duncan* 1996 SLT 428; *Jackson v McDougall* n 14 above.
16 *Anderson v British Coal Corporation* 1992 SLT 398.
17 Rule 37.1(2)(a); *McGee v Matthew Hall Ltd* 1996 SLT 399.
18 *Brogham v O'Rourke* 2005 SLT 29.
19 *Anderson v British Coal Corporation* 1992 SLT 398.

judging may be entrusted to fifth-rate minds or whether it is not so difficult and important that only the best minds available are good enough"[20].

1.17 In reality this is a two-part argument and it may well be true that if the evidence is truly of a highly complex and technical nature then the case could be better dealt with by a single judge than by a jury. However, this is what, in effect, already happens within the Scottish system because a party can apply to have a proof on the basis that the case is too complex on its facts or law for a jury to deal with, particularly if the evidence is likely to be of a highly technical nature. Competing expert evidence may be a problem in that a jury may find it difficult to choose between the different positions advanced although, of course, we expect criminal juries to do this in circumstances where the liberty of an individual is at stake, and perhaps it is easy to underestimate the ability of a jury to deal with complex issues such as medical or psychiatric evidence[21]. The more general argument, that of the unsuitability of jurors to decide issues of fact, is a curious one. We expect jurors in criminal trials to decide issues of fact which may be both contentious and convoluted[22] and, although it is true that they are only being asked to return a single verdict relating to the guilt of the accused rather than having to analyse the evidence and make findings in relation to the matters set out in the schedule of damages, what is sometimes overlooked is that there exists a mechanism for overturning the jury's decision on the facts where it can be shown that the verdict was returned contrary to the evidence, a safeguard which can be invoked even though the jury makes no formal findings in fact or gives no reasons for its decision.

(b) Juries often reach verdicts on irrelevant considerations

1.18 Irrelevant considerations might include sympathy for a pursuer, a desire to punish the defenders, the championing of the small man against the monolith of the mighty insurer or even a liking or dislike of the counsel involved in the case. It cannot be denied that this never happens in hearings before a jury or, for that matter, a single judge, since human bias is difficult if not impossible to eradicate from any legal system unless it has been rendered so mechanistic and inflexible so as to eliminate all possible considerations of equity and justice. It is generally felt that Scottish juries are fairly discriminating and that bias perhaps cuts both ways but, in the absence of objective as opposed to anecdotal evidence, it is difficult to form any real view on the matter. In America extensive research has been carried out on the psychology of the civil jury and the results of such research would suggest that on the whole the perceived bias of

---

20 Gibb, *Law From Over the Border*, p 49.
21 See e.g. Lord Philip's comments in *Livingstone v Fife Council* 2004 SLT 161 in relation to psychiatric evidence.
22 Lord Eassie in *Currie v Strathclyde Regional Council Fire Brigade* 1999 SLT 62.

jurors is perhaps greater than the actual bias which they display when entrusted with the difficult task of administering justice.

(c) Jury trials are more expensive to run than proofs

1.19 In 1959 the Strachan Committee, which was appointed to consider whether the civil jury trial should be retained, did not find that a jury trial was inherently more expensive to run than a proof[23] and, apart from the cost of the jury precept and the motion roll or procedure roll hearing where the mode of inquiry is in dispute, it would seem that this is still true at the present day so far as taxations are concerned[24]. The evidence at the trial may well be shorter in compass since there is a danger of prolix questions and witnesses who, if their testimony is not kept in short compass, will bore the jury with irrelevancies but this, of course, has to be balanced against the fact that a trial will also include opening speeches, a judge's charge and a time for the deliberations in the jury room, all of which a proof will not. Modern jury trials tend to last for between two and four days[25] with trials spilling over into a second week being comparatively rare. In one notable example a trial involving damages payable to a widow and children following upon a death for which liability was admitted was completed within a couple of hours[26]; indeed a generation ago it was commonplace for counsel to conduct two jury trials per week while in the sheriff court two in a single day was not unknown.

(d) On occasions juries get things wrong and their verdicts are inscrutable

1.20 No judge would claim to be infallible in his assessment of the evidence or in computing damages but, it is argued, judges' decisions can be challenged at a reclaiming motion and the reasons which they gave in explanation, however sparse, provide a basis for an appeal[27]. This is not so in the case of jury trial where the jury gives no reasons and thus, it is said, it is far more difficult

---

23 *The Civil Jury in Scotland*, Cmnd 851, para 37.
24 Confirmed by the Auditor of the Court of Session in discussions with the author in 2004.
25 In written answers (nos S2W 14045 and 14057) given to a member of the Scottish Parliament on 25 February 2005, it was said that the average duration of a civil jury trial in the Court of Session was, in 2002, 3.2 days, in 2003, 3.7 days and in 2004, 3.7 days while the comparable figures for all proofs were 3.9, 3.5 and 3.0 days respectively.
26 *Kempton v British Railways Board*, Lord Prosser, 18 May 1993★. The motion sheet in this action (01377/5/91) reveals that the jury was empanelled at 10.35, junior counsel's opening speech was at 11.01, the first witness called at 11.07, the second at 11.24 and the third at 11.27, no evidence was led by the defenders, the closing speeches commenced at 11.29 and 11.45 respectively, the charge began at 12.00, the jury adjourned at 12.15 and delivered its verdict at 12.55.
27 Research in the US suggests that there is a 78 per cent correlation between judge and jury verdicts in civil trials: see H Kalven and H Ziesel, *The American Jury* (Boston, 1966).

for a party to mount a successful appeal. The argument has been developed within the context of the human rights legislation and has some force even though mechanisms exist for asking the jury to specify its findings on matters highlighted in issues and, in the case of non-patrimonial damages, the schedule of damages will usually give enough detail upon which to challenge the jury's decision. Few other jurisdictions have managed to resolve this question satisfactorily, but it may be that the price to pay for having both civil and criminal juries is that their decisions are to some extent inscrutable.

(e) Existence of jury trials leads to two-tier system of justice

1.21 The argument that jury trials lead to a two-tier justice system principally relates to the fact that there is a perception that in an appropriate case a jury might well award a greater sum by way of damages than a judge might, particularly in relation to solatium although, curiously, not for damages for defamation. Judges, particularly in the Outer House, are constrained by precedent as to what non-patrimonial damages they can award[28] but the Inner House is not so rigidly constrained and can, and indeed does, consider jury awards where appropriate[29] as, indeed, can the court at first instance, but neither are bound by such awards[30]. Juries are not so bound and in our present system there is no mechanism whereby the jury can be informed of previous awards, scales or tariffs or even, in the case of a second trial, what the first jury awarded. Jurors are left to consider with open minds what a fair and reasonable award might be and the only constraints placed upon them are the sum sued for and, where their award is considered by the Inner House to be excessive or inadequate, for their verdict to be quashed and a new trial before a different jury ordered. In two particular areas, that of solatium awarded for serious and permanent injury and the damages awarded to the relatives of a deceased person, it is quite clear that jury perceptions are clearly different from those of judges and the discrepancy between the two bodies is both noticeable and consistent, so much so that all other things being equal pursuers would be well advised to opt for jury trial in these circumstances and defenders to resist it.

(f) Juries are drawn solely from Edinburgh area

1.22 The argument that juries are drawn from the Edinburgh area is two-

---

28 See e.g. Temporary Judge J G Reid QC in *Murray v Greenock Dockyard Co* 2004 SLT 346 (OH).

29 *Shaher v British Aerospace Flying College Ltd* 2003 SC 540; *McLean v William Denny & Bros* 2004 SC 656; *Murray's Exrx v Greenock Dockyard Co* 2004 SLT 1104 (IH); see also A Hajducki, "Changing Values: Bereavement Awards in the post-Shaher World" 2003 SLT (News) 189.

30 *Martin v James & Andrew Chapman* 1995 GWD 2-77; *Currie v Kilmarnock and Loudon District Council* 1996 SC 55; *Swan v Hope-Dunbar* 1996 GWD 29-1750.

fold, namely (a) that it places an unfair additional burden of jury service on persons living in Edinburgh and the Lothians, and (b) that juries are consequently unrepresentative of Scotland as a whole. Strachan considered and rejected the first criticism – in 1956 the proportion of the population of that area summoned for civil jury service amounted to 16 persons per thousand and the current figure would be much lower. The second argument is based on the fact that an Edinburgh jury might have different cultural perceptions and a different view of credibility and reliability from, say, a Glasgow jury[31]. Whether this is true in relation to criminal juries is a moot point but the remedy would be to have cases regularly tried in venues other than Edinburgh – an expedient that was tried and largely abandoned in Victorian times.

(g) Mere threat of civil jury may be enough to cause defenders to settle a case which has little merit

1.23 A contrary view would be that if the case has little merit there would be little commercial advantage in making a settlement other than for a nominal nuisance value. Again Strachan considered the matter and concluded that if it were true that by obtaining issues the pursuer was in a position to exert undue pressure on a defender this was "a matter for the legal profession"[32]. Another view might be that if this were so then it was due to ignorance or misconception on the part of the defender's agents. Better disclosure of documents and reports and the pre-trial meetings required in the new Chapter 43 personal injuries actions might well nowadays tend to ensure a more level playing field, if it is indeed not level.

(h) Civil juries are not part of legal heritage of Scotland

1.24 A rather arcane objection that civil juries are not part of Scotland's legal heritage is sometimes voiced but does not merit serious consideration given the fact that civil juries in their present form have been part of Scottish practice since 1815. The institution is now entering its third century and, in any event, was preceded in medieval times by a civil assize. Nowadays both civil and criminal juries are part of the Anglo-Norman heritage of Scots law and have gained public acceptance and trust.

Arguments in favour of jury trials

1.25 Lord President Cooper once remarked that the occasional jury trial

---

31 In *Macpherson v Caledonian Railway Co* (1881) 8 R 901, it was argued unsuccessfully that a civil trial should be heard in Edinburgh "because the jury would be more impartial than [a jury] in Glasgow"!
32 Report, para 43.

introduced "a little light relief into the weary existence of the practitioner and on that account enjoys a measure of popularity in Parliament House"[33]. Although a pertinent observation, the positive reasons for retaining the institution are usually thought to be somewhat stronger than this.

(a) Relative finality of jury's verdict

1.26 The relative finality of the verdict is said to be a good argument in favour of the retention of civil juries and is particularly relevant when the pursuer does not have the benefit of legal aid and is a person of modest means[34]. Notwithstanding the grounds on which the verdict can be reviewed, it does have a certain degree of finality and is not easily overturned. Sometimes it is said to be easier for parties to accept the jury's contemporaneous judgment rather than wait for a judgment after avizandum.

(b) Public involvement in administration of justice

1.27 "The intervention of the lay mind has a value which might be set off against any disadvantage arising from the subjectivity of a lay tribunal."[35] Interestingly enough, many practitioners and members of the judiciary see this, the democratic involvement of the lay Scot in a system designed to protect his rights, as the most important argument in favour of retaining jury trials, particularly when allied with the following argument.

(c) Juries may be more in touch with reality when assessing damages

1.28 It is widely felt that the levels of damages awarded by judges are inadequate, particularly where solatium is involved, and that the disparity between judicial and jury awards merely reflects this; as Lord McCluskey remarked: "12 jurors from different walks of life and with different incomes and needs might be thought to be better placed to understand the value of money than a judge such as myself"[36]. It also raises the interesting question of how solatium is assessed by judges, and a comparison with Victorian times shows that in real terms many solatium awards have fallen considerably. A system which updates awards for inflation by reference to the retail price index may be somewhat out of date in an era of low inflation, rising wages and high

---

33 Cooper, *Selected Papers* (1956), p 70.
34 *Graham v Paterson & Sons* 1938 SC 119 per Lord Justice-Clerk Aitchison.
35 Strachan Committee Report, para 53.
36 *Girvan v Inverness Farmers' Dairy (No 2)* 1996 SLT 631; similar sentiments were expressed by Lord Stott in *Pullar v National Coal Board* 1969 SLT 62 at 63; by Lord President Hope and Lord Prosser in *Currie v Kilmarnock and Loudon District Council* 1996 SC 55 and in *McLeod v British Railways Board* 2001 SC 534 at 540. Similar views have been expressed in the US but the Law Commission for England and Wales thought otherwise: Consultation Paper No 140, paras 4.82–4.83.

house prices and this may well in itself be the answer to why juries, when they come to look at solatium in a particular case, start at a higher base level than a judge might. If the assessment of damages is truly a jury matter then is it reasonable to complain when juries award what they think is fair?

(d) Jury trials work and should therefore be retained

1.29   Notwithstanding the experience of other jurisdictions, there is a feeling that in Scotland the institution works and that juries are capable of properly assimilating facts and assessing liability, contributory or apportioned liability and damages. There is, of course, the old adage that "if it works, don't change it", and if trial by jury is at least as good a way as a proof of achieving the ends of justice, then there is little point in abolishing it. This is not to say that it is a perfect institution and cannot be adapted and modernised to suit present-day conditions but it is important to ensure that any alterations to the present practice and law do not detract from the basic principle of allowing the jury to function effectively as a decision-making body with as few unnecessary constraints as possible.

1.30   Perhaps Scotland should take heed from sister jurisdictions in the British Isles where the use of the civil jury has become greatly diminished and where, in the words of one commentator:

> "It has enjoyed the widespread popular approval and confidence amongst the common people of England . . . [but now] like the Cheshire Cat, trial by jury in civil cases has to all intents and purposes vanished leaving behind its grin, which has remained to mock us."[37]

The Strachan Committee, having carefully considered the merits and demerits of the retention of the civil jury in Scotland, concluded in rather less colourful language that:

> "Balancing the arguments on both sides and the evidence relating to them, we do not find that there is any preponderance in favour of abolishing jury trial. We therefore recommend that jury trial in the Court of Session be not abolished."[38]

---

37 Jacob, *The Fabric of English Civil Justice* (Hamlyn Lectures, 1987), p 158; McMahon, *Judge or Jury: The Jury Trial for Personal Injury Cases in Ireland* (Cork, 1985) gives a similar warning in relation to Ireland.
38 Report, para 56.

Chapter 2

The historical perspective

ORIGINS AND ANTECEDENTS OF THE CIVIL JURY

2.01   Although Scotland can justly claim to have been the birthplace of many inventions and institutions, trial by jury is not one of them. The origins of a system of juries or lay assessors being used to determine factual issues within a legal context is unclear and, although the Franks and Saxons probably had such a system, it was in the England of medieval times that anything remotely like the modern jury, in both the criminal and civil sense, first evolved as part of the coeval development of central government and legal procedure. Then, with the gradual northward permeation of Anglo-Norman influences, the idea of the jury or assize crossed the border and within a fairly short period began to be established as part of the legal process within the northern kingdom.

2.02   The initial form of the civil jury trial in Scotland bore little resemblance to that currently in use and appears to have originated with the system of brieves introduced in the reign of David I. A brieve consisted of an order issued by the king's Chancery to the sheriff or other local representative of the Crown, requiring him to summon a jury or assize of "twelve leal men" for the purpose of obtaining their verdict on a particular matter in dispute – effectively, for the determination of the relevant facts in the light of the jury's personal or local knowledge. An essential difference from the modern system was, of course, that there was never any requirement for the jury to hear evidence from witnesses and it was not required, when giving its verdict, to assess monetary damages. This early use of a civil jury subsisted from the thirteenth century for some three hundred years or so until, with the growing sophistication of legal procedures in the sixteenth century concomitant with the gradual evolution of the Court of Session, the brieve system fell out of use and the determination of facts in civil disputes became the sole preserve of the judge or sheriff-substitute[1].

---

1 For a full and scholarly account of the early history see Willock, *The Origins and Development of the Jury in Scotland* (Stair Society, 1966); for England and Wales see Cornish, *The Jury* (1968).

2.03 In certain respects, however, the concept of the use of a lay assize to determine factual issues never quite died out in Scotland and, apart of course from criminal trials where the jury system flourished and was seen as an indispensable part of the administration of justice, assizes continued to be used in a number of peculiar and *sui generis* proceedings such as the service of heirs, the apportionment of the widow's terce, cognition of the insane and, at least initially, in the settlement of boundary disputes. By contrast, in England and Wales the civil jury developed into a very powerful institution and was so highly regarded that it became effectively the sole means by which issues of fact could be determined in causes pending before the courts of common law and could be described as "the hallmark of English civil justice and the bulwark of liberty which . . . imprinted itself in the English-speaking countries"[2].

THE MOVEMENT FOR REFORM

2.04 Although the practice of the Court of Session had often been criticised it was not until the latter half of the eighteenth century that a general and widespread dissatisfaction with its procedures and processes began to be widely voiced. In 1785 Ilay Campbell, the then Lord Advocate, introduced a Bill which was regarded as being the precursor of the movement for the reform of the court and this seems to have promoted a lively debate[3]. One particular grievance focused upon the peculiar and anachronistic organisation of Outer House business, whereby a single Lord Ordinary would, for a week at a time, be sent to hear all pending civil proofs with the inevitable result that, given this almost impossible workload expected from one person, evidence had to be taken on commission in virtually all cases. It was felt that this practice led to a system of verbose and virtually incomprehensible pleadings and, more importantly, to considerable and unacceptable delay and expense to litigants.

2.05 In 1785 James Boswell, the celebrated biographer, diarist and member of the Scots Bar, issued a pamphlet which contained not only a trenchant criticism of Campbell's proposals but also a suggestion that it was high time that the civil jury was reintroduced in Scotland[4]. The popularity of this view was echoed at public meetings in Ayr, Haddington and elsewhere by Henry Erskine in his capacity as Dean of the Faculty of Advocates and, most cogently, by one of the judges, Lord Swinton, who suggested that jury trial should be used in the Court of Session for all actions of reduction, restitution,

---

2 Jacob, *The Fabric of English Civil Justice* (Hamlyn Lectures, 1987).
3 See generally Phillipson, *The Scottish Whigs and the Reform of the Court of Session 1785–1830* (Stair Society, 1990).
4 Boswell, *A Letter to the People of Scotland* (1785).

damages for fraud and injury and "in other causes of great importance and perplexity, where the evidence depends on parole testimony"[5]. Swinton concluded:

> "that to obtain justice is the sole end of legal trials: that without finding out the truth, justice cannot be obtained: that the best manner of taking evidence is in the presence of the court, which is to judge of it: that a court is best composed of established judges to decide the law, and of juries to try the fact; that in Great Britain, including both kingdoms, jury-trial is the palladium of liberty in criminal matters; that in England the security of property and of reputation in civil matters; and for these reasons, in civil questions of great importance, Scotland is also intitled to a revival of their native and ancient privilege."

Despite such eloquence, nothing further was done and the hiatus of the French Revolution and the Napoleonic Wars effectively put such reforms on the back burner.

2.06 With the advent of a Whig government in 1806, the issue of reform was once more to the fore. In that year James Grahame, an advocate, issued a pamphlet on the subject of civil jury trial[6], and in the following year a further Bill to reform the Court of Session, including the introduction of civil juries, was published but met considerable opposition from, among others, Walter Scott, poet, novelist and Member of Faculty. The Bill came to naught and the Scottish judges stated that they were "very doubtful of the expediency of jury trials in civil causes". However, in 1808 a revamped Bill, which deleted the provision of civil jury trial, passed into law and the first major reform of the court was then undertaken. A commission, under the chairmanship of Ilay Campbell, who was now in retirement, was set up to consider the matter again and in 1810 a majority of its members came out in favour of an experiment whereby the court, in certain cases, might be authorised to remit issues of fact in a cause to a jury for its determination[7].

2.07 There the matter might have rested had it not been for two further factors. The first of these was the feelings harboured by the rising middle classes in Scotland who, in those pre-Reform Act days, were given few opportunities to participate in public life and were accordingly looking for the chance to serve in the administration of justice; the second was altogether more surprising and, ultimately, persuasive. For many years the House of Lords, as the ultimate appellate court for Scotland, had been dissatisfied with both the number and content of the "Scotch Appeals" and one particular bone of con-

---

5 Swinton, *Considerations concerning a Proposal for Dividing the Court of Session into Classes or Chambers and for Limiting Litigation in Small Causes and for the Revival of Jury-Trial in Certain Civil Actions* (1789).
6 Grahame, *Thoughts on Trial by Jury in Civil Causes* (1806).
7 The chairman had already previously published his own views in *Hints upon the Question of Jury Trial* (1809).

tention, most keenly felt by those schooled in the English common-law tradition, was that their Lordships often had to remit cases back to Edinburgh so that questions of fact could be elucidated and clarified prior to the determination of the appeal[8]. In one perhaps all too typical case Lord Chancellor Eldon commented that "this is one of those cases which compelled one extremely to lament the want of inclination which prevailed in Scotland to adopt trial by jury in civil proceedings"[9], and it is therefore not surprising that it was Lord Eldon himself who was one of the sponsors of a Bill "to extend trial by jury to civil causes in Scotland". Notwithstanding criticism (partly on the grounds that this was an English measure being foisted upon Scotland by an English court whose very jurisdiction in Scotland was suspect) the Bill received widespread Scottish support and, accordingly, passed into law in May 1815.

THE JURY COURT

2.08   The Jury Trials (Scotland) Act 1815 created, for an experimental period of seven years only, a separate Jury Court in Scotland, independent of the Court of Session. The court was presided over by a Lord Chief Commissioner and two other commissioners, and the Inner House of the Court of Session, acting upon the report of a Lord Ordinary or judge of the Admiralty Court, could remit a cause for trial to the Jury Court, there being no right of appeal against the grant or refusal of such a remit. In general the procedure followed was based upon the contemporary jury trial practice adopted in England and Wales, the jury consisting of 12 persons and their verdict had to be unanimous. A limited right of review of jury verdicts was given and, although the court was usually held within Parliament House in Edinburgh, it was also empowered to go on circuit.

2.09   This reintroduction of the civil jury into Scotland was generally acknowledged as a success and within four years the beneficial effects were felt to be sufficiently great as to justify the retention of the Jury Court on a more permanent basis. Accordingly the Jury Trials (Scotland) Act 1819 took this step and, in addition, made it mandatory to try certain types of action, namely assault, defamation, breach of promise and seduction, before a jury. Further reforms followed in the Court of Session Act 1825 and in terms of section 28 of that Act there was set out a list of the causes appropriate to be heard by juries – the so-called "enumerated causes" – which included those covered by the 1819 Act as well as injury to moveables and land, certain actions of mercantile character such as insurance, charterparties, freight, the carriage of goods

8 For a readable, if somewhat partisan, account see Gibb, *Law From Over the Border* (1950).
9 *Smith v Macneil* (1836) 2 Dow 538 at 544.

by land and sea, the praetorian liability of innkeepers and stablers, nuisance and actions for the wages of masters of ships and vessels and of mariners.

2.10 The Lord Chief Commissioner of the Jury Court, William Adam, was a somewhat remarkable man and it was largely through his efforts and lobbying that civil jury trials became a permanent feature of Scottish legal procedure. A relative of the famous Adam brothers, he was a close friend of Walter Scott and practised at both the Scots and English Bars, served as an English MP and, at the age of 65, returned to his native land to preside over the Jury Court with these somewhat unusual credentials. Described by Lord Cockburn as having a "plain and well-bred manner", he was said to be

> "though well read for a busy gentleman . . . not a person of either learning or general ability. His true merits resolved into industry, practical sense, agreeable deportment, and a conscientious ambition to secure the success of the Jury Court. No one else could have either launched or piloted it with the same understanding or enthusiasm as Adam. He . . . retired with the respect and affection of the whole legal profession and of the public."[10]

The other commissioners were two of the existing judges of the Court of Session, Lords Meadowbank and Pitmilly – the former died shortly after his appointment and was succeeded by Lord Gillies. In later years the total number of commissioners was raised to five.

2.11 The flavour of everyday life in the Jury Court comes over well in the five-volume dedicated series of reports edited by John Murray, advocate. These include, unusually for their time, verbatim judgments, beginning with a case in which the painter and proprietor of an estate in Stockbridge, Sir Henry Raeburn, together with a number of feuars in Great King Street, unsuccessfully brought an action in nuisance against the proprietor of New Town laundry who used "an improved steam engine" in his premises[11]. In addition to case reports, Murray's reports contain introductions and general discussions, model pleadings and observations about jury trial practice and procedure and, in the first volume, the long introductory speech of William Adam which the very first civil jury, summoned on 22 January 1816, had to sit through before hearing the "improved steam engine" case[12]. In that speech the Lord Chief Commissioner, perhaps somewhat optimistically, observed that:

10 Cockburn, *Memorials of His Time* (1855), chapter V.
11 *Raeburn v Kedslie* (1816) 1 Mur 1.
12 1 Mur xv. Adam also published *Observations respecting the Further Extension of Trial by Jury to Scotland in Civil Causes* (1828) and during his retirement and when he was virtually blind he dictated *A Short View of the Difficulties which surrounded the Introduction of Trial By Jury to Civil Causes in Scotland and of the Ultimate Success of the Experiment* (1835) and the monumental *Practical Treatise and Observations on Trial by Jury as now Incorporated with the jurisdiction of the Court of Session* (1836).

"our inquiries here are not into hidden and occult acts of crime, where the discovery of truth may often be involved in intricacy and difficulty, and in doubtful testimony, from the very nature of the acts. We shall have here to deal
with the open acts and transactions of men in the ordinary course of life and
intercourse of the world. In such transactions . . . there is nothing likely to
happen but an easy solution in every case."[13]

LATER DEVELOPMENTS

2.12   Within time it was felt that the business of the Jury Court could be
dealt with more conveniently and economically if it were to be incorporated
within the main body of the Court of Session and, following upon the recom-
mendation of a commission set up under section 56 of the 1825 Act, the separate jurisdictions of the separate Jury, Consistorial and Admiralty Courts
were abolished by the Court of Session Act 1830 and their functions were
transferred to the single and ancient supreme court of Scotland. The duties of
the erstwhile commissioners devolved upon the judges of the Outer House
and from then onwards jury trials became part of the ordinary administration
of civil justice by that court. There were no substantive changes and all actions
which would have been tried in the Jury Court prior to 1830 were now tried
in the Court of Session. In 1837 Robert Macfarlane WS published what was
to be regarded as the standard textbook on the subject, namely *The Practice of
the Court of Session in Jury Causes*[14], and followed this up with a book on issues
and a further series of jury trial reports[15]. However, a certain distrust of the
institution remained and as late as 1839 it could be said that:

> "The law of the Jury Court, no one knows,
> It has rules for its friends and rules for its foes."[16]

2.13   The exclusivity of the enumerated causes was short-lived and in 1850
a proof on commission was allowed in place of jury trial in all of the enumerated causes except actions for libel or nuisance or causes which were properly
and in substance actions for damages[17]. The appropriation or reservation of
causes to juries was then further substantially derogated from in 1866 when,
for the first time, the concept was introduced whereby if both parties consented or if one of them could show special cause then, notwithstanding the
fact that the cause was an enumerated one, the Lord Ordinary was given the

---

13 1 Mur xxv–xxvi.
14 Born in 1802, Macfarlane became an advocate, "was successful with juries in civil
    actions, although not an orator" (*Dictionary of National Biography*), reached the bench as
    Lord Ormidale and died in 1880.
15 Only the first volume (1838–39) was ever published.
16 Maidment, *Court of Session Garland*, 1839 supplement.
17 Court of Session Act 1850, s 49.

power to order a proof[18]. In 1868 a Royal Commission was appointed to look at legal procedures and *inter alia* it considered the position of the civil jury. By no means uncritical of the institution and commenting that "the plant has not taken root and growth", the Commission recommended the retention of the civil juries but it did feel that the court should have an unfettered discretion as to whether to proceed by way of proof or trial in any particular case and that the distinction between enumerated and other causes should be abolished[19]. These recommendations were ignored and the provisions of 1866 continued to be followed[20].

2.14   Civil juries not only continued but the institution seemed to grow in strength although there were cyclical fluctuations in its use brought about largely by the prevailing attitudes of the court to how special cause was to be interpreted. Another Royal Commission, this time under the chairmanship of Lord President Clyde, was appointed in 1926 and its members recommended the retention of the civil jury albeit with the abolition of the concept of enumerated causes and its replacement by a general power for the parties (or, where they could not agree, by the court) to choose the appropriate means of inquiry. In the event only minor changes to jury trial procedure were made by the ensuing Administration of Justice (Scotland) Act 1933. What was surprising was that between 1900 and 1926 there were an average of 21 civil jury trials heard every year but in the following decade this rose to an average of 46 per annum, largely due to the appalling rise in the number of persons involved in "running-down" actions caused by the now ubiquitous motor car.

2.15   Civil juries were effectively suspended during the Second World War[21] but became popular again in the 1950s and 1960s, a period which many have regarded in retrospect as forming their golden age. Between 1954 and 1959 a total of between 86 and 104 cases annually were being disposed of by juries and between 1960 and 1965 the annual average was some 85. There were many reasons for this, the principal ones being the fact that contributory negligence was no longer a bar to recovering damages and the increasing willingness to litigate for industrial injuries, particularly in the mines and on the railways. In April 1958 it was said that there were some 395 cases awaiting trial, including some 280 workplace-related accidents and some 86 road traffic cases. It was therefore appropriate that it was within this period that the most thorough and far-reaching review of civil jury trials was undertaken, that of the Strachan Committee[22]. Having considered the contemporary position, the

---

18 Evidence (Scotland) Act 1866, s 4.
19 Royal Commission on the Courts of Law in Scotland, Fourth Report (1870).
20 See the observations of Lord President Inglis in *Nicol v Britten & Owden* (1872) 10 M 351.
21 Administration of Justice (Emergency Provisions) (Scotland) Act 1939, s 4.
22 Its report was published as *Civil Jury Trial in Scotland*, Cmnd 851.

Committee reported in November 1958 that it favoured the retention of the civil jury trial by a majority of seven to three, albeit with a very powerful minority dissent expressed by Sheriff Kermack. The Committee did, however, make a number of recommendations in respect of revising the list of enumerated causes and of taking a broader view of the special cause requirements and made a number of quite far-reaching proposals in respect of procedural matters which it felt would alleviate certain of the perceived defects in the system and in the review of jury verdicts.

2.16   The Strachan proposals were, however, never put into effect and civil jury trials continued along their previous path although the number of cases which got to trial began to show a slow and seemingly inexorable decline. Between 1966 and 1970 the annual average was 42 but in the period 1971 to 1975 it had declined to 23 and between 1976 and 1980 it was down to seven. The decline continued and in 1981 the figure was one, in 1983 four and in 1984 two, the actual nadir being in 1982 when, for the first time since 1816 and excluding wartime, not a single jury trial took place in the Court of Session. It seemed, indeed, as if an endangered species was facing extinction.

THE SHERIFF COURT

2.17   With the exception of fatal accident inquiries[23] and the assessment of compulsory purchase compensation[24] the use of civil juries in the sheriff court was all but unknown although there was a power to remit any cause to the Court of Session to be tried by a jury[25]. However, in 1907 a limited power was given to sheriffs to hear, with a jury of seven, actions which were brought under the provisions of the Employers' Liability Act 1880[26], and in 1913 this power was amended to allow for jury trial by an employee against his employer at common law and, following upon the repeal of the 1880 Act in 1948, this became the sole type of civil action which could be tried by a jury in the sheriff court[27]. There were certain peculiarities in the procedure, including the fact that the jury consisted of seven persons, the damages claimed had to exceed £50, the sheriff had no discretion akin to the special cause provisions and there was a difference in the way that the verdict was taken. Because of these limitations, and in particular because of the exclusion of road

---

23 The procedure is explained in Dobie, *Law and Practice of the Sheriff Courts in Scotland* at pp 452–454 and such juries were abolished by the Fatal Accidents and Sudden Deaths Inquiry (Scotland) Act 1976.

24 Under the provisions of the Land Clauses Consolidation (Scotland) Act 1845 a jury of 13 could assess compensation when a claim exceeded £50.

25 Sheriff Courts (Scotland) Act 1907, s 30 repealed by Law Reform (Miscellaneous Provisions) (Scotland) Act 1980, Sch 3.

26 Sheriff Courts (Scotland) Act 1907, s 31.

27 For procedure see Dobie, chapter XV.

traffic accident cases, civil jury trial in the sheriff court never became as popular as in the Court of Session and between 1960 and 1965 an average of only 15 trials per annum took place, the most popular venues being the sheriff courts of Glasgow, Paisley and Dumbarton. The Strachan Committee recommended their abolition and the Grant Committee studying the procedures of the sheriff court[28] concurred. Civil jury trial in the sheriff court was, however, not finally abolished until 1980[29].

THE MODERN RENAISSANCE

2.18 In the Court of Session the civil jury had all but died out in the mid-1980s and it was thought that the eventual abolition of the institution was only a matter of time. Then, following the recommendations of the Scottish Law Commission, the Court of Session Act 1988 was passed. This was a general consolidating and tidying-up measure which nevertheless preserved a statutory basis for civil jury trials and, at the same time, the Lord Advocate, through the Scottish Courts Administration, issued a consultation paper inviting views on whether or not such trials should be abolished. The response was largely in favour of retention and although various suggestions were put forward such as the giving of guidance to juries, an increase or decrease in the number of jurors and the inversion of onus in special cause arguments[30], the institution was retained with little change.

2.19 Throughout the 1990s jury trials continued to be heard and there were a number of motions for a new trial on the grounds of an excess of damages culminating in the high-profile action of *Girvan v Inverness Farmers' Dairy* which reached the House of Lords in 1997[31]. With an increasing tendency for awards to be reported, perceptions, especially within the profession, became heightened and the number of cases set down for jury trial began to increase, evidenced by the sharp rise in the number of reported decisions on the question of proof or jury trial. More publicity ensued with a defamation action involving a priest, a challenge to the institution under the European Convention on Human Rights, some surprisingly low awards and, paradoxically, the highest ever awards in successive cases for solatium of £250,000 and £300,000 respectively, together with an attempt to raise relatives' death awards following upon a number of relatively high jury awards. The new personal injury actions procedures which commenced in April 2003 have, it is said, theoretically made it easier to obtain jury trials in the Court of Session although it is too early to tell whether in fact the new rules have made any sig-

---

28 *The Sheriff Court*, Cmnd 3248 (1967).
29 Law Reform (Miscellaneous Provisions) (Scotland) Act 1980, s 11.
30 See e.g. the recommendations of the Scottish Legal Action Group in 1989 SCOLAG 150.
31 1998 SC (HL) 1.

nificant difference whatsoever in this area. On any view the present number of cases in which a trial actually proceeds may still be comparatively low[32] but the number of cases in which issues are allowed is significantly higher and it is clear that a renewed interest in the civil jury has led to a greater awareness and potential use of the institution in Scotland.

32 The author estimates that the number of civil jury trials that actually ran to the point where a verdict was given amounted to four in 1997, three in 1998, eight in 1999, two in 2000, five in 2001, five in 2002, three in 2003, four in 2004 and three in 2005. In May 2004 133 new procedure personal injury actions were signetted and one proof and two jury trials proceeded to a conclusion. In the session 2004–05 an average of six jury trials per month were appearing on the rolls. According to Scottish Courts statistics a total of 43 jury trial diets were assigned in 2003 and 66 in 2004; the comparable number of proof diets assigned were 1,331 and 2,014 of which, respectively, 68 and 91 proceeded to proof.

Chapter 3

Civil juries and human rights

INTRODUCTION

3.01 In the United Kingdom it is unlawful for a court or tribunal to act or fail to act in a way which is incompatible with a right contained in the European Convention on Human Rights[1], and these rights include *inter alia* the right to a fair trial, the right to respect for private and family life and the right to freedom of expression. This chapter examines how those rights are alleged to have been infringed and what measures, if any, could be taken to remedy such breaches.

RIGHT TO A FAIR TRIAL

3.02 Article 6(1) provides that in the determination of his civil rights and obligations, everyone is entitled to a fair and public hearing within a reasonable time by an independent and impartial tribunal established by law and that judgment shall be pronounced publicly. It has been held that it is an integral part of that right that the court must indicate with sufficient clarity the grounds on which it based its decision since it is this, *inter alia*, which makes it possible for a person to exercise usefully the grounds of appeal available to him[2]. In a subsequent case it was held that Article 6(1) obliges the court to give reasons for its judgments, but that this does not require a detailed answer to every argument and that the extent to which the duty to give reasons applies may vary according to the nature of the decision. The diversity of different legal systems, statutory rules, legal opinions and the presentation and drafting of judgments has to be taken into account and the question of whether or not a court has failed to fulfil the obligation to state reasons can only be determined in the light of the circumstances of the case[3].

---

1 Human Rights Act 1998, s 6.
2 *Hadjianastassiou v Greece* (1992) 16 EHRR 219, para 33.
3 *Hiro Balani v Spain* (1994) 19 EHRR 566, para 61.

3.03 It is certainly arguable that trying a civil case before a jury is a breach of Article 6(1) in that a jury in Scotland never gives reasons for its decision and in the first of three cases dealing with the matter, *Gunn v Newman*[4], a personal injury action where liability was admitted, the defenders opposed the granting of issues on the basis that trial by jury was incompatible with the defender's right to a fair hearing. The argument was based upon the fact that, in relation to solatium, (a) the defender had no rational basis for calculating an appropriate figure to found a tender upon, (b) that she could not rely upon previous awards when addressing the jury and thus would not, as a matter of comparative justice, have a fair hearing, (c) that a jury had no previous experience in assessing solatium and would be likely to be swayed by irrelevant factors, (d) that whereas a judge would give reasons for his award a jury would not, (e) that a jury award could *per se* be grossly unfair, and (f) that the unfairness inherent in the system could not be remedied under the provisions for review since the circumstances in which an award could be successfully challenged as being excessive were limited and the only power available to the Inner House was to order a new trial rather than to requantify the damages awarded[5]. These arguments failed because the defenders failed to show "special cause" in terms of the relevant statutory provisions[6], and since these arguments would apply to any case involving solatium "a universal characteristic cannot, without the total abuse of language, be special"[7].

3.04 The second in the trio of Scottish cases was *Sandison v Graham Begg Ltd*[8] where the argument was put forward in relation to a pre-existing disability that jury trial should be refused because reasons would not be given by the jury as to why a particular body of medical evidence might be preferable to another. The court held that the defender's rights under Article 6(1) were not infringed and that the Inner House had little difficulty in dealing with motions for a new trial without having before it the reasons for the jury's decision either on liability or on the quantum of the damages awarded. After considering the relevant case law[9] it was held that the fact that the jury's award was broken down into various heads in the schedule of damages meant that it was not necessary for detailed reasons to be given before a party dissatisfied with the jury's decision on quantum could exercise his statutory right to a new trial[10].

---

4 2001 SC 525. A similar unsuccessful attack was mounted on criminal juries in *Transco plc v HM Advocate* 2004 SLT 995.
5 Court of Session Act 1988, ss 29–31.
6 Court of Session Act 1988, ss 9, 11.
7 Lord Hamilton at 531F. The decision was reclaimed but the case settled shortly before the appeal was due to be heard.
8 2001 SC 821.
9 *Maltman v Tarmac Civil Engineering Ltd* 1967 SC 177 at 183 and *Tate v Fischer* 1998 SLT 1419 at 1421C–D.
10 The point was argued again, unsuccessfully, in *MacInnes v Owen* 2004 GWD 38-776.

3.05   The matter was revisited in rather more detail by the Inner House in *Heasman v J M Taylor & Partners*[11] and although the view was taken that civil jury trials were not in themselves inherently unfair in terms of Article 6(1) a number of interesting points were raised. Lord Coulsfield held that:

> "there is little difficulty in concluding that the procedures followed in a civil jury trial are adequate to give the assurance that the jury are directed to the proper questions. Trial by jury is, in the absence of some special circumstances, trial by an impartial and independent tribunal. The matters in controversy in the pleadings are defined by the pleadings. The issue (and counter-issue, if there is one) specify a question or questions for the jury to answer. The heads of damages, and the sums sued for, which set a maximum for the award, are also set out in the issue. The questions in the issue are often posed in general terms, but the court has the power to direct that the issue should include a special question or questions, if circumstances make it appropriate to do so. The jury are given directions by the judge as to the law to be applied and the proper approach for them to take. The jury does not give reasons but as a general rule it is possible to see what view the jury have taken of the evidence, and in that context the absence of reasons can be regarded, as it was in *R v Belgium*[12], as inherent in the system and acceptable. In any event, in regard to the assessment of solatium in particular, the question is what is a reasonable award and, as the pursuer argued, even a judge can say little more than that he considers a particular sum to be reasonable."

3.06   Lord Coulsfield went on to comment that in the landmark House of Lords case of *Girvan v Inverness Farmers' Dairy (No 2)*[13] there were passages

> "which may be interpreted as approving of a less stringent test for determining whether a jury award is excessive, or indeed inadequate. I do not think, however, that at this stage it is possible to give further consideration to that issue: it should be discussed, in my view, in relation to a particular award, and in particular circumstances."

Lord Johnston, agreeing with Lord Coulsfield that the defenders' arguments in relation to unfairness should properly be considered after the jury trial had taken place and at the motion for a new trial, went on to say that:

> "I am not convinced that the lack of reasons *per se* invalidates the jury system in terms of the Convention since it is recognised by some European jurisprudence that reasons are not necessarily essential to the obtaining of a fair trial. But if the issue of lack of reasons is taken in the context of *Girvan* a much more difficult problem arises in the sense that it is highly arguable that a defender is effectively required to accept a jury's verdict without reasons because the parameters of appeal are so narrowly stated. It is significant that Lord Clyde in *Girvan* does not appear to go as far as Lord Hope in adopting the Victorian

11   2002 SC 326.
12   (1992) 72 DR 195.
13   1998 SC (HL) 1.

language of established cases and to my mind there is at least a stateable argument that in the context of 2002 the word 'gross' is perhaps to be given a more broad meaning than the extreme position which applied to it in Victorian times. It also seems to me highly desirable that *Girvan* should be revisited in an appropriate case in the context of the Convention which did not of course feature in the arguments presented to the House of Lords at that particular time. In this context the case of *McLeod v British Railways Board*[14] is not without significance."

3.07 Lord Hamilton, in concurring with the view that the granting of a jury trial was not an inherent breach of Article 6, observed that "more troubling, in my view, is the absence before the jury of any information about sums awarded by judges or juries in comparable cases". After reviewing the current position[15] and the various suggestions made in past cases to support the view about informing the jury[16] he stated that:

"While the continuation of this [present] practice is . . . regrettable, I am not persuaded that a jury, denied such guidance, is inevitably disabled from making a fair award. There is no compelling evidence that jury awards even for the same injuries are, as a generality, widely discrepant. While the two juries in *Girvan*[17] returned figures which were to some extent diverse, those returned in *McCallum v Paterson*[18] were very similar. It is also necessary, as discussed below, to bear in mind the control available by review of the verdict in the Inner House. In any event it must, in my view, be borne in mind that, so far at least as drawn to our attention, there is no rule of law (whether based on primary legislation, rule of court or binding judicial decision) which prevents a judge presiding at a jury trial from giving, if the circumstances so indicate, fuller directions on damages than has been traditional. Indeed such a judge now has an obligation to act in a way which is compatible with the parties' Convention rights [Human Rights Act 1998, s 6(1)]. An 'act' includes a failure to act [s 6(6)]. If in a particular case a failure to give fuller directions on damages would be incompatible with the right of a pursuer or defender or both to a fair trial, the presiding judge will have an obligation to give such directions. Any such directions would, of course, include a direction that any figures referred to were for guidance only and were not prescriptive. I am not persuaded that any perceived difficulties in giving such directions are serious, far less insuperable."

3.08 It is perhaps interesting to note that Lord Hamilton was of the view that "this opinion may raise more questions than it answers" and in

14 2001 SC 534.
15 With reference to *Traynor's Exrx v Bairds and Scottish Steel* 1957 SC 311.
16 Lord Abernethy in *Girvan v Inverness Farmers' Dairy (No 2)* 1996 SC 134 at 153 and Lord Hope at 1998 SC (HL) 1 at 20–21; Lord President Rodger in *McLeod v British Railways Board* 2001 SC 534 at 540–541.
17 1995 SLT 735; cf 1996 SLT 631.
18 1968 SC 280; cf 1969 SC 85.

the context of supplying the jury with more information this is certainly so. Juries can and are supplied with copies of actuarial tables when computing patrimonial loss but to date no successful motion has been made to put previous awards or tables before a jury in relation to solatium[19]. One commentator states that:

"it is now arguable that the jury should be provided with, e.g. relevant pages from *McEwan & Paton*, or the *Judicial Studies Board Guidelines*. Of course, the jury should be advised that they are free to ignore such guidance, but such a practice would quickly show whether judicial awards are too low, or whether juries make high awards in the mistaken belief that that is what judges already do."[20]

A more traditionalist view is that such guidelines would be of little real assistance as the jury would be unsure of what to do with them and that, even if previous jury awards were included in the information given to the jurors, this would only detract from the duty to make a fair and reasonable award in the light of their own experience of life[21]. Interestingly in the majority of American jurisdictions advocates are not permitted to offer expert opinion on the dollar value of pain and suffering and in many jurisdictions they are not permitted to argue for such damages in specific sums.

3.09 Another possible infringement of the Article 6(1) right to a fair trial might be any purported restriction of legal aid or other financial consideration which would prevent a pursuer having his action tried before a jury as opposed to in the sheriff court[22] but it is unlikely that a pursuer would succeed in such an argument if funding was given to allow the pursuer to access any court even if it were not his tribunal of choice.

---

19 Interestingly in *Cameron v Lanarkshire Health Board*, reported on another matter at 1997 SLT 1040, counsel for the defenders, prior to his closing speech, made a motion to be allowed to address the jury on quantum with reference to reported cases and the motion was refused on the basis that he could cite no precedent or point to any practice for adopting such a course.

20 R Milligan, *Scottish Human Rights Service*, para C2.020. A response to the Lord Advocate's Consultation Paper on Civil Juries in 1989 included a suggestion that: "Such guidance might . . . take the form of the submission by counsel of appropriate judicial precedents, coupled with guidance by the judge on whether the [precedents] were in fact comparable or the provision to the jury of a range or band of amounts within which an award might be made": 1988 SCOLAG 66. In 1982 the Prices Advisory Committee (Motor Insurance) in Ireland recommended that "the judge should be allowed to inform the jury as to what he or she estimated to be the going range of general damages for the sort of injuries provided in the circumstances of the particular case." In *Sneddon v Deutag Services*, Lord Carloway, 1 Nov 2004★ the sum claimed for solatium in the pursuer's valuation was put to the pursuer in the course of cross-examination and the line was allowed on the basis that in Chapter 43 personal injury actions such valuations were, effectively, part of the pleadings. See also **20.15** below.

21 A Hajducki, "Civil Juries and Solatium" 2002 SLT (News) 271.

22 *Airey v Ireland* (1979) 2 EHRR 305.

FREEDOM OF EXPRESSION

3.10   Article 10 provides that everyone has the right to freedom of expression
which, since it carries with it duties and responsibilities, is subject to such conditions and restrictions as are prescribed by law. When balanced with the right
to respect for privacy and family life in terms of Article 8 this has an effect
upon the law of defamation. In the case of *Tolstoy v United Kingdom*[23], in which
a jury awarded the plaintiff the sum of £1,500,000 in damages for having been
branded a war criminal by the defendant, it was argued that Articles 6(1) and
10 had been contravened. The complaint under Article 6(1) was that the applicant's rights to a fair trial had been infringed by an order for security for costs
made against him but the principal argument was that the amount of the
award plus costs and an injunction amounted to a disproportionate interference with his rights under Article 10 and were not as "prescribed by law"
under Article 10(2). His case was based on the lack of guidance given to the
jury, the disproportionate nature of the remedy and the fact that it could only
be overturned if the court were to hold that the jury had acted capriciously,
unconscionably or irrationally, and the fact that the jury was not required to
give reasons for its decision. The court rejected the arguments relating to lack
of guidance and lack of reasoning but upheld the appeal on the basis of the lack
of proportionality. The matter has been touched upon several times in
England[24], but such arguments have not yet been directly advanced in Scotland. In the former jurisdiction, however, the court has the power to substitute
its own assessment of damages for that awarded by the jury[25]; in Scotland it
does not and can only grant a motion for a new trial.

RIGHT TO PRIVACY

3.11   In terms of Article 8 everyone has the right to respect for his private
and family life and this has already been considered above in respect of defamation actions. Where a video recording or surveillance has been carried out
in a personal injuries action such a course of conduct may be arguably a breach
of Article 8 subject to any counter argument in relation to proportionality and
the regard to the fair balance which must be struck between the respective
competing interests[26]. Similar arguments might be advanced in relation to the
recovery of medical or employment information under a specification of
documents[27], particularly if such documents were to be put before a jury.

---

23 (1995) 20 EHRR 442.
24 *Reynolds v Times Newspapers Ltd* [1999] 4 All ER 609 at 625, [2001] 2 AC 127; *Ashworth
     Hospital Authority v MGN* [2002] 1 WLR 2033; *Grobelaar v News Group Newspapers*
     [2002] 4 All ER 732 and *Kiam v MGN* [2003] 3 WLR 1036.
25 Courts and Legal Services Act 1990, s 8(2).
26 *Martin v McGuiness* 2003 SLT 1424.
27 *MS v Sweden* [1998] EHRLR 115.

Chapter 4

Experience of other jurisdictions

4.01   There are a number of other jurisdictions where civil juries are used to a greater or lesser extent and, almost without exception, these jurisdictions have a common-law heritage and to a greater or lesser extent follow English or American practice. In this chapter the sister jurisdictions of the British Isles are examined first, followed by North America, Australasia and, finally, the rest of the world.

ENGLAND AND WALES

4.02   Until the passing of the Common Law Procedure Act of 1854 the jury was the sole means by which issues of fact could be tried in the courts of common law but the Act then altered things by making provision for trial by judge alone in most actions if, but only if, both parties consented. In 1933 the right to a civil jury trial was, however, greatly curtailed and became limited to certain types of action only and there now exists a right to a civil jury trial solely in cases of libel and slander, false imprisonment and malicious prosecution or to a defendant against whom a claim is made involving a charge of fraud. This right exists in both the county courts[1] and in the Queen's Bench Division of the High Court[2], but is qualified by the fact that the court may, if it feels that the trial involves a prolonged examination of documents or accounts or a scientific or local investigation, order that the case be tried before a judge alone unless there are special circumstances to justify jury trial, such as a person's honour or reputation being at stake[3]. In other cases not covered by the statutory list, such as personal injury actions, trial by jury may be granted at the discretion of the court, and whereas this discretion was once "completely untrammelled"[4], in practice it is now difficult if not impossible

---

1 County Courts Act 1984, s 66.
2 Supreme Courts Act 1981, s 69.
3 E.g. *Goldsmith v Pressdram* [1987] 3 All ER 485; *Aitken v Preston*, The Times, 21 May 1997.
4 *Hope v Great Western Railway* [1937] 2 KB 130 per Lord Wright MR.

to obtain a jury trial in such actions[5] except where exemplary damages are claimed[6].

4.03   Prior to 1965 some 2 per cent of trials in the Queen's Bench Division took place before a jury – the figure has now declined somewhat with the exception of actions for defamation[7] and false imprisonment[8]. In the remaining cases which are still heard by juries, their freedom has been somewhat curtailed in recent years so that in defamation actions, where the jury is told to ensure than any award it makes is proportionate to the damage which the claimant has suffered[9], the court is now given the power to substitute its own assessments of damages for that of juries[10] and, following upon a particularly controversial award, judicial guidelines can now be given to juries in relation to the quantum of damages in defamation actions[11]. In addition there is an alternative statutory method of judicial assessment of damages in such actions[12], and although some have felt that the "golden age" of jury trials in defamation actions has come to an end there is still a relatively high number of such trials. In relation to false imprisonment and wrongful arrest actions, the Court of Appeal has introduced damages guidelines for juries and, once again, a departure has been made from the notion that the jury is to award a reasonable sum untrammelled by any judicial interference[13].

4.04   In the High Court there are 12 persons on the jury and in the county court eight, and verdicts should be unanimous although majority verdicts respectively of 10:2 and 7:1 can be accepted. Despite the atavistic English attachment to juries and their retention in coroners' courts[14] there is no strong movement to reintroduce them to any extent[15].

---

5 *Ward v James* [1966] 1 QB 273 following on from what were seen to be two unreasonably high jury awards in *Warren v King* [1963] 3 All ER 521 and *Morey v Woodfield (No 2)* [1964] 1 QB 1. See also *Williams v Beesley* [1971] 1 WLR 1295 and *Hulse v Chambers* [2001] 1 WLR 2386, para [9].

6 *H v Ministry of Defence* [1993] 2 QB 103.

7 For some recent examples see *Safeway Stores plc v Tate* [2001] QB 1120 and *Alexander v Arts Council for Wales* [2001] 1 WLR 1840.

8 For an interesting discussion on the role of the jury in such actions see *Ward v Chief Constable, West Midlands Police*, The Times, 15 Dec 1997; *Safeway v Tate* (n 7 above) and *Kiam v MGN* [2002] 3 WLR 1036.

9 *Rantzen v Mirror Group Newspapers* [1994] QB 670 at 696.

10 Court and Legal Services Act 1990.

11 *John v MGN* [1996] 2 All ER 35 – the guidelines include referring the jury to other defamation awards which have been made or approved by the Court of Appeal, to the scale of awards in personal injury actions (but see the criticism of this by the Privy Council in the Jamaican case of *The Gleaner Co v Abrahams* [2003] 3 WLR 1038) and by suggesting to the jury what the appropriate brackets or awards might be, although they are not then bound to make an award within these brackets – *Kiam v MGN* (n 8 above).

12 Defamation Act 1996.

13 *Thompson and Hsu v Commissioner of Police for the Metropolis* [1997] 2 All ER 762.

14 Coroners Act 1988, s 8(2).

15 See e.g. the comments of the Law Commission Consultation Paper No 140 *Damages for Personal Injuries: Non-Pecuniary Loss* (1995).

NORTHERN IRELAND

4.05   In the Supreme Court of Northern Ireland an action or issue of fact in an action in which a claim for libel and slander, malicious prosecution or false imprisonment is made shall be tried by a jury unless it involves matters of accounting, the protracted examination of documents or technical or scientific evidence, is likely to take a long time or is for another specified reason unsuitable for jury trial; any other action or issue of fact is tried without a jury unless the court orders to the contrary because there are allegations of fraud, undue influence or some other specified reason[16]. In personal injury actions jury trial will only be ordered in exceptional circumstances[17] notwithstanding the fact that retention of such jury trials had been recommended by a committee set up to consider civil procedures in the province[18]. In Northern Ireland the civil jury consists of seven members. The number of actions still heard by juries is, however, only a small percentage of the total[19].

REPUBLIC OF IRELAND

4.06   It has often been observed that the Irish appear to enjoy litigation and until the 1980s the civil jury trial was both a popular and well-used form of procedure, particularly in relation to actions for personal injuries, although it was remarked in one case with some justification that:

> "the proliferation of personal injuries claims and the significant high number of serious cases appear to me to have been induced among those concerned with processing such claims, lawyers, insurers and other indemnifiers alike, a degree of monetary punch drunkenness that has tended to remove reality from such settlements."[20]

However, in 1988, following upon the near collapse of the motor insurance industry in Ireland, allegedly caused by the high levels of damages awarded by juries, the right to trial by jury was severely curtailed and, in actions for personal injuries and actions arising out of wrongful deaths, abolished altogether; in the lower courts jury trial had already been abolished. The motivation behind this move appears to have been a political one and was controversial[21]. The spectre of the jury award still lives on though, as the level

16 Judicature (NI) Act 1987, s 62.
17 *Simpson v Harland & Wolff plc* [1988] NI 432.
18 *Report of the Committee on the Supreme Court of Judicature of Northern Ireland* (1970) Cmnd 4293.
19 In 1992 for example out of the 422 civil actions heard in the Supreme Court, only one involved a jury.
20 *Sinnott v Quinsworth, Coras Iompair Eireann and Durning* [1984] ILRM 531 at 535.
21 For a passionate defence of the civil jury in Ireland see McMahon, *Judge or Jury: The Jury Trial for Personal Injury Cases in Ireland* (Cork, 1985) and see annotations in Irish Current Law to the Act below.

of general damages for personal injury actions awarded in Ireland is still considerably in excess of the equivalent awards in Britain. In the Republic, civil juries of 12 members are still authorised to hear certain specific types of action, namely defamation, assault, false imprisonment, malicious prosecution and negligent or intentional harm to certain types of property[22] and, in respect of the first category alone, jury trial is still relatively common.

ISLE OF MAN

4.07 In the High Court of the Isle of Man certain types of civil action are to be heard by a jury, namely claims of fraud, libel, slander, malicious prosecution or false imprisonment, provided that the Deemster is not of the opinion that the trial would require a prolonged examination of documents or accounts or any scientific or local investigation which could not be conveniently made by a jury[23]. A jury has six members and is drawn from a panel of ten arrived at after a list of 36 potential jurors has been drawn up, and the parties alternatively strike off one name each until only ten names are left – an ingenious solution to picking a jury in a small jurisdiction where many of the Island's inhabitants may be known to each other[24].

CORONERS' COURTS

4.08 In those jurisdictions where the coroner is part of the system of civil administration, juries regularly sit when he officiates to determine the cause of death, albeit now usually in a minority of cases[25]. The size of the coroner's jury varies so that in England and Wales and Northern Ireland it normally comprises between seven and eleven members and elsewhere in the world the normal number is six.

UNITED STATES OF AMERICA

4.09 In the majority of state jurisdictions within the United States the civil jury trial is regarded as being an important institution and a significant number of cases, often of high value, are heard. Any litigant can claim the right to trial by jury in those types of cases for which such a right exists, and among the types of action competent to be tried in this way are personal injury actions,

22 (R o I) Courts Act 1988, s 1.
23 (I o M) High Court Act 1991, s 14; Jury Act 1980, s 18.
24 (I o M) Jury Act 1980, s 19.
25 Section 8(3) of the Coroners Act 1988 provides that in England and Wales a jury shall be summoned where a death has occurred in certain prescribed circumstances and s 8(4) provides that in all other cases the coroner has a discretion to dispense with a jury.

product liability cases, commercial disputes such as alleged patent infringement and (in large numbers) medical malpractice suits; indeed the range of causes which can be tried before civil juries is probably the greatest available in any country in the world[26]. The Seventh Amendment to the US Constitution guarantees a civil jury trial in virtually all federal court actions for damages. In the US the size of the civil jury varies, with six being the prescribed number for federal juries, and in the state courts the size varies with juries having between six and 12 members.

4.10 Americans regard the civil jury as a valuable everyday part of the machinery of justice in their country and it has been said that "no institution reflects the strengths and weaknesses of America more accurately than the jury. The inefficiency which often results from jury trial is accepted as a virtue of the system which scrupulously protects individual rights"[27]. In seeking to understand why the country so favours civil juries one view is that:

> "chief among the theoretical considerations is that the United States relies on a robustly adversarial form of justice. This means that Americans trust neutral and passive bodies to render decisions on the basis of the sharp clash of proofs presented by adversaries in a highly structured forensic setting. The jury is the most neutral and passive decision-maker available."[28]

CANADA

4.11 The civil jury in Canada was imported prior to the confederation in 1867 but it is now not used as extensively as in the neighbouring jurisdiction of the United States. However, the institution is still available for use in a wide variety of cases in Ontario and British Columbia, where it is regarded as a substantive personal right which is not to be derogated from except for cogent reasons. The civil jury is used to a lesser extent in Alberta and Saskatchewan, where more restrictions are placed upon its availability, and not at all in Quebec or the Canadian Federal Court, both of which expressly prohibit civil jury trials. "Civil juries are not widely used in Canada. However, there is no clear evidence that their use imposes any burden on the justice system or that their verdicts are aberrant."[29] The same commentator observes that civil juries are most widely used in motor vehicle accident cases and that they are

---

26 Texas is, apparently, the only state in either the US or the world in which child custody cases can be heard before a jury – a recent example was *Marinkovich v Linden* (2001), in which the defendant, believing that the judge who had been presiding over the case for four years was biased against her, took the unusual step of opting for jury trial. In the event the jury awarded custody to the plaintiff and visitation rights to the defendant.

27 Lynn, *Jury Trial Law and Practice* (New York, 1986); see also Litan (ed), *Verdict – Assessing the Civil Jury System* (Washington DC, 1993).

28 Vidmar (ed), *World Jury Systems* (Oxford, 2000), per Lansman at p 384.

29 Bogart in Vidmar, p 487.

favoured by insurance company defendants, and is of the view that if the constraints that are placed on obtaining jury trials in Canada were removed or loosened then their use would be greatly increased there and they would become much more common.

AUSTRALIA AND NEW ZEALAND

4.12 Civil juries still exist in both Australia and New Zealand and derive directly from colonial influences from the late nineteenth century. However, in Australia relatively insignificant numbers of cases are still tried by juries, whose size varies by state from between four and 12 members depending on the state jurisdiction, and their use is largely confined to a small category of civil actions. In New Zealand only a handful of cases annually is tried before a jury and, since the imposition of no-fault compensation for personal injuries, have been largely confined to actions of defamation and abuse of government power. The recent partial revival of personal injury actions based on negligence may, however, lead to an increase in the number of New Zealand civil jury actions.

THE REST OF THE WORLD

4.13 The civil jury exists in a number of jurisdictions throughout the world although in some countries it appears to be hardly ever used, either because of the small size of those jurisdictions or because trial before a judge alone is preferred. Those jurisdictions which have retained it are almost all countries which were, or are, in the British or US spheres of influence and most, if not all, also have their criminal cases tried before a jury. In most cases the jury has 12 members but the number can vary considerably. Those countries which retain civil juries at the time of writing are Malawi, Tonga, Guam, the Northern Marina Islands, Anguilla, Montserrat, St Vincent and the Grenadines, the Virgin Islands, Bermuda, the Cayman Islands, the Turks and Caicos Islands, St Christopher and Nevis, Jamaica, Puerto Rica and Belize[30].

---

30 Vidmar, chapter 13.

Chapter 5

Competent actions

BASIC CONSIDERATIONS FOR JURY TRIAL

5.01　There are three basic considerations which must be taken into account before any decision can be made as to whether or not a civil cause should proceed before a jury. Although these considerations may occur at different stages in the process it is nevertheless convenient to deal with them all at this juncture since they are fundamental matters which will affect each and every potential action. The three basic considerations are whether:

(a)　the action can competently proceed by way of jury trial, i.e. whether the action falls within the ambit of one of the enumerated causes or would otherwise be deemed suitable for jury trial and there exists no statutory bar to issues;

(b)　either party would be able to show special cause and thereby defeat the other party's right to a jury trial; and

(c)　it is in the best interests of a party to seek issues, i.e. the tactical and practical considerations which might arise when considering the respective merits of proof or jury trial.

The first matter, competence, is dealt with in this chapter while special cause and the tactical and practical considerations are dealt with in chapters 6 and 7 respectively.

THE ENUMERATED CAUSES

5.02　The expression "enumerated cause" arose from section 28 of the Court of Session Act 1825 in which a lengthy list of causes was set out and enumerated as being specially appropriate for trial by jury. The position was subsequently modified in 1850 when a proof on commission was allowed in place of jury trial in all of the enumerated causes except actions for libel and nuisance or causes which were properly and in substance actions of damages[1]. How-

1　Court of Session Act 1850, s 49.

ever, by the end of the nineteenth century there were few, if any, trials held in actions covered by the majority of these categories[2] and the Scottish Law Commission had, therefore, little hesitation in recommending the repeal of section 28 and its replacement by a shorter and more concise list of enumerated actions[3].

5.03   The current list of enumerated causes is to be found in section 11 of the Court of Session Act 1988 wherein it is provided that, subject to the consent of the parties or the showing by them of special cause in terms of section 9(b) of the Act, the following actions if remitted to probation *shall be tried by a jury*, namely:

(a)   an action of damages for personal injuries,
(b)   an action of damages for libel or defamation,
(c)   an action founded on delinquency or quasi-delinquency where the conclusion is for damages only and expenses, and
(d)   an action of reduction on the ground of incapacity, essential error or force and fear.

5.04   The effect of the current provision is that it is mandatory for a Lord Ordinary to remit all cases which fall within the ambit of the enumerated causes to trial by jury rather than proof unless either (a) the parties consent to a proof, or (b) one or other of the parties successfully argues that there is special cause for granting a proof rather than a trial.

ACTIONS OF DAMAGES FOR PERSONAL INJURIES

Definition

5.05   The first category of enumerated cause is that which, in recent years, has provided the bulk of civil actions tried before juries in the Court of Session, namely actions for personal injuries. No special meaning attaches to the words "personal injuries" in this context and accordingly the words are to be construed according to their normal meaning, i.e. all causes which would reasonably be thought of as falling within this category. The 1825 Act refers to "all actions on account of injury to the person, whether real or verbal", and since section 11 of the 1988 Act was only a consolidating provision it did not alter the position in regard to claims which would have fallen within the ambit of the 1825 Act. Accordingly a claim for loss of society and loss of support made in terms of section 1(3) and (4) of the Damages (Scotland) Act 1976 was held to be an action of damages for personal injuries falling within

2 In *Mitchell v Glickman* 1952 SLT (Notes) 51 it was said that this was "a case in which the main claim is one for damages for breach of contract, an issue which has not been tried before a jury for at least the past fifty years"; trial by jury was refused and the case was remitted back from the Court of Session to the sheriff court for a proof.
3 Scottish Law Commission Report No 111 (1988), p 11.

the meaning of section 11 of the 1988 Act[4]. Claims for transmitted solatium following upon a death and made in terms of section 2 of the 1976 Act are also heard by juries[5]. However in an action where the pursuer sustained personal injury after being a passenger in a car where the driver was uninsured and a question arose with the Motor Insurers' Bureau as to whether the pursuer knew or ought to have known that the driver was uninsured, the court held, this being a vital question to establish liability on the part of the defenders and minuters, that the cause was a "hybrid" action and thus did not fall properly within the definition of an enumerated cause[6]. The Administration of Justice (Scotland) Act 1982 defines "personal injuries" as including "any disease or any impairment of a person's physical or mental condition and injury resulting from defamation or any other verbal injury or injury to reputation"[7], and accordingly it could be argued that the enumerated causes include injuries resulting from verbal injury or other injury to reputation by reason of this definition[8].

Optional procedure

5.06 Where the pursuer in an action for personal injuries elected to use the optional procedure of the Court of Session[9], service of a summons in that form constituted a waiver by the pursuer of the right to jury trial[10] but the defender was still entitled to seek a jury trial unless he waived the right to do so[11].

Chapter 43 procedure

5.07 Actions for personal injuries raised under the provisions of the new

---

4 *Morris v Drysdale* 1992 SLT 186 at 188H–I and 188K–189A per Lord Morison.
5 E.g. *Wells v Hay* 1999 Rep LR 44.
6 *McFarlane v Thain* [2006] CSIH 3. Perhaps the term "hybrid" is not strictly a necessary one given that special cause was established in that action. In *Vetco Gray UK Ltd v Slessor* [2006] CSIH 11, where the court divided an inquiry into two stages to allow a separate proof between the defender and third party on the validity of an indemnity clause and then thereafter a proof or jury trial on liability as between the pursuer and defender or third party depending on the outcome of the first proof, *McFarlane* was (at para [15]) distinguished on the ground that "the Motor Insurers' Bureau was not a third party but had entered the process as a minuter and the second defender seemed to contemplate, wrongly in the view of the court, that the issue of the Motor Insurers' Bureau indemnity should also be determined by the jury. . . . In our view the word hybrid was a fair description in the circumstances of that case".
7 Section 13(1); this is in the same terms as s 10(1) of the Damages (Scotland) Act 1976.
8 For the meaning of "personal injury" and whether or not it includes injury to feelings, see *Barclay v Chief Constable, Northern Constabulary* 1986 SLT 562; *Fleming v Strathclyde Regional Council* 1992 SLT 161 and *Smith v City of Glasgow District Council* 1991 GWD 16-955. For the elements of verbal injury see *Steele v Scottish Daily Record & Sunday Mail Ltd* 1970 SLT 53.
9 Former Chapter 43 Part V abolished with effect from 1 April 2003.
10 Former rule 43.19(a) abolished in new actions as from 1 April 2003.
11 Former rule 43.19(b), 43.22.

Chapter 43 procedure introduced in 2003 can be tried by way of proof or jury trial and the Rules make specific reference to jury trial. The use of the procedure is mandatory for all personal injuries actions. "Personal injuries" are defined as "any disease or impairment, whether physical or mental", and "personal injuries action" as "an action of damages for, or arising from, personal injuries or death of a person from personal injuries" and, although it has been said that this definition demonstrates an intention to embrace every action which could possibly qualify in terms of the new definition[12], an action for professional negligence arising out of a failure to raise or prosecute a personal injuries action would be excluded from the procedure[13], even though this type of action can be tried by a jury[14].

Provisional damages

5.08   Where a claim for provisional damages is made[15], it has been said that, because of the fundamental difficulties which a jury would face in assessing such a claim, Parliament has, by implication, deprived the pursuer of the right to a jury trial[16]; it should be noted, however, that there is no express provision prohibiting the same.

Actions brought outwith the triennium

5.09   In general all actions for personal injuries or death consequent thereon require to be raised within three years of the date upon which the injury was sustained or the death occurred[17] and, provided that such actions are raised within the triennium, then there is no reason why issues may not be applied for, qualified only by considerations of *mora* where it is alleged that a party has been materially prejudiced by the delay in raising or prosecuting an action[18]. However, where the pursuer seeks to rely on the statutory provisions that allow an action to be brought later than three years after the date of death or of the sustaining of the injury but within three years of the date upon which the pursuer was or ought to have become aware of certain material facts[19] then trial

12   Lady Paton in *Tudhope v Finlay Park (t/a Park Hutchison, Solicitors)* 2003 SLT 1305.
13   Lord Cameron in *Tudhope v Finlay Park (t/a Park Hutchison, Solicitors)* 2004 SLT 783.
14   See further **5.13** below.
15   Administration of Justice (Scotland) Act 1982, s 12; rule 43.2(3).
16   *Potter v McCulloch* 1987 SLT 308 at 311L per Lord Weir, although whether this decision is correct in law has been doubted by many practitioners. See also *McFadyen v Crudens Ltd* 1972 SLT (Notes) 62 and *Winchester v Ramsay* 1966 SC 41. It is possibly less contentious to hold as correct Lord Weir's alternative formulation that in the circumstances of that case special cause could be found.
17   Prescription and Limitation (Scotland) Act 1973, ss 17, 18.
18   See **6.40** *et seq* below.
19   Prescription and Limitation (Scotland) Act 1973, ss 17(2)(b), 18(2)(b).

by jury is excluded[20]. Where the pursuer seeks to invoke the equitable power of the court to override the triennium then a jury trial is also ruled out[21]. If there is any question of whether or not the action was as a matter of fact raised within the triennium then it may be possible for this to be determined at a preliminary proof and issues may then be applied for at a later date[22].

ACTIONS OF DAMAGES FOR LIBEL AND DEFAMATION

5.10 Defamation has been defined as "the wrong or delict which is committed when a person makes an injurious and false imputation, conveyed by words or signs, against the character or reputation of another"[23]. The term covers both spoken and visual matter so that the phrase used in section 11 of the Court of Session Act 1988, "libel and defamation", is somewhat otiose. Strictly, however, the term "defamation" does not cover verbal injury, i.e. injury indirectly done by words not in themselves defamatory of the pursuer, slander of title and property, business or goods, *convicium*, malicious falsehood[24] or other forms of verbal injury but, as already explained, some forms of verbal injury may fall within the "personal injury" head[25]; in practice it has been suggested that the distinction between defamation and verbal injury "is sometimes so subtle that this alone will normally justify withholding [a verbal injury case] from a jury"[26]. Whether or not this view is correct, it is certainly true that as a matter of fact verbal injury actions have rarely, if ever, been tried by a jury.

5.11 An action for defamation must be brought within three years of the date on which the right of action accrued, being the date of publication or communication or the date upon which publication or communication first came to the notice of the pursuer[27], and although the pursuer can seek to invoke the equitable power of the court to override this time limit the right to jury trial is, in those circumstances, lost[28]. A further statutory exclusion to trial by jury in a defamation action occurs when the alleged defamer has made an offer to make amends and that offer has been accepted[29]; in such cases all

---

20 Prescription and Limitation (Scotland) Act 1973, s 22(4).
21 Prescription and Limitation (Scotland) Act 1973, s 19A(4).
22 *Haddow v Lord Advocate* 1959 SLT (Notes) 48.
23 Cooper, *The Law of Defamation* (2nd edn, 1906), p 1; see also Norrie, *Defamation and Related Actions in Scots Law* (1995).
24 See e.g. *Joyce v Sengupta* [1993] 1 WLR 337.
25 See **5.05** above.
26 Norrie, p 163.
27 Prescription and Limitation (Scotland) Act 1973, s 18A(1), (4)(b).
28 Prescription and Limitation (Scotland) Act 1973, s 19A(4).
29 Defamation Act 1996, ss 2 and 3, applied to Scotland by s 18(2).

remaining matters in contention are decided by a single Outer House judge sitting without a jury[30].

ACTIONS FOUNDED ON DELINQUENCY AND QUASI-DELINQUENCY

5.12 As in the two previous categories of enumerated cause, the expression "actions founded on delinquency and quasi-delinquency" is derived directly from the 1825 Act and refers in substance to delict in the sense of a deliberately inflicted wrong and quasi-delict in the sense of negligence or unintentional harm. For the purpose of jury trial this definition encompasses not only delicts such as assault, rape[31] and wrongful diligence[32] but also fault and violation of duty such as in the invasion of personal liberties by individuals or by representatives of the state, for example actions for malicious prosecution[33], wrongful imprisonment[34] or assault by police[35] or prison officers[36] – specific areas where the Strachan Committee thought that jury trial was preferable to proof before a judge and which, in practice, are the principal actions tried under this head[37]. A complex example of an action under this head being allowed to proceed before a jury was one which involved allegations of malicious and unjustified arrest and assault by the police and the making by them of false and malicious reports to the procurator fiscal[38].

5.13 This head of enumerated cause is, however, a wide one and covers virtually any cause which is, in substance, an action of damages *ex delicto*. Thus it would include an action for professional negligence where, for example, a solicitor failed to raise an action for personal injuries timeously[39] even though this was an action to which the Chapter 43 procedure might not apply[40]. Note, however, the general qualification in section 11 of the Court of Session Act 1988 that the conclusions in an action for delict or quasi-delict must be limited to damages and expenses only[41].

30 Defamation Act 1996, s 3(10).
31 *Black v Duncan* 1924 SC 738; that case involved a right to sue by the husband of the victim, a matter which would now be dealt with by a consideration of the modern law of primary and secondary victims.
32 *Hutchison v Provost, Magistrates and Councillors of Innerleithen* 1933 SLT 52.
33 *Douglas v Main* (1893) 20 R 793; *Peffers v Lindsay* (1894) 22 R 84.
34 *Munro v Holmes* 1949 SLT (Notes) 51.
35 *Macarthur v Chief Constable, Strathclyde Police* 1989 SLT 517.
36 *Campbell v Secretary of State for Scotland*, The Scotsman, 7 Oct 1989.
37 A similar view is taken in England and Wales, Northern Ireland and the Irish Republic.
38 *Robb v Sutherland; Irvine v Sutherland* 1994 GWD 38-2251; see also *Davidson v Chief Constable, Fife Police* 1995 SLT 545.
39 *Robertson v Bannigan* 1965 SC 20, per Lord Wheatley, although special cause was found in that case.
40 *Tudhope v Finlay Park (t/a Park Hutchison, Solicitors)* 2004 SLT 783.
41 Court of Session Act 1988, s 11.

ACTIONS OF REDUCTION ON GROUNDS OF INCAPACITY, ESSENTIAL ERROR OR FORCE AND FEAR

5.14 The 1825 Act provided that actions of reduction on the heads of furiosity and idiotcy, facility and lesion and force and fear should be heard before a jury. The Court of Session Act 1988 made a number of changes to the first of these grounds to take into account changes in practice and reflect the fact that a small number of actions of reduction on the grounds of essential error had also been sent to jury trial but that actions on the ground of undue influence in practice had always proceeded by way of proof; the remaining 1825 ground was left unchanged.

5.15 Incapacity may arise out of a number of factors such as insanity or mental incapacity including drunkenness[42] or non-age[43]. "Error becomes essential whenever it is shown that but for it, one of the parties would have declined to contract"[44], the usual ground being because of a misrepresentation by one of the parties. Force and fear encompasses a contract which has been entered into by reason of threats or violence sufficient to overcome the fortitude of a reasonable man, the true ground of reduction being fear induced by force[45].

5.16 It is, perhaps, interesting to note that although the questions of fact arising in actions of reduction might appear to be eminently suitable for determination by a jury, the Strachan Committee thought otherwise and stated that "we have been told that juries are particularly likely to err in actions of reduction, perhaps because of the difficulty of a simple direction in law being given, perhaps because the circumstances of these cases are more remote from everyday experience than, say, the nature of an accident causing physical injury"[46]. Note, however, that reduction on the ground of forgery is not an enumerated cause[47].

JURY TRIAL IN OTHER CAUSES

5.17 Although the list of enumerated causes cannot be added to, i.e. there is no automatic right to a jury trial in any action other than those set out in section 11 of the 1988 Act, the court has an overriding power to determine in any non-consistorial action the tribunal before which a proof in a particular

---

42 *Taylor v Provan* (1864) 2 M 1226.
43 Age of Legal Capacity (Scotland) Act 1991, s 1(1)(a).
44 *Menzies v Menzies* (1893) 20 R (HL) 108 at 142 per Lord Watson; *Stewart v Kennedy* (1890) 17 R (HL) 25 at 28.
45 Stair, I, ix, 8; *Priestnell v Hutcheson* (1857) 19 D 459 at 499 per Lord Deas.
46 Strachan Committee Report, para 66.
47 *Watson v Lloyd* (1897) 5 SLT 73; *Blount v Watt* 1953 SLT (Notes) 39 and see **5.17**.

cause may be led[48]. Thus the Lord Ordinary may, after a motion has been made to have a cause which is not an enumerated one, order a jury trial, provided that it is done solely on the basis of the facts of the case and not upon some other general consideration. In the past this power was exercised to allow a jury trial in an action of reduction on the grounds of essential error (when this was not at the time an enumerated cause) and the Inner House refused to interfere with this exercise of the Lord Ordinary's discretion[49]. In another case the court refused to allow jury trial in actions of reduction on the ground of fraud although it was not doubted that the judge had the power to do so and, in the words of Lord Guthrie, "if there were a practice that reductions on the ground of forgery were sent to jury trial, I should have followed it, but there is no such practice"[50], notwithstanding the fact that criminal cases involving fraud and forgery are regularly tried before juries in Scotland[51]. Therefore, although in theory a jury trial can be obtained in any cause which is not an enumerated one, it may as a matter of current practice be difficult, if not virtually impossible, to convince a Lord Ordinary to grant issues in such circumstances[52].

AGREEMENTS BETWEEN PARTIES AS TO MODE OF INQUIRY

5.18   Since 1866 the Lord Ordinary has had the power to grant a proof rather than a jury trial in any action falling within the enumerated causes in two specified circumstances, namely (a) where the parties consent to this, or (b) where special cause is shown[53]. In relation to such consent, the parties are free to agree to a debate, preliminary proof, proof, proof before answer or jury trial as appropriate[54] and the general rule is that where parties have agreed on a particular mode of inquiry, be it jury trial or otherwise, then the Lord Ordinary in the exercise of his discretion should comply with their wishes and give effect thereto[55] even if he had some doubts as to the propriety of their choice[56]. Moreover if the parties agree to a particular mode of inquiry then the cause will so proceed and the agreement between them will be regarded as binding unless either of the parties subsequently agrees to a different mode of inquiry or the pleadings are amended in such a manner as to justify the court considering the matter de novo or there is a material change in circumstances[57].

48 Maclaren, p 545; Maxwell, p 326.
49 *Fletcher v Lord Advocate* 1923 SC 27.
50 *Blount v Watt* 1953 SLT 73; see also *Campbell's Trs v Lloyd* (1897) 5 SLT 73.
51 *Currie v Strathclyde Regional Council Fire Brigade* 1999 SLT 62.
52 In *McFarlane v Thain* [2006] CSIH 3 an unsuccessful attempt was made to invoke this power in an action which the court held was not an enumerated cause.
53 Court of Session Act 1988, s 9(b).
54 Rule 22.3(5) and, in actions to which the Chapter 43 procedure applies, rule 43.
55 *Dent v North British Railway Co* (1880) 17 SLR 368.
56 *Gallagher v National Coal Board* 1962 SLT 160 at 162.
57 See chapter 13 below.

Chapter 6

Special cause

GENERAL CONSIDERATIONS

6.01 Where the parties cannot reach an agreement as to the mode of inquiry in an enumerated cause, the party who seeks a proof rather than a jury trial must satisfy the court that there is special cause as to why the other party should be deprived of his right to a trial[1]. This statutory right is not affected by the Rules of Court[2] or by any other legislation unless it can be shown that the rule or legislation expressly or by implication affects the right to a jury trial by excluding or otherwise placing a restriction on that right[3]. The appropriate stage at which the matter would normally be considered by the court is in the case of an ordinary action at a procedure roll hearing and, in a Chapter 43 action, a motion roll hearing[4].

6.02 A "special cause" must be a cause which is special to the particular case being considered and it must relate to some factor inherent in the case itself which renders it unsuitable for trial by jury[5]. Lord Clyde once observed that:

"A special cause implies some speciality or other about the case or its circumstances, but the Court has always refrained from any attempt to lay down rules on the subject; nor is anything gained by pointing out that this or that general consideration will not be enough in itself to constitute special cause. Whether this or that special feature – or some combination of special features – amounts to special cause is a question to be determined, not by reference to any legal principle or category, but as a matter of sound discretion, and the discretion rests mainly, and in the first instance, with the Lord Ordinary whose duty it is to try the case."[6]

1 Court of Session Act 1988, s 9(b).
2 *Graham v Paterson & Sons Ltd* 1938 SC 119.
3 *McFadyen v Crudens Ltd* 1972 SLT (Notes) 62 per Lord President Emslie; cf *Potter v McCulloch* 1987 SLT 308 at 311L per Lord Weir and *Winchester v Ramsay* 1966 SC 41.
4 See further **9.02–9.05** below.
5 *Taylor v Dumbarton Tramways Co* 1918 SC (HL) 96 at 108 per Lord Shaw of Dunfermline; *Anderson v Grieve* 1970 SLT (Notes) 39.
6 *Walker v Pitlochry Motor Co* 1930 SC 565.

6.03   In a subsequent case Lord Justice-Clerk Aitchison held that:

> "Special cause means some real ground of substance making the case unsuitable
> for jury trial. It must not be a mere hypothetical difficulty conjured up by the
> ingenuity of counsel[7]. It ought to be something that is capable of articulate for-
> mulation, and not a mere generality."[8]

More recently it has been said that the question of special cause in any case
"is essentially a matter for the discretion of the court, the object being to select
as between the alternative methods of inquiry which type of tribunal would
best secure justice as between the parties to the action"[9].

6.04   In considering special cause there are, therefore, no general rules which
are applicable to any particular set of circumstances, so that precedent can only
provide a guide to practice and thus the attitude of the court to, say, special
cause in an action founded upon a breach of a particular statutory provision
will not set a precedent in relation to special cause in another case based on a
breach of the same provisions[10]. Thus any particular case must be considered
solely on its merits and must have some difficulties in itself which would make
it unsuitable for trial by jury[11]. In a recent case[12] Lord Eassie commented
that:

> "Only limited assistance is to be gained from looking at other cases in which
> the question of proof or jury trial may have been decided on particular aver-
> ments. There is obviously a considerable borderline area in which the judge, in
> the exercise of his discretion, has to reach a view as to the suitability or not of
> the case for hearing before a jury."

Whether or not these difficulties constitute special cause is very much a
matter for the impression of the court[13] and the discretion of the Lord
Ordinary in finding whether or not special cause has been established is para-
mount; the Inner House will be slow to interfere with the exercise of that
discretion and overturn his decision[14].

6.05   In considering whether or not special cause has been established, the
court should have regard only to considerations special to the particular case
involved and not to those which are general in character and might apply in
other circumstances[15]. These considerations should be strictly related to the

---

7   See also *Patterson v Somerville* [2005] CSOH 19.
8   *Walker v Pitlochry Motor Co* 1930 SC 565.
9   *Graham v Associated Electrical Industries Ltd* 1968 SLT 81 at 82 per Lord President Clyde.
10 *Swan v Jute Industries Ltd* 1968 SLT (Notes) 8; *Anderson v Grieve* 1970 SLT (Notes) 39.
11 *McLellan v Western SMT Co* 1950 SC 112 at 116.
12 *Currie v Strathclyde Regional Council Fire Brigade* 1999 SLT 62.
13 *Taylor v Scottish Boiler & General Insurance Co* 1951 SLT (Notes) 36.
14 *Vallery v McAlpine & Sons* (1905) 7 F 640; *Walker v Pitlochry Motor Co* 1930 SC 565;
    Graham v Paterson & Sons Ltd 1938 SC 119 at 136; *McLellan v Western SMT Co* 1950 SC
    112 at 116.
15 *Rice v Borland* 1961 SC 16.

factual or legal matters raised by the action itself and not to any unconnected matters, so that the fact that the case might be of particular interest to the general public because it involved football ("Scotland's national game") is not a relevant factor when considering special cause[16]. In a similar fashion the fact that a jury trial might have practical advantages for a party is not a special cause[17], or the fact that, *per se*, there is a multiplicity of questions in the issues which the jury will be required to answer[18]. In England it has been held that the fact that a party is a fugitive from justice[19] or that a case might have to depend to a great extent on hearsay evidence[20] has not been sufficient to deprive a person of his right to a civil jury. It should, however, be borne in mind that since jury trial is available as of right in all cases which fall within the ambit of the enumerated causes and that special cause is an exception to that right, one party cannot deprive the other of a jury trial by manipulating the pleadings, for example by admitting liability only after the other has been refused issues because of a difficult question of law relating to liability[21]. Although it is usually the defender who seeks to establish special cause, the pursuer has the same statutory right to avoid issues and the considerations are identical irrespective of which party is seeking a proof[22].

6.06   Bearing in mind that the finding of special cause is a matter dependent on the exercise of discretion by the Lord Ordinary, each case will tend to turn on its own peculiar facts and circumstances and one example therefore may be of little guidance in considering what should be done in another case[23]. There are, nevertheless, certain categories under which decisions can be broadly grouped in order to demonstrate how the courts have approached the matter in the past. Cases decided under the previous Scottish statutory provision relating to special cause[24] have been held to still be of relevance[25], but English authority and practice in this area have been held to be of no assistance at all[26]. It should be emphasised that the following categorisation is not intended to be exhaustive and that if there is any single and overriding principle which can be applied in this area it is that cases which are straightforward in respect of both the facts and the law will always be allowed to be tried by

---

16 *Peat v News Group Newspapers Ltd* 1996 GWD 16-952.
17 *Englert v Stakis plc* 1996 Rep LR 130.
18 *McKeown v Sir William Arrol & Co Ltd* 1974 SC 97; *Smith v T & J Harrison* 1973 SLT (Notes) 92; *Scott v Vieregge* [2005] CSOH 42.
19 *Polanski v Condé Nast Publications Ltd* [2005] UKHL 10.
20 *O'Brien v Chief Constable, South Wales Police* [2003] EWCA Civ 1085 at paras 68–69 per Brooke LJ cited with approval in *Polanski* at para 36.
21 *Higgins v Burton* 1968 SLT (Notes) 14.
22 For a recent example of where the second defender sought issues and the pursuer and minuters argued special cause see *McFarlane v Thain* [2005] CSOH 22, 2005 SLT 221; [2006] CSIH 3.
23 *Walters v National Coal Board* 1961 SLT (Notes) 82.
24 Evidence (Scotland) Act 1866, s 4.
25 *Shanks v British Broadcasting Corporation* 1993 SLT 326 at 336J–K.
26 *Millar v London & North Eastern Railway* 1927 SLT 499 at 503; *Shanks* at 337I–J.

a jury and that any significant departure from the straightforward may justify the finding of special cause. This is especially true where there are a multiplicity of such departures from the norm and in these circumstances the court will more readily find special cause even if the individual matters raised might not in themselves have been sufficient to justify a finding of special cause.

6.07 Traditionally all debates on the question of special cause have been conducted solely on the basis of the averments which have appeared in the pleadings[27] and it has not been the practice to consider extraneous matter[28]. However, in Chapter 43 personal injury actions a practice seems to have developed whereby the mandatory statement of valuation and the documents in support thereof have been referred to when the matter of special cause is before the court and their contents have been considered in deciding whether fair notice of the pursuer's claim has been given[29], whether a claim is too complex to be heard by a jury[30], and whether a claim was specific in relation to loss of employability or loss of support[31] but not where the pleadings were so inspecific that they did not identify the persons on whose behalf a particular claim was made[32]. However, it has been said that a party cannot simply point to the potential complexities in a particular claim that may or may not arise without any suggestion in his averments as to why matters might be difficult and thus hope to avoid a jury trial[33].

DIFFICULT QUESTIONS OF FACT

6.08 The members of the jury are the "masters of the issues within their province, namely the questions of fact"[34] and it is only where the facts are in some way particularly difficult or complex that special cause will normally be established. Thus, in a case in which it was said that the matter between the parties was relatively straightforward and turned principally upon a single question of fact, i.e. the state of a set of traffic lights immediately prior to a collision, Lord Eassie concluded that: "Having regard to the relative complexity of matters regularly addressed by juries in criminal cases, it cannot be said that the merits of this claim raise any issue rendering its determination unsuitable for a jury"[35].

---

27 The exception to this are pleas based on *mora* – see **6.41** *et seq* below.
28 However, where documents have been lodged in terms of rule 27.1(1) as having been founded upon by a party or adopted as incorporated into the pleadings, then such documents may be referred to at the motion roll or procedure roll hearing but see also *Prophit v British Broadcasting Corporation* 1997 SLT 745.
29 *Easdon v A Clark & Co (Smethwick) Ltd* [2006] CSOH 12.
30 *Millar v Watt* Lady Smith, 2004 GWD 16-530.
31 *Scott v Vieregge* [2005] CSOH 42; *May v Jeeves Parcels Ltd* [2005] CSOH 71.
32 *Jones v Leslie* 2004 Rep LR 136.
33 *Crawford v Renfrewshire Council*, Lord Wheatley, 2000 GWD 40-1476.
34 *Macintosh v Commissioners of the Burgh of Lochgelly* (1897) 25 R 32 at 34.
35 *Currie v Strathclyde Regional Fire Brigade* 1999 SLT 62; cf *Beaton v Cain* 2000 SLT 920.

6.09 It should be recognised that, *per se*, the existence of questions of fact which might involve the jury in some thought or the existence of evidence which might be complex or technical in nature is not sufficient to establish special cause – the difficulties must be of such a nature as to justify withholding the case from the jury[36]. It is always to be assumed that, however difficult the facts are in a particular case, if the judge can properly direct the jury then special cause would not be found but "while it must be accepted that our system of civil as well as criminal jury trials largely depends upon juries faithfully following directions given by the trial judge, there will always be exceptional cases where that may be doubted or even unlikely"[37]. Where the multiplicity of facts are of such a nature that there is a real danger that the jury might "miss the point altogether", special cause might be found[38] so that, for instance, in a case which involved questions relating to an extremely complex chemical process, a proof was allowed[39]. By way of contrast in a case arising out of a road traffic accident, the mere complexity of facts which the jury would have to take into account, including the inferences which they would be required to draw from evidence including locus measurements, was held not to be sufficient to constitute special cause and issues were allowed notwithstanding these factors[40].

6.10 Some consideration has been given by the courts to cases involving the causation and extent of personal injuries sustained and the medical treatment received therefor. Medical complexity is not necessarily a reason not to send a case to a jury[41] nor is the fact that the pursuer suffers from a number of readily understandable medical conditions[42] and issues should be allowed where the injuries and their sequelae are not out of the ordinary[43]. The onus is on the defender to show that there is a real likelihood, as opposed to a purely hypothetical possibility, of the issues being of such controversy or novelty or complexity that they would render jury trial inappropriate[44].

> "The mere fact that a number of surgeons have to give evidence does not necessarily mean that the conditions or symptoms they describe will be difficult or complex. The fact that different results have been produced from a series

36 *Thompson v Home* 1994 GWD 12-778.
37 *Morris v Fife Council* (Extra Div) 2004 SLT 1139.
38 *Barbour v McGruer* 1967 SLT (Notes) 41; *Gardner v A B Fleming & Co Ltd* 1969 SLT (Notes) 93.
39 *Robertson v T & H Smith Ltd* 1962 SC 628.
40 *Shearer v Bevan's Exrx* 1986 SLT 226.
41 *Thomson v McAlear* 1996 Rep LR 128; *Irvine v Balmoral Hotel Edinburgh Ltd* 1999 Rep LR 41; *MacInnes v Owen*, Temporary Judge C J Macauley QC, 24 Nov 2004; *Annandale v Santa Fé International Services Inc* [2006] CSOH 52.
42 *Stewart v Nicoll* 2003 SLT 843; *Devaney v Yarrow Shipbuilders* 1999 SLT 561; *Graham v Dryden* 2002 Rep LR 104.
43 *Wells v Stenhouse* 2000 GWD 21-828.
44 *King v Negro* 2002 GWD 40-1323.

of tests is exactly the kind of issue which juries are expected to assess in many cases."[45]

However, the severity of the injury sustained does not in itself amount to a special cause, so that a case involving the permanent and severe disablement and the inability to enjoy physical recreation was held to be suitable for trial by jury[46]. The fact that the pursuer is claiming for an industrial disease does not constitute special cause[47]. A conflict of medical[48] or psychiatric[49] opinion as to causation is not in itself enough to form special cause and juries are frequently called upon to decide on a broad basis of common sense where there is an apparent conflict of medical opinion in which it is not suggested that an area of medical science is involved which is neither novel nor unexplained[50]. Thus, in a case where blindness supervened after a blow on the nose a jury trial was refused on the basis that medical science improperly understood the pursuer's condition[51].

6.11 Special cause has not been established in the following circumstances: (a) in a case involving pleural plaques consequent upon exposure to asbestos where physically the condition was asymptomatic but the pursuer was anxious and depressed and there was a possibility that he could develop the fatal condition of mesothelioma[52]; (b) where the pursuer was suffering from 13 different medical conditions, most of which were disputed, and which would require evidence from orthopaedic surgeons, neurologists, psychologists and employment consultants[53]; (c) where a pursuer had suffered shock with no outward physical signs of injury[54]; (d) in the case of an executor's transmitted claim for the pain and suffering of a person prior to his death, both where the death occurred as a result of the accident forming the subject-matter of the action[55] and where the death was unrelated[56]; and (e) where there was an unusual head of claim (loss of a holiday) provided that the loss sustained could be said to be foreseeable[57].

6.12 Where complex matters involving the standard of care applicable to

---

45 *Werfel v Norfrost Ltd* 2002 GWD 1-12; see also *Potts v McNulty* 2000 SLT 1269.
46 *Shearer v Bevan's Exrx* 1986 SLT 226.
47 *Beattie v Ross Dairies Ltd* 1955 SLT (Notes) 50.
48 *Meechan v McFarlane* 1996 SLT 208; *Miller v Clarke Chapman & Co* 1952 SLT (Notes) 27; *McKenna v Sharp* 1998 SC 297; *McGuire v Morris & Spottiswood Ltd* [2005] CSOH 82; *Toner v McLeod* [2006] CSOH 22.
49 *Livingstone v Fife Council* 2004 SLT 161.
50 *McAllister v Strathclyde Regional Council* 1993 GWD 1-65.
51 *Fyfe v Barnet & Morton Ltd* 1965 SLT (Notes) 52.
52 *Gibson v McAndrew Wormald & Co* 1998 SLT 562.
53 *Stewart v Nicoll* 2003 SLT 843.
54 *Cowie v London, Midland & Scottish Railway* 1934 SC 433.
55 *Wells v Hay* 1999 Rep LR 44 (where the death occurred several days later).
56 *Gartley v R McCartney (Painters) Ltd* 1997 Rep LR (Q) 18 (the death occurred three years later).
57 *Potts v McNulty* 2000 SLT 1269.

professional persons such as nurses and doctors and which would involve precise considerations of detailed anatomical evidence are concerned, special cause
may be found[58]. However, if the relevant averments have been made to enable
a jury to be properly directed[59] and the jury can, in the circumstances of the
case, be properly directed, then issues will be allowed[60] especially if the negligence alleged is relatively simple in nature, for example where an accepted
proper practice was not followed[61] or where there was a failure to diagnose a
reasonably obvious condition[62].

6.13 Some other examples of where the court has allowed issues despite an
argument being advanced in relation to factual complexity include: (a) where
a pursuer was injured in a fall and then received further injuries when as a
result of a road traffic accident he was thrown out of the vehicle conveying
him to hospital, it was held that the jury would be able to discriminate
between medical opinions expressed before it and to assess what loss was attributable to the road traffic accident and what was attributable to the original
fall[63]; (b) where, after amendment, the medical issues at stake were held no
longer to be difficult and the only real issue at stake was the pursuer's credibility[64]; and (c) where the defender averred that the pursuer might have been
predisposed to the onset of depression and that the development of a psychiatric injury could be cumulative[65].

6.14 Some examples of where the court has found a case too complex for
a jury include where: (a) the matters in dispute concerned the extent of brain
damage suffered by an incapax, the issue of his alleged epilepsy, causation of
his symptoms and the question of whether he suffered from functional overlay
and post-traumatic stress disorder and here it was said that there was an abnor-
mally large volume of medical evidence in addition to other factors[66]; (b) there
was a combination of lengthy medical history independent of the accident,
an exaggeration of symptoms and an attempt to produce misleading results in
tests, a poor work record and difficulties in relation to the calculation of future
wage loss and the assessment of actuarial evidence[67]; (c) there was complicated
evidence relating to brain stem lesions with detailed reference being made to

---

58 *Miller v Lanarkshire Health Board* 1993 SLT 453.
59 *Hunter v Hanley* 1955 SC 200.
60 *Murray v Lanarkshire Acute Hospitals NHS Trust*, Lord Wheatley, 2003 GWD 6-135 –
   see also **6.33** below.
61 *Murray*, n 60 above.
62 *Devlin v Ghosh*, Lord McEwan, 4 May 2005★ – this case involved a failure to exclude,
   in diagnosis, the possibility that the pursuer, a 39-year-old woman with a significant
   past history of heart problems, had had an infarction when she was doubled up in pain,
   having difficulty in breathing and was distressed and anxious; issues were allowed.
63 *McKenna v Chief Constable, Strathclyde Police* 1998 SLT 1161.
64 *Meldrum v Crolla* 2001 GWD 13-461.
65 *Livingstone v Fife Council* 2004 SLT 161.
66 *McKechnie's Curator Bonis v Gribben* 1996 SLT 136.
67 *Meechan v McFarlane* 1996 SLT 208.

x-rays and MRI scans, in combination with other factors[68]; (d) it was said that the merits of the case were straightforward but a jury might have difficulty in determining the extent to which the accident caused the injury and conse-quent loss to the pursuer given a pre-existing condition and a history of depression[69]; (e) a pursuer suffered several distinct and serious injuries to his lower limbs and the question arose as to how these injuries related to his pre-sent disability and pain, discomfort and restriction of movement in his leg and back[70]; (f) the pursuer had suffered depression greater than grief and loss of society and the value of the services and by whom they were rendered was insufficiently pled it was said to be difficult to direct the jury accord-ingly[71]; (g) the medical records were 1,000 pages long and related to multiple and serious injuries and there was a conflict of evidence as to life expectancy[72]; (h) there were averments of physical and psychological injury and the jury would have to decide whether one or both or neither rendered the pursuer unfit for some types of work or were indeed relevant[73]; (i) the pursuer's evi-dence in cross-examination would be likely to have such an effect on the jury's mind that a serious risk of prejudice would occur that no direction by the judge could realistically remove and, further, that there was a risk that aver-ments, now removed, that a third party had contributed to the pursuer's con-dition might result in difficulties for the jury in attributing the loss to the defender[74]; (j) the pursuer had left open for inquiry a range of factual, statis-tical and opinion issues which created uncertainty and would leave the jury a multiplicity of possible situations relating to causation[75]; and (k) inadequate notice had been given to the defender on the pathology existing between the injury sustained as a result of an accident and the devastating consequences now said to be the direct result of that injury[76].

DIFFICULT QUESTIONS OF LAW

6.15 Notwithstanding the principle that it is for the judge to direct the jury in relation to the applicable law, there may be cases in which it would be diffi-cult to properly direct the jury because of the complex legal question or

68 *Thomson v Kvaerner Govan Ltd* 1997 GWD 12-493.
69 *Pietryea v Strathclyde Regional Council* 1998 SLT 184.
70 *McInnes v Kirkforthar Brick Co* 1998 SLT 568.
71 *Beaton v Cain* 2000 SLT 920.
72 *Sharp v Henderson* 1999 GWD 29-1359.
73 *McCormack v CSC Forestry Products Ltd* 2001 GWD 40-1499; *Kennedy v Forrest-Jones* 2001 SLT 630.
74 *Morris v Fife Council* (OH) 2003 SLT 926 upheld (IH) 2004 SLT 1139; cf *Livingstone v Fife Council* 2004 SLT 161.
75 *Forrest v Gourlay* 2003 SLT 783; cf *Annandale v Santa Fé International Services Inc* [2006] CSOH 52.
76 *MacInnes v Owen*, Temporary Judge C J Macauley QC, 24 Nov 2004.

questions involved and therefore issues should be refused[77]. Examples of this might include (a) where consideration was needed of the meaning of "serious" and "risk" in the context of a new statutory provision which had not previously been judicially interpreted[78], (b) where common law liability for bulls had never previously been decided in the context of the circumstances of the case[79], and (c) where it is suspected from the averments that problems of admissibility of evidence are likely to arise and it can be said that it is in the best interests of both parties to have a proof allowed[80].

6.16 Special cause has not been found (a) merely because there is contributory negligence[81], (b) because there is a difficult question relating to statutory construction[82] unless there is some material and relevant complication in the case to make it so[83], (c) where there was an issue of whether or not the pursuer was a primary victim when an explosion occurred in his vicinity[84], (d) where the pursuer had suffered an emotional reaction to bereavement which amounted to a psychiatric injury[85], (e) where there were questions relating to *res ipsa loquitur* and strict liability imposed by statutory duties[86], and (f) where a question relating to the allocation of limited resources did not of itself render a case unsuitable for jury trial[87], and (g) where there was uncertainty as to the precise meaning of the phrase "knew or ought to have known" within a specific statutory context[88].

DIFFICULT QUESTIONS OF FACT AND LAW

6.17 Where there are difficult questions of fact and law is something of a hybrid category but the same principles apply, namely that the main consideration in finding special cause is that of whether or not an effective direc-

---

77 *Caldwell v Wright* 1970 SC 24.
78 *Potter v McCulloch* 1987 SLT 308 at 312C (provisional damages), cf *Wells v Hay*, Lord Kingarth, 4 March 1998★ where it was held that "grief and sorrow" in terms of s 1(4) of the Damages (Scotland) Act 1976 had no special meaning and issues were allowed.
79 *Henderson v John Stuart (Farms) Ltd* 1963 SC 245; *Sneddon v Baxter* 1967 SLT (Notes) 67.
80 *Boyle v Glasgow Corporation* 1949 SC 254 at 261 per Lord Justice-Clerk Thomson; *Holt v Drever* 1970 SLT (Notes) 49; *Robertson v Leslie & Saddler Ltd* 1970 SLT 44.
81 *Gardner v Hastie* 1928 SLT 497 at 499 per Lord Fleming; *Belford v Jones* 1973 SLT (Notes) 85; *Ross v Pryde* 2004 Rep LR 129 and note the specific wording of s 1(6) of the Law Reform (Contributory Negligence) Act 1945.
82 *Macintosh v Commissioners of Burgh of Lochgelly* (1897) 25 R 32.
83 *Morrison v Cults Lime Ltd* 1961 SLT (Notes) 31; *McLean v Robert W Douglas (Contractors) Ltd* 1969 SLT (Notes) 21.
84 *Forey v RHI Refractories (UK) Ltd* 2004 GWD 9-198 – note that in this case the pursuer gave a specific undertaking to limit the scope of the evidence led at the trial.
85 *Gillies v Lynch* 2002 SLT 1420 and *Gillies v Lynch (No 2)*, Lord Macfadyen, 2004 GWD 35-710; cf *Ross v Pryde* 2004 Rep LR 129.
86 *Johnston v J T Inglis & Sons Ltd*, Lord Bonomy, 2000 GWD 1-6.
87 *Ireland v Dunfermline District Council* 1998 SLT 231.
88 *McFarlane v Thain* [2006] CSIH 3.

tion can be given to the jury[89]. Where it can, issues will be allowed – an example of this being a case where it was said that there had been an unjustified and malicious arrest, assault and the making of false and malicious reports to the procurator fiscal and in which it was held that a civil jury could properly be charged to address the question of whether the police had acted maliciously and without justification and whether they were guilty of assault, these all being matters which were commonly considered by juries in criminal proceedings[90]. However, in some cases it will be difficult or impossible to properly charge the jury because of the existence of complex questions of both fact and law and issues will be refused.

6.18 Examples of cases which have been held to be difficult on the facts and law for a jury to try include where: (a) there was a difficult and novel question arising out of statutory questions relating to access to the workplace[91], (b) there was an accident in a slaughterhouse and consideration had to be given to the relative responsibilities of employers and occupiers and to the suitability of the layout of purpose-built premises[92], (c) questions arose in relation to loss of society and support where a widow was now cohabiting with another man who had accepted her child into family[93], (d) an 11-year-old boy had sustained severe injuries and a consideration of his future employment prospects was required[94], (e) it was averred that an injured passenger was aware that the driver of the vehicle in which he was travelling had been drinking[95], (f) the pursuer was suffering from industrial dermatitis and it was said that in consequence difficult questions of fact and law arose[96], (g) two separate and distinct standards of care could be applied to the same incident[97], (h) there was some doubt as to the legal status of a party, for instance where the pursuer was said to have been a volunteer rather than an employee[98], (i) an employee was killed while being given a lift home in one of the company's lorries and a question arose in relation to whether or not there was any contract of carriage between the employer and employee[99], (j) two buses collided and the operators of one blamed the roads authority and thereby raised difficult questions of fact and law[100], (k) one set of defenders adopted averments of fault against the pursuer but made

---

89 E.g. *Robertson v Lothian Health Board* 1989 GWD 27-1223; *Cheeseman v International Travel Service* [2005] CSOH 164.
90 *Robb v Sutherland; Irvine v Sutherland* 1994 GWD 38-2251.
91 *McCormick v Fairfield Shipbuilding & Engineering Co Ltd* 1964 SLT (Notes) 34.
92 *Bygate v Edinburgh Corporation* 1967 SLT (Notes) 65.
93 *Morris v Drysdale* 1992 SLT 186.
94 *Timoney v Dunnery* 1984 SLT 151.
95 *McGinnigle v McLuskie* 1974 SLT (Notes) 34.
96 *Rigley v Remington Rand* 1964 SLT (Notes) 100; *Cauley v Thomas Boag & Son Ltd* 1962 SLT (Notes) 63.
97 *Black v Angus Hospitals Management Board* 1960 SLT (Notes) 7.
98 *Vallance v Easson Brothers Ltd* 1949 SLT (Notes) 7.
99 *McKie v NorWest Construction Co* 1931 SN 126.
100 *Craigens v Central SMT Co* 1937 SLT 139.

further averments of fault against the other which were denied by the pursuer[101], (l) drawing a fair and reasonable dividing line, as a matter of degree, between the illegitimate and legitimate actings of three arresting police officers was considered to be difficult enough for an experienced judge and it would be exceedingly difficult for proper jury directions to be framed[102], (m) the pursuer's pre-existing dyslexia might give rise to complications in assessing patrimonial loss because of the difficulty in directing the jury in relation to causation, remoteness of damages and mitigation of loss[103], and (n) there was a question as to whether "reasonably practicable" measures had been taken in relation to a statutory duty[104].

6.19 Cases which, though potentially complex on the facts and law, have been held to be suitable for issues include (a) where there were averments relating to risk assessments on a building site combined with statutory and common law cases and where substantial expert evidence would be required[105], and (b) where a statutory case had been pled but where the jury only had to decide if the equipment had been maintained in an efficient state, in efficient working order and in good repair[106].

DIFFICULTIES IN ASSESSING DAMAGES

6.20 Where there are difficulties in assessing damages, either because of difficult questions of fact and law or because of the lack of specification in relation to a head of claim, this may constitute special cause[107], but it should be noted that the fact that the jury may be presented with a difficult task in assessing damages does not, *per se*, mean that a case is necessarily unsuitable for jury trial[108], and "difficulty in quantifying a claim which is inherently non-specific in character is, if anything, a reason for sending a case to jury trial rather than the reverse"[109]. Much will depend, once again, on whether or not an effective direction can be given to the jury and it has been said that when different heads of damage have to be put to a jury that the trial judge will always be assisted by the formulae put by counsel in their speeches[110]. Since in Chapter 43 personal injury actions a statement of valuation now has to be lodged, this should

101 *McKenzie v Donachie* 1969 SLT (Notes) 3.
102 *McKie v Orr*, Lord Emslie, 2002 GWD 7-246, (IH) 2003 SC 317.
103 *Elwis v Consignia*, Lord Reed, 2004 GWD 38-775; cf *Baillie v ECG Group Ltd* [2005] CSOH 40 and *Annandale v Santa Fé International Services Inc* [2006] CSOH 52.
104 *Baillie v ECG Group Ltd* [2005] CSOH 40.
105 *Warnock v Clark Contracts Ltd* 2003 GWD 19-569.
106 *Kelly v First Engineering Ltd*, Lord Abernethy, 1999 GWD 21-1016.
107 Conversely where there is no suggestion by the defenders that the claim cannot be properly valued the court will be slow to find special cause – e.g. *Patterson v Sommerville* [2005] CSOH 19.
108 *McKeown v Sir William Arrol Ltd* 1974 SC 97; *Timoney v Dunnery* 1984 SLT 151.
109 *Stark v Ford (No 2)* 1996 SLT 1329.
110 *Muir v Leitch*, Lord McEwan, 2003 GWD 25-708.

assist the defender in assessing whether or not the claim being put forward is, in fact, capable of being assessed by a jury or whether the difficulties raised would properly constitute special cause and any minor discrepancies can be clarified either before or during the proof[111].

6.21 Examples of where special cause has been found on this basis include where: (a) there was a possibility that an overlap between a loss of society award and damages for post-traumatic stress suffered by the surviving family members would be likely to confuse a jury in conjunction with an element of speculation as to the earnings of the pursuer and his deceased spouse[112], although it has been doubted whether there is any general proposition that if parents claiming damages sought to aver specific injury to them rather than loss of society and bereavement they would necessarily be deprived of their right to a jury trial[113], (b) the fact that the pursuer was prosecuting a parallel case against a third party founding partly on the circumstances of the present action in a situation where it would be bound to confuse and complicate the jury's task in assessing damages in the present case[114], (c) there might have been difficulty for a jury to distinguish between a number of potentially overlapping claims relating to past loss of wages, compensation for loss of employment and premature retirement and loss of pension rights[115], (d) there were difficulties in dealing with the relationship between wage loss and handicap on the labour market in conjunction with other factors[116], and (e) in a paraplegic case a combination of factors, namely the fact that the pursuer had claimed for private care costs but the defenders contended that all or part of those costs would be met from public funds, that there was a novel claim for sperm harvesting and injection fertility treatment, that there was a claim for additional housing costs part of which related to the expense of adaptation which might or might not form part of the resale value of the property, and that because the pursuer might be capable of earning a living the future wage and pension loss claims were uncertain, amounted together to a potential complexity of elements which would justify withholding the case from a jury[117].

6.22 Examples of where special cause has been refused and issues allowed include where: (a) there was psychological trauma for the loss of a child *in utero* and it was held that a trial judge could provide the jury with lucid directions about the difference between damages for the loss of society of a child and

---

111 *Higgins v DHL International* 2003 SLT 1301.
112 *Bromham v Highland Regional Council* 1997 SLT 1137.
113 *Boyce v Sherrie* 1998 SLT 611; see also *Green v Chief Constable, Lothian and Borders Police* 2004 SCLR 301.
114 *McKie v Orr*, Lord Emslie, 2002 GWD 7-246.
115 *Johnston v Clark (No 1)* 1997 SLT 923; *(No 2)* 1998 SLT 139.
116 *Thomson v Kvaerner Govan Ltd* 1997 GWD 12-493; *Easdon v A Clarke & Co (Smethwick) Ltd* [2006] CSOH 12.
117 *Easdon v A Clarke & Co (Smethwick) Ltd*, n 116 above.

damages for the trauma caused by the loss of the child[118], (b) a claim was made for a child *in utero* at the time of the parent's death[119], (c) the pursuer suffered a number of medical conditions, the averments relating to her working life and loss of job were complex and future loss was uncertain[120], (d) there was a claim for pension loss[121], (e) the retiral age of the pursuer was not averred, it being within the competence of the jury to decide such a matter[122], (f) the claim was for a share of partnership profits but all necessary material was available for such a calculation to be made or could be sought by way of specification[123], (g) the averments relating to the pursuer's working life and her loss of a job were complex but did not call for any special directions to the jury[124], and (h) it was clear that the pursuer was seeking a full wage loss on a multiplier/multiplicand basis allowing for a small reduction to cover the chance of his getting some work of a non-manual nature in the future[125].

6.23 Particular attention has been paid in recent years to the question of multipliers, especially in connection with the introduction of the approved "Ogden" actuarial tables and their application by the courts[126]. It was observed by Lord McCluskey that:

> "for decades in Scotland, juries have been computing damages with only the most general guidance from the court as to how to calculate multipliers and multiplicands for the purpose of computing loss of financial support. The introduction of tables which can be explained by articulate experts may render the task of computing damages more technical but it hardly makes the task more difficult."[127]

Although initially some doubt was expressed[128] it has now been held that the mere fact that a jury might be required to consider the application of the Ogden tables in a particular case would not constitute special cause[129]. Although there is no universal rule that all cases involving an application of the Ogden tables would necessarily be suitable for jury trial[130] issues have been allowed where some percentage reduction in the multiplier would have to

118 *McMartin v Gindha* 1995 SLT 523.
119 *Cohen v Shaw* 1992 SLT 1022; *MacIntosh v Findlay* 2001 Rep LR 66; *Mulholland v Morrison*, Lord Philip, 3 March 2003* and see **6.27** below.
120 *Stewart v Nicoll* 2003 SLT 843.
121 *Crawford v Renfrewshire Council* 2000 GWD 40-1476; *Graham v Dryden* 2002 Rep LR 104; *Johnston v J T Inglis & Sons Ltd* 2000 GWD 1-6.
122 *Muir v Leitch* 2003 GWD 25-708.
123 *McAllister v McKechnie* 2000 GWD 38-1421.
124 *Stewart v Nicoll* 2003 SLT 843.
125 *Kelly v First Engineering Ltd* 1999 GWD 21-1016.
126 *Wells v Wells* [1999] 1 AC 345; *McNulty v Marshalls Food Group* 1999 SC 195.
127 *Reid v BP Oil Grangemouth Refinery Ltd*, Lord McCluskey, 2001 GWD 16-589.
128 *Dunn v Rigblast Energy Services Ltd* 1999 SLT 531.
129 *Robertson v Smith* 2000 SLT 1012; *Tait v Diamond Offshore Drilling Ltd*, Lord Wheatley, 2001 GWD 1-15; cf *Sharp v Henderson* 1999 GWD 29-1359; *Kennedy v Forrest-Jones* 2001 SLT 630.
130 *Meldrum v Crolla* 2001 GWD 13-469.

be used to allow for the uncertainties in future childbearing or retaining or changing employment[131]and, in a fatal case, where the jury might require to apply different tables for different members of the family[132]. In practice it is interesting to note that the Ogden tables appear to present few difficulties to a jury when it assesses damages[133].

CLAIMS LACKING IN SPECIFICATION

6.24   One of the most contentious areas in dealing with special cause has been that of the question of whether claims being pursued are specific enough to allow a jury to deal with them. In a recent case the matter was succinctly put by Lord Eassie as follows: "In many ways a plea as to lack of specification really goes to the question of fair notice. That will arise whether the case is being heard by a judge or a jury."[134] It is therefore submitted that the only true test of specification is that of whether or not the case is specific enough to allow it to proceed to either a proof or a jury trial and that accordingly a lack of specification is not a proper ground upon which to found special cause.

6.25   The principle of fair notice is important, so that where a party has not provided specification in relation to certain of his claims and, having been asked to do so by the other party, does not, then this may be a decisive factor in establishing special cause[135]. However, as already noted above[136], the courts have expressed a willingness to look outside the record to see whether fair notice has, in fact, been given and in Chapter 43 personal injury actions reference has been made both to the statement of valuation and to the documents lodged therewith. However, it is only legitimate to look at these where they amplify or otherwise detail the specific heads of claim pled in the summons and they will be of little assistance if the head of claim does not appear in the summons[137] or if there is a significant variance between the heads pled on record and those which feature in the statement of variation[138].

6.26   Recent examples of where the court has held that a lack of specification would preclude jury trial include where: (a) there were no averments that the pursuer's continuing symptoms arose as a consequence of the accident rather

---

131 *Stewart v Nicoll* 2003 SLT 843.
132 *Warnock v Clark Contracts Ltd,* Lord McCluskey, 2003 GWD 19-569; *Graham v Dryden* 2002 Rep LR 104; *Crawford v Renfrewshire Council* 2000 GWD 40-1476; cf *Potts v McNulty* 2000 SLT 1269.
133 See **21.02** below.
134 *Currie v Strathclyde Regional Council Fire Brigade* 1999 SLT 62; see also *Easdon v A Clarke & Co (Smethwick) Ltd* [2006] CSOH 12 at para [10].
135 *Marshall v PLM Helicopters Ltd* 1997 SLT 1039.
136 See **6.07** above.
137 However, see *Towers v Jack,* Lord Drummond Young, 27 May 2004★: **15.21**, n 51.
138 Cf *May v Jeeves Parcels Ltd* [2005] CSOH 71.

than having been caused or contributed to by some other factor[139], (b) there were no averments from which any inference of reasonable foreseeability of injury could be drawn[140], (c) a widow's claim for loss of support contained no averments relating to her or her husband's pre-accident earnings, benefits in kind or company dividends and thus any claim would have to be speculative[141], (d) the jury would be given no guidance in the pleadings as to the nature of the pursuer's disability and the prospects of employment[142], and (e) a fellow employee for whom the defenders were vicariously liable was not named[143]. However, issues were allowed despite the fact that the pursuer had not specified which of the psychological consequences of the accident were shortlived and which were continuing[144].

6.27 It should be remembered that a judge or jury has to wield a broad axe in assessing all aspects of quantum – "where one is dealing with a claim which is of a kind which defies precise quantification, a jury is in as good as, or even better, position than a judge to make an assessment"[145] – but that does not mean that claims can be so vague as to be completely meaningless. In considering individual heads of claim for loss of support in fatal actions it has been said that the matter must be approached on a broad basis and that there is no need for detailed averments as to the extent to which the deceased supported his family or the extent to which spouses shared[146]. Future wage loss and disadvantage on the labour market are also approached on a broad brush basis[147] and the assessment of such matters has been held to be primarily a jury question[148] even though it is common that some aspects of a claim may remain unspecific[149]. Issues have been allowed in respect of children[150] and posthumous children, notwithstanding that in the former it is often difficult to specify losses which might be incurred later in life and in the latter such matters as loss of society, support and services may all, to a great extent, be little more than conjecture on the part of the jury. In both cases it has been argued that where losses are of necessity so incapable of specific quantification

139 *Sandison v Graham Begg Ltd* 2001 SC 821.
140 *Higgins v DHL International* 2003 SLT 1301.
141 *Muir v Cameron* 2004 Rep LR 47.
142 *Dunn v Rigblast Energy Services Ltd* 1999 SLT 531.
143 *Devaney v Yarrow Shipbuilders* 1999 SLT 561.
144 *Irvine v Balmoral Hotel Edinburgh Ltd* 1999 Rep LR 41.
145 *Stark v Ford (No 2)* 1996 SLT 1329; *Scott v Vieregge* [2005] CSOH 42.
146 *Smith's Exrs v J Smart (Contractors) plc* 2002 SLT 779; *Scott v Vieregge* [2005] CSOH 42 (a claim for loss of accommodation by a relative allowed to go to trial).
147 *Skakle v Downie* 1975 SLT (Notes) 23; *Stark v Ford (No 2)* 1996 SLT 1329; *McLaughlin v Shaw* 2000 SLT 794; *Stewart v Nicoll* 2003 SLT 843.
148 *Hendrie v The Scottish Ministers*, Extra Div, 2003 GWD 13-394.
149 *Wells v Stenhouse* 2000 GWD 21-828.
150 *Robertson v Smith* 2000 SC 591.

what remains is a "classic jury question"[151]. A good modern example is found in a recent case where complex children's claims were allowed including claims for loss of support and services for children who were likely to proceed into further education – "a jury is well able to assess the measure of the likely parental support in terms of such practical domestic assistance as might be afforded to student offspring and to value it accordingly"[152]. In relation to employment prospects of adults, in one case involving an offshore worker it was said that "a jury was in a sound position to judge on employment prospects generally and in relation to the long-term prospects for the oil industry"[153]. Pension loss claims for adults have been allowed[154] and there seems no reason why an expert should not be able to give evidence to the jury as to how it should value such a claim[155].

6.28 Services claims have been particularly problematic for pursuers even though a jury should take a broad approach to the assessment of such damages[156] and issues have been refused where there has been no specification of the care or value of care received[157]. However, with the advent of statements of valuations in Chapter 43 personal injury actions and with a growing practice to send detailed valuations to defenders in other actions such objections will rarely be met in the future except, perhaps, where the persons rendering the services and on whose behalf the claim is accordingly being made are not specified in the summons[158]. Issues have been allowed where it was pled that the pattern of care is likely to change in the future and it was held that in the circumstances there was nothing difficult or vague about the claim[159].

---

151 In *Mulholland v Morrison*, Lord Philip, 3 March 2005★, issues were allowed for a posthumous child where it had been pled that the deceased would have kept in touch with his son, rendered "normal" services to him and been active in his support. Interestingly the deceased had been unemployed at the date of his death but his likely career progression had been pled and was supported by an employment expert's report. The case of *MacIntosh v Findlay*, Lady Paton, 11 Feb 2000 (unreported), where *inter alia* the posthumous child's claim for support was held to be unsuitable for jury trial because of a lack of specification should be treated with caution as the pursuer was allowed issues on appeal – the Inner House judgment was an *ex tempore* verbal decision and is unreported although the outcome of the trial can be found at 2001 Rep LR 66.
152 *Scott v Vieregge* [2005] CSOH 42.
153 *Tait v Diamond Offshore Drilling Ltd* 2001 GWD 1-15.
154 E.g. *Stewart v Nicoll* 2003 SLT 843; *Crawford v Renfrewshire Council* 2000 GWD 14-476.
155 As it can in a proof – see *Allison v Orr* 2004 SC 453.
156 *Ingham v John G Russell (Transport) Ltd* 1991 SC 201.
157 E.g. *Beaton v Cain* 2000 SLT 920; cf *Smith v Forth Ports plc* 2004 GWD 16-357; *Graham v Dryden* 2002 Rep LR 104; *Harte v Dalkeith Demolitions Ltd* 2004 GWD 12-277; *Irvine v Balmoral Hotel Edinburgh Ltd* 1999 Rep LR 41; *Keane v Walker Contracts (Scotland) Ltd* 1999 GWD 9-410; *May v Jeeves Parcels Ltd* [2005] CSOH 71.
158 *Jones v Leslie* 2004 Rep LR 136; cf *Muir v Leitch* 2003 GWD 25-708.
159 *Werfel v Norfrost Ltd* 2002 GWD 1-12.

AVERMENTS OF DOUBTFUL RELEVANCY

6.29   The general question posed in the issue is based upon the averments made on record. These averments may not all be relevant but the relevant averments must be proved before the pursuer can obtain a verdict[160]. When a case is clearly irrelevant then it is suitable neither for proof nor jury trial and should be dismissed[161].

> "Averments are not of doubtful relevance because one party maintains that they are relevant and the other maintains that they are irrelevant. In the face of such a dispute, the court may hold either that the averments are relevant or that they are irrelevant. In the former case, the plea to relevancy will be repelled, and either the case will be remitted to proof or (in the absence of any special case for not doing so) issues will be allowed. It is only if the court takes the view that it cannot be satisfactorily determined whether the averments are relevant or irrelevant without first hearing evidence that the averments can properly be described as being of doubtful relevance. In that event, inquiry must be made by proof before answer, and the possibility of jury trial is excluded."[162]

Thus an action which was based upon a breach of occupiers' liability where the deceased, in a state of inebriation, fell asleep on a floor and was drowned by an ingress of water, was held to be not only unsuitable for jury trial but wholly irrelevant and thus dismissed[163]. The real problem, however, arises in connection with averments which are of doubtful (as opposed to patent or obvious) relevance.

6.30   "When a case is to go for proof before a judge there is perhaps no great necessity for over-strictness. The judge can always allow a certain latitude and when his patience is exhausted he can indicate that an amendment is desirable and, if the amendment is of a substantial character, there is room for adjournment or for facilities for allowing further evidence. But [in a] jury trial very different considerations obtain. A properly drawn record is essential for jury trial, and the points at issue ought to be clearly focused. One wants to avoid wrangling as to the admissibility of evidence. That is undesirable in itself and sometimes operates prejudicially against the party taking objection. In jury trials there is little scope for amendment and none for adjournment. Mistakes may be fatal. It seems to me that it is in the interests of all parties that the relevant and substantial points should be stated and clearly stated in the record, and that the facts relied upon, the grounds of action and the pleas-in-law should be adequately presented. . . . The function of a record is to convey what the case is about and to make the legal issues clear, and it is really intolerable that it

---

160 *Haughton v North British Railway Co* (1892) 20 R 113; *Crannie v Glengarnock Iron & Steel Co Ltd* (1908) 12 SLT 864.
161 E.g. *Kemp v Secretary of State for Scotland* 1997 SLT 1174.
162 *Gillies v Lynch* 2002 SLT 1420 at 1422L–1423B per Lord Macfadyen.
163 *McCann v Secretary of State for Trade and Industry* 1997 GWD 32-1644.

should be left to the court, with the assistance of counsel, to try to extricate from the averments what the points in the case are."[164]

6.31   It follows, therefore, that, as a general proposition, where averments on record are of doubtful relevancy this would normally in itself constitute a special cause[165].

> "There is no room for trial before answer. The subsumption on which a jury trial proceeds is that all questions of relevancy have been disposed of and that the trial is to proceed on the basis of the record, which is looked on as conclusive of relevancy. This is shown by a number of considerations. No judge could exclude evidence from the jury's consideration if the party leading it could show that he had sufficient record for it. So, too, the courts, when invited to send a case to proof rather than to jury trial, are frequently affected by the consideration of the doubtful relevancy of the record, and the courts have frequently emphasised the desirability of records in cases going to juries being clearly stated so as to focus for the jury the points in controversy. Of the expediency of conducting a jury trial on the basis of a relevant record and of the chaos which would result if it were sought to conduct a jury trial before answer there can be no doubt. It is only on a relevant record that the proper respective functions of judge and jury can satisfactorily be operated."[166]

6.32   In virtually any case where the law applicable to the facts cannot be stated with precision until the facts are determined, special cause may be found. "A useful test in these cases is to consider whether on the pursuer's pleadings an adequate and effective direction could be given to, and applied by, the jury on the contentious question."[167] Thus where it was claimed that solicitors had failed to raise an action timeously[168], or where an accident occurred on an unfenced river bank adjoining a children's playground and there was some doubt as to the extent of the occupiers' liability[169], or where it was unclear as to whether an electricity undertaking "controlled" a manhole within the context of statutory regulations[170], issues were refused on the grounds of doubtful relevancy since in each case the elucidation of the facts was necessary before the

---

164 *Boyle v Glasgow Corporation* 1949 SC 245 at 261 per Lord Justice-Clerk Thomson. It should be noted that the latter remarks were made in connection with contemporary sheriff court pleadings, this case being remitted for jury trial from Glasgow. Interestingly, neither *Haughton* nor *Crannie* were cited in this case.

165 *Sutherland v James Taylor* 1970 SLT (Notes) 62 per Lord Cameron.

166 *Moore v Alexander Stephen & Sons* 1954 SC 331 at 333–334 per Lord Justice-Clerk Thomson; see also *O'Malley v Multiflex (UK) Inc* 1995 SCLR 143 and **18.44**, n 118.

167 *O'Malley v Multiflex (UK) Inc* 1995 SCLR 143 at 145 per Lord Gill *Fallone v Lanarkshire Acute Hospitals NHS Trust* [2006] CSOH 51.

168 *Robertson v Bannigan* 1964 SLT 318.

169 *O'Hara v Glasgow Corporation* 1966 SLT (Notes) 24; cf *Oldcorn v Purdon* 2003 GWD 1-4 and *Gibb v International Paper Ltd*, Lord Johnston, 26 Oct 2005*, where issues were allowed in an occupiers' liability case where a four-year-old drowned in an unfenced and disused canal on the defenders' land and the defenders held the pursuer (the child's mother) wholly or partly to blame through a lack of proper supervision.

170 *Michael v Argyll Stores (Properties) Ltd* 1989 GWD 11-484.

precise legal duties could be identified. It therefore follows that where a pursuer has a good and relevant statutory case but a weaker common law case which may be of doubtful relevancy, or vice versa, then if he wishes to obtain issues he would be advised to proceed only with the stronger of the two cases to avoid the defender being able to establish special cause.

6.33 Examples of where special cause has been found on the grounds of doubtful relevancy include where: (a) there were possibly inconsistent technical averments relating to the complex processes carried out at a chemical works[171], (b) the pursuer failed to aver a relevant case in relation to two reasonable constructions which could be put upon a particular statutory provision[172], (c) the pursuer himself was allegedly in breach of a statutory duty incumbent upon him[173], (d) there were collateral issues involving mechanical defects which the defender should allegedly have been aware of[174], (e) there were "exceptional, novel and important" matters arising out of averments relating to a fire having been caused by another visitor to the premises having dropped a cigarette[175], (f) there were averments that road racing was taking place and that one party had been inciting the other to drive at an excessive speed[176], (g) there was a demand for an "immediate" system of cleaning up spillages[177], (h) an accident occurred on an ungritted road and it was not clear as to whether it was being alleged that the road was never gritted at any time or that there might have been a failure to institute a priority system of gritting[178], (i) a domestic worker in a mental hospital was injured by a patient running for his lunch after another member of staff shouted out "Dinner Time!,"[179] (j) a nurse was injured lifting a patient and the correct type of lift to be used was said to be a matter of judgment in the particular circumstances and it was unclear as to whether the pursuer had in any event made a decision as to what type of lift to use and where her pleadings relating to the duty to provide a safe system of work were ambiguous[180], (k) there were inconsistencies, difficulties and a lack of specification in relation to services provided to the pursuer and confusion in relation to his life expectancy[181], (l) a police officer sued her former employers for wrongs com-

171 *Robertson v T & H Smith Ltd* 1962 SC 628.
172 *Walters v National Coal Board* 1961 SLT (Notes) 82.
173 *McLachlan v L K Mackenzie & Partners Ltd* 1961 SLT (Notes) 29; *Weldon v William Grant & Sons Ltd* 1964 SLT (Notes) 29; *Rankin v FMP (Farm Supplies) Ltd* 1962 SLT (Notes) 46.
174 *Pitt v Graham* 1967 SLT (Notes) 108.
175 *Stewart v Astor & Faith* 1925 SLT 7.
176 *Purden's Curator Bonis v Boyd* 1963 SC (HL) 1.
177 *Reid v Galbraith's Stores* 1970 SLT (Notes) 83.
178 *Murray v Grampian Regional Council* 1993 GWD 9-642; cf *Travers v William Collins Sons & Co Ltd* 1990 GWD 39-2276 where issues were allowed in a case where it was admitted that gritting had been carried out but the pursuer claimed that the gritting was inadequate.
179 *Cassidy v Argyll and Clyde Health Board* 1997 Rep LR 76.
180 *McFarlane v Lothian Health Board* 1989 GWD 39-1827.
181 *Sharp v Henderson* 1999 GWD 29-1359.

mitted when she was arrested for perjury and it was held that the pursuer's averments on malice and assault could only be determined after an inquiry into the facts[182], (m) an auxiliary nurse in a mental hospital was injured in his haste to reach a patient attempting to commit suicide[183], (n) there were problems as to the reasonable inferences that could be drawn depending upon which combination of factual averments were proved[184], (o) imputed knowledge was in issue and it was necessary to hear the facts first[185], (p) there were questions in relation to what sedentary work the pursuer could undertake[186], (q) in a case of alleged professional negligence there were no averments relating to what an ordinary dentist acting with reasonable care and skill would have done or failed to do[187], and (r) there was an alleged failure to make an earlier diagnosis of a cancerous condition, the timescale of that earlier diagnosis and the reason why any chemotherapy would have been unnecessary were not averred and the effect of the pursuer having lost faith in the medical profession was not explained[188].

6.34   Whether a precaution is reasonably necessary[189] or whether a particular type of injury was foreseeable[190] may, however, be suitable questions for a jury to answer. Whether any particular duty of reasonable care is owed by one party to another is a question of law but the question of whether, on the facts in a particular case, there was or was not a failure to take reasonable care is, properly, a question for the jury and in this area "there was not, and could not be a complete uniformity of standard. One jury would attribute to the reasonable man greater degree of prescience than another."[191]

CRIMINAL CONVICTIONS RELIED UPON

6.35   The fact that a party has been charged with a criminal offence arising out of the incident forming the basis of the action is not, *per se*, a special cause[192], even when it was the pursuer who was convicted[193] or acquitted[194] of the offence, but where a party founds upon a conviction[195] and there are

---

182 *McKie v Orr* 2002 GWD 9-268.
183 *Barr v Tayside Health Board* 1992 SLT 989.
184 *Harte v Dalkeith Demolitions Ltd* 2004 GWD 12-277.
185 *Keane v Walker Contracts Scotland Ltd* 1999 GWD 9-410.
186 *O'Malley v Multiflex (UK) Inc* 1997 SLT 362.
187 *Toner v McLeod* [2006] CSOH 22.
188 *Fallone v Lanarkshire Acute Hospitals NHS Trust* [2006] CSOH 51
189 *Singh v Glasgow Corporation* 1962 SLT (Notes) 6; *Sutherland v James Taylor* 1970 SLT (Notes) 62.
190 *O'Hara v Glasgow Corporation* 1966 SLT (Notes) 24.
191 *Qualcast (Wolverhampton) Ltd v Haynes* [1959] AC 743 at 757 per Lord Somervell approved in *Barr v British Railways Board* 1965 SLT (Notes) 40.
192 *King v Paterson* 1971 SLT (Notes) 40.
193 *Shearer v Bevan's Exrx* 1986 SLT 226.
194 *Robb v Sutherland, Irvine v Sutherland* 1994 GWD 38-2251.
195 Law Reform (Miscellaneous Provisions) (Scotland) Act 1968, s 10(1), (2).

doubts as to the exact facts upon which the conviction was based and the standard of proof necessary to dispute those facts, special cause has been found[196]. Where the defender intends to prove that he did not commit the relevant offence[197] or where he was convicted of one relevant charge but acquitted on two other relevant charges[198] issues have been refused; jury trial was, however, allowed in a case where the defender claimed that he had pled guilty to the offence while he was still suffering from the effects of a head injury[199]. However, in all cases in which jury trial is sought the court has to be satisfied that the conviction upon which the party seeking issues founds is relevant to the matters which form the subject-matter of the action[200].

UNUSUAL ONUS OF PROOF

6.36 The fact that the onus of proof has been inverted does not, in itself, make the case unsuitable for jury trial[201] particularly if the pursuer accepts the inverted onus in his pleadings and this is the correct position in law[202]. Where, however, there are difficulties such as a shifting onus of proof[203] or there is conflicting authority as to upon whom the onus falls[204] then special cause may be found. Examples include a case where an unlit stationary lorry was run into after lighting-up time[205] and a case where an unsuitable vehicle ran off the road[206] – both of these cases were ones in which it was said that difficult questions of onus were involved and accordingly issues were refused.

SEVERAL GROUNDS OF ACTION

6.37 Examples of special cause being found where there are several grounds of action include an inquiry into an arrangement between two companies which had a bearing on their vicarious liability for the fault of a driver[207] and an action which involved two alternative cases against a stevedore employer and a firm of coal merchants concerning a defective system of work, *pro hac*

196 *Caldwell v Wright* 1970 SC 24.
197 *Fardy v SMT Co* 1971 SLT 232; cf *Garnett v Gowans* 1971 SLT (Notes) 77.
198 *Gemmell v McFarlane* 1971 SLT (Notes) 36.
199 *King v Patterson* 1971 SLT (Notes) 40.
200 *Cronie v Messenger* 2004 GWD 22-479.
201 *Jack v Guardbridge Paper Co* 1968 SLT (Notes) 8; *Gault v James Templeton & Co Ltd* 1968 SLT (Notes) 37.
202 *Donno v British Railways Board* 1964 SLT (Notes) 108.
203 *Sinclair v National Coal Board* 1963 SC 586; *McNeil v National Coal Board* 1965 SLT (Notes) 32; *Galbraith v Scottish Stamping & Engineering Co Ltd* 1958 SLT (Notes) 7; *Crawford v Peter McAinsh* 1962 SLT (Notes) 26.
204 *Duncan v Smith and Phillips* 1965 SLT (Notes) 16; cf *Donno v British Railways Board* 1964 SLT (Notes) 108.
205 *Crawford v Peter McAinsh Ltd* 1962 SLT (Notes) 26.
206 *O'Donnell v D & R Ferrying Co* 1965 SLT (Notes) 75, 1966 SLT (Notes) 71.
207 *McKie v NorWest Construction Co* 1931 SN 126.

vice employment and vicarious liability where it was said that for the purposes of jury trial there were "too many grounds of action, and too many alternatives on record to make it safe to send the case to such a tribunal without serious risk of a miscarriage of justice"[208].

TWO DIFFERENT FORMS OF INQUIRY UPON SAME FACTS

6.38 If there are likely to be two or more different forms of inquiry arising out of the same incident this may cause difficulties. Thus where a number of actions relating to the same accident or incident have been raised and a proof has already been granted in some of those actions, it might amount to a special cause to refuse issues in the remaining actions[209]. However, the mere fact that a pursuer in another action arising out of a single incident had indicated that he did not wish to exercise his right to jury trial would not prevent issues being allowed in the case under consideration[210], but where a widow was claiming damages in respect of her husband's death but was, at the time, the defender in his action of divorce on the grounds of her cruelty, special cause was found because the jury might have to determine whether or not a reconciliation would have taken place and thus determine what would have happened in the consistorial action[211]. Issues were refused in a case where there might have to be two separate forms of inquiry in a single action where there was a dispute between the defender and a potential indemnifier as to whether the pursuer was acting within the course of his employment with the defenders at the time of the accident[212]. It has been said that it is not appropriate to have a jury trial in relation to quantum of damages and a separate proof in relation to liability in the same action[213].

A THIRD PARTY IS BROUGHT IN

6.39 Where a third party has been brought into an action, the court has the power to allow the action, so far as directed against the third party, to proceed to a proof or jury trial before, at the same time, or after the proof between the pursuer and defender as the court thinks fit[214]. It is competent for such an inquiry to be conducted in stages by two different modes, e.g. in the case of an accident where the defender brought in a third party on the basis of an indem-

208 *Mackenzie v John Smith & Sons* 1955 SLT (Notes) 25 per Lord Walker.
209 *Murphy v Kirkcudbright County Council* 1955 SLT (Notes) 26.
210 *Hatherley v Smith* 1989 SLT 316.
211 *Longster v British Road Services* 1967 SLT (Notes) 9 and see also *Dornan v Forrest* 1932 SC 562.
212 *Winchester v Ramsay* 1966 SC 1 – whether such a course would be followed today is a matter of conjecture.
213 *Bruce v John Toole & Sons (Cable Contractors) Ltd* 1969 SLT (Notes) 26.
214 Rule 26.7(3).

nity between himself and the third party, a proof was allowed between defender and third party on the indemnity question (which did not involve the pursuer) on the basis that a decision could thereafter be taken as to whether a proof or jury trial should be allowed between the pursuer and whoever remained liable to compensate him[215]. In every case where third party notice procedure is used, the pursuer's statutory right to a jury trial is subject to the discretion of the court to decide the modes of inquiry[216] but the mere presence of a third party does not constitute special cause[217]. Exercise of the court's discretion does not depend on whether or not the pursuer has concluded for damages against the third party[218] and a motion to bring in a third party has been refused where it would be unfair to delay the pursuer's claim for damages[219]. In deciding whether to grant an order for service of a third party notice in an action, the court does not take into account the fact that the party may lose his right to jury trial if the order is granted, it not being a relevant factor[220].

INTEREST IS CLAIMED

6.40 If, in a case where interest on any aspect of the damages is being sought, it is impossible for the court properly to identify the elements of a lump sum awarded by the jury for the purposes of interest thereon then this might amount to special cause[221], but in a normal case where the issue has been broken down into the various heads of claim so that interest may be apportioned thereto[222] then this difficulty does not arise.

DELAY IN RAISING OR PROSECUTING ACTION

6.41 If a party has been materially prejudiced by delay (*mora*) then this can constitute special cause[223]. Mere delay, however, is not enough[224] and any

---

215 *Vetco Gray (UK) Ltd v Slessor* [2006] CSIH 11 at para [15], *Winchester v Ramsay*, n 212.
216 *Vetco*, para [17]; *Winchester v Ramsay*; *Bruce v John Toole & Son (Cable Contractors) Ltd*; *Rodgers v James Crow & Sons Ltd* 1971 SC 155.
217 Rule 26.7(3); cf *Algeo v Melville, Dundas & Whitson* 1973 SLT (Notes) 90; *Cairnie v Secretary of State for Scotland* 1966 SLT (Notes) 57; *Tait v Leslie and Saddler* 1971 SLT (Notes) 79. See also B Gill, "Aspects of Relevancy in Third Party Procedure" 1968 SLT (News) 65.
218 *Garnett v Gowans* 1971 SLT (Notes) 77; *Harley v Forth Ports Authority* 1973 SLT (Notes) 7.
219 *Tait v Leslie & Saddler* 1971 SLT (Notes) 79.
220 *Rodgers v James Crow & Sons Ltd* 1971 SC 155.
221 *Cooper v Pat Munro (Alness) Ltd* 1972 SLT (Notes) 20; *McMahon v J & P Coats Ltd* 1972 SLT (Notes) 16; *McFadyen v Crudens* 1972 SLT 62.
222 *Macdonald v Glasgow Corporation* 1973 SC 52; *Crowe v Norman Stewart & Co (Roofing Contractors) Ltd* 1972 SLT (Notes) 12; *Smith v T & J Harrison* 1973 SLT (Notes) 92; *McKeown v Sir William Arrol & Co* 1974 SC 97.
223 *Hunter v John Brown & Co* 1961 SC 231 at 235–236; *Rutherford v Harvey & McMillan* 1954 SLT (Notes) 28; *McDonald v A & J Wade Ltd* 1962 SLT (Notes) 19; *McLachlan v Atholl Houses Ltd* 1964 SLT (Notes) 56; *McManus v Liquidators of Kelvin Shipping Co* 1966 SLT (Notes) 45.
224 *Ferris v Union Castle Steamship Co* 1964 SLT (Notes) 72; *McDermid v Underhill Heating Engineering Ltd* 1971 SLT (Notes) 12.

delay which has been occasioned must be what can be described as inordinate, i.e. beyond that which normally occurs in litigation[225]. Such inordinate delay can be a delay in intimating a claim, in raising an action, or in proceeding with it[226] and the delay can be exacerbated by the absence of any reasonable explanation therefor[227]. Other factors which might, in conjunction with delay, suggest to the court special cause may include the subsequent destruction of the locus of an accident[228], the disappearance or death of a material witness[229], the disposal of the instrument which caused the accident[230], or any other circumstances connected with delay which raise difficult questions of fact and law[231].

6.42   The delay must be due to circumstances outwith the control of the party seeking to rely on it as a special cause[232] and, most importantly, the party relying upon it must be able to show that he is, or is likely to be, materially prejudiced by it. Material prejudice may occur in various ways, for example the late intimation of a claim or a subsequent change of tack by a pursuer may make it difficult for a defender to prepare his case properly[233], or the delay may have caused a likely impairment of the quality of evidence by the dimming of the recollection of essential witnesses[234], including the pursuer himself[235]. Where the impaired evidence can be gained from another source, such as official meteorological records, delay may not necessarily amount to special cause[236]. Sufficient notice of the alleged prejudice must be given in the pleadings so that where a delay occurred but the parties had full and detailed pleadings relating to the merits of the cause and the defender had the benefit of inquiries made after the accident and a fatal accident inquiry had been held, a jury trial was allowed since the evidence led at the inquiry had covered similar ground and the transcript thereof would at least constitute a valuable aide memoire[237].

225 *Hunter v John Brown & Co* 1961 SC 231; *Conetta v Central SMT Co* 1966 SLT 302.
226 E.g. *Porter v Gordon* 1952 SLT (Notes) 80; *Leys v Torry Animal Products* 1964 SLT (Notes) 97; *Milne v Glasgow Corporation* 1951 SC 340.
227 *Leys v Torry Animal Products* 1964 SLT (Notes) 97.
228 *Black v Duncan Logan (Contractors) Ltd* 1969 SLT (Notes) 19.
229 *Woods v ASC Motors* 1930 SC 1035.
230 *McLeish v James Howden & Co* 1952 SLT (Notes) 73.
231 *Cumming v British Railways Board* 1968 SLT (Notes) 5; *Mooney v BMC (Scotland) Ltd* 1970 SLT (Notes) 24.
232 *Ferris v Union Castle Steamship Co* 1964 SLT (Notes) 72.
233 *Rice v Borland* 1961 SLT 16; *Morrison v John G Kincaid & Co* 1969 SLT (Notes) 6.
234 *Hunter v John Brown & Co* 1961 SC 231; *Carmichael v Thomas Usher & Son* 1964 SLT (Notes) 30; *Davidson v Chief Constable, Fife Police* 1995 SLT 545.
235 *Mackinnon v North British Aluminium Co* 1960 SLT (Notes) 22.
236 *Carmichael v Thomas Usher & Sons* 1964 SLT (Notes) 30.
237 *Sutherland v Chief Constable, Fife Police* 1994 GWD 29-2326.

DEFENDER INSURED

6.43 Although the jury should not take into account the fact that a defender is insured[238], the fact that it might be reasonably obvious to a jury that the defender will be covered by a compulsory insurance policy does not *per se* constitute special cause[239]. The same applies where from the instance of the action it is obvious that an insurer or third party will meet the damages awarded so that if the action in a road traffic accident has been raised against an insurer[240] or against the Motor Insurers' Bureau this will not constitute special cause[241]; in any event such an action could not be held to be a special cause as, if this were correct, issues would have to be refused irrespective of the pleadings or merits in every action of a similar type[242].

MISCELLANEOUS FACTORS WHICH MIGHT CONSTITUTE SPECIAL CAUSE

6.44 Miscellaneous special causes might include where: (a) the court finds it difficult to adjust the issues and counter-issues to ensure a just and proper verdict being reached because of the complicated circumstances of the case[243]; (b) there are questions relating both to the admissibility and evaluation of evidence to be led[244] although difficulties as to the admissibility of evidence may arise during the course of any jury trial and, if they can be dealt with satisfactorily by the presiding judge, then a trial may be allowed[245]; (c) the procedure in the case has already been unusual or protracted[246]; (d) there was a possibility that the jury's attention might be distracted by the passing of unusual correspondence between the parties following the accident[247]; (e) the stated cause of

---

238 *Stewart v Duncan* 1921 SC 482; *McFarlane v Thain* [2006] CSIH 3.
239 *Dickson v Condie* 1931 SLT 494 (car insurance); the same principle would apply to employers' insurance.
240 Under the European Communities (Rights Against Insurers) Regulations 2002 (SI 2002/3061) the first case of this nature in which issues were allowed was *Gardner v Royal & Sun Alliance Insurance*, Temporary Judge R F MacDonald QC, 22 Sept 2004★.
241 If, however, the MIB sought to avoid liability by relying on the specific exclusion thereof in relation to persons who "knew or ought to have known" that the driver was uninsured etc, then, because the proper construction and application of that phrase awaited a final decision (see *White v White* [2001] 1 WLR 481 (HL)) the case would not be suitable for jury trial: see *McFarlane v Thain* [2006] CSIH 3.
242 The position might be different if the pleadings deliberately and improperly mentioned the insurers in order to unduly influence the jury: *McFarlane v Thain* [2006] CSIH 3. See also **18.11** below and A Hajducki, "Insurers, Indemnifiers and the Jury" 2005 SLT (News) 49.
243 *McQuillan v Glasgow Daily Mail* (1902) 9 SLT 393; cf *McKeown v Sir William Arrol & Co* 1974 SLT 143.
244 *MacDonald v Mackinnon* 1958 SLT (Notes) 51; affd 1959 SLT (Notes) 25; *Rice v Borland* 1961 SLT 116; *Kemp v Secretary of State for Scotland* 1997 SLT 1174.
245 *Stevens v Cremonesi* 1998 SLT 838 at 840.
246 *Graham v Associated Electrical Industries Ltd* 1968 SLT 81.
247 *Rice v Borland* 1961 SLT 116.

the accident had changed between intimation of the claim and the making of the averments on record[248]; (f) the relationship between two of the heads of claim was unclear[249]; (g) the pursuer had a speech impediment which might obstruct the performance of the jury's function[250]; and (h) in any case there are a number of fairly minor reasons which individually might not amount to special cause but which do so in combination[251].

MISCELLANEOUS FACTORS HELD NOT TO CONSTITUTE SPECIAL CAUSE

6.45   Examples of miscellaneous factors which have not been held to constitute special cause include where: (a) the evidence available in the case is scanty[252], hearsay[253], or might require to be taken on commission[254], (b) an injured person has allegedly already been compensated for an accident[255], (c) in an ongoing action the executrix of a defender has been sisted in his place[256], (d) a defender does not propose to give evidence[257], (e) there may be an obligation upon the pursuer to repay certain advances made[258], (f) the issue required the jury to make fourteen separate awards[259], (g) the defender raises the question of whether or not the pursuer was acting in the course of his employment[260], (h) the existence of previous similar accidents was known[261], (i) the accident was due to a latent defect[262], (j) there was a probability that only a trifling award of damages might be awarded since the size of any damages likely to be recovered is irrelevant[263], and (k) it was said that the jury might be prejudiced against a party because of his unpopular political views[264].

248 *Macfarlane v Industrial Engineering Ltd* 1961 SLT (Notes) 30.
249 *O'Malley v Multiflex (UK) Inc* 1995 SCLR 1143.
250 *Thomson v Kvaerner Govan Ltd* 1997 GWD 12-493. The rationale used was that the pursuer's evidence was vital and that it would be more difficult for the individual members of the jury to seek clarification of what the pursuer had said than for counsel and the judge. In the event the pursuer's speech was comprehensible at the proof notwithstanding the fact that he lost the action for unconnected reasons. The case eventually ended up in the House of Lords – see 2004 SLT 94.
251 *Murphy v Kirkcudbright County Council* 1955 SLT (Notes) 26; *Shields v George Smith & Sons* 1948 SLT (Notes) 24; *Rosie v Samuel B Allison Ltd* 1950 SLT (Notes) 56; *Strawthorn v Kilmarnock Magistrates* 1952 SLT (Notes) 83; cf *McFarlane v Thain* [2006] CSIH 3.
252 *Bullett v British Railways Board* 1964 SLT (Notes) 102.
253 *Shearer v Bevan's Exrx* 1986 SLT 226.
254 *Mackinnon v Wierse* (1904) 12 SLT 101; *Nicol v McIntosh* 1986 SLT 104 and *Stevens v Cremonesi* 1988 SLT 838 where it was remarked that it was not uncommon for juries to hear evidence on commission.
255 *Purden's Curator Bonis v Boyd* 1963 SC (HL) 1.
256 *Shearer v Bevan's Exrx* 1986 SLT 226.
257 *Nicol v McIntosh* 1986 SLT 104.
258 *Barbour v McGruer* 1967 SLT (Notes) 41.
259 *Smith v T & J Harrison Ltd* 1973 SLT (Notes) 92.
260 *McIntosh v Cameron* 1929 SC 44.
261 *Eccles v Archibald Thomson* 1959 SLT (Notes) 47.
262 *Bottomley v SMT Co* 1948 SLT (Notes) 25.
263 *Rhind v Kemp & Co* (1893) 21 R 275.
264 *Brown v Anderson* (1900) 8 SLT 113 (support of the Boers).

DEFAMATION ACTIONS

6.46   In determining whether or not special cause is shown, defamation cases are, in principle, treated no differently from other types of enumerated cause. It is for the court to determine as a matter of law whether the words complained of are capable of bearing the defamatory meaning which the pursuer seeks to ascribe to them[265]. This must be done prior to the issues being allowed so that the pursuer's pleadings should clearly state what meaning is being ascribed to them if the words are not ex facie defamatory together with any of the circumstances surrounding the uttering of the words which may throw light on their true meaning[266]. If this is done then the court can determine whether the facts stated are such as to entitle the pursuer to have the case sent to jury on an issue which sets forth the innuendo or secondary meaning which the pursuer seeks to prove[267]. The jury then determines whether, as a matter of fact, the statement has defamed the pursuer. Provided that there are sufficient averments with which the jury can construe the words complained of as being defamatory, issues will normally be allowed[268].

6.47   Historically the plea of special cause was rarely taken in defamation actions and, even where it was, a number of extremely complex cases were tried by jury[269]. The principle is still applicable and in a recent case where the main issue of fact was whether or not a particular statement had been made and pleas of *veritas* and fair comment were to be argued by the defenders, it was held that these factors did not amount to special cause and that if *veritas* and fair comment were to be regarded as "difficult and delicate questions of mixed fact and law . . . then the statutory provision that libel and defamation cases are ordinarily to be tried by a jury would be very considerably eroded, if not rendered virtually ineffective", especially when, in reality, the main question was one of whether or not the statement had been made[270]. It should also be noted that whereas in personal injury actions the inversion of the onus of proof may be a ground upon which special cause can be established[271] this would not be the case in defamation actions where the onus of proving *veritas* will normally lie upon the defender.

6.48   Where there were averments of doubtful relevancy such as the relation-

---

265   *Russel v Stubbs Ltd* 1913 SC (HL) 14.
266   *Gollan v Thompson Wyles Co* 1930 SC 599.
267   *Sexton v Ritchie & Co* (1890) 17 R 680.
268   E.g. *Hannah v Scottish Daily Record & Sunday Mail Ltd* 2000 SLT 673.
269   E.g. *Cunningham v Duncan & Jamieson* (1889) 16 R 383; *Lever Bros v The Daily Record (Glasgow) Ltd* 1909 SC 1004; *Lamond v The Daily Record (Glasgow) Ltd* 1923 SC 512; *Macdonald v Martin* 1935 SC 621; *Ogston & Tennant Ltd v The Daily Record (Glasgow) Ltd* 1909 SC 1000; *Rogers v Orr* 1939 SC 121; *Winter v News Scotland Ltd* 1991 SLT 828.
270   *McCabe v News Group Newspapers Ltd* 1992 SLT 707 at 709 per Lord Morison. The case was settled before the trial. See also *McCormick v Scottish Daily Record & Sunday Mail Ltd*, Lord Menzies, 18 Jan 2006*, at **18.44** below.
271   See **6.36** above.

ship of parties, questions of whether the innuendos pled were capable of being defamatory and a dispute as to whether the statement constituted fact or comment, these might well constitute mixed questions of fact and law which could be determined only after hearing the facts and thus, because of these uncertainties, jury trial may be held to be inappropriate[272]. Where factual issues relating to malice and qualified privilege need to be explored and the facts elicited before any decision in law could be made, issues may also be refused[273]. In a similar way to all other actions where there are a number of separate or interlinked difficulties for a jury, special cause may be established even if each difficulty *per se* might not have led to this result. An example is provided by a case where it was held that the jury was likely to be confused by the complexity of averments relating to the pursuer's professional activities, standards of professional conduct and duty, the substantial volume of documentary evidence required, the range and variety of issues and defences, averments of doubtful relevancy which would make it difficult to charge a jury, confused and unclear averments of loss, difficult questions of fact and law concerning the fiduciary duties of company directors and possible conflicts of interest in the pursuer's conduct[274].

ACTIONS OF REDUCTION

6.49   In actions of reduction on the grounds of incapacity, essential error or force and fear, special cause can be found on the same basis as in all other types of action tried by juries[275] so that where a jury might be faced with real difficulties in assessing the reliability of witnesses[276], where there are difficult questions relating to the conduct of professional persons and their duties[277] or where the case was substantially concerned with averments of undue influence[278], issues may be refused.

272 *Peat v News Group Newspapers Ltd* 1996 GWD 16-952.
273 *Nicol v Caledonian Newspapers Ltd* 2003 SLT 109; see also *Reynolds v Times Newspapers Ltd* [2001] 2 AC 127; *Loutchansky v Times Newspapers Ltd* [2002] QB 783; *Galloway v Telegraph Group Ltd* [2004] EWHC 2786 (QB); *Jameel v Wall Street Journal Europe SPRL (No 2)* [2005] EWCA Civ 74; *McCartan Turkington Breen v Times Newspapers Ltd* [2002] 2 AC 277 (NI).
274 *Shanks v British Broadcasting Corporation* 1993 SLT 326; see also *Hay v Institute of Chartered Accountants of Scotland*, Lady Paton, 2002 GWD 28-978 and *Thomson v Ross*, Lord Eassie, 18 July 2000 (unreported).
275 *MacDonald v Mackinnon* 1959 SLT (Notes) 25.
276 *MacDonald v Mackinnon*, n 275 above.
277 *Young v Healy* 1909 SC 687; cf *McCaig v Glasgow University Court* (1904) 6 F 918.
278 *Ross v Gosselin's Exrs* 1926 SLT 239.

Chapter 7

Tactical and practical considerations

INTRODUCTION

7.01 The question of whether or not it is desirable to have any particular cause tried before a jury must, at the end of the day, be a matter for the discretion of the parties involved and, although it has to be stressed at the outset that each case must be considered on its own peculiar facts and circumstances, there are nevertheless a number of tactical and practical considerations which might be common to virtually all cases. Whatever the final choice of hearing, however, it is vital that in all cases which might potentially be suitable for jury trial at least some serious thought be given to the mode of inquiry at an early stage and that counsel and agents discuss the matter with their clients while the pleadings are still at the adjustment stage. Indeed some practitioners have gone so far as asserting that the failure to do so might, in certain circumstances, be tantamount to professional negligence.

7.02 At the outset an action suitable for trial by jury must fall within one of the enumerated causes and not otherwise be excluded from such trial by reason of any statutory provision. On the assumption that it is a cause which could competently be tried by a jury, the pursuer's advisers must consider whether or not it would be desirable to opt for trial or proof at the earliest stage possible, preferably prior to the actual raising of the action even though, of necessity, this will have to be done before the defenders declare their hand as to whether or not they intend to raise the question of special cause. Similar considerations apply in respect of defenders who have only the limited time between the intimation of the action and the closing of the record to decide on whether or not they intend to seek issues. In all cases whether to subsequently risk the expenses of a procedure roll or motion roll hearing on the matter of special cause must be balanced against the perceived gain whether in relation to quantum of damages, liability or both. Then serious consideration should be given to the pros and cons of seeking issues. What follows in this chapter is some general guidance drawn from the example of recent jury trials in the Court of Session and the author has attempted to avoid both "perceived wisdom" and the results of psychological studies of the workings of the civil jury in other jurisdictions, informative though these might be[1].

LIABILITY

7.03 Notwithstanding the pleadings, liability in a personal injury action is seldom clear-cut but in the vast majority of cases it should be fairly obvious either that the pursuer has a fairly good chance of succeeding on liability or that liability is at least to some extent in question. If liability is in question then it should be reasonably clear that this is because the defender has mounted a serious factual challenge to the pursuer's account of the accident, that he raises a real legal issue or that there is a question arising as to the apportionment of liability either in relation to contributory negligence on the part of the pursuer or as between defenders. Sharp issues of fact or apportionment of liability are readily suited to jury trial but questions of law are rarely so. At the time an action is raised (particularly if there has been little pre-litigation communication between the parties) the stance to be taken by the defenders may, however, not be readily apparent to the pursuer and, conversely, the defenders may be uncertain as to what their preferred mode of inquiry might be and, where the Chapter 43 personal injuries procedure is being used, there may be little time for either side to properly consider the matter but some of the points dealt with below might be helpful even if only to confirm a preliminary view.

7.04 Although corroboration in civil causes where liability is in issue is no longer essential, independent witnesses who can verify a pursuer's account of an incident or the circumstances surrounding it are certainly helpful in proving a case before a jury, but where a pursuer is thought to be a credible and reliable witness the absence of other witnesses to speak to the primary facts is by no means fatal[2]. An analysis of decisions in jury cases where the pursuer failed on liability does not necessarily lead one to the conclusion that the result would have been any different if the case had been heard by a judge, as the following examples would illustrate.

- An auxiliary nurse claimed to have been taking an elderly patient to his lunch when he lost his balance and, in trying to help him, she caught his weight and thus suffered injury. There were no witnesses to the accident and the patient had died before the trial date. In cross-examination the pursuer conceded that the patient was being fed intravenously at that time and

---

1 Two good recent works are Greene and Bornstein, *Determining Damages: The Psychology of Jury Awards* (Washington DC, 2003) and Feigenson, *Legal Blame: How Jurors Think And Talk About Accidents* (Washington DC, 2nd edn, 2001). Most US research is based on the mock jury: see Bornstein, "The Ecological Validity of Jury Simulations" (1999) Law and Human Behaviour 23–75.

2 E.g. *Cameron v Lanarkshire Health Board* 1997 SLT 1040.

this factor cast some doubt as to what she had actually been doing and thus her credibility and reliability were put in issue. The result was a verdict assoilzing the defenders after the jury had deliberated for only 12 minutes[3].

- A school cleaner claimed to have tripped on an admittedly defective step and fallen to her injury. The only witness was a schoolteacher who said that the pursuer had tripped at a point much higher up on the stairway. Once again the pursuer's credibility was challenged on a separate point since a video recording shown to the jury appeared to suggest that, in fact, she was substantially exaggerating the extent of her disabilities. The pursuer lost her action[4].

- An auxiliary nurse slipped on an "excessively" wet floor which had just been cleaned and claimed that she had not seen any warning signs prior to her accident. The defenders pled sole fault and produced a witness whom the pursuer had told that she had seen such signs before falling. The jury found for the defenders by a majority of seven to five[5].

7.05 One could, perhaps, argue that in these cases had the pursuers' integrity as witnesses not been impugned on subsidiary matters, then the jury might well have been more inclined to find in their favour but then so might a judge. Examples of analogous cases where pursuers were successful in establishing liability before a jury include the following:

- A care assistant slipped on a recently cleaned wet floor while carrying a tea-pot. The jury returned a unanimous verdict in her favour subject to a finding of contributory negligence of 12.5 per cent[6].

- A hospital cleaner of small stature operating a large buffing machine was injured when it dragged her across a polished floor. Here liability was established by a majority and she received agreed damages of £2,500[7].

It is interesting that in both of these cases there were no eye witnesses to corroborate the pursuer's account.

7.06 Where pursuers come across as honest (particularly if they are elderly, a child[8] or in a category of occupation with which the public might have some sympathy, e.g. nurses, doctors, firemen) and are apparently neither fabricating nor exaggerating their claims then it has been suggested that a jury might be more inclined to find in their favour by giving them the benefit of the doubt when considering both the facts and the legal duties applicable and this may

---

3 *Reid v Lanarkshire Health Board*, Lord Kingarth, 13 Feb 1999★; cf *Ross v Fife Healthcare NHS Trust* 2000 SCLR 621.
4 *Corkindale v East Dunbartonshire Council*, Lord Mackay of Drumadoon, 25 Oct 2002★.
5 *Fidler v Ayrshire and Arran Health Board*, Lord Penrose, 14 Oct 1992★.
6 *Baillie v Leafield Nursing Home*, Lord Kirkwood, 31 March 1994★ but see the note to the report in Appendix III, 2 [29] below.
7 *Bishop v Queensberry House Hospital*, Lord Milligan, 9 Dec 1992★.
8 But by way of caution cf *Christie's Curator ad litem v Kirkwood* 1996 SLT 1299.

be doubly so where the pursuer's injuries are catastrophic or otherwise distressing. By way of example, in a recent case where the pursuer was a paraplegic and total damages were agreed at £800,000, liability was in issue in a situation where two lorries were approaching each other on a country road which was wide enough for both to pass safely. The pursuer, thinking a collision would ensue, panicked and swerved off the road. The defender was at the time travelling at 50 mph, which was 10 mph in excess of the speed limit applicable to his vehicle. The jury found for the pursuer[9]. However, it would have to be conceded that in the vast majority of cases where jury awards have been made liability is either admitted or, where liability is in dispute, on a strict analysis of the facts it would be difficult to say that the outcome would have been any different had liability been assessed by a judge. The position might, however, be different in the case of a pursuer who was an obvious wrongdoer for whom a jury may have less sympathy than might a judge and where the jury might be reluctant to award any damages at all on the basis, possibly, that the pursuer deserved what he got[10].

Contributory negligence

7.07 Views differ on whether or not findings of contributory negligence are affected by the mode of trial, but it may be that the real question here is not whether a jury would find a person partially responsible for an accident where a judge would not but more one of the eventual apportionment of liability between pursuer and defender. Some recent examples include the following findings of contributory negligence by juries: (a) 5 per cent for a man working on a roof who fell through a rooflight and died. He had no helmet on (although apparently this would have made little difference to the head injuries sustained) and no safety harness – the contribution on his part appears to have been that he failed to contact his supervisor when he found that there were no certified anchor points for harnesses on the roof in question[11]; (b) 10 per cent for a motor cyclist who collided with an ice-cream van turning across his path[12]; (c) 12.5 per cent for a care assistant who slipped on an obviously wet

---

9 *Dickson v Scottish Borders Council*, Lady Paton, 9 July 2003★.
10 In *Carson v Chief Constable, Lothian and Borders Police*, Lord McEwan, 6 Feb 2003★, a man with a criminal record was, after a car chase, being pursued on foot by police officers through a wood when he received certain injuries as a result, allegedly, of those officers using excessive force. The jury, by a majority, declined to make an award to him.
11 *Warnock v Clark Contracts*, Lord Wheatley, 18 Nov 2004★.
12 *Bryce v Adam Stark Ltd*, Lord McEwan, 20 June 2005★ – the pursuer was riding a powerful motorbike in a 40 mph zone at a speed estimated by him to be "between 40 and 45 mph", by a road traffic expert at "in the high fifties at a conservative guess" and by an independent witness at "70 or 80 mph". The van driver, who had admitted "cutting the corner", had been convicted of an offence under s 3 of the Road Traffic Act 1988.

floor[13]; (d) 20 per cent for a track worker struck by a train while examining the line[14]; (e) 25 per cent for a 12-year-old youth who sustained extensive burning injuries when he fell onto high-voltage electric cables[15]; (f) 35 per cent for a nurse who on leaving an operating theatre in a hurry collided with a carelessly parked trolley[16]; (g) 60 per cent for a woman who slipped on a substance spilt on a floor[17]; (h) 80 per cent where a woman slipped in the bath of a holiday cottage where there was no bath mat and where the defenders pled *volenti*[18]; and (i) 95 per cent in the case of a young boy who hanged himself in a police cell and had not been put on "suicide watch" despite making previous threats to kill himself[19]. Perhaps the best advice that can be given is to be cautious of putting to a jury cases where the pursuer's contribution is, on any view, likely to be high and to avoid situations where a jury might well on a "common-sense" basis take a higher assessment of contributory negligence than a judge would. A good example of the latter might be a situation where a judge would make a 25 per cent finding in relation to the pursuer's failure to wear a seatbelt but the evidence might suggest that had the pursuer been wearing a belt injury would have been avoided or lessened. On the other hand, findings by a judge of contributory negligence of less than 25 per cent are relatively uncommon so it is possible to argue that juries might, if they regard the contribution as slight, tend to downplay such negligence in reaching a figure.

Contribution between defenders

7.08 Although juries are asked to apportion liability between defenders in relatively few cases other than road traffic accidents there is no evidence to suggest that their apportionments are made on any different basis from those of a judge. However, in a recent case where the pursuer was a pillion passenger on a motorbike driven by the second defender and the first defender was the driver of a van at the front of a line of traffic who turned right while being overtaken by the bike, the jury made a 95 per cent / 5 per cent apportionment between first and second defenders, apparently finding the second defender liable because he admitted travelling slightly in excess of the speed limit at the

---

13 *Baillie v Leafield Nursing Home*, Lord Kirkwood, 31 March 1994★.
14 *Kirkland v British Railways Board* 1978 SC 1 and see **24.17** below.
15 *McLeod v British Railways Board* 2001 SC 534.
16 *Cameron v Lanarkshire Health Board* 1997 SLT 1040.
17 *Mitchell v North Glasgow Hospitals NHS Trust* 2004 Rep LR 100 and see article by R G Milligan in (2002) Rep L Bul 2.
18 *Manton v Commissioners of Northern Lights* 2004 Rep LR 100 and see article by C Connal, "Jury Trials in the Court of Session" (2003) 48 JLSS Nov/54.
19 *Davidson v Chief Constable, Fife Police*, Lord Hamilton, 18 May 1995 although it is understood that the evidence suggested that he may not have actually intended the result of his attempt to have been successful.

time despite there being no clear evidence that the speed made a material contribution to the accident[20].

QUANTUM OF DAMAGES

Solatium[21]

7.09 In personal injury actions there is considerable evidence to suggest that where the injuries sustained are of a serious and permanent nature and have an adverse effect upon the pursuer's enjoyment of life then the damages likely to be awarded by a jury will be considerably in excess of those which might be expected from a judge. Examples of this can be found in cases involving paraplegia or tetraplegia, serious multiple injuries[22], amputated limbs[23], severe and disfiguring scars[24], sexual dysfunction[25], post-traumatic distress or other psychological conditions[26], transmitted solatium in distressing circumstances[27] and residual injuries which impacted on the pursuer's enjoyment of life[28]. These categories of case include those in which the highest ever awards of solatium have been made and several examples of where the defenders have unsuccessfully sought a new trial on the basis of an excess of damages. The next raft of cases[29] involves awards which, although marginally higher than that which might have been expected from a judge, are not significantly so. Interestingly these cases were all ones where liability was in dispute but there is no particular common thread to them. However, the last category of cases illustrates well the principle that the jury should not always be regarded as a fairy godmother and here awards have (from the pursuer's point of view) been distressingly low and pursuers have even, on occasions, failed to beat what can

20 *Shaw v Russell*, Lord Carloway, 10 May 2004★.

21 For case notes on jury awards for solatium see Appendix III, section 2 below.

22 E.g. *Shaw v Russell* 2004 Rep LR 99; *Leeder v Advocate General for Scotland* 2004 Rep LR 99; *Towers v Jack* 2004 Rep LR 100; *Marnoch v British Railways Board* (1993) McEwan & Paton, CN3-00D.

23 E.g. *Mill v British Railways Board* (1996) McEwan & Paton, CN17-00; *Middleton v Smith* (1992) BPILS Bulletin 11; *Currie v Kilmarnock and Loudon District Council* 1996 SC 55: for amputated fingers see *Carmichael v Isola Werke (UK) Ltd*, Lord Bracadale, 19 May 2005; Appendix III, 2 [10].

24 E.g. *McLeod v British Railways Board* 2001 SC 534; *Walker v Moncur* 2001 Rep LR 67.

25 E.g. *Adamson v Lothian Health Board* 2000 Rep LR (Quantum) 44: for a full account of the case see L Sutherland, "Medical Negligence and Civil Juries" (2000) 32 Rep L Bul 1.

26 E.g. *Tate v Fischer* 1998 SLT 1419; *Gartley v R McCartney (Painters) Ltd* 1997 Rep LR (Quantum) 18; *Masse v Lord Advocate* 1999 Rep LR (Quantum) 75; *Stuart v Lothian & Borders Fire Board* 1997 Rep LR (Quantum) 17.

27 E.g. *Wells v Hay* 1999 Rep LR 44.

28 E.g. *Girvan v Inverness Farmers' Dairy (No 2)* 1998 SC (HL) 1; *Davis v Bryson* 2004 Rep LR 99.

29 E.g. *George v Bank of Scotland* 1997 Rep LR (Quantum) 18; *Harmer v West Lothian NHS Trust* (1998) McEwan & Paton, CN4-044A; *Malcolm v Lothian and Borders Fire Board*, 23 Nov 1990; *Ross v Fife Healthcare NHS Trust* 1999 Rep LR (Quantum) 75.

only be described as not ungenerous tenders. The cause of such low awards is not clear but may be because either the jury has rejected evidence of injuries more serious than proved[30], because the injuries were comparatively trivial[31], perhaps because the pursuer was serving a prison sentence[32], or for reasons that were not even clear to the counsel and agents involved in the cases[33]. The only conclusion one can perhaps draw from looking at awards is that juries are generous to genuine pursuers who have suffered greatly and can be mean to unsympathetic pursuers with minor injuries especially where there is an element of exaggeration involved. Whether or not liability is admitted seems to have little effect on solatium but a defence strongly insisted upon and which the jury may think has little moral merit may possibly make it inclined to view damages in a more favourable light.

Relatives' claims under Damages (Scotland) Act 1976, s 1(4)

7.10   There is clear evidence that relatives with claims for bereavement, grief, loss of society and guidance are normally awarded sums considerably in excess of those awarded by judges applying a quasi-tariff system[34] and this trend seems likely to continue. Thus, in the absence of any complicating factor (such as an unsatisfactory relationship with the deceased or a complex or potentially valuable loss of support claim[35]) a pursuer might be best advised to seek issues. An exception to this general rule might be found in the case of a person of potentially bad character, the loss of whom the jury might feel to be of little consequence or where the jury felt that a relationship was unstable, fraught or devoid of any genuine feeling[36]. An interesting departure from the practice

30 E.g. *Buchanan v Mason* 2001 Rep LR 67, an admitted liability road traffic accident case where there was evidence to suggest that the pursuer was exaggerating the extent of his disabilities.

31 E.g. *Manton v Commissioner for Northern Lights* 2004 Rep LR 100 and article in (2003) 48 JLSS Nov/54; *Kirkpatrick v Secretary of State for Scotland*, 24 April 1997.

32 E.g. *Campbell v Secretary of State for Scotland*, The Scotsman, 7 Oct 1989; *Kirkpatrick v Secretary of State for Scotland*, 24 April 1997; *Davidson v Chief Constable, Fife Police*, Appendix III, 1 [6]; cf *McLeod v British Railways Board* 2001 SC 534.

33 E.g. *Tait v Campbell* 2004 Rep LR 100; *Mitchell v North Glasgow University Hospitals NHS Trust* 2004 Rep LR 100; *Jamieson v Higgins* 1998 Rep LR (Quantum) 23.

34 See Appendix III, section 1, the tables in A Hajducki, "Changing Values: Bereavement Awards in the Post-Shaher World" 2003 SLT (News) 189 and the Inner House awards in *McLean v William Denny & Bros* 2004 SC 656 and *Murray's Exrx v Greenock Dockyard Co* 2004 SLT 1104.

35 E.g. in *MacIntosh v Findlay* 2001 Rep LR 66, it was apparently felt that the jury's loss of support award to a posthumous child was less generous than that which might have been expected from a judge.

36 One can only speculate in the absence of any reasons given by the jury. In *Davidson v Chief Constable, Fife Police*, Lord Hamilton, 18 May 1995, the jury made a nil award to the cohabiting girlfriend of a petty criminal who killed himself in police custody and found contributory negligence of 95 per cent which resulted in his mother and posthumous child getting minimal awards.

followed by judges in relation to damages for children of varying ages is that whereas they would tend to award the greatest sums for younger children (on the basis that they will have suffered the greatest amount of loss of society and guidance), juries tend to award siblings similar amounts, presumably either on the basis of balancing factors such as the enhanced grief of an older child who is more aware of their loss or because they believe that equity is best served by equal treatment[37].

Patrimonial loss

7.11   Because there is much less scope for divergence in awards for patrimonial loss between a judge and a jury, patrimonial loss being "capable of reasonably precise calculation"[38], there is no particular tactical advantage to be gained by either side in insisting on a jury trial merely because it is felt that a jury would award more. The one area which might, however, be more contentious is that of necessary services rendered to a pursuer and there is at least one camp who would maintain that since this head of damage is largely an artificial one created by statute then a jury might have more of a problem in making a generous award under this head. There are certainly examples of nil[39] and low[40] awards by juries, but provided that services are properly considered under individual headings in the schedule to the issues then the jury should be considered to be able to make an appropriate award. However, provided the jury is given all of the relevant facts, including agreed figures, multiplicands or multipliers, and is properly directed, then there is no reason to suspect that its awards for patrimonial loss would differ from that of a judge.

REASONS WHY DEFENDER MIGHT OPT FOR JURY TRIAL

7.12   With few exceptions[41] it is invariably the pursuer who seeks issues and the defender who resists them. However, in other jurisdictions, notably Canada, this is not always the case and from some of the cases discussed above it seems clear that there may well be circumstances in which defenders might be advised either to agree to the pursuer's motion for issues or even to insist on a jury trial when the pursuer wishes for a proof and is prepared to argue

---

37 E.g. *Kempton v British Railways Board*, Appendix III, 1 [3] and *Warnock v Clark Contracts*, Appendix III, 1 [1] – in the latter case the jury also made identical awards for loss of services and support to the three children notwithstanding the fact that at the time of their father's death they had been aged nine, six and three respectively.

38 *Girvan v Inverness Farmers' Dairy (No 2)* 1998 SC (HL) 1 at 17 per Lord Hope.

39 E.g. *Manton v Commissioners for Northern Lights* 2004 Rep LR 100; *Buchanan v Mason* 2001 Rep LR 67.

40 E.g. *Mitchell v North Glasgow University Hospitals NHS Trust* 2004 Rep LR 100 (£750).

41 E.g. *Buchanan v Mason*, Lord Johnston, 9 June 2000 – see **13.04** below; *McFarlane v Thain* [2005] CSOH 22, 2005 SLT 221.

special cause. These circumstances might include cases (a) where liability is admitted but where the pursuer is exaggerating or manufacturing physical symptoms of injury especially if there is evidence such as a videotape of the pursuer behaving in a clearly inconsistent manner; (b) where there is doubt as to whether the accident actually occurred because the injuries or prior statements are inconsistent or there is a good supporting witness or witnesses who can negate the pursuer's account; (c) where on any view the pursuer's account is incredible; (d) where the pursuer can be shown to have been dishonest in his dealings with the defender or police or other agencies[42]; (e) where the medical records are clearly at odds with the injuries claimed or the nature of the accident; (f) where liability might rest on somewhat technical grounds; or (g) where a jury might see the situation as being a "but for the grace of God" one[43]. Where liability is admitted but the injuries are trivial and the pursuer has rejected a reasonable tender then a defender may wish to consider putting the matter to a jury. Where quantum is agreed at a low sum but liability is still in issue, particularly if a substantial degree of contribution is alleged, then a defender may also wish to insist on a trial.

7.13 What is, however, important is that defenders consider carefully what the matters in contention between the parties actually are and how those matters can best be adjudicated upon and, having done so, if they then feel that a jury is the best mode for trying those matters they should insist upon a trial. It has, however, to be admitted that the very tight time scales of the Chapter 43 personal injuries procedures often make it difficult for defenders to analyse such questions at their leisure and there is a real danger that cases which, from the defenders' point of view, would be better being tried by a jury end up with a proof being allocated by default.

DEFAMATION ACTIONS

7.14 In relation to defamation actions it has often been observed that "the only person who can contemplate with equanimity bringing an action . . . is one with ample means, whose reputation is unblemished, whose past contains no skeletons, and whose complaint is of a damaging and clear public misstatement of a specific fact"[44], and this is especially true when considering whether or not to seek a jury. The function of the jury is to determine ques-

---

42 E.g., possibly, *Carson v Chief Constable, Lothian and Borders Police*, Lord McEwan, 6 Feb 2003★ – see n 10 above.

43 An example of this might be *Christie's Curator ad litem v Kirkwood* 1996 SLT 1299 where a three-year-old girl emerged from between cars parked outside a shop and was struck by a car. Evidence was led to the effect that the driver had no opportunity to see her prior to that moment and thereby had no means of avoiding the accident. The jury returned a verdict in the defender's favour.

44 Gatley, *Libel & Slander* (10th edn, 2004), para 24.2.

tions of fact and often it is called upon to determine what the words complained of actually mean. Thus, from a pursuer's point of view if the words are clear, unequivocal and obviously damaging and the pursuer is seen to be beyond reproach, trial by jury might be seen as being preferable, but if the pursuer is a person of outspoken or unpopular views, wealthy or controversial or otherwise seen as a person who can well take care of himself then he might be advised to seek a proof whereas a defender might be encouraged to seek issues. The mode of inquiry will thus depend on factors such as the nature and identity of both the pursuer and defender, the nature of the statement, the method of publication, the existence of any previous dispute between the parties, the degree of actual or perceived damage done to the pursuer and the fact that, inevitably, a jury trial for defamation will attract more publicity in Scotland than, say, an action raised in the sheriff court.

7.15   When it comes to damages for defamation, juries in Scotland do not tend to award the largesse that their counterparts in England were once wont to do[45] and, indeed, the fairly modest awards that juries have tended to award in recent years are not so dissimilar from the levels of award that one might expect from a judge in similar circumstances[46], although punishing the tabloids may still be seen as a legitimate jury goal[47] even if this is carried out on a discriminating basis[48].

45 For Scottish jury awards see case notes in Appendix III, section 3 below and for English awards by juries and by judges between 1990 and 2003 see Appendix 3 to Price and Duodo, *Defamation Law, Procedure and Practice* (3rd edn, 2004). The reason for this apparent discrepancy may be either due to the innate sense and moderation of Scots juries or the fact that in England such damages can have a punitive element absent in Scotland.
46 Cf *Winter v News Scotland Ltd* 1991 SLT 828 and *Wray v Associated Newspapers Ltd* 2000 SLT 869.
47 Perhaps the award in *Clinton v News Group Newspapers Ltd*, 18 Dec 1999, Appendix III, para 3 [1] is an example of this.
48 Cf *Clinton*, n 47 above, and *Barry v News Group Newspapers Ltd*, 18 Dec 1999, Appendix III, para 3 [3] below.

Chapter 8

To the closing of the record

8.01 This chapter deals with procedural issues in jury causes up to the stage of the closing of the record and, in particular, identifies specific matters which might arise and affect the mode of inquiry insofar as this might relate to trial as opposed to proof. Such matters are, of course, in addition to those which have already been identified in the preceding chapters relating to the causes which can competently be tried before a jury, the question of special cause and the tactical and practical considerations which might influence a party in the choice between proof and jury trial.

RAISING THE ACTION

Ordinary actions

8.02 In all actions to which the new Chapter 43 procedure does not apply an action in which the pursuer intends to seek jury trial should be raised in the normal manner and the summons should be prepared, signetted and served as usual[1]. In the case of personal injuries actions raised before 1 April 2003, the rules relating to ordinary actions still apply along with relevant modifications[2] but the optional procedure for such actions no longer applies[3]. All defamation actions[4], actions for malicious prosecution or wrongful imprisonment, actions for professional negligence arising from personal injury actions[5] and actions of reduction should accordingly be raised under the ordinary procedure, but

---

1 Rules, Chapters 13 and 16.
2 See [old] Chapter 43 reproduced at pp C352/24 *et seq* of Morrison.
3 [Old] rules 43.18–43.28; note that under the optional procedure the service of the summons in such an action constituted a waiver by the pursuer of his right to jury trial although the defender could still seek issues unless he waived his right thereto.
4 Injuries resulting from defamation or other injury to reputation, whilst included in the relevant definitions of "personal injuries" found in s 10(1) of the Damages (Scotland) Act 1976 and s 13(1) of the Administration of Justice (Scotland) Act 1982 have no place in the definitions within rule 43.1(2): *Tudhope v Finlay Park (t/a Park Hutchison, Solicitors)*, Lord Cameron, 2004 SLT 783; see also Practice Note No 2 of 2003.
5 *Tudhope v Finlay Park (t/a Park Hutchison, Solicitors)* 2004 SLT 783, despite the fact that jury trial is competent in such actions: see **5.13** above.

actions for damages for a delictual wrong such as rape and assault would now fall within the new Chapter 43 procedure since they would qualify as personal injury actions.

Chapter 43 actions

8.03 In respect of all personal injuries actions raised in the Court of Session on or after 1 April 2003, new mandatory rules based in part on the Cullen and Coulsfield Reports[6] apply irrespective of the proposed mode of inquiry. In deciding whether or not the rules apply to a particular action certain statutory definitions have been provided. "Personal injuries" include "any disease or impairment, whether physical or mental" and a "personal injuries action" means "an action for damages for, or arising from, personal injuries or death of a person from personal injuries"[7]. It was not, however, intended that any actions which are not, in ordinary parlance, concerned with personal injuries are covered by Chapter 43[8] and the expression "arising from" does not include a situation where a defender who, although not responsible in law for causing such injuries, allowed a valuable right based upon a claim for negligence to become time-barred[9]. With certain exceptions[10] all of the rules applying to ordinary actions apply to Chapter 43 actions as do the rules specifically relating to jury trials[11] and in a personal injury action the form of summons must be in the prescribed form[12]. In terms of the Rules of Court the fact that an action has been raised under the ordinary or Chapter 43 procedure has no effect upon a party's entitlement to jury trial[13].

Legal aid

8.04 The Scottish Legal Aid Board requires that detailed reasons be given by a pursuer's agent when an application is made to raise an action in the

---

6 *Review of Business of the Outer House in the Court of Session*, Dec 1995, *Report of the Working Party on Court of Session Procedure* 2000 (www.scotcourts.gov.uk/session/report/coulreport.htm) and supplementary report July 2002 (www.scotcourts.gov.uk/session/report/supplementary.htm).
7 Rule 43.1(2).
8 Practice Note No 2 of 2003.
9 *Tudhope v Finlay Park (t/a Park Hutchison, Solicitors)* 2004 SLT 843 involved an action for professional negligence of solicitors who had allowed an action to become time-barred. The action was remitted to proceed as an ordinary action in terms of rule 43.5(1) despite having been originally raised as a Chapter 43 action: see *Tudhope v Finlay Park (t/a Park Hutchison, Solicitors)* 2003 SLT 1305.
10 The exceptions being listed in rule 43.1(3).
11 Rule 37.4; the only specific exemption being rule 36.3 relating to the lodging of productions.
12 Form 43.2-A as amended by SSI 2004/291; this form is broadly similar to the old Form 43.1 used in optional procedure actions.
13 Cf the now defunct ordinary procedure: see **8.02** and n 3 above.

Court of Session where the sum sued for is less than £50,000. If the case is a personal injury action seen as being suitable for raising under the Chapter 43 procedure, full information must be given as to why the action should be raised under this procedure rather than in the sheriff court. In addition, where it is disclosed that a jury trial is sought, detailed arguments to show that a jury trial would be appropriate and reasonable in the circumstances must be made and simply stating that a jury may make a higher award than a sheriff or judge is not, in itself, sufficient justification for Court of Session proceedings[14].

PRINCIPLES OF PLEADING

Ordinary actions

8.05   The two cardinal rules of pleading in any civil action are that the averments should be precise and that they should give fair notice. This is particularly important in the context of civil jury actions since, in the words of Lord Justice-Clerk Thomson: "once a jury is empanelled, there is little room for amendment and none for adjournment. Parties are held to their records, and their records ought to give fair notice of the points which parties intend to make."[15]

8.06   As in the case of any ordinary action irrespective of the mode of inquiry, the articles of condescendence and answers in the record should be as brief and pointed as possible as is consistent with clarity and should contain no argument or irrelevant or scandalous averments[16]. In the specific context of jury trials it has been observed that the object of the pleadings

> "ought to be, clearly and distinctly to state the averments and the pleas of the parties opposed to each other, to state the facts, and to aver the truth, in as few and distinct terms as possible . . . to make the averments in direct and precise terms, avoiding entirely all matter which goes merely to show the probability of the statement, and . . . then making the averment, that these facts being true, the conclusion is clear for the pursuer or defender"[17].

8.07   It is accordingly important in any case in which either of the parties desire a jury trial that the averments are clearly and distinctly stated and that the issue between the parties is focused in a clear and distinct manner[18] or, in

---

14   *The Recorder*, 39 (SLAB, May 2004). The additional requirement only applies where the reason put forward for the Court of Session is the desire for jury trial rather than a more general wish to use the Chapter 43 procedure.

15   *Lawrie v Glasgow Corporation* 1952 SC 361 at 363; see also *Littlejohn v Brown & Co Ltd* 1909 SC 169 at 176–177 per Lord Justice-Clerk Macdonald and *Boyle v Glasgow Corporation* 1949 SC 254 at 261 per Lord Justice-Clerk Thomson.

16   Maclaren, p 311.

17   Introduction to Murray's *Jury Court Reports*, 5 Mur xix.

18   Lord Commissioner Adam in his speech at the opening of the Jury Court, reported at 1 Mur 1.

other words, that the pursuer's averments are relevant and specific on all material points[19]. In an early leading case, Lord Justice-Clerk Hope observed that, when comparing jury trials to proofs:

> "Jury Trial has innumerable and inappreciable advantages for the attainment of truth: but it must all be over in the current progress of the trial, it is quite plain that if each party has not full and fair notice of the adversary's case, he cannot be able to meet it in evidence: and if a verdict passes in consequence of parties entering on a line of inquiry, of which the adversary got no notice, and on which he could not be prepared, a trial would be the most imperfect and defective mode of investigation which could be conceived. . . . The beauty of the Scotch system [of pleadings] is that, without disclosing what is properly called evidence, you must at least state the line of defence, and the main facts and points in the inquiry on which you rest, so that the other party shall be fully able previously to investigate the case, and be prepared for it."[20]

Putting it perhaps a little more succinctly, over a century later Lord Justice-Clerk Thomson remarked that a party "is entitled to conduct his case on the footing that the closed record discloses his adversary's case"[21].

8.08   Thus, a party should not be taken by surprise by the leading of evidence in relation to matters of which there is fair notice in the pleadings[22] and it should be noted that the failure to plead a case in accordance with the evidence may prove to be fatal[23]. In another case Lord Justice-Clerk Thomson said that:

> "the court is often charitable to records and is slow to overturn verdicts on technical grounds. But where a pursuer fails completely to substantiate the only grounds of fault averred and seeks to justify his verdict on a ground which is not just a variation, modification or development of what is averred but is something which is new, separate and distinct, then we are not in the terms of technicality."[24]

It should, of course, not be overlooked that one important reason why the pleadings should relate to the evidence is that amendment during the course of the trial and after the evidence has come out may prove to be difficult or even impossible[25].

---

19 *Cassidy v Argyll and Clyde Health Board* 1997 SLT 934; see also *McCormack v CSC Forestry Products Ltd* 2001 GWD 40-1499.
20 *Neilson v Househill Coal and Iron Co* (1842) 4 D 1187 at 1193.
21 *Lawrie v Glasgow Corporation* 1952 SC 361 at 365.
22 *Wilson v Thomas Usher & Sons* 1934 SC 332; *Christie's Curator ad litem v Kirkwood* 1996 SLT 1299; *Cameron v Lanarkshire Health Board* 1997 SLT 1040.
23 *Cleisham v British Transport Commission* 1964 SC (HL) 8; *Mulligan v Caird (Dundee) Ltd* 1973 SLT 72; *Sheridan v George Wimpey & Co Ltd* 1964 SLT (Notes) 106.
24 *Burns v Dixon's Iron Works* 1961 SC 102.
25 See e.g. *Cameron v Lanarksire Health Board* 1997 SLT 1040.

Defamation actions

8.09 An adherence to the strict rules of pleading may be particularly necessary in cases of defamation where the roles of judge and jury are quite distinct. Before issues are allowed it is essential for the pursuer to set forth in his pleadings the precise words complained of, any meaning which he ascribes to those words and, if the statement is not defamatory *per se*, he must aver extrinsic facts and circumstances which render it so. In those circumstances "it is for the court to determine whether the facts stated are such as to entitle the pursuer to have the case sent to a jury on an issue setting forth the innuendo or secondary meaning which he undertakes to prove"[26].

Chapter 43 personal injury actions

8.10 In Chapter 43 procedure personal injury actions these same basic principles apply. However, the prescribed form for a summons states that averments are to be made in numbered paragraphs relating only to those facts necessary to establish the claim[27]. Therefore what is required in most cases to which the procedure applies in relation to liability is (a) the briefest description of the events on which the claim is based, together with a brief indication of the grounds of fault alleged and a specific reference to any statutory provision which is founded upon[28]; (b) the name of every medical practitioner from whom, and every hospital or other institution in which the pursuer or, if applicable, the deceased, received treatment[29]; and (c) an indication of the individual heads of claim which the pursuer is putting forward[30]. Averments should be "couched in such a way as to require individual answers to particular averments of fact"[31]. Pleas-in-law are not to be included[32]. It should, however, be remembered that

> "although the [statutory] phraseology selected was intended to create a departure from what had become over elaborate and formulaic forms of pleadings in personal injuries actions, the new rules simply reflect what was always the fundamental principle in written pleadings, namely to aver only the facts which need to be proved to establish the case, and not the evidence or argument"[33].

26 *Sexton v Ritchie & Co* (1890) 17 R 680 at 696 per Lord Maclaren.
27 Rule 43.2(1)(a) as amended by SSI 2004/291.
28 Practice Note No 2 of 2003.
29 Rule 43.2(1)(b) as amended by SSI 2004/291.
30 The detailed sums involved are now included in the statement of valuation of claim required under rule 43.9 – see *May v Jeeves Parcels Ltd* [2005] CSOH 71 and *Easdon v A Clarke & Co (Smethwick) Ltd* [2006] CSOH 12.
31 Working party supplementary report, which also contains styles.
32 Lord Coulsfield, Introductory Address at Seminars on new personal injury procedures; Alexander v Metbro, 2004 SLT 963 per Lady Paton; Practice Note No 3 of 2004.
33 *Baillie v ECG Group Ltd* [2005] CSOH 40 per Lord Carloway.

8.11 Where such simplified pleadings have been used, it has been said that
a requirement of fair notice in a broad rather than a technical sense is one
which should be reasonably met[34]. However, in relation to the pleadings in
Chapter 43 actions it has been observed that, although they were designed to
simplify written pleadings and avoid complexity where possible, nothing in
the rules detracted either from the principle that defenders were entitled, when
presented with a summons, to be able to ascertain without undue difficulty the
nature of the case against them or from the fundamental principle that a pursuer ought not to raise an action against a defender except in circumstances
where he had information upon which he was able to make a relevant case[35].
It is suggested that this principle applies to all actions, whether they are to be
tried before a jury or at a proof and that accordingly no distinction should be
made in relation to the proposed mode of inquiry, i.e. that the pleadings are
either relevant or irrelevant except in that small number of cases where it can
truly be said that the brief statements of fact with brief references to common
law and/or statute which might suffice in a personal injury summons under the
new procedure might give rise to questions of law which can only be decided
after the facts can be elicited[36]. Nevertheless in order to secure a jury trial there
would still require to be sufficient factual averments in the pleadings to entitle
the pursuer to lead evidence in relation to foreseeability and the specific statutory duty which it is alleged that the defender breached must be specified[37]
and alternative cases should still be pled[38]. However, in general, personal injuries actions are pled in a shorter and simpler form than that used in ordinary
actions[39].

The sum sued for

8.12 One important consideration which should be addressed at the initial
stage, whether the action is an ordinary action or one to which the Chapter 43
procedure will apply, is the question of the sum sued for since this sum will
appear in the issue and may well prove to be of the greatest importance at the
stage when the jury is considering its quantification of damages. The sum
should be expressed in sterling although juries can be asked to award component parts of patrimonial loss in other currencies if appropriate[40]. In both
ordinary and Chapter 43 actions the conclusion must include a specific total

---

34 *McFarnon v British Coal Corporation* 1988 SLT 242 at 243B.
35 *Clifton v Hays plc* 2004 Rep LR 73 (note).
36 *Hamilton v Seamark Systems Ltd* 2004 GWD 8-167 per Lady Paton.
37 *Higgins v DHL International (UK) Ltd* 2003 SLT 1301.
38 *Rodgers v British Steel plc* 1992 SLT 642.
39 *Alexander v Metbro Ltd* 2004 SLT 963; *Easdon v A Clarke & Co (Smethwick) Ltd* [2006]
    CSOH 12.
40 E.g. in *Towers v Jack* 2004 Rep LR 100, where a jury awarded medical expenses of US
    $7,114.

sum (or sums) for damages[41], and some care should be given to selecting a sum which is both reflected in the statement of valuation of claim which must be produced under the latter procedure but, more importantly, will reflect an adequate sum to form a cap on the jury's award. For example, where there are claims for solatium and patrimonial loss, the element for solatium in the total sum sued for should, so far as possible, relate to a sum which the jury might realistically award and be neither too high (in which case the jury might feel that the claim is so unrealistic that it inadvertently penalises the pursuer for having such venial expectations) or too low (in which case the jury might feel constrained to award what it feels was, in reality, an inadequate sum). There is, therefore, an art at pitching the sum sued for at an amount which balances out these factors but does not leave the award of a generous jury open to challenge on the basis of excess of damages – an art which, like all arts, is difficult to explain but more obvious in practice.

DEFENCES

8.13 Appearance is entered in the normal manner and there are no special features of defences in actions in which a jury trial is sought other than the fact that in an ordinary action a plea-in-law is included if the defenders wish to resist issues[42]. In Chapter 43 actions no pleas-in-law are now allowed but a brief outline of legal points to be raised may be included[43].

SUBSEQUENT PROCEDURE

Ordinary actions

8.14 During the period in which the cause is on the adjustment roll the parties may adjust their pleadings in the usual manner, and the period for adjustment automatically extends to eight weeks although at any time and on the motion of any party the court may pronounce an interlocutor closing the record or continuing the cause on the adjustment roll for such period as the court thinks fit[44]. However, once the court has pronounced an interlocutor closing the record the pursuer must, within four weeks after the date of that interlocutor, lodge in process three copies of the closed record and send to the

---

41 The variable sum concluded for in the optional procedure was only possible because such actions were excluded from trial by jury.
42 See **9.06** below.
43 See **9.07** below.
44 Rule 22.2.

other parties six copies each[45] and, at the same time, enrol a motion for further procedure[46].

Chapter 43 actions

8.15 On the lodging of the defences in a Chapter 43 personal injuries action or, where there is more than one defender, on the lodging of the first set of defences the Keeper of the Rolls allocates a diet for the hearing of the action[47] (the mode of which is, as yet, undetermined) and issues the statutory time-table[48] which provides currently for, *inter alia*, an adjustment period of eight weeks[49]. Ten weeks after the lodging of defences, i.e. two weeks after the closing of the record, the record has to be lodged and a motion for further procedure enrolled.

8.16 If any party wishes to make a motion to have the action withdrawn from the Chapter 43 procedure and transmitted to the ordinary procedure then, within 28 days of the lodging of the defences, that party must make such an application by way of motion[50]. Such a motion will only be granted if the court is satisfied that there are exceptional reasons for doing so[51], and particular care should be taken to include as much information as possible on the motion sheet when such a motion is enrolled[52]. Although medical negligence actions are, in practice, often transferred to the ordinary roll under this provision it cannot be assumed that merely because an action involves professional negligence it would necessarily be so transferred[53]. The mere fact that an action has been transferred or remains as a Chapter 43 action does not, of course, mean that it is necessarily suitable or unsuitable for jury trial although the factors which might influence the court in granting a motion[54] might possibly have a bearing on the matter. Although a subsequent motion for sist or variation of the statutory timetable may be made[55], it is most unlikely to be granted if no previous motion to have the action transferred to the ordinary

---

45 Rule 22.3(1), (2).
46 Rule 23.5.
47 Rule 43.6(1)(a). Diets of trial are normally four days but if a longer period is required then this should be intimated to the Keeper of the Rolls – Practice Note No 2 of 2003. It should be borne in mind that there is no provision for a continued diet of jury trial so any estimate should err on the generous side.
48 Rule 43.6(1)(b).
49 The periods in the timetable are found in the Appendix to Practice Note No 2 of 2003.
50 Rule 43.5(1).
51 Rule 43.5(2).
52 *Broadfoot's Curator Bonis v Forth Valley Acute Hospitals NHS Trust* 2003 GWD 26-729; Practice Note No 2 of 2003.
53 *Broadfoot*, n 52 above.
54 Set out in rule 43.3(3).
55 Under rule 43.8.

roll has been made or granted[56]. The practice of the courts has, however, varied with some Lords Ordinary refusing sists on the basis that the statutory timetable should be rigidly adhered to and others taking a more pragmatic view based on the circumstances before them.

8.17 The pursuer's statement of valuation must be lodged within eight weeks of the lodging of defences, the defender's within 16 weeks; in both cases a list of the documents supporting the valuation must be lodged at the same time[57]. The purpose of these valuations is to disclose the position of the parties after allowing them a limited but realistic time to prepare for such disclosure[58] but they are not binding on the parties[59]. Although the mode of inquiry has not been fixed at the time that the statements are required, on the assumption that the pursuer does, or in any event may, wish to seek issues, then it is suggested that solatium be valued at what a jury might realistically award[60] rather than by adhering to Judicial Studies Board guidelines or levels of judge-made awards. Any such estimate would, however, have to be on the basis merely of an educated guess and a pursuer would be wise to err on the generous side whereas a defender might well be expected to value solatium on a conservative basis. It should be borne in mind that these valuations may be brought to the attention of the jury at the time of the trial[61]. Although the Rules do not provide for subsequent amendment or substitution of statements of valuation, it would appear that in practice such documents are frequently produced and exhibited to the other parties.

REMITS FROM SHERIFF COURT

8.18 Any ordinary cause brought in the sheriff court can be remitted to the Court of Session on the motion of any of the parties if the sheriff is of the opinion that the importance or difficulty of the cause makes it appropriate to do so[62]. A Full Bench considered the question of remit at some length[63] and one judge alone was of the view that the availability of jury trials in the Court of Session might in itself be a factor favouring such a remit[64]. However, in a subsequent case the Inner House decided otherwise and held that the availability of and desire for jury trial was not in itself a relevant consideration to

---

56 Practice Note No 2 of 2003; however in Feb 2004 of the 24 applications made to have the timetable varied all were granted.
57 Rule 43.9; Appendix to Practice Note No 2 of 2003.
58 Coulsfield Working Party Report.
59 Practice Note No 2 of 2003; see also *Easdon v A Clarke & Co (Smethwick) Ltd* [2006] CSOH 12.
60 For a table of actual jury awards in recent cases see Appendix III.
61 See **19.06** below.
62 Sheriff Courts (Scotland) Act 1971, s 37(1)(b).
63 *Mullan v Anderson* 1993 SLT 835.
64 Lord Justice-Clerk Ross at 840G.

favour remit[65]. This does not, of course, mean that an action can never be remitted from the sheriff court when one or more parties desires a jury trial but the justification for such a remit would have to be made with reference to the statutory criteria of importance or difficulty. On receipt of the process from the sheriff clerk when an action has been remitted, the Deputy Principal Clerk will give written intimation to each party and thereafter the process is lodged in the General Department and the party lodging it will then apply by motion for such further procedure (such as jury trial) as he desires[66].

REMITS TO SHERIFF COURT

8.19 An application can be made by either party to an action to, or the court may of its own volition, remit a cause from the Court of Session to the sheriff court having jurisdiction, if, in the opinion of the court, the nature of the action makes it appropriate to do so[67]. "Nature of the action" refers to the particular case not to any class of actions so that the fact that a claim might be a small and straightforward one is not in itself sufficient to justify a remit to the sheriff court, and the court should have regard to any practical and procedural advantages of the Court of Session, such as the availability of jury trial[68] and/or the existence of the Chapter 43 procedure[69].

---

65 *Donnelly v Safeway Stores plc* 2003 SC 235. That case involved a pursuer who alleged that she had been wrongfully detained for shoplifting and that the goods in question had been "planted" upon her. A proof before answer had already been granted in the sheriff court.
66 Rule 32.3 and 32.4(2).
67 Law Reform (Miscellaneous Provisions) (Scotland) Act 1985, s 14.
68 *McIntosh v British Railways Board* 1990 SC 338.
69 *Wilson v Glasgow City Council* 2004 SLT 1189.

Chapter 9

The allowance of issues

DECIDING FURTHER PROCEDURE

9.01   The next stage in the proceedings is to have the further procedure in the cause, and in particular the mode of inquiry, formally determined. Where a party seeks to have a cause determined by a jury, he must seek issues in relation to the whole of his case and it is not open to him to seek separate trials in relation to liability and quantum as there is no equivalent to the rule of court which allows for a divided proof[1].

Personal injury actions

9.02   In actions to which the Chapter 43 procedure applies the pursuer is required to lodge in process two copies of the record by the date specified in the timetable (i.e. not later than 10 weeks after the defences have been lodged[2]) and at the same time enrol a motion craving the court to allow a preliminary proof on specified matters, to allow a proof, to allow issues for jury trial or to make some other specified order[3] although it is anticipated that an order for inquiry (i.e. proof or jury trial) will usually be made[4]. It is considered good practice for the parties to discuss how the action will be heard before the motion is enrolled[5] and if the motion for a jury trial is unopposed then issues will normally be allowed.

9.03   If the other party or parties do not agree with the cause being tried by a jury then they must oppose the motion to allow issues and they will be expected to specify fully, in the notice of opposition, the grounds upon which the motion is opposed[6]. The matter will then normally be dealt with on the

---

1 Rule 36.1; see also *McFarlane v Thain* [2005] CSOH 22, 2005 SLT 221; [2006] CSIH 3.
2 Practice Note No 2 of 2003.
3 Rule 43.6(5).
4 Practice Note No 2 of 2003.
5 Practice Note No 3 of 1991.
6 Forms 23.2 and 23.4 are used.

motion roll although, if it is anticipated that the motion will last more than
20 minutes, the Keeper should be informed accordingly[7]. Should the person
opposing the motion for issues wish the cause to be appointed to the procedure roll then this should be marked on the motion, but as a matter of
principle, such a request will not be granted lightly[8]. If the pursuer fails to
lodge the record timeously then the Keeper will have the case put out by order
where an explanation therefor will be required[9]. Where a party enrols for jury
trial, the diet assigned in the original timetable will, where practicable, be
adhered to[10].

Ordinary actions

9.04   In all other actions if the parties are agreed as to further procedure then,
of consent, they may move the court to appoint the cause to the procedure
roll, to allow a preliminary proof on specified matters, to allow a proof before
answer, a proof, issues for jury trial or some other specified order, and an
unopposed application for the allowance of issues is usually dealt with by way
of an unopposed motion. It is only when the parties cannot reach an agreement as to what further procedure would be appropriate that the cause is
appointed to the by order (adjustment) roll[11] from where it will be set down
for a hearing on the procedure roll.

9.05   Where the cause is appointed to the procedure roll the court will
require the party or parties seeking to debate their pleas to lodge in process,
within 28 days or such other period as the court may order, a note of their
arguments consisting of numbered paragraphs stating the grounds on which
they propose to submit that their preliminary pleas relating to the mode of
inquiry should be sustained and a copy of this note should be sent to all the
other parties[12].

THE PLEADINGS

Pleas-in-law

9.06   It is incumbent upon the party who seeks to deny the other his right
to a jury trial to establish special cause and he should give fair notice of his

7 [Practice] Notice: 7 March 1990 and see comments of Lord Wheatley in *May v Jeeves
   Parcels Ltd* [2005] CSOH 71, para [19].
8 Practice Note No 2 of 2003.
9 Rule 43.6(7); Practice Note No 2 of 2003.
10 Practice Note No 2 of 2003.
11 Rule 22.3(5).
12 Rule 22.4 as qualified by Practice Notes No 3 of 1991 and No 4 of 1997; for the failure
   to do so see *Fairbairn v Vayro*, Lord Osborne, 2000 GWD 22-843.

argument both in the pleadings and in the plea[13]. Although in the past it was not thought appropriate to argue special cause without a specific plea[14] the current practice in ordinary actions is that there should be a specific plea directed at the mode of inquiry, for example, "The case being unsuitable for jury trial, issues should not be allowed." No reason need be stated in the plea-in-law unless a plea of *mora* is being taken and with the modern requirement to disclose arguments prior to the procedure roll diet there is, perhaps, less necessity for the once more common detailed special cause plea. In the absence of a plea directed towards the mode of inquiry it may not be possible to argue special cause and the courts have discouraged "back door" arguments where full notice thereof has not been given. An example was a case where the defenders sought to rely upon delay as a factor exacerbating problems of relevancy when their pleadings stated that there was special cause for withholding the case from jury trial by reason of "difficult questions of mixed fact and law"[15]. On occasions, however, special cause arguments have been heard in the absence of a plea where the pursuer either consents to this[16] or raises no objection[17] or where the court allows the defenders to amend at the bar by adding an appropriate plea[18].

9.07 The foregoing does not apply in personal injury actions to which the Chapter 43 procedure applies since pleas-in-law are no longer allowed in the pleadings in such actions[19]. Should the defender wish to give the pursuer notice of his intention to oppose a motion for jury trial prior to marking opposition to that motion then he is at liberty to include in his last answer a statement such as, "The defender contends that the action is not suitable for jury trial."[20] The defender can, presumably, elaborate on this quasi-plea and in theory should the pursuer be intending to prevent a defender from seeking a jury trial he could include a similar statement within his pleadings.

Averments on record

9.08 In an ordinary action, as well as a specific plea, there should also be sufficient supporting averments upon which the plea is founded[21], and in the case

13 *Rigley v Remington Rand* 1964 SLT (Notes) 100 per Lord Kilbrandon; *Irvine v Balmoral Hotel Edinburgh Ltd* 1999 Rep LR 41.
14 *Boyce v Sherrie* 1998 GWD 8-428.
15 *Anderson v British Railways Board* 1974 SLT (Notes) 10.
16 As in *McLaughlin v Scott's Shipbuilding Co* 1960 SLT (Notes) 58.
17 *Rigley v Remington Rand* 1964 SLT (Notes) 100.
18 *Boyce v Sherrie* 1998 GWD 8-428.
19 *Alexander v Metbro Ltd* 2004 SLT 963; Practice Note No 3 of 2004.
20 *Alexander v Metbro Ltd*, n 19 above.
21 *McFaull v Compania Navigacion Sota y Anzar* 1937 SLT 123 per Lord Russell.

of *mora* and delay prejudice must be expressly averred[22] and specification given as to the reason therefor, for example that the recollection of specified witnesses[23] has been dimmed in relation to specified and material matters[24]. A general averment of prejudice is, by itself, not enough[25]. If the party seeks to put forward a defence or explanation upon which he seeks to found in relation to a special cause, for example that he did not commit a crime of which he was found guilty, then this must also be specified[26]. The position in relation to personal injury actions to which the Chapter 43 provisions apply is, in this respect, unclear but there is no specific prohibition in the Rules to prevent parties making averments of this nature.

FORM OF HEARING

9.09   Since there is no provision for trial before answer[27] all outstanding preliminary pleas require either to be repelled of consent or dealt with on the procedure roll or at the motion roll hearing before issues can be allowed and this includes any pleas directed towards relevancy and specification. It is, however, incumbent upon the parties to discuss with each other the further procedure which would be appropriate with the aim of avoiding a debate if at all possible, and the failure to do so may be taken into account when deciding the question of expenses[28]. Should a party seek a discharge of a procedure roll diet already allocated, he will require to make application by way of motion for discharge of the diet and for further (specified) procedure[29].

GRANT OR REFUSAL OF ISSUES

9.10   Deciding upon the mode of inquiry is a discretionary matter on the part of the Lord Ordinary, the object being to select the tribunal which would best secure justice between the parties[30]. The allowance of issues can therefore be subject to a condition so that if the Lord Ordinary is of the view that to secure such justice issues will only be allowed subject to the party seeking them giving an undertaking, noted in the minute of proceedings, then there would

22 *McLachlan v Atholl Houses Ltd* 1964 SLT (Notes) 56; *Morrison v John G Kincaid & Co Ltd* 1969 SLT (Notes) 6 and *Russell v National Coal Board* 1963 SLT (Notes) 20.
23 *Duncan v British Railways Board* 1964 SLT (Notes) 73.
24 *McDermid v Underhill Heating Engineering Ltd* 1971 SLT (Notes) 12; *Sutherland v Chief Constable, Fife Police* 1994 GWD 39-2326.
25 *Morrison v Ellis & McHardy Ltd* 1965 SLT (Notes) 27; *McManus v Liquidators of Kelvin Shipping Co* 1966 SLT (Notes) 45.
26 *Fardy v SMT Co* 1971 SLT 232.
27 *Moore v Alexander Stephen & Sons Ltd* 1954 SC 331 at 334–335.
28 Practice Note No 3 of 1991.
29 Practice Note No 7 of 2004.
30 *Graham v Associated Electrical Industries Ltd* 1968 SLT 81 at 82 per Lord President Clyde; *Walker v Pitlochry Motor Co* 1930 SC 565.

appear to be no reason why such a procedure would not be competent[31]. Where the Lord Ordinary, after debate, wishes a party to clarify his position in relation to an averment in the pleadings which, if deleted, would allow issues to be granted, he can have the cause put out by order "so that the party concerned can state his current position"[32].

The interlocutor

9.11 The court must then decide upon the mode of inquiry having heard the parties and, if a jury trial is to take place, the correct form of the interlocutor is to repel any preliminary pleas and to allow issues[33]. If a plea relating to prejudice is repelled, all of the averments relating to prejudice are nevertheless left standing on record[34]. Where issues have been allowed, the court may allow any counterclaim to proceed to trial before, at the same time as, or after, the action as it thinks fit. In a Chapter 43 personal injuries action where there are no pleas to repel the interlocutor will merely allow a jury trial.

Onus of establishing special cause

9.12 In relation to jury trials it is specifically provided that any action which falls within the enumerated causes[35] shall be tried by a jury unless either of the parties consents to a proof or one of them shows special cause[36]. Thus if any party seeks to argue that an action which would be competent to be tried by a jury should not be so tried and the other party or parties insists upon their statutory right to jury trial, the onus is on the party seeking to deny that right to establish that special cause exists and that issues should not be allowed.

EXPENSES

9.13 The expenses of the motion or procedure roll hearing will normally follow success, i.e. if special cause is shown then the party establishing it will be entitled to his expenses and if issues are allowed then the party insisting on his right to a trial will be awarded them. Expenses are, of course, at the dis-

---

31 An example of this is *Fleming v Sneddon*, Lady Paton, 12 May 2004★ where the pursuer was required to give an undertaking that no claim for future wage loss would be advanced and that the issues would only contain a claim for damages arising out of the loss of opportunity of promotion during the period which the pursuer was absent from work.
32 *Baillie v ECG Group Ltd* [2005] CSOH 40.
33 Rule 28.1(3)(d).
34 *Devine v Beardmore & Co* 1956 SLT 129; *McLachlan v Atholl Houses Ltd* 1964 SLT (Notes) 56.
35 Court of Session Act 1988, s 11.
36 Court of Session Act 1988, s 9(b).

cretion of the court and if a party has amended at the hearing he may still be entitled to his expenses where such an amendment was a "belt and braces" exercise "which did not affect the court's underlying view that enough had already been averred"[37].

TRIAL WITHOUT ISSUES

9.14   Although it was formerly competent to allow a jury trial to take place without issues the provisions in the Rules of Court to allow the same were not incorporated into the present Rules, the practice being thought to have fallen into desuetude. The last reported case of trial without issues occurred in 1965[38] and the decision to allow the same was subsequently criticised by Lord Justice-Clerk Grant who thought that the practice was unsatisfactory and could lead to confusion[39].

---

37 *Patterson v Sommerville* [2005] CSOH 19.
38 *Ryan v Orr* 1965 SLT 12.
39 *McKenzie v Donachie* 1969 SLT (Notes) 3.

Chapter 10

Issues

GENERALLY

10.01 An issue can be defined as the formal question of fact which is to be put to the jury after it has heard all of the evidence in the case and which it will be required to answer in order to return a verdict. An issue does not form part of the pleadings but is "a mere memorandum of what the party suggests as the issue to be tried"[1]. The issue should therefore be a concise statement of the question or questions of fact[2] and, being a device to simplify the jury's task, it should be expressed in ordinary language which a jury can understand[3]. The issue ought to be in conformity with the record[4] and as uncomplicated as is compatible with a fair presentation of the rival pleas of the parties[5]. Since the jury can only answer the question posed in the issue in the affirmative or negative, it should be framed in such a manner as to allow this and avoid the situation where the jury might, in effect, be being asked two questions at once, for example whether in a case involving two defenders it finds "either of the defenders or both of them" liable.

10.02 There are no prescribed forms of issue but the courts have sometimes laid down suggested forms and it has been suggested that in modern times the framing of issues has become something of a lost art[6]. Wherever possible and expedient, the current practice in relation to issues and counter-issues has been adapted to meet the demands of new circumstances and where a point of general principle has arisen (such as how to deal with new statutory matters such as interest on damages or the calculation of repayable benefits) the Lord Ordinary before whom the issues have been placed for approval may proceed by way of a report to the Inner House for its guidance[7].

1 *Anderson v Glasgow & South Western Railway* (1865) 4 M 259 per Lord President McNeill.
2 Bell, *Dictionary*, p 586.
3 *Macfarlane & Co v Taylor & Co* (1867) 6 M (HL) 1 at 5.
4 *Lawrie v Glasgow Corporation* 1952 SC 361 at 366.
5 *Taylor v National Coal Board* 1953 SC 349 at 354.
6 *Christie's Tutor v Kirkwood* 1991 SLT 805 per Lord McCluskey.
7 Rule 34.1; *MacDonald v Glasgow Corporation* 1973 SLT 107 at 110; *Mitchell v Laing* 1998 SC 342.

10.03   If in any action the onus of proof has shifted from the pursuer to the defender then the defender, for all practical purposes, will become the pursuer for the purpose of drafting and lodging the issue[8].

10.04   Appendix I to this work gives suggested styles for issues, these examples being largely drawn from actual styles which have received the sanction of the courts.

GENERAL AND PARTICULAR ISSUES

General issues

10.05   Issues can be categorised as general and particular. A general issue is one which is specific as regards time and place but general as to other facts and is used in personal injury actions where there are no separate or severable grounds of action[9].

Particular issues

10.06   Particular issues are usually used either where the pursuer must obtain a verdict upon some particular averment upon which he founds, for example "while in the course of his employment with the defenders"[10], or where a person was at a locus for some particular purpose, for example "for the purpose of meeting a passenger"[11]. Other examples of particular issues include where the defender has put forward a defence which the general issue of the pursuer will not disclose, for example where the defender averred that when the pursuer was injured he was travelling without a ticket, the pursuer was required to state "while travelling as a passenger"[12], or where it was said that an employee of the defender was acting outwith the scope of his employment, the pursuer was required to put into the issue words which raised sharply the question of that employee's scope of employment[13]. If, however, the matter of vicarious liability is not under challenge then the words "whilst in the course of his employment with the defenders" need not be inserted.

WHERE MULTIPLE ISSUES REQUIRED

10.07   Although usually a single issue will suffice in a cause, there are certain

---

8 Maclaren, p 589.
9 Maclaren, p 565; cf *Ireland v North British Railway Co* (1882) 10 R 52 at 59.
10 *Robertson v Primrose & Co* 1910 SC 111 at 112.
11 *Wilson v North British Railway Co* (1873) 1 R 172.
12 *Hamilton v Caledonian Railway Co* (1856) 18 D 999.
13 *Wood v North British Railway Co* (1899) 1 F 562; cf *McIntosh v Cameron* 1929 SC 44.

circumstances in which it may be necessary to have more than one issue. The general principle is that separate issues are required for separate wrongs done by the same defender[14] unless the wrongs can be said to form a single occurrence[15]. Thus where the pursuer sues in respect of wrongful arrest, police assault, malicious prosecution and wrongful detention, or where he sues in respect of the giving of false information to the police and the subsequent repetition of it to bystanders[16], separate issues with separate schedules of damages will be required. Where the pursuer complains of several wrongs done to him at the same time (such as several defamatory statements made in a single letter) the practice is to have separate issues corresponding to each statement with a single schedule of damages appended to the last issue and containing the single lump sum sued for[17]. In an action for damages against two defenders in which their liability was pled on separate grounds and therefore there was no question of any apportionment, there must be a separate issue against each defender[18].

WHERE THERE ARE SEVERAL PARTIES

10.08 Where there are several pursuers, the general rule is that where they have a community of interest they may sue in one action but have separate issues, so that where two persons alleged that they had been defamed in a single statement, it was held competent for them to claim damages in one action provided that the claims were separately concluded for and that each pursuer took a separate issue[19]. However, where several pursuers, including the executor, are suing in respect of the death of a relative they may have separate conclusions but a single issue with separate schedules thereto[20]. Where there are several defenders one general issue against all is sufficient[21], unless there is doubt as to the liability of one or other of them in which case wording such as "either of the defenders or both of them" will be used[22], but the pursuer does not ask in his issue for the jury to decide upon the apportionment *inter se* between the defenders[23]. One general issue is also suitable where the same pursuer is suing different defenders in different actions and the actions are all con-

---

14 *Paton v Brodie* (1857) 20 D 258.
15 *Gray v Maitland* (1896) 4 SLT 38.
16 *Douglas v Main* (1893) 20 R 793.
17 *Falconer v Docherty* (1893) 20 R 765; *Barclay v Manuel* (1902) 10 SLT 450.
18 *Cooper v Brown & The Rosebank Foundry Ltd* (1893) 1 SLT 44.
19 *Mitchell v Grierson* (1894) 21 R 367.
20 *McPhail v Caledonian Railway Co* (1903) 5 F 306; *Gray v Caledonian Railway Co* 1912 SC 339.
21 *McCosh v McCosh* (1832) 10 S 579; cf *Cooper v Brown and The Rosebank Foundry Co* (1893) 1 SLT 44 where separate issues were allowed against each defender.
22 *Goodall v Forbes* 1909 SC 1300.
23 In *Brown v Murray Motors*, Lord Menzies, 13 Feb 2003*, where the question posed in the pursuer's issue related to liability between two defenders, the words "and if so, in what proportion" were deleted at the motion for the approval of issues.

joined to be heard together[24]. Where there is a third party then the issue will normally include the words "to any extent" since the pursuer would be entitled to recover against the defender if he were found to be at blame at all[25], but unless the pursuer has convened the third party as a defender he will be unable to take an issue against the third party[26].

ISSUES IN PARTICULAR TYPES OF ACTION

Personal injury actions

10.09 Where the pursuer in an action for damages for personal injuries founds upon both a breach of statutory duty and a breach of common law, a single issue containing the word "fault" will suffice and it is not necessary to specify separately the statutory breach[27]. Where contributory negligence is pled by the defenders, the words "to any extent" are usually inserted but these words should not otherwise be used in issues[28]. If the very existence of the accident is in dispute then the wording of the issue should reflect this and thus the normal form of issue, i.e. "whether the accident to the pursuer . . . was caused by the fault of the defender"[29], should be replaced by the form "whether the pursuer . . . sustained injury through the fault of the defenders"[30]. When the case is based on vicarious liability, the question in the issue is normally whether injury was caused "through the fault and negligence of the defenders' employee"[31], and where the insurer is being sued directly it may be appropriate to use the wording "through the fault of X, for which the defenders are liable"[32].

Where liability is admitted

10.10 Where liability is admitted and the only matter for the consideration of the jury is that of the quantification of the damages due therefor, the issue will still be in the usual form, i.e. the question of whether the accident was caused by the fault of the defender will be asked and require to be answered, notwithstanding the fact that there is only one answer that can be given to that

---

24 *West v Edinburgh Tramways Co* (1903) 10 SLT 524.
25 *Cairnie v Secretary of State for Scotland* 1965 SLT (Notes) 57; Appendix I, style A5.
26 *Jack v Glasgow Corporation* 1965 SLT 227; *Aitken v Norrie* 1966 SC 168.
27 *Matuszczyk v National Coal Board* 1955 SLT 26.
28 *MacLean v The Admiralty* 1960 SC 199; *Thomson v David J Clark Ltd* 1954 SLT (Notes) 11.
29 *Hayden v Glasgow Corporation* 1948 SC 143.
30 *Stewart v Blythswood Shipbuilding Co* 1951 SLT (Notes) 48.
31 E.g. *Younger v Strathclyde Fire Board* (1998) 20 Rep L Bul 4.
32 E.g. *Gardner v Royal & Sun Alliance Insurance Co*, Temporary Judge R F MacDonald QC, 22 Sept 2004*.

question and that the presiding judge will have to direct the jury to answer the issue in the affirmative[33]. The practice was recently brought to the attention of the Inner House where it was said to cause little difficulty in practice and it was observed by Lord President Rodger that:

> "It must be recalled that in a case where a jury trial takes place, the decree of the court is based upon the verdict of the jury. That being so, the jury's answer to the question on liability forms the proper basis for any eventual decree by the court finding the defender liable to pay a specific sum of damages."[34]

The degree of negligence is, however, not a matter for the jury's consideration and the issue should only contain the word "fault" without any qualification thereof[35].

Defamation actions

10.11   Where a defamatory statement has been made verbally (i.e. slander), then the time and the place where the statement was made and the persons to whom it was made must all be included in the issue[36]. When the statement is made in writing (i.e. libel), the recipient thereof should be identified in the issue but if the statement was published in a newspaper or other document issued to the public then the mere fact of publication will suffice for the issue, for example the name and date of the newspaper in which it was printed[37]. The issue must be as specific as possible, but some latitude as to the date of publication or repetition of the statement may be allowed[38]. When a lengthy document or documents is founded upon in the issue, the normal procedure is to append these documents in a schedule annexed to the issue rather than incorporate them into the body of the issue itself[39].

10.12   Where the pursuer relies on an innuendo, this must be set out in both the pleadings and the issue[40] and the words "meaning thereby that the pursuer" or "falsely and calumniously representing the pursuer" should be used. Where the defamatory statement was made in a foreign language, the English equivalent should be set out in the issue in the same manner as an innuendo

---

33 *Black v North British Railway Co* 1908 SC 444, a Full Bench decision following upon the earlier case of *Morton (Cooley's Factor) v Edinburgh & Glasgow Railway* (1845) 8 D 288.

34 *Mitchell v Laing* 1998 SLT 203; see also *Benson's Exr v Scottish Lion Engineering Ltd* 2002 SC 228 (a fuller report appears at 2002 SLT 435).

35 *Hillcoat v Glasgow & South Western Railway Co* (1907) 15 SLT 433; *Black v North British Railway Co* 1908 SC 444.

36 *Broomfield v Greig* (1868) 6 M 992.

37 *Morrison v Ritchie & Co* (1902) 4 F 645.

38 *Grant v Fraser* (1870) 8 M 1011; *Lockhart v Cumming* (1852) 14 D 452; cf *Smith v Paton* 1913 SC 1203 and *Martin v McLean* (1844) 6 D 981.

39 *Mackay v McCankie* (1883) 10 R 537 at 538; *Falconer v Docherty* (1893) 20 R 765.

40 *Scoullar v Gunn* (1852) 14 D 920; *James v Baird* 1915 SC 23, 1916 SC (HL) 158.

would be[41]. Where a general charge such as dishonesty was made and specific instances thereof were given, the pursuer may select one or more of the instances but he need not put all of them into the issue[42]. Where the statement was made on a privileged occasion the words "falsely, calumniously and maliciously" should be used but there must be relevant averments of malice on record if the word is to appear in the issue[43]. "Without probable cause" should be inserted into the issue where the pursuer requires to prove this[44].

Assault, wrongful arrest and unlawful detention

10.13   Where the wrong founded upon is a delict such as assault, then the issue will simply ask if the defender "assaulted the pursuer to his loss, injury and damage"[45]. In cases of wrongful arrest the issue will normally include the words "maliciously and without probable cause"[46] but, according to the particular facts of the case, the expressions "wrongfully and illegally"[47] or "wrongfully and with unnecessary force and violence"[48] may be appropriate. Where false reports were given by the defender to the police or by them to the procurator fiscal then the words "maliciously and without probable cause" will be used[49], but where an arrest was instructed in the absence of any accusation of a crime having been committed, the words "wrongfully and illegally" will suffice[50], and in one case these words were used in respect of a passenger for failure to pay a fare following upon a false charge thereof being made by an employee of the defenders[51]. In respect of wrongful detention or imprisonment the words "wrongfully and illegally" will usually be appropriate[52].

Actions of reduction

10.14   In the case of reduction on the grounds of incapacity, the issue merely asks whether the deed is not the deed of the purported granter thereof[53].

41 *Bernhardt v Abrahams* 1912 SC 748; cf *Martin v McLean* (1844) 6 D 981.
42 *Powell v Long* (1896) 23 R 534.
43 *Gorman v Moss Empires* 1913 SC 1; see also *McEwan v Watson* (1904) 12 SLT 248 in relation to confidentiality.
44 *Craig v Peebles* (1876) 3 R 441; *Suzor v Buckingham* 1914 SC 299. There may, however, be a query as to the correct form of issues in a case involving the "responsible journalism" defence run in *Reynolds v Times Newspapers* [1999] 4 All ER 609.
45 E.g. *Kirkpatrick v Secretary of State for Scotland*, 24 April 1997★.
46 *Young v Magistrates of Glasgow* (1891) 18 R 825.
47 *Shields v Shearer* 1914 SC (HL) 33.
48 *McGilvray v Main* (1901) 3 F 397.
49 *Douglas v Main* (1893) 20 R 793.
50 *Peffers v Lindsay* (1894) 22 R 84.
51 *Percy v Glasgow Corporation* 1922 SC (HL) 144.
52 *Mackintosh v Smith & Lowe* (1864) 2 M 389; cf *Mackenzie v Cluny Hill Hydropathic Co* 1908 SC 200 at 207.
53 E.g. *Gibson's Exr v Anderson* 1925 SC 774.

Where essential error is the ground, this is most commonly because of a misrepresentation and the issue will seek to ask if the deed was signed while the pursuer was under essential error as to the material part of the contract induced by misrepresentation of the defender[54]. Where the misrepresentation was fraudulent it is enough to ask if the pursuer was induced to sign the deed by the fraudulent misrepresentation of the defender or, if it was made by another person, that person should be named in the issue and the words "on behalf of the defender" should be added[55]. Where the reduction is sought on the grounds of force and fear, the issue should simply ask if the deed was obtained "by force and fear, without the pursuer having received any [or the proper] value thereof"[56].

THE SCHEDULE OF DAMAGES

10.15 Since it is the duty of the jury to assess damages if it returns a verdict for the pursuer[57], it is necessary to attach to the issue a schedule of damages which sets out both the sum sued for and each individual head of claim, notwithstanding the fact that, in law, the award of the jury is a single indivisible sum of damages[58].

> "How, and to what extent, different 'heads' of damages will be required to be set out in an issue is not a reflection of separate 'claims', but merely a suitable way of discovering the make-up or break-down of the jury's award in such a way as to make it possible where part of the award is attributable to past loss and damages to give the pursuer appropriate interest on the part of the principal sum."[59]

However, on one recent occasion issues were allowed where there was no schedule of damages because the pursuer was not seeking any interest although whether the verdict which would then be given as a single sum would comply with Article 6 of the European Convention on Human Rights is debatable.

10.16 The schedule of damages is not strictly regarded as being part of the issues and can therefore only be looked at to show the limit of the claims put forward[60].

10.17 The individual heads of claim in the schedule may be numbered for the sake of convenience although it is more common not to do this. Each

54 *Hart v Fraser* 1907 SC 50.
55 *Beresford's Trs v Gardner* (1877) 4 R 363.
56 *Gelot v Stewart* (1870) 8 M 649; cf *Young v Healy* 1909 SC 687; see also *McDougall v McDougall's Trs* 1931 SC 102.
57 Court of Session Act 1988, s 17(4).
58 *Tate v Fischer* 1998 SLT 1419.
59 *Hill v Wilson* 1998 SC 81.
60 *Welsh v Stewart* (1818) 1 Mur 400; *Benson's Exr v Scottish Lion Engineering Ltd* 2002 SLT 435 at 437.

separate head of claim should be listed, for example solatium, wage loss, services and miscellaneous patrimonial loss and specification of the services, by having different heads of claim relating to necessary personal services rendered to the pursuer and the loss of services rendered by the pursuer. There should be separate heads in respect of services rendered by different individuals, for example "services rendered by wife", "by stepmother", "by daughter Jane", "by daughter Susan" etc, the rationale behind this being that each of these persons may have a separate right of action against the pursuer to recover the sums awarded by the jury in relation to these services[61]. The wording of the heads should reflect the record, so that a claim for loss of employability in the pleadings should be mirrored by a similar claim in the issue[62]. In the case of the relative's claims for non-patrimonial loss arising out of a death it is not necessary to separate out the various components of distress and anxiety, grief and sorrow and loss of society and guidance and such a claim should be simply described in the schedule as "Section 1(4) Damages (Scotland) Act award"[63]. Miscellaneous patrimonial loss such as the cost of a funeral, holiday cancellation, ruined clothing or private medical care or prescriptions should all be covered in individual heads of claim and not lumped together under a single omnibus heading[64].

10.18   There may be a single schedule of damages or more than one according to the circumstances of the case. In general where the pursuer sues for a single wrong there is merely one issue and one schedule of damages. Where there are multiple wrongs and therefore separate issues then there will be multiple schedules of damages. Where, however, several pursuers all sue in respect of the death of a relative there will be a single issue but a separate schedule of damages in respect of each pursuer. Where a single pursuer sues in a number of separate capacities for damages arising out of a single wrong, such as a wife and executrix suing for transmitted solatium, loss of society and support and services, there will only be one issue but several schedules appended thereto.

Interest

10.19   For the purpose of interest calculation, it is necessary to frame the issues in such a way so as to allow the jury to distinguish that part of any continuing head of claim which it was awarding for loss sustained to date and that part of the loss which relates to the future. Thus where solatium is to be

---

61 See e.g. *Yule v Forbes* 2003 GWD 29-814.
62 *Hill v Wilson* 1998 SC 81.
63 Approved by Lord Kingarth in *Wells v Hay*, 4 March 1998★, where the terms "solatium" and "grief award" were held to be inappropriate.
64 Although issues were allowed with a "miscellaneous patrimonial loss" head, the issue was amended at the trial diet by deletion of this head with the approval of the presiding judge: *Tate v Fischer*, 12 June 1997★.

awarded in respect of a continuing injury, the heads of claim in the issue should be listed as "past solatium" and "future solatium"[65] or "section 1(4) Damages (Scotland) Act award (past)" and "section 1(4) Damages (Scotland) Act award (future)"[66]. The same principle applies where there is a continuing patrimonial loss such as "past wage loss" and "future wage loss" or "past loss of employability" and "future loss of employability"[67].

Recoverable benefits

10.20   Where in a personal injuries action the pursuer has received certain benefits which he will require to repay to the government either in part or in full[68] then it will be necessary for him to frame the issues in such a way as to enable the statutory scheme of recovery to be carried out[69] although the jury is not required to actually determine what sums will be repayable by the pursuer[70]. The "relevant date" for the purposes of the repayment legislation must therefore be identified[71] and, once identified, must be reflected in the appropriate head of patrimonial claim in the issue. It is suggested that the most efficacious way of so doing is to have a sub-head in brackets which relates to the relevant period so that the jury can assess the total amount under that head (which is the sum reflected as a component of the total damages awarded) and then deal with the apportionment of that sum as between the relevant and non-relevant periods thereof[72].

---

65 *Macdonald v Glasgow Corporation* 1973 SLT 107; *Plaxton v Aaron Construction (Dundee) Ltd* 1980 SLT (Notes) 6.
66 *McAllister v Abram* 1981 SLT 815 (a case involving the old loss of society award).
67 *Hill v Wilson* 1988 SC 81.
68 Social Security (Recovery of Benefits) Act 1997, Sch 2.
69 Practice Note No 3 of 1997.
70 *McKenna v Sharp* 1999 SC 297.
71 *Mitchell v Laing* 1998 SLT 203.
72 See e.g. A Paton, "Recovery of Benefits: Issues for Juries" (1998) 19 Rep L Bul 4 and 20 Rep L Bul 3.

Chapter 11

Counter-issues

GENERALLY

11.01 Counter-issues are the formal questions of fact which the defenders wish to put to the jury and serve the same purpose as the issues for the pursuers. They should only be lodged if they are necessary, should only raise a question of fact[1] to be answered by the jury and should be in conformity with the record[2]. A counter-issue should meet the pursuer's issue[3] but it may include any question of fact which is made the subject of a specific averment on record or is relevant to a plea-in-law of the party lodging it notwithstanding that it does not in terms meet the proposed issue[4], in which case the facts which the defender will have to establish to support his counter-issue, which are different from the facts the pursuer will have to establish to support the issue, may be contained in a counter-issue[5].

WHERE COUNTER-ISSUES APPROPRIATE

11.02 There are a number of circumstances in which counter-issues may or may not be deemed appropriate, and in the leading case of *Taylor v National Coal Board*[6] the Inner House considered at some length the history and use of counter-issues and laid down some helpful guidelines as to when they should or should not be used.

11.03 Counter-issues are most widely used in cases where contributory negligence has been pled[7] but there are many other circumstances in which they

---

1 *Gallagher v National Coal Board* 1962 SLT 160.
2 *Lawrie v Glasgow Corporation* 1952 SC 361 at 366.
3 *British Workman's and General Assurance Co v Stewart* (1897) 24 R 624; *Blasquez v Lothians Racing Club* (1889) 16 R 893; *Milne v Walker* (1893) 21 R 155.
4 Rule 37.1(5).
5 *Taylor v National Coal Board* 1953 SC 349 at 365 per Lord Patrick.
6 1953 SC 349 at 365–368.
7 *Hayden v Glasgow Corporation* 1948 SC 143 at 146 per Lord President Cooper; *Lawrie v Glasgow Corporation* 1952 SC 361; *Gallagher v National Coal Board* 1962 SLT 160; *Christie's Tutor v Kirkwood* 1991 SLT 805; Appendix I, Style B1.

are appropriate. These include cases where there are questions of liability between different defenders[8] or between defenders and third parties[9], and otherwise they may be appropriate where it is expedient for the due administration of justice and where the Lord Ordinary, in exercise of his discretion, deems them to be necessary. They are needed when a plea of *volenti non fit injuria* is being taken by the defenders[10], where it is alleged that the defender breached a statutory duty and he wishes to show that it was not reasonably practicable to comply with that statutory duty[11], and where there are questions of a fellow employee being at fault in a case pled upon an unsafe system of work and defective plant[12]. A counter-issue was allowed after the defender alleged that the driver of his vehicle, in which the pursuer was injured as a passenger, was at the time of the accident prohibited from carrying passengers[13], and in a case where the defenders pled that liability for an injury was excluded by reason of the terms of a contract printed on a ticket[14].

11.04 It has been suggested that counter-issues could be more widely used and that since they can cover "any question of fact" in the record or pleas[15] they can be used to refine a jury's verdict and render it more open to scrutiny. However, the attitude of the courts to this suggestion is at present unclear in that in a recent case a counter-issue was approved in the following terms, "Had the pursuer fully recovered within one year of the accident?"[16], whereas in a subsequent case a similar question, "Had the pursuer fully recovered from her injuries within four months, of the accident?" was refused, it being held that it was not proper to use a counter-issue for the purposes of an advocacy tool and that in any event such a counter-issue was unnecessary[17].

Where liability apportioned

11.05 Where the pursuer raises an action against two defenders, only one joint counter-issue should be lodged by the defenders since there is only a single question, that of apportionment *inter se*, which they require the jury to answer[18]. Where two separate defenders both seek to establish contributory negligence against a pursuer, even when there is a third party, they can do this

8 *Christie's Tutor v Kirkwood* 1991 SLT 805; Appendix I, Style B2.
9 Appendix I, Style B3.
10 *Rowand v Saunders & Connor (Barrhead) Ltd* 1953 SC 292; Appendix I, Style B4.
11 *Gallagher v National Coal Board* 1962 SLT 160; *Taylor v National Coal Board* 1953 SC 349.
12 *Heath v Colvilles Ltd* 1950 SLT (Notes) 10.
13 *Taylor v R L Williamson & Sons* 1956 SLT (Notes) 59.
14 *Grieve v Turbine Steamers Ltd* (1903) 11 SLT 379.
15 Rule 37.1(5).
16 *Livingstone v Hardie*, Lord Nimmo Smith, 15 Jan 2003★.
17 *Hutcheson v C P Blair (t/a Truck Plant Services)* Lord Brodie, 29 June 2004★.
18 Appendix I, Style B2.

in a single counter-issue[19]. Where the first defender seeks to establish contributory negligence and the second defender does not, then two counter-issues will be required, the first asking "whether the accident was caused partly by the fault of the pursuer and, if so, what proportion of the blame is attributable to him", and the second being a joint counter-issue in the usual form for two defenders with no contributory negligence[20]. Where a child, in the charge of its parents, was injured in the street and the defender pled that there was negligence both on the part of the child or his parents or both of them, a counter-issue in the form "whether the said accident was partly caused by the fault of said child, and if so, to what extent" was approved[21].

Defamation actions

11.06 Counter-issues are appropriate in defamation actions where it is intended to prove *veritas* as a complete defence to the statement[22] or an innuendo[23] and, indeed, without a counter-issue the defender will not be allowed to lead any evidence relating to the truth of the statement[24] even when *veritas* is being pled merely to prove the circumstances in which the statement was made in order to reduce damages[25]. The substance of the alleged defamation should be set out in the counter-issue so as to mirror, as closely as possible, the substance alleged in the issue[26]. The counter-issue must not be so vague as not to give the pursuer fair notice of what the defender intends to prove against him[27] and it must meet the statement which the pursuer has put in issue and take the sting out of the alleged defamation[28]. Where there were two separate material charges against the defenders, it was open to them to justify these charges either by two separate counter-issues or by a composite counter-issue which separated out the charges from one another[29]. It is competent to take a counter-issue which justifies a separate part of the statement complained of even if this leaves other parts remaining of which the defender does not or is not able to prove the truth and the success of such a counter-issue may have an

---

19 Appendix I, Style B3.
20 *Christie's Tutor v Kirkwood* 1991 SLT 805.
21 *Turner v Simpson* 1948 SLT (Notes) 4.
22 Appendix I, Style B4; *Torrance v Weddel* (1868) 7 M 243.
23 *Christie v Craik* (1900) 2 F 380.
24 *Paul v Jackson* (1884) 11 R 460 at 467 per Lord Fraser.
25 *McNeill v Rorison* (1847) 10 D 15; *Craig v Jex-Blake* (1871) 9 M 973.
26 *Powell v Long* (1896) 23 R 534.
27 *Paul v Jackson* (1884) 11 R 460.
28 *McDonald v Begg* (1862) 24 D 685; *Fletcher v H J & J Wilson* (1885) 22 SLR 433; *British Workman's and General Assurance Co v Stewart* (1897) 24 R 624; *C v W* 1950 SLT (Notes) 8.
29 *O'Callaghan v D C Thompson & Co* 1928 SC 532.

effect of limiting the damages awarded[30]. The counter-issue in a case where the defence is one of fair comment should express this clearly[31].

WHERE COUNTER-ISSUES NOT APPROPRIATE

11.07 "No counter-issue is in general justified unless it raises a defence which is a complete counter to the pursuer's issue, so that if the jury answer the counter-issue in the defender's favour, he will be entitled to the verdict. No counter-issue in general is necessary or desirable where the defence is simply a direct negative of the pursuer's issue, the controversy between the parties being sufficiently focused and emphasised by the jury having to answer 'yes' or 'no' to that issue. Thus where the defender wishes to ask the jury whether or not the accident was caused by the sole fault of the pursuer, a counter-issue is unnecessary[32]. On the other hand where the facts which the defender will have to prove in order to support the counter-issue differ substantially from the facts which the pursuer will have to prove in order to support his issue, a counter-issue will in general be useful and appropriate in order to emphasise the separation between the issues of fact which it is the onus of the different parties to prove, and to ensure that the jury consider each of them separately."[33]

Counter-issues are also not appropriate where they seek to raise the question of the alleged negligence of persons who are not parties to the action where, even if their negligence was proved, this would be relevant only to the assessment of damages[34].

Defamation actions

11.08 Counter-issues are not appropriate in defamation actions where they do not in substance cover the alleged defamatory statement[35], and were held to be unnecessary where the pursuer claimed to have been defamed in a newspaper report of a court action and the defenders had pled that the report was a fair and accurate report of those proceedings[36]. A counter-issue would, however, be appropriate where the defender sought to attribute to the words used a different meaning from that contended by the pursuer and was offering to prove the truth of that alternative meaning.

---

30 *O'Callaghan v D C Thompson & Co*, n 29 above; cf Defamation Act 1952, s 5.
31 *Moffat v London Express Newspapers Ltd* 1951 SLT (Notes) 8.
32 *Burke v London and North Eastern Railway* 1947 SN 174.
33 *Taylor v National Coal Board* 1953 SC 349 at 367 per Lord Patrick.
34 *Rowand v Saunders & Connor (Barrhead) Ltd* 1953 SC 292.
35 *Bertram v Pace* (1885) 12 R 798.
36 *Wright & Grieg v Outram & Co* (1889) 16 R 1004.

Chapter 12

Lodging and approval of issues

LODGING OF ISSUES

12.01 Within 14 days after the date of the interlocutor allowing issues, the pursuer must prepare and lodge in process a draft or proposed issue together with a copy of it for the use of the court[1]. When the pursuer fails to lodge a proposed issue within the 14 days allowed, any other party may, within seven days, lodge in process a proposed issue and a copy thereof for the court[2].

12.02 A proposed issue may be defective in form but is nevertheless to be treated as a proposed issue since the lodging of it signifies the desire of the pursuer to have a jury trial. Thus, a proposed issue which omitted a material element can still be authenticated for trial provided that it is adjusted to cure the alleged defect since if a proposed issue that omitted a material element was *ipso facto* invalid, it could never be subject to adjustment as the Rules of Court contemplate[3].

12.03 The consequence of the failure by the pursuer or any party who seeks a jury trial to lodge a proposed issue timeously is that he or she will be held to have departed from their right to insist upon a trial and any other party to the action may then apply by way of motion for a proof[4]; given that issues can only be allowed after all preliminary pleas have been dealt with, irrespective of whether or not the defender has previously agreed to a jury trial, a proof and not a proof before answer is the only appropriate form of inquiry in these circumstances[5].

12.04 However, where a party fails to lodge a proposed issue within the 14-day period allowed and no proposed issue has been lodged by any other party, then the party in default may lodge a proposed issue late, which will be

---

1 Rule 37.1(1).
2 Rule 37.1(3).
3 *Benson's Exr v Scottish Lion Engineering Ltd* 2002 SC 228.
4 Rule 37.1(2).
5 *Benson's Exr v Scottish Lion Engineering Ltd*, n 3 above.

allowed on cause shown at the discretion of the court[6]. Although "cause shown" is not defined it may include the inadvertence of agents if a suitable explanation is given therefor, but does not include a situation where the failure to lodge issues timeously was due to a general indifference of agents to the Rules of Court[7]. "Where an honest mistake has been made by one side and no prejudice is being suffered by the other, the discretion [to allow late lodging of issues] ought generally to be exercised."[8] The specific provision in the rules relating to the late lodging of issues should be used when appropriate rather than the rather wider general powers of relief contained in rule 2.1 which, in this context, will not be exercised "except in extraordinary circumstances"[9].

12.05 The exercise of the Lord Ordinary's discretion in allowing or refusing late issues can be challenged on appeal, although the Inner House will be slow to overturn his discretion[10]. The party seeking to reclaim against the allowance or refusal of late issues can do so without leave providing that the appeal is marked within 14 days of such refusal or grant[11].

LODGING OF COUNTER-ISSUES

12.06 Where a proposed issue has been lodged any other party may, within seven days after the pursuer has lodged the proposed issue, lodge in process a proposed counter-issue together with a copy of it for the court[12].

12.07 Where a defender has failed to lodge a proposed counter-issue timeously then, there being no specific power to lodge counter-issues late, he should use the general powers of relief contained in rule 2.1[13].

APPROVAL OF ISSUES AND COUNTER-ISSUES

Procedure

12.08 The pursuer or party who lodges the proposed issue must, on the day after the period for lodging a proposed counter-issue expires, i.e. seven days after the lodging of the proposed issue[14], apply by way of motion to the court

---

6 Rule 37.1(2)(a).
7 *McGee v Matthew Hall Ltd* 1996 SLT 399.
8 *Wyllie v Wyllie* 1911 SC 1.
9 *McGee v Matthew Hall Ltd*, n 7 above.
10 *Flynn v Morris Young (Perth) Ltd* 1996 SC 255; *Benson's Exr v Scottish Lion Engineering Ltd* 2002 SLT 435 at 439C.
11 Rule 38.3(4)(b).
12 Rule 37.1(4).
13 For general observations on the use of rule 2.1 see **1.14** above.
14 Rule 37.1(4).

for approval of the proposed issue[15]. In a case to which the Chapter 43 procedure does not apply, an estimate of the likely duration of the jury trial must be given and a request must be made for a diet to be allocated accordingly[16]. Where there are multiple issues the court may approve only some of the issues and disallow others[17].

12.09   Where there are counter-issues, the defender or party who has lodged them must, within seven days after the enrolment of the motion for the approval of the proposed issue, apply by way of motion to the court for the approval of the counter-issue[18]. Where a proposed counter-issue has been lodged then the motions for approval of the proposed issue and counter-issue will be heard at the same time[19].

12.10   If a party fails to move timeously for approval of the issues or counter-issues then he may seek to have them approved late by asking the court to invoke the general relieving provision of the Rules of Court[20]. Where a jury trial has already been allowed it may be competent for a party to seek to oppose the motion for approval of the proposed issue and to have the cause sent to the procedure roll, providing that he can successfully persuade the court to do so by using the general relieving provision of rule 2.1[21], but the court would probably now be reluctant to do this in the absence of some compelling reason.

Adjustment

12.11   At the hearing of the motion for the approval of the proposed issue and counter-issue, the court can insist on any modifications to the issue and counter-issue which it thinks fit in order that the matters of fact are sharply focused for the jury[22]. Although in the majority of cases issues and counter-issues are approved without modification, the court can modify or adjust them, this being a matter for the discretion of the judge hearing the motion in the light of special circumstances of each case and in the light of what is expedient for the doing of justice between the parties[23]. The approval of issues can be delayed, where the court is otherwise prepared to do so, until a con-

15 Rule 37.1(6).
16 Rule 6.2(5). It should, of course, be borne in mind that since there is no provision for a continued trial diet parties would, where there is any possibility of a trial spilling over into the second week, err on the cautious side and ask for a longer diet.
17 *McEwan v Watson* (1904) 12 SLT 248.
18 Rule 37.1(7).
19 Rule 37.1(8).
20 Rule 2.1; *Flynn v Morris Young (Perth) Ltd* 1996 SC 255.
21 Rule 2.1; *McFaull v Compania Navigacion Sota y Anzar* 1937 SLT 118; **1.14** above.
22 *Hayden v Glasgow Corporation* 1948 SC 143 at 145.
23 *Taylor v National Coal Board* 1953 SC 349 at 350; *Black v Duncan* 1924 SC 738 at 744–745 per Lord Justice-Clerk Alness.

dition precedent relating to the payment of expenses has been fulfilled[24]. If there is no opposition to the motion by either party, the matter is usually dealt with by way of an unopposed unstarred motion.

Authentication

12.12 When the Lord Ordinary grants the motion for the approval of a proposed issue or counter-issue, he authenticates the adjusted issue or counter-issue with his signature[25] and this then becomes the actual issue or counter-issue to be put to the jury. The usual form of any such interlocutor is:

> "The Lord Ordinary approves of the proposed issue [and counter-issue] No[s].
> . . . [and . . . . .] of process and allows them as now authenticated to be the
> issue [and counter-issue] for the trial of the cause; appoints the said issue [and
> counter-issue] to be tried by jury on the . . . . . day of . . . . . . 20 . . at 10
> o'clock in the forenoon and appoints a jury to be summoned for this purpose
> in common form."[26]

Any interlocutor dealing with the approval of issues must be heard by a Lord Ordinary and not by a clerk of session. The party whose issue or counter-issue it is must then lodge 18 copies of the issue or counter-issue for the use of the court and the copies need not contain the authentication of the Lord Ordinary[27].

12.13 An interlocutor adjusting the issues in a jury trial may be reclaimed[28] but if no such challenge is made then, in theory, the issues and counter-issues cannot be subsequently attacked, although when the defenders at a trial diet challenged what was clearly an incompetent head of damages contained in the schedule to an issue which had previously been allowed by the court, the parties agreed to amend the issue and record and to delete the offending claim[29].

SUBSEQUENT AMENDMENT OF ISSUES

12.14 Issues may be amended at any time before final judgment at the discretion of the court for the purpose of determining the real question in controversy between the parties[30] and the rules relating to the amendment of issues are the same as those governing amendment of the record. Thus the

24 E.g. *Haughton v North British Railway Co* (1892) 20 R 113.
25 Rule 37.1(9).
26 Morrison, p 177.
27 Rule 37.1(10).
28 See **23.06** below.
29 *Tate v Fischer*, 12 June 1997*.
30 Rule 24.

court has frequently in practice allowed issues to be amended to increase the sum claimed[31] and to delete a head of claim[32] but will not allow a variation or new issue to be lodged where this is based upon an entirely separate ground of action from that on record[33]. Where there is a single issue relating to a number of separate pursuers and the cause has been settled in advance of the trial diet by some but not all of those pursuers, it is the normal practice by agreement between the remaining parties to amend the issue so as to delete all reference to parties whose claims are no longer before the jury[34].

---

31 *McDonald v Caledonian Railway Co* (1909) 2 SLT 20; such amendment is now commonplace and is often done by the parties at a late stage in the process including up to the first day of the trial diet. Any such amendment should, however, still only be done with the specific approval of the court.
32 *Tate v Fischer*, 12 June 1997★. In *Shaw v McKinlay*, Lord Hardie, 18 Oct 2005★ the pursuer was made to delete, on the first day of the trial, a claim for loss of employability from the allowed issues on the basis that the pleadings contained only a direct wage loss claim.
33 *Burns v Diamond* (1896) 23 R 507.
34 An example of this was in *Honer v Wilson*, Lord Menzies, 25 Jan 2005★.

Chapter 13

Altering the mode of inquiry

13.01 Although the mode of inquiry may already have been determined by the agreement of the parties or order of the court, this may be subject to subsequent alteration when (a) the parties agree to do so[1], (b) the record has been subsequently amended, or (c) there has been a material change of circumstances. In each case it will be necessary to enrol a motion to obtain the approval of the court to the proposed alteration in the mode of inquiry, whether or not the parties are in agreement thereto, and subsequently the issues and counter-issues will require to be approved in the usual manner.

AFTER AMENDMENT OF THE RECORD

13.02 Since any party to the cause may, subject to the discretion of the court, amend his pleadings at any time before final judgment[2], the court is not precluded from reconsidering or altering the mode of inquiry at any time after amendment on the motion of a party[3] but whether or not the court does reconsider the question is, however, a matter for the discretion of the Lord Ordinary[4]. Thus the allowance of a proof may be recalled after amendment and the case sent to jury trial, for example where a services claim was substantially amended[5]. Conversely, the allowance of a jury trial may be recalled and a proof allowed instead, for example where further heads of claim were added in by way of amendment to the pleadings and these claims included matters which would amount to special cause for withholding jury trial[6].

13.03 Where a party does not seek to amend at the procedure roll or motion roll hearing dealing with further procedure, fails timeously to reclaim the

---

1 See **5.18** above.
2 Rule 24.1.
3 *Bendex v James Donaldson & Sons Ltd* 1990 SC 259; *Gillies v Lynch (No 2)* 2004 GWD 35-710.
4 *Johnston v Clark* 1998 SLT 139.
5 *Stark v Ford (No 2)* 1996 SLT 1329.
6 *McKechnie's Curator Bonis v Gribben* 1996 SLT 136; see also *Nicol v McIntosh* 1987 SLT 104.

interlocutor allowing proof and then subsequently amends, a motion for issues may be refused as not being in the best interests of justice[7]. Where the record has been specifically amended in order to obtain issues, the party who amended may be liable to the other not merely in the expenses of the amendment process but also for the whole of the expenses up to the date of the amendment[8]. In an ordinary action it is competent to amend the pleadings by adding pleas to specification and relevancy after issues have been allowed[9] but it may be refused if no good reason therefor can be given[10]. If an amendment adding such a preliminary plea is allowed, this would require to be addressed before the mode of inquiry was further determined.

ON A MATERIAL CHANGE OF CIRCUMSTANCES

13.04 Where there has been a material change in circumstances after the mode of inquiry has been determined, the matter may be considered *de novo*. Such a material change would include the death of a party or an admission of liability at a later stage in the proceedings. An example of the latter was where there were circumstances amounting to special cause in relation to one of the pursuers, and the defenders subsequently settled or admitted liability in relation to that pursuer's claim and it was held that the defenders would not be able to deprive the pursuer of a jury trial by manipulation of the pleadings in this way[11]. By contrast, where a pursuer tried to have a proof before answer substituted for a jury trial which he had obtained at his own instigation on the basis of his now confused mental condition, the defender successfully opposed the motion and the court refused to change the mode of inquiry already allocated on the basis that the pursuer's evidence could be taken on commission and read out at the trial[12].

13.05 Although there is no procedure whereby parts of a trial, for example liability and quantum, can be separated at the stage when the initial inquiry mode is chosen[13], where liability has been separately determined and all preliminary pleas have been repelled, this may constitute a change in circumstances enabling parties to return to the court and ask for quantum to now be determined by a jury if no special cause for withholding issues now exists.

13.06 Where the defenders failed to attend the procedure roll debate and

7 *Johnston v Clark* 1998 SLT 138.
8 *Haughton v North British Railway Co* (1892) 20 R 118.
9 *McKenna v British Transport Commission* 1960 SLT (Notes) 30.
10 *McFarquhar v British Railways Board* 1967 SLT (Notes) 102 – in that case the only reason put forward was that senior counsel, having reviewed the pleadings in the closed record, came to the view that an argument on relevancy could now be advanced.
11 *Higgins v Burton* 1968 SLT (Notes) 14.
12 *Buchanan v Mason*, Lord Johnston, 9 June 2000★.
13 Cf proofs – rule 36.1 is excluded from jury trial by the application of rule 37.4.

oppose the granting of issues, they could not subsequently have the inter-locutor allowing jury trial recalled or reviewed notwithstanding that there was a good reason for their non-attendance at the original debate[14].

WHERE INNER HOUSE HAS LAID DOWN THE MODE OF PROOF

13.07   Where the Inner House has laid down the mode of inquiry, for ex-ample where it has granted a motion for a new trial, and there is subsequent amendment of the pleadings or a change in circumstances, then should any party seek a change in the mode of inquiry the correct procedure is for the Lord Ordinary to report the matter to the Inner House for its consideration[15]. When on the procedure roll it was held that part of the pursuer's case was ir-relevant and a proof before answer was allowed on the remaining part, the Inner House allowed issues when the irrelevant averments were deleted by amendment[16].

---

14 *Black v Somerfield Stores Ltd* 1998 SLT 1315.
15 Rule 34.1; *Ewart v Ferguson* 1932 SC 277; *Kerr v John Brown & Co* 1965 SC 144.
16 *Elliot v Secretary of State for Air* 1957 SLT (Notes) 3.

Chapter 14

Preparing for the trial diet

ALLOCATION OF A DIET

14.01 In an action to which the Chapter 43 procedure applies the trial diet will already have been allocated at the time when the statutory timetable was drawn up[1] and the trial will normally have been set down for four days. In all other actions the interlocutor of the Lord Ordinary which approved the issues will also have provided for the hearing to be fixed but it is the Keeper of the Rolls who is responsible for the actual allocation of the trial diet[2]. The length of the diet to be fixed will depend on the estimates which the parties submitted at the motion to approve the issues[3] and as soon as it is convenient after the approval of issues, the Keeper will give written intimation to each party of the diet[4]. Where the trial is expected to be of exceptional length or complexity the parties must attend on the Keeper for the purpose of fixing the diet[5], and where they require a special diet (in practice usually an accelerated diet) of consent or on cause shown an application must be made to the Keeper prior to the allocation of the diet[6].

Conjoined diets

14.02 It is competent to seek to have two separate jury trial actions conjoined so that they will be heard together in a single diet, usually in a situation where different pursuers raise separate actions of damages arising out of a common wrong[7] – an example being where two persons claimed to have been defamed by the same newspaper article[8]. Where separate families sue in respect of the deaths occurring in the same accident, the actions may be conjoined and

---

1 Rule 43.6; Practice Note No 2 of 2003.
2 Rule 6.2(1), (2)(b).
3 Rule 6.2(5), (6).
4 Rule 6.2(7).
5 Rule 6.2(15)(a).
6 Rules 6.2(13), 6.2(14).
7 E.g. *Simpson v Imperial Chemical Industries* 1983 SLT 60.
8 *Clinton v News Group Newspapers Ltd* 1999 SC 367.

a common trial diet assigned[9] but parties may wish such actions to run separately and be tried at different diets if, for example, the different pursuers have suffered greater or lesser psychological trauma as a result of the deaths[10]. At the time that the actions are conjoined, one action will be designated as the leading action, i.e. the one in which that pursuer's evidence is led before the other pursuer's. Conjoined actions may be disjoined at any time prior to the empanelling of the jury[11].

PLACE OF DIET

14.03 All trial diets are now held in Edinburgh. It was formerly possible to have civil jury trials in the Court of Session held on circuit but the last reported example of this taking place was a trial held in Stirling in 1885[12] and the last reported successful motion for a circuit trial was made in 1905[13]. By the 1930s the practice was described as no longer competent[14] and was formally abolished in 1988[15].

CITATION OF JURORS

14.04 The jurors for the trial are summoned by virtue of an authority or precept signed by a Lord Ordinary or clerk of court[16], and not less than 14 days prior to the diet of trial the pursuer's agent must attend at the General Department of the Court of Session and request the issue of a jury precept[17]. Where the pursuer has failed to request the issue of a jury precept, any other party may request one not less than 10 days before the trial diet[18], and where no party has requested the issue of a jury precept then each party shall be held to have departed from the application for a jury trial and inquiry into the facts of the cause shall be taken by proof[19]. The court, however, has the power under the general powers conferred by rule 2.1, to allow a precept to be issued late and has exercised this power when the reason for the late issue was con-

---

9 E.g. *Morral v LeBrusq, Strang v LeBrusq*, **15.12** below.
10 E.g. *Gillies v Lynch; Fettes v Lynch* 2002 SLT 1420.
11 See **15.10** below.
12 *Mackin v North British Railway Co* (1885) 22 SLR 775.
13 *Laing v Hay* (1905) 12 SLT 820.
14 Thompson and Middleton, p 103.
15 Jury Trials (Scotland) Act 1815, s 15 repealed by Court of Session Act 1988.
16 Court of Session Act 1988, s 12. The form of precept is found in Form 37.2-A by virtue of rule 37.2(3).
17 Rule 37.2(1).
18 Rule 37.2(2).
19 Rule 37.2(6).

fusion and error on the part of the pursuer's agents[20] and when, in a situation
where the pursuer's agents had withdrawn from acting, the defender had
made a motion to allow the precept to be issued five days prior to the assigned
trial diet in order that the diet be preserved[21]. A fee is payable for the issue
of the precept and the fee is a composite one which includes all outlays
incurred in the citing and countermanding of jurors[22]; if the fee is not paid
then the jury cannot be summoned and in consequence the trial diet may have
to be discharged at the pursuer's expense[23].

14.05   Where a jury precept has been issued it is then transmitted by a Clerk
of Session to the Sheriff Principal of the Sheriffdom of Lothian and Borders
who causes a list of potential jurors to be prepared; this list contains an equal
number of men and women[24] – it is no longer possible to request an all-male
or all-female jury[25]. A list of 36 persons, 18 men and 18 women, is then drawn
up by the sheriff clerk at Edinburgh from the register of those eligible for jury
service and resident in the sheriff court districts of Edinburgh, Haddington and
Linlithgow, i.e. the City of Edinburgh and former counties of East, West and
Mid Lothian. The sheriff clerk cites each person on the list by first class
recorded post[26].

QUALIFICATION AND ELIGIBILITY OF JURORS

Persons qualified for jury service

14.06   The following persons are qualified to serve as jurors in a civil jury
trial: namely all persons who are registered as parliamentary or local government electors in the Lothians who are aged between 18 and 65, have been
ordinarily resident in the United Kingdom, the Channel Islands or the Isle of
Man for any period of at least five years since the age of 13 and are not otherwise disqualified or ineligible to serve[27].

---

20 *Wilkie v Dakers*, Lady Smith, 3 June 2003★; agents had made a premature application
    for a precept and then due to an internal misunderstanding the pursuer's agents omitted
    to make a further application within the proper time. The precept was only reapplied
    for seven days prior to the trial diet but the pursuer had taken the wise precaution prior
    to the hearing of the motion of getting the General Department to confirm that the
    jury could still be cited timeously.
21 *Pall v Fulton*, Lady Smith, 12 May 2005★. In the event a full panel of jurors appeared
    but the diet was discharged on the pursuer's motion – see **15.12** below, n 22.
22 The level is laid down in the Court of Session, etc Fees Order 1984 (SI 1984/256) as
    amended.
23 Juries Act 1949, s 6; for an example of the consequences of non-payment of the fee
    see *Center v Duncan* 1965 SLT 168.
24 Rule 37.2(4).
25 Statute Law (Repeals) Act 1989, Sch 1 repealed proviso (b) to s 1 of the Sex Disqualifi-
    cation (Removal) Act 1919.
26 Rule 37.2(5); the form of citation is found at Form 37.2-B.
27 Law Reform (Miscellaneous Provisions) (Scotland) Act 1980, s 1(1); rule 37.2(4).

Persons ineligible for jury service

14.07 The following persons are ineligible for jury service[28]:

(a) the judiciary, namely Lords of Appeal, Senators of the College of Justice, sheriffs, justices of the peace, stipendiary magistrates, the chairman, president or registrar of any tribunal and their deputes and any person who has held any of these positions within the last 10 years[29];

(b) persons connected with the administration of justice, namely advocates and solicitors (whether in practice or not), advocates' clerks, solicitors' apprentices and trainees, certain court staff and officers, clerks of the peace and their deputes, inspectors of constabulary and their assistants, police constables and cadets, members of certain authorities connected with the police, officers of prisons and similar institutions, procurators fiscal and their clerks and assistants, messengers-at-arms and sheriff officers, members of children's panels, reporters and their staffs, directors of social work, members of the Parole Board for Scotland, members of the Scottish Criminal Cases Review Commission and any persons who have held any of these positions within the last five years[30]; and

(c) the mentally disordered, namely inpatients and certain outpatients receiving treatment for mental disorder and persons who have a guardian or *curator bonis*[31].

Persons disqualified from jury service

14.08 The following persons are disqualified from jury service[32]:

(a) persons who have been sentenced in the United Kingdom, Channel Islands or Isle of Man to life imprisonment or a term of five years or more in custody or persons who have been ordered to be detained during Her Majesty's pleasure;

(b) persons who have been sentenced to three months or more in a prison or youth institution and who have not been rehabilitated under the Rehabilitation of Offenders Act 1974; and

(c) persons who have been convicted of an offence and sentenced to probation, community service or drug treatment orders except where they have been rehabilitated under the 1974 Act.

---

28 1980 Act, s 1(1)(d).
29 1980 Act, Sch 1, Part 1, Group A.
30 1980 Act, Sch 1, Part 1, Group B.
31 1980 Act, Sch 1, Part 1, Group C.
32 1980 Act, Sch 1, Part 2 as amended by the Criminal Justice Act 1988, Sch 9, para 4 and the Criminal Justice (Scotland) Act 2003, s 78.

EXCUSAL OF JURORS

14.09   Any person who is qualified and eligible to serve as a juror but excusable as of right from jury service and who either attends for jury service in compliance with his or her citation or gives prior notice thereof to the clerk of court, is excused from service[33]. Those excusable as of right[34] include Members of Parliament (including the devolved parliaments and the European Parliament), full-time serving members of the forces[35], members of the medical and similar professions, ministers of religion, persons who have attended for jury service within the last five years and persons who have been excused jury service by a court for an as yet unexpired period.

14.10   Any person not excusable as of right may, as soon as possible after receipt of his citation, apply in writing to the Deputy Principal Clerk of Session to be released from his or her citation and if the Deputy Principal Clerk is satisfied that there are good and sufficient grounds for excusal, he or she may be excused[36]. There is no statutory definition of "good and sufficient grounds" and a subjective test is applied so that, for example, work, holiday or family commitments, illness or disability can all be taken into account. If a person fails to make such an application then he must attend the trial diet and make a further application to the clerk of court or presiding judge before the jury is empanelled[37] and if she or he fails to attend then an offence has been committed[38].

OFFENCES BY JURORS

14.11   Any person who, knowing that he or she is ineligible, not qualified or disqualified from jury service, knowingly serves on a civil jury commits an offence and is liable on summary conviction, if ineligible or not qualified, to a fine not exceeding level 3 on the standard scale and, if disqualified, to a fine not exceeding level 5[39]. However, the fact that a person who serves on a jury is ineligible or not qualified for jury service and that jury returns a verdict, then the validity of that verdict is not in itself affected[40]. Any person who falsely claims to be excusable from jury service as of right commits an offence and is liable on conviction to a fine not exceeding level 3 on the standard

---

33 1980 Act, s 1(2).
34 1980 Act, Sch 1, Part 3.
35 Subject to the provisions of the 1980 Act, s 1(3).
36 1980 Act, s 1(5); rule 37.3(1).
37 Rule 37.3(2).
38 1980 Act, s 2 (1).
39 1980 Act, s 3(1)(b), (c).
40 1980 Act, s 1(4); for a recent example of this in a criminal trial see *AR v HM Advocate* [2005] HCJAC 94.

scale[41]. Those cited to attend are given full details of whether they are qualified, ineligible, disqualified or excused as of right[42].

ASSESSORS

14.12   An assessor does not determine the issues of fact but provides expert advice on which the court might rely in determining the issues[43]. However, it has been held that parties to a jury trial cannot seek to have an assessor appointed in order to assist with technical matters requiring special knowledge and the court cannot *ex proprio motu* appoint an assessor since questions appropriate for an assessor are of their nature unsuitable for a jury to answer[44].

PRODUCTIONS

Documents

14.13   All documents founded upon by a party or adopted as incorporated in his pleadings require to be lodged with the summons or defences and a failure to do so may result in an adverse finding in expenses[45]. All other productions require to be lodged by a due date and, in an action to which the Chapter 43 procedure applies, all productions must be lodged by the date specified in the timetable[46] which will normally be eight weeks prior to the trial date; a production which is not lodged by that date may not be used or put in evidence at the trial except by the consent of the parties or by leave of the court on such conditions, if any, as to expenses or otherwise as the court thinks fit[47]. In ordinary actions productions must be lodged not later than 28 days prior to the trial[48] and a production not so lodged cannot be used or put in evidence at the trial unless the parties consent or the court gives leave on cause shown and subject to the same conditions as apply in Chapter 43 actions. In both types of action documents which are used to test the credibility of witnesses can be produced at the trial without having been previously lodged[49].

41   1980 Act, s 3(1)(a).
42   Form 37.2-B.
43   Rules, Chapter 12.
44   *McLean v Johnstone* (1906) 8 F 836; *Williamson v Richard Irvine & Sons Ltd* 1960 SLT (Notes) 34.
45   Rules 27.1, 27.2.
46   Rule 43.6(2)(vii).
47   Rule 43.8; Practice Note No 2 of 2003.
48   Rule 36.3(1) applied to jury trials by rule 37.4.
49   See **18.19** below.

Real evidence

14.14 Physical objects which constitute real evidence should be lodged within the same time-scale as documents and should not be in a dangerous, fragile or perishable condition so as to render them unsuitable for examination. Since the article itself is evidence only of its appearance at the time and can be used only for drawing certain limited inferences thought should be given to the suitability or otherwise of the object as a production before the jury and whether or not it is capable of being shown more clearly in photographs or video recordings[50].

Copies for the jury

14.15 Productions which a party intends to seek to place before the jury should be copied before the trial diet and the copies should resemble the originals as closely as possible, i.e. not be "topped or tailed", be coloured if the originals are coloured, and be copied in whole where practicable. Normally six copies will suffice for the use of the jurors.

Photographs

14.16 Where it is intended that photographs should be put before the jury, care should be taken as to how effective these photographs are and what effect they might have on the jurors. The identity and location of the photographer, date on which the photograph was taken and a description of the locus should be retained and, unless these can be agreed with the other party, a witness will be required to speak to these matters. It is helpful if a scale can be indicated on the photograph – a scale rule placed in view being an easily understandable way of achieving this. In fatal claims photographs of the deceased prior to the accident have been shown to juries[51] and in personal injury actions photographs of scars which the pursuer is too embarrassed to exhibit have been provided for jury members.

Plans

14.17 Plans should be scaled and clearly drawn and of a size that can either be put on a board before the jury or replicated in a size which would be convenient for distribution to the jury. Scales should be marked. An extract from an ordnance survey or street map is usually of lesser assistance, not having been

---

50 For a recent explanation of the "best evidence rule" in relation to real evidence, see *Haddow v Glasgow City Council* [2005] CSOH 157.
51 E.g. in *Wells v Hay* 1999 Rep LR (Quantum) 44.

produced for the case, unless a wide locus is being shown, for example the area of a town or route that a person followed.

Video recordings

14.18 The production of videotapes or digital recordings is now becoming more common in jury trials and such videos usually fall into one of four categories, namely (a) an illustration of how a particular operation should properly be carried out or how specific items of plant and equipment work, (b) the locus of an event, (c) a "day in the life of" video of a badly permanently injured pursuer[52], and (d) a video designed to show that a pursuer has or does not have a particular set of injuries or disabilities claimed.

14.19 In relation to the first of these categories care should be taken to ensure that the task shown is being carried out in a way that conforms to the testimony of expert or lay witnesses and is not so confused that the jury will have trouble in understanding it. Locus may be more clearly seen, particularly in relation to other areas of a factory or workplace, in a video rather than in photographs but in this context videos and photographs should not be regarded as mutually exclusive. A "day in the life" video may depict more accurately than oral evidence the hardships which an injured person must endure in order to overcome his or her handicaps. In the case of surveillance videos care should be taken that the making of such a video does not infringe upon the human rights of the pursuer[53] and that what is shown will clearly and unequivocally demonstrate to the jury whatever it is intended to demonstrate as experience in proofs would tend to suggest that this is often not the case – a "damp squib" is of little evidential or tactical advantage. Appropriate arrangements will of course require to be made in connection with showing the video in court and parties should be aware that it is their responsibility to provide both a video player and enough monitors to enable the judge and jury to properly view the video.

WITNESSES

14.20 In Chapter 43 actions a witness list requires to be lodged not later than eight weeks prior to the trial diet[54] and there is no express provision prohibiting the calling of a witness not on the list. In all other actions parties must

---

52 Commented on in the American case of *Bannister v Town of Noble*, 812 F 2d 1265 – see also *Magee v City of Glasgow Council* 2003 GWD 13-423.
53 *Martin v McGuiness* 2003 SLT 1424 where it was held that in the circumstances of that case the video evidence neither infringed the pursuer's right to privacy under Article 8 of the ECHR or a fair trial under Article 6 – see also R Milligan, "The Admissibility of Video Evidence" (2004) 58 Green's Civil Law Bulletin 3.
54 Rule 43.6(1)(vii); Practice Note No 2 of 2003.

exchange lists of witnesses 28 days prior to the trial diet[55]. In all actions a party who seeks to call as a witness a person not on the list may do so subject to such conditions, if any, as the court thinks fit[56] and these might include a postpone-ment of the trial to allow the other party to consider matters or precognosce the additional witness or a discharge of the trial diet.

14.21   Care should be taken in the selection of witnesses to give evidence at the trial and it is undesirable to lead a surfeit of evidence before the jury when one or two good witnesses would do, and any attempt to "gild the lily" may incur the suspicion of the jury. It should, however, be remembered that the weight to be given by a judge to the uncorroborated testimony of a single witness where a crucial witness was not led to substantiate his or her position may not be great[57] and a jury may have even deeper reservations. Witnesses for a jury trial are cited in the normal manner[58] but some thought should be given to the order in which the witnesses are to be led at the trial as the order in which evidence is adduced before the jury may have an important part to play in its appreciation of the facts of the case. The Keeper should be informed in advance of the trial diet of any special needs which any party or witness might need, for example wheelchair access.

SKILLED WITNESSES

14.22   Evidence from skilled witnesses (the proper name for expert witnesses in Scotland) may be of use, and often is essential, in proving a case before a jury, particularly if the parties are in dispute in relation to medical or technical matters and where there are productions which may require an explanation, such as tachographs, wage records or medical records. However, it should be remembered that expert witnesses, however skilled, can give no more than evidence and that their duty is to provide the jury with the necessary scientific criteria for testing the accuracy of their conclusions so as to enable the jury to form its own independent judgment by the application of those criteria to the facts proved in evidence[59]. It should always be remembered that the pur-pose of a skilled witness is to present to the jury some technical knowledge on the basis of which he forms his opinion, and thus a road traffic expert can speak to the direction, position or speed of a vehicle from such things as vehicle or pedestrian impact damage or skid marks, but should not be asked to give a view as to which party was to blame on the basis of precognitions or

---

55 Practice Note No 8 of 1994.
56 Practice Note No 8 of 1994.
57 *Rae v Chief Constable, Strathclyde Police* 1998 Rep LR 63.
58 Rule 36.2 applied to jury trials by rule 37.4.
59 Per Lord President Cooper in *Davie v Magistrates of Edinburgh* 1953 SC 34 at 40; see also *Assessor for Lothian Region v Wilson* 1979 SC 341 at 349.

evidence led from lay witnesses. The expert must be more than a mere fact-finder[60] and care should be taken to choose an expert who is both eminent in his field, articulate and not likely by his manner to alienate a jury.

14.23 It is usually helpful if, in cases where expert evidence is to be led, a consultation can be arranged with each expert in order that the way in which his or her evidence will be put over to the jury can be discussed. If this is not possible, then agents should at least make it clear to the expert that he will be giving evidence before a civil jury rather than in the probably more usual setting of a proof. It is often of use to explain to expert witnesses that they should face the jury and direct their answers to them rather than to the presiding judge and that they should try to ascertain from the jurors' reactions as to whether or not they are following what is being said. Useful advice to a skilled witness might include the observation that when giving evidence

> "eye contact with the questioner should be maintained and . . . the witness should avoid memorising testimony and should talk towards the jurors, looking at them most of the time. . . . The expert's tone of voice should be sufficiently clear and loud for the furthest juror to hear without difficulty. However, it should not be louder; otherwise the expert may be perceived as pushy and excessively assertive. The expert should be serious both on and off the stand."[61]

14.24 Any models, plans or other productions which the expert would find to be of use can be discussed and thought should be given as to how to counteract any expert evidence given by the other party's witnesses. A consideration should also be taken of whether or not the expert truly can add anything to the parties' case – for instance would the reconstruction evidence of a road traffic expert be counter-productive if the accident is easily explainable by the witnesses, or does the fact that the police witnesses have advanced their own theories require backing up by refuting by such an expert?

14.25 In the case of medical witnesses care will have to be taken to ensure that they are able to explain what might be, to a lay person, complicated or detailed matters in a way which is neither patronising nor too technical, and it is often preferable if such witnesses can be persuaded to give their evidence without merely reading out their reports but by explaining matters to the jury in a logical and straightforward manner. Psychological or psychiatric evidence can potentially be more difficult, but many of the concepts involving conditions such as post-traumatic stress, clinical depression and other disorders may nowadays be fairly commonplace and easier for a modern jury to understand[62], although the expert witness should always assume that an explanation of any condition should still be given as lay persons may have a far from accu-

60 *Donnelly v FAS Products Ltd* 2004 GWD 12-266.
61 Freckleton, *The Trial of the Expert* (Melbourne, 1987), p 144.
62 See e.g. the comments of Lord Philip in *Livingstone v Fife Council* 2004 SLT 161.

rate grasp of particular medical or psychiatric terms. Even where medical evidence is agreed, thought should be given as to the effect on a jury of merely reading out an agreed medical report or of having the expert give parole evidence to the jury even if it is uncontroverted and notwithstanding any adverse effect which this might have in expenses[63]. Where issues of proper medical care, professional negligence or a missed chance are involved the experts should be aware of the relevant tests and careful to frame their evidence so that it can be applied by the jury in the light of the directions of the judge.

14.26 Some controversy arises out of the use of services experts and there have been adverse findings in expenses in relation to the use of them in certain cases[64]. If the services claimed are by family members and for relatively small amounts over a limited period such an expert will not be needed when the hours of and remuneration for such services can be easily ascertainable[65] but where they are of a considerable extent and may require professional help (e.g. in the case of a paraplegic) then an expert may be needed and copies of his or her report could be laid before the jury while his or her evidence is being led[66]. Employment consultants are useful where they can give evidence which cannot readily be led from lay witnesses, particularly when the pursuer is no longer able to continue in his pre-accident employment with his former employers and where that loss is considerable and continuing, but not so necessary where they are called upon merely to assist the court in valuing a claim for loss of employability or assessing the pursuer's promotion prospects if the jury could work these matters out for itself from the other evidence led and, in such circumstances, any expenses incurred in the instruction of such an expert may not be recoverable[67]. An actuary may be required if there is some difficulty in the evidence which cannot be resolved by agreement or an application of the Ogden tables by the jury, such as a complicated valuation of pension loss[68].

DEMONSTRATIVE EVIDENCE

14.27 In the course of a trial it may sometimes be helpful to be able to put before the jury evidence that has been specially prepared for the purpose of illustrating the primary facts in the case. This type of evidence, known in America as "demonstrative evidence", consists of productions which either explain the oral testimony of the witnesses to be called (such as models, video

---

63 See R G Milligan, "Jury Trial Awards: A Case Study" (2002) 43 Rep L Bul 2, where he felt that the failure to do so had an effect on the outcome of the trial.
64 E.g. *Donnelly v FAS Products* 2004 GWD 12-266; *Fallon v Lamont* 2004 GWD 24-519.
65 *Donnelly; Fallon*, above.
66 *Forsyth's Curator Bonis v Govan Shipbuilders Ltd* 1988 SLT 321.
67 *Allison v Orr* 2004 SC 453.
68 *Allison v Orr*, n 67 above.

recordings, maps, plans or photographs) or in some way synthesises several separate sources of evidence into one easily understood and effective exhibit (such as charts or diagrams or a plan showing the various positions of eye-witnesses and vehicles at the time of a collision). Some care should be given whether or not such evidence would in fact be helpful and if in a relatively simple case (e.g. a typical slip and fall case) the jury might conclude that the preparation by a party of a sophisticated model might be designed to over-come shortcomings in that party's evidence[69]. "The general rule of thumb . . . should be that the equipment must fit the case. The fact that advanced technology is available does not mean that it will assist the trier of fact in every case."[70]

14.28 In contrast, where there are competing and inconsistent theories as to how a road traffic accident occurred, a scale model complete with vehicles might be of assistance to the jury although care should be taken to ensure that the vehicles are, so far as possible, of the correct make and colour as the originals[71]; alternatively a video showing the road layout at the locus and the sight lines of vehicles approaching it could be used[72]. The cost of preparing any demonstrative evidence should be proportionate, although in a recent case where the not inconsiderable expenses of preparing a video for a proof before answer that subsequently settled were allowed, the court remarked that "the pursuer is entitled to present their case in the most persuasive manner possible, whether to persuade a judge or a jury", and "the proper use of modern technology was to be commended and encouraged, not penalised"[73].

EVIDENCE ON COMMISSION

14.29 Evidence may be taken on commission where a witness resides beyond the jurisdiction of the court, is unable to attend court by reason of age, infirmity or sickness or for some other special cause found[74] and although "it is not uncommon for juries to consider this type of evidence"[75] care should be taken if a witness is considered crucial and his or her evidence is likely to be the subject of attack on the grounds of credibility and/or reliability since the effect of a commission will be to deprive the jury of a chance to form its own impression of that witness. This is particularly true where the jury might have a certain sympathy with or hostility to a witness or in the situation where two

69 Dombroff, *Demonstrative Evidence* (New York, 1983), p 6.
70 Litan (ed), *Verdict: Assessing the Civil Jury System* (1991), p 369.
71 This was done in the trial in *Davis v Bryson*, Lord Philip, 24 May 2002★.
72 As in *Dickson v Scottish Borders Council*, Lady Paton, 9 July 2003★.
73 Temporary Judge J G Reid QC in *Magee v Glasgow City Council* 2003 GWD 13-423.
74 Court of Session Act 1988, s 10(b); rule 35.11; see generally Morison, p 245 and Macsporran and Young, *Commission and Diligence*.
75 *Stevens v Cremonesi* 1988 SLT 838.

essential witnesses are in stark disagreement as to a matter essential to the cause, for example lay witnesses who contradict each other as to material facts or expert witnesses who disagree as to the cause or effect of, say, the pursuer's injuries, and it is even more unsatisfactory to have both experts give their evidence on commission.

14.30 If evidence on commission has been allowed the commission should be held early enough to allow the transcript to be available at the trial but a report by the commissioner in relation to the credibility of the witness examined at the commission is not usually thought to be appropriate in a jury trial action[76]. Where the evidence is from an aged, infirm or ill person and is thus in danger of being lost the court may order that the evidence taken on commission is to lie *in retentis*. In a recent case authority was given to have the evidence on commission videotaped[77]; the presiding judge acted as commissioner and the whole of the proceedings were recorded by a shorthand writer. The tapes were then played back to the jury at the trial and this proved to be a most effective way of bringing the evidence of that witness before the jury[78]. It should be noted, however, that evidence taken on commission may not be used at the trial if the witness becomes available to attend the trial diet[79].

EVIDENCE VIA LIVE TELEVISION LINK

14.31 As an alternative to taking evidence on commission an effective way of presenting to the jury the evidence of a witness unable to attend the trial would be to take evidence from him via a live television link. Although there is no specific provision in the Rules of Court to allow this[80] the procedure was used in a recent proof in the Court of Session, apparently to great effect[81]. The objective of taking evidence in this way should be to make the part of the trial where the live-link evidence is being taken "as close as possible to the usual practice in a trial"[82], and its use is at the discretion of the presiding judge[83]. Although there may be instances when evidence via a video link is less preferable than evidence on commission (e.g. where the witness is seriously ill and requires a nurse or doctor at hand and where therefore it might be thought that a commissioner should be physically present), English experience suggests

76 *Stevens v Cremonesi* at 840.
77 *Dickson v Scottish Borders Council*, Lord Drummond Young, 27 June 2003★.
78 *Dickson v Scottish Borders Council*, Lady Paton, 9 July 2003★.
79 Rule 35.14(3).
80 Cf the provisions in the Criminal Justice (Scotland) Act 1995, ss 271(5) and 273.
81 *Penny v J Ray McDermott Diving International Inc*, Lord Bonomy, 9 Oct 2003 – see, in particular, para [16] of the judgment; this point was not mentioned in the note of the case at 2003 GWD 33-948.
82 English Civil Procedure Rules, rule 32.3 and Practice Direction: Annex 3 (Video Conferencing), para [3].
83 *Rowland v Bock* [2002] 4 All ER 370.

that such a method of taking evidence is "as natural as when a witness is present in the courtroom"[84], and evidence has been allowed via a live link in a civil jury trial in that jurisdiction[85]. Prior authority should, accordingly, be sought so that the appropriate arrangements can be made, and it is the responsibility of the party seeking to use such a link to ensure that the equipment to be used has been properly installed in the courtroom and is ready for use.

AGREEING THE EVIDENCE

14.32 In any action due to be heard by a jury it is desirable to agree such parts of the evidence as are no longer in dispute and this can usually be done by way of a joint minute which is then read (and explained if necessary) to the jury at the trial diet. It is a requirement that where a party admits any matter of fact (whether in the pleadings or not) or the authenticity of any document or copy thereof which has not been admitted in the pleadings or in respect of which a notice to admit has not been intimated, a minute of admission or joint minute must be lodged in process and can be used in evidence at the trial if otherwise admissible in evidence[86]. In taxing the account of expenses the Auditor is expressly directed to disallow the expenses of leading any evidence on matters covered by a minute of admission[87], and the court may refuse certification for the attendance at the diet of an expert witness if his or her evidence was not in issue and could have been covered by a joint minute[88]. This has a particular effect in jury trials where a party may have to take the risk of not recovering the expense of a skilled witness when the expert evidence spoken to is not controversial but where it is felt that the report will not adequately explain to the jury the matters covered therein – for example, where the oral and unchallenged evidence of a medical witness may be wanted to help the jury understand the gravity of the pursuer's injuries and the nature of any disabilities from which he or she now suffers[89].

14.33 Agreement is especially important where there are any heads of damage which are no longer in contention, whether it be solatium or patrimonial loss. In most cases it should be possible to agree individual items relating to actual loss sustained such as damaged property or clothing, wasted expenses (e.g. the cost of a holiday lost because of the accident), funeral

---

84 *Polanski v Condé Nast Publications Ltd* [2004] 1 WLR 387 (CA) at 402. It should be noted that, on the whole, this does not seem to have been the experience of Scottish practitioners to date.

85 *Polanski v Condé Nast Publications Ltd* [2005] UKHL 10 (House of Lords overruled the Court of Appeal by a majority and allowed the claimant to give evidence via such a link).

86 Rule 36.7(1) and (2) applicable to jury trials by rule 37.4.

87 Rule 36.7(3) applicable to jury trials by rule 37.4.

88 *Ayton v National Coal Board* 1965 SLT (Notes) 24.

89 See R G Milligan, "Jury Trial Awards: A Case Study" (2002) 48 Rep L Bul 2.

expenses or past wage loss (whether in total or on the basis of loss up to certain specified dates from which the jury is then left to choose the most appropriate "back to work" date) and other miscellaneous matters as well as small claims for lost services, nominal future losses and the like should also be agreed if possible. If matters which may be of assistance to the jury but still leave a final quantification to it can be agreed then this is generally of benefit to both parties. Examples of this would be multiplicands for wage loss or services lost or rendered, retirement age, appropriate multipliers whether or not linked to any actuarial tables, likely wage increases and similar matters.

The pre-trial meeting

14.34   In actions covered by Chapter 43 procedure the parties are required to meet not later than four weeks prior to the trial diet[90] in order to discuss settlement of the action and to agree, so far as is possible, the matters which are not in dispute between them[91]. It is expected that the parties' legal advisers (presumably both counsel and agents) will be present at the pre-trial meeting[92] and the representatives of each party must have access to the party or to another person (such as an insurer) who has the authority to commit the party in the settlement of the action[93]. A record of the meeting in the form of a minute in prescribed form[94] is to be lodged in process by the pursuer not less than three weeks prior to the trial diet and the minute is to be signed by counsel or the solicitor advocate for each party; the signatories accept responsibility to the court for the conduct of the meeting and the recording of what took place at it[95]. The failure to lodge the minute timeously will result in the case being put out by order[96].

14.35   The matters to be covered at the pre-trial meeting include admissions of liability or agreeing quantum, answers to notices to admit, an estimate of the length of the trial, agreements as to solatium, wage loss and services with multipliers and/or multiplicands where agreed. The practical effect of all of this has obvious repercussions at the trial diet itself for if, say, multiplicands have been agreed at the meeting or the appropriate Ogden actuarial tables identified, then the task of the jury in assessing patrimonial loss becomes more straightforward and there will be less margin for error when it comes to quantify damages. It is said that it is the obligation of each party to take all such

---

90   It may, of course, sometimes be desirable to have the pre-trial meeting earlier than this – see comments of Lady Paton in *Zimmerman v Armstrong* 2004 SLT 915.
91   Rule 43.10(1).
92   Practice Note No 2 of 2003.
93   Rule 43.10(4).
94   Form 43.10.
95   Practice Note No 2 of 2003.
96   Rule 43.10(3).

steps as are necessary to comply with the letter and spirit of the rule[97] and the task of the jury should be eased if parties adhere to this exhortation. Since the minute of the pre-trial hearing will normally not be placed before the jury it will be necessary for parties to enter into a joint minute prior to the trial diet in order that the jury can be properly informed of what is, and what is not, still in dispute.

OTHER PREPARATIONS FOR TRIAL

14.36 Where in a personal injuries action there are repayable benefits then the defenders should apply to the Benefits Agency for the appropriate certificate in advance of the trial diet[98]. A copy of every documentary production, marked with the appropriate process number, requires to be lodged for the use of the presiding judge not later than 48 hours prior to the trial diet and all steps of process and productions which have been borrowed out are to be returned to process before 12.30 pm on the day preceding the trial diet[99]. If it is desired that any documents be placed before the jury, an appropriate number of copies (usually six) should be made. If it is desired that any party other than the pursuer be ordained to lead at the trial then an appropriate motion should be enrolled in good time[100].

14.37 It cannot be too strongly emphasised that in preparation for a jury trial, even more so than for a proof, a consultation between party and counsel who is to conduct the trial is of the greatest assistance and provides an invaluable method by which counsel can assess the weakness or strengths of the pursuer or defender and the way in which they will give evidence, and inform the parties about the basic procedure that will be followed at the trial. It is also of benefit to allow counsel to consult with skilled witnesses prior to the trial diet for similar reasons.

LATE SETTLEMENT OF ACTIONS

14.38 If parties reach a settlement of the action after the jury precept has been issued then, in order to cause those summoned for jury service as little inconvenience as possible, the Keeper of the Rolls should be informed as soon as practicable that the trial diet will no longer be required. The fee paid for the jury precept includes the contingency of countermanding the jurors and is thus not refundable if the trial does not proceed.

---

97 Practice Note No 2 of 2003.
98 Social Security (Recovery of Benefits) Act 1997, s 4.
99 Rules 36.4 and 36.5 applied to jury trials by rule 37.4.
100 E.g. in a defamation action where the defence of *veritas* is relied upon and publication is admitted. See also *Macfarlane v Macfarlane* 1947 SLT (Notes) 34.

14.39 If the Keeper is advised that the case has settled on or before the Thursday prior to the trial diet, he will inform the sheriff clerk at Edinburgh of this and the sheriff clerk will accordingly countermand the jurors by letter which, in the ordinary course of post, will be delivered by the Saturday of that week. If the Keeper is informed after Thursday then he will arrange for a message to be put on the answering machine on the free phone number which has been highlighted in the juror citation instructions given to each potential juror. Such instructions direct each potential juror to contact that number after the close of business on the Monday, i.e. the day before the trial diet is due to commence. Settlement on the Monday may, however, create difficulties although it is now the practice to give parties the e-mail address of the clerk of the Lord Ordinary who has been allocated to hear the trial so that should settlement be achieved after normal office hours it may still be possible for him to contact the panel of potential jurors prior to the trial diet. It should be borne in mind that the parties' agents have no authority to make direct contact with those cited for jury service.

14.40 If timeous information that the case has settled is not given then it may be necessary for counsel to formally appear at the trial diet and give the presiding judge an explanation for why the settlement was so late.

Chapter 15

Preliminary matters

ALLOCATION OF TRIAL JUDGE

15.01 Where possible the Keeper will allocate a Lord Ordinary to preside at a jury trial several days prior to the diet and the nominated Lord Ordinary will not normally deal with any other business on the first day of the trial. Any permanent judge of the Court of Session may hear a civil jury trial but, by direction of the Lord President, temporary judges are currently not allocated to such actions.

DUTIES OF CLERK

15.02 Prior to the commencement of the trial diet, it is the duty of the clerk of court to ensure that all of the productions in the case are in process and that they have been laid out by the macer, that the record accurately reflects all of the amendments thereto and that the issue properly contains the sum or sums currently being sued for. He will have a copy of the amended jury list which will contain the names and addresses of all of the potential jurors who are expected to attend at the trial diet. Those who have already been excused from attendance prior to the diet[1] or those in respect of whom the postal citations have been returned as undelivered should already have been deleted from this list. From the amended list the clerk or an executive officer will prepare the ballot slips. These are separate and identical pieces of paper each of which will contain the name of a potential juror appearing on the amended list[2].

INITIAL ROLL CALL OF JURORS

15.03 At "the appointed hour" (i.e. the time at which those who appear on the jury list have been cited to appear on the first day) the clerk of court will call over the names of the potential jurors and retain the ballot slip for

---

1 In terms of rule 37.3.
2 Court of Session Act 1988, s 13(2).

each person who answers. He will then roll up each of those ballot slips "as nearly as may be in the same shape" and place them in a box or glass container on the table in front of him and will then mix up all of them[3]. This procedure normally takes place prior to the judge taking his seat on the bench. If an insufficient number of potential jurors are in attendance, i.e. a number insufficient to form a jury after peremptory and other challenges have been made, then it may be necessary for the court to discharge the diet and adjourn the trial, it being no longer competent at the diet to add extra jurors ("tales") on to the list[4]. A note should be kept of those persons who have been cited to attend but have failed to appear since their failure to appear constitutes an offence[5].

15.04   After the clerk of court has called over the list of potential jurors, he will usually explain to them what is about to happen in court and will inform them of the names of the parties and the nature of the case to be tried and tell them that if they have any knowledge of the parties or are personally aware of the circumstances giving rise to the action then they should make this fact known to him. In the code applicable to criminal jury trials in Scotland it is suggested that if a person is of sufficient importance to be named in the indictment then the jurors should be asked to declare if they know that person[6]. It could be argued that perhaps a similar practice should be used in civil jury trials in respect of persons to whom an event was reported or who are alleged to have caused an event for which the defenders are vicariously liable.

15.05   The clerk will then outline the method by which the jurors are to be chosen, explaining to them that their names will be drawn and that, if no objection is made, those chosen should make their way to the jury box. He should also inform them of the nature of peremptory challenges and emphasise that a challenge to a drawn juror should not be seen as a reflection on his personal suitability to serve in that capacity. He may tell them that they will have an opportunity to place their coats etc in the jury room and to make any necessary arrangements before the trial commences. He usually concludes by explaining to the potential jurors the procedure in respect of the claiming of expenses by those who are not chosen to serve.

3 1988 Act, s 13(2).
4 Jury Trials (Scotland) Act 1815, s 28, which contained this power, was repealed by the Court of Session Act 1988 although the practice had, in fact, fallen into desuetude. Note that in a recent Justiciary Appeal, a conviction was quashed when it followed upon the verdict of a jury of 15 balloted out of a panel of only 22 potential jurors which, the court felt, "lacked the appearance of fairness. The ballot was plainly unsatisfactory and . . . in our opinion, there was a miscarriage of justice": *Brown v HM Advocate* [2006] HCJAC 09. The court did not, in that case, deal with a supplementary argument concerning the imbalance in numbers between male and female jurors.
5 Law Reform (Miscellaneous Provisions) (Scotland) Act 1980, s 2; a fine of up to £200 for non-attendance can be imposed although this can be remitted at the discretion of the court.
6 *Pullar v HM Advocate* 1993 SCCR 514.

15.06 If the trial is not to proceed then the clerk, in consultation with the presiding judge, can release those summoned for jury service but, since the pool of potential jurors has been cited to deal with one specified action only, care must be taken to ensure that the correct pool has, in fact, been released. A graphic example of this occurred in March 1997 when two trials were due to be heard on the same day and, following upon the late settlement of the first, the pool of jurors cited to hear the second case was discharged in error with the result that the trial diet in the second action had to be adjourned.

PLACES IN COURT

15.07 Parties and counsel will, as at a proof diet, usually sit so that the pursuer is at the right of the bar of the court and the defender to the left (i.e. to the left and right, respectively, of the presiding judge). There is, however, a convention (sometimes not observed in practice) that where the jury box is situated at the left of the bar this order will be reversed and that the pursuer will sit to the left (i.e. the judge's right) and thus next to the jury. Parties are entitled to be present in court throughout the proceedings unless the presiding judge directs otherwise.

FAILURE OF PARTY TO APPEAR AT THE TRIAL

15.08 If a pursuer or person upon whom the burden of proof lies appears at the trial diet but his opponent does not then he is entitled to lead his evidence (which will, of course, be uncontroverted) and at the conclusion of it ask the jury for a verdict in his favour[7]. As an alternative, that party may instead exercise his option of seeking to have the party who has failed to appear held by the court to be in default and thus obtain in the usual manner decree by default with expenses[8].

15.09 On the other hand, if the pursuer or person upon whom the burden of proof lies fails to appear at the trial diet, then the defender or person upon whom the burden of proof does not lie is entitled to obtain a verdict in his favour without the necessity of leading any evidence[9]. As an alternative, the court has the power either to grant decree against the pursuer or person upon whom the burden of proof lies or to pronounce decree of dismissal with expenses[10].

15.10 However, a possibly less contentious way of proceeding would be to seek a postponement of the trial as detailed below, particularly if the party fail-

7 Rule 37.5(a).
8 Rule 20.1(4).
9 Rule 37.5(b).
10 Rule 20.1(2), (3).

ing to appear is a party litigant. Where there are conjoined actions and one set of pursuers fails to appear, the diets can be disjoined and the trial proceed with the remaining pursuers although this would normally require the consent of the party who has appeared. An example of where this was done involved the parents of one of two young persons killed in an accident who were unable to attend the diet because of the weather conditions prevailing on that day[11]; the trial then proceeded in relation to the claim of the parents of the other victim[12].

POSTPONEMENT OF THE TRIAL

15.11 Until the jury has been empanelled and sworn it is competent for any party to the cause to apply for a postponement of the trial on account of the unavoidable absence or sickness of a material witness[13], or for some other sufficient cause proved to the satisfaction of the court[14]. Such a motion should be made immediately the reason for it becomes apparent and will normally be dealt with in the same way as a motion for the discharge of a trial diet although the court may also wish to take into account the additional inconvenience which such a postponement would cause to potential jurors already cited.

Where postponement allowed

15.12 Examples of where the court has held that there has been sufficient cause for postponement of a trial include the temporary illness of the pursuer[15], the temporary illness of a material witness[16], the impending hospitalisation of an expert witness[17], a very recent accident to one of the parties[18], a party being unable to reach court because of adverse weather conditions[19], the pursuer's counsel being unable to attend for the same reason[20], a last-minute change of agents[21], the withdrawal of the pursuer's agents and consequent absence of

11 *Morral v LeBrusq*, Lord Mackay of Drumadoon, 7 Feb 2001★.
12 This disjoined trial resulted in the award in *Strang v LeBrusq* 2001 Rep LR 52.
13 In *Duncan v Kvaerner Govan Ltd*, Lord Maclean, 16 June 1993★, the pursuer only became aware after the jury was empanelled that an essential witness was on holiday in Majorca and the cause was continued until the following day when the presiding judge then refused a postponement and discharged the diet, substituting a proof in its place.
14 Maclaren, pp 602–603.
15 *Mackintosh v Fraser* (1851) 21 D 783.
16 *Leadhills Mining Co v Scots Mine Co* (1869) 22 D 989; *McKie v Western SMT Co* 1951 SC 776.
17 *Davis v Bryson*, Lord Penrose, 23 Feb 2001.
18 *Nixon v Houston* (1898) 1 F 78.
19 *Morral v LeBrusq*, Lord Mackay of Drumadoon, 7 Feb 2001★.
20 *Davie v McCowans Ltd* Lord Clarke, 27 Feb 2001★.
21 *Scott v Christie's Trs* (1856) 19 D 195.

witness citations[22], the fact that the pursuer was still undergoing active medical treatment and was due to undergo further investigation[23], where the defender claimed to have discovered certain information late which would entitle him to further adjust the pleadings[24], and where there were some doubts at the trial diet as to the pursuer's fitness to give instructions and accordingly investigations were needed to ascertain whether or not the appointment of a curator might be necessary[25].

Where postponement refused

15.13 Examples of where postponement of a trial has been refused by the court include where the defender wished to have additional time to take the evidence on commission of a witness resident abroad[26], where a party wished to await the result of a commission for which he had not been diligent in applying[27]; where a material witness was abroad and the address of another material witness was unknown[28], where the defender desired additional time to examine documents eight days prior to the trial diet[29], and where it was held that there would be undue prejudice to the pursuer if the defender were allowed a discharge five days prior to the trial diet because certain medical records were missing and he had been aware of this problem for some time[30].

Expenses

15.14 Formerly payment of the expenses occasioned by the postponement of the trial by the party seeking the postponement was peremptory[31] but the modern practice is that the presiding judge can exercise his discretion as to expenses in the normal manner, and in recent cases orders have been made that the expenses occasioned by the postponement are payable by that party[32] to be found in the cause[33] or that no expenses were due to or by either party[34]. In

---

22 *Pall v Fulton*, Lord Kingarth, 17 May 2005*.
23 *Duncan v Kvaerner Govan Ltd*, Lord Cullen, 26 May 1992*.
24 *Gillies v Lynch*, Temporary Judge T G Coutts QC, 5 Nov 2003*; for the sequel see 2004 GWD 35-710.
25 *Buchanan v Mason*, Lord Kingarth, 8 Dec 1999*.
26 *Conacher v Conacher* (1859) 21 D 597.
27 *Simmies v Burnet & Reid* (1875) 12 SLR 622.
28 *Casey v Casey* 1912 SC 1325; see also *Duncan v Kvaerner Govan Ltd*, Lord Maclean, 16 June 1993*, at **15.11**, n 13 above.
29 *British Workman's and General Assurance Co v Stewart* (1897) 21 R 624.
30 *McAvera v Rankin*, Lord Cameron of Lochbroom, 27 Nov 2003*.
31 *McKie v Western SMT Co* 1951 SC 776.
32 *Pall v Fulton*, Lord Kingarth, 17 May 2005*: see **15.12** above, n 22.
33 *Buchanan v Mason*, Lord Kingarth, 8 Dec 1999*: see **15.12**, above, n 25.
34 *Duncan v Kvaerner Govan Ltd*, Lord Cullen, 26 May 1992*: see **15.12** above, n 23; *Davis v Bryson*, Lord Penrose, 23 Feb 2001*: see **15.12** above, n 17; *Davie v McCowans Ltd*, Lord Clarke, 27 Feb 2001*: see **15.12**, n 20.

certain circumstances the payment of the expenses may be made a condition precedent of continuing with the action[35].

APPLICATIONS TO VIEW

15.15   Any party to the cause may make a request that the jury be allowed to view any heritable or moveable property which is relevant to the action and the presiding judge may grant the application if he considers that it is proper and necessary for the jury to view that property[36]. Heritable property will normally be limited to the locus of an accident or event and moveable property will include any immoveable object which cannot be uprooted or any production which is too large to be brought into court and will thus require the jury to view it outwith the courtroom.

15.16   The grant of such a view is at the discretion of the court and there are no specific rules or regulations which govern the matter. The application to view should normally be made before the jury has been empanelled so that the matter of procedure can be dealt with and any provisional arrangements with affected persons (e.g. the owner or custodian of the locus or property in question) can be confirmed and any transport proposals considered. It is suggested that the appropriate time for a view would be after the opening speech for the pursuer in order that the jury is able to understand what it is viewing in the context of the case which it has to try, but there is no reason why a view cannot take place at any time prior to the jury beginning its deliberations if it is thought that this would be more suitable[37].

15.17   Whether or not a view is allowed is a matter for the discretion of the presiding judge and must depend on his opinion as to it being both proper and necessary[38]. It has been said that great care should be exercised in considering whether or not to allow a view because there might be a danger that the jury might form an erroneous impression before it has heard the evidence in a cause[39], but this statement should perhaps be treated with caution since it was expressed in the context of the old procedure when views were held prior to the opening speeches of counsel. It should, however, be borne in mind that a view is not to be regarded as an investigatory exercise in which evidence

---

35 E.g. *Nixon v Houston* (1898) 1 F 78.
36 Court of Session Act 1988, s 14. The very elaborate rules dating from the 1815 Act, s 29, were not re-enacted. Under the former procedure views usually took place prior to the trial diet but it seems to have been contemplated that a view could competently take place during the course of a trial: *Redpath v Central SMT Co* 1947 SN 177.
37 Note, however, that in *Hattie v Leitch* (1889) 16 R 1128 Lord Justice-Clerk Macdonald commented that it would be unsatisfactory to have a view after all of the evidence in a case had been led.
38 Court of Session Act 1988, s 14.
39 Note to *Arrott v Whyte* (1828) 4 Mur 149.

would be gathered and that it should only be allowed where it would make the evidence which the jury will hear more comprehensible to it[40].

15.18   An application should be refused if what in essence is being proposed is that each juror should put him or herself in a position of being a witness and making up his or her own mind as to what could be seen from a particular viewpoint[41]. There is an obvious danger if the locus or property in contention is close at hand to the court or in an easily accessible or well-known place since one or more of the jurors might be tempted to carry out their own informal view and to report their findings to the other jurors. This could then result in a successful motion for a new trial on the basis that the jury may have reached its verdict partly on the basis of such "evidence"[42]. Thus, for example, where the locus of an accident had been the ramparts of Edinburgh Castle, barely half a mile from the courtroom, a view was felt to be desirable for that reason and a motion to allow it granted[43]. On the other hand, where the site to be viewed was an open one where there was a risk that the jury would see potential evidence not spoken to by witnesses, a locus inspection in a criminal case was refused[44].

INCIDENTAL MOTIONS

15.19   Before the trial commences there may be a number of procedural matters which counsel may wish to raise and have the presiding judge deal with and whether or not such motions would be heard before the jury would very much depend on the nature of the motion. Provided that the outcome of any motion would not result in a postponement of the trial or otherwise make the empanelling of the jury unnecessary, it might be thought to be more convenient to have all such matters reserved until the jury has been empanelled as it is the normal practice to grant the jurors a short recess and the hearing

40 *Hoekstra v HM Advocate (No 5)* 2002 SLT 599.
41 *Rodden v HM Advocate* 1995 SLT 185 where the High Court pointed out that there was an additional difficulty if the jurors disagreed between themselves as to what they could or could not see from any particular point.
42 *Sutherland v Prestongrange Coal and Fire Brick Co* (1885) 15 R 494; cf *Hope v Gemmell* (1898) 1 F 74. See also the criminal cases of *Aitken v Wood* 1921 JC 84; *Brims v MacDonald* 1993 SCCR 1061 and *Gray v HM Advocate* 2005 SLT 159 where Lord Eassie at para [28] observes that: "Crimes are commonly committed in public places of which some of the jurors will have direct knowledge from their own personal activities or places which members of the jury may not avoid in the carrying out of their own personal activities during the course of a trial." If such a visit has been made and the presiding judge is aware of this then he can specifically direct to proceed only on the basis of the evidence led during the trial.
43 *Stuart v Lothian and Borders Fire Board*, Lord Eassie, reported in *The Scotsman*, 26 April 1997.
44 *Rodden v HM Advocate* 1995 SLT 185 at 188C where additional factors also taken into account were the uncertain weather at the time and the fact that the jury would have to walk several hundred yards across exposed land to reach the site.

of such a motion prior to this might result in delaying or prolonging the trial. However, for the sake of clarity, all preliminary motions are dealt with in this chapter.

15.20 The following is not intended to be an exhaustive list of all the motions which might be made but is merely an illustration of the matters which might be competently dealt with prior to the selection of the jurors and, in general, any incidental motion which could be made prior to the commencement of a proof can be made at this stage or indeed after the jury has been empanelled but before the pursuer's opening speech. These motions include those relating to the correction of clerical errors in the issues or pleadings[45], additions to or substitutions in the list of witnesses, the lodging of amended records or issues[46], motions in respect of allowing an expert witness to remain in court during the whole or any part of the evidence[47], and any other similar matters. A motion to allow evidence to be taken on commission may be made at the start, or indeed during the course, of the trial but it would be unusual for such a motion to be granted at such a late stage unless the witness had only just become ill or otherwise unavailable and the party needing his or her evidence was placed in an emergency as a result[48]. The lodging and allowance of late productions may also be dealt with at this stage although late lodging without prior intimation to the other party is discouraged and, in a recent case where the record stated that "vouching will be produced" of certain costs and the pursuer attempted to lodge the relevant receipts on the morning of the diet, the court refused to allow the same[49]. Leave to lodge a video recording made by the defenders, of the contents of which the pursuer has had no warning, may also be refused if tendered at the trial diet on the basis of lack of fair notice and as a contravention of Article 6 of the European Convention on Human Rights.

Amendments

15.21 It is competent to seek to amend the pleadings at the trial diet but, unless such amendments are minor and incidental, such late amendment may prove to be difficult[50] and, if allowed, may result in the court discharging the trial diet on the motion of counsel or *ex proprio motu*[51] if it is felt necessary to do so, for example if the other party requires time to investigate or answer any

---

45 Macfarlane, p 118.
46 Rule 37.4.
47 See further **18.03** below.
48 *Forbes v Leys* (1820) 5 Mur 289; Mackay, p 369.
49 *Manton v Commissioners of Northern Lights*, Lord Carloway, 22 Jan 2003★.
50 E.g. *Dryburgh v National Coal Board* 1962 SC 485 at 489; *Strachan v Caledonian Fishselling and Marine Stores Co Ltd* 1963 SC 157.
51 E.g. *Johnston v Tayside Regional Council* 1988 GWD 5-208.

new points raised and there is not time to do so during the course of the trial[52], or if a relevancy or time-bar point will be taken as a result of the amendment. The principle, however, should always be regarded as one of fair notice so that in Chapter 43 procedure actions when one party has given the other adequate notice of a proposed alteration to his case, an amendment may be allowed in circumstances where otherwise it might have been refused[53].

52 Cf the situation in *Cameron v Lanarkshire Health Board* 1997 SLT 1040.
53 In *Towers v Jack*, Lord Drummond Young, 27 May 2004*, where the pursuer was allowed to include a claim for plastic surgery worth US$7,114 the claim had been intimated at a pre-trial hearing and outlined in a medical report lodged several months previously. The pursuer successfully argued that following the decision of Lord Mackay of Drumadoon in the commercial cause action of *Tolley v Abbey Life Assurance Co*, 7 May 2004 (unreported) he did not need to amend the pleadings to include the head of claim since "fair notice of the parties' contentions on the issues before them can be given in a variety of ways including correspondence exchanged between the parties". Whether, following the amendment to rule 43, the pursuer would still be able to claim for a head of damages not specifically stated in the pleadings is a moot point but in the circumstances of that particular case there would seem no reason why the presiding judge would not have allowed an amendment at the bar.

Chapter 16

Empanelling the jury

SIZE OF JURY

16.01 The civil jury in Scotland has 12 members[1], the number being derived from English practice and possibly as a reflection of the 12 apostles. It is, however, competent once a jury of 12 has begun to hear a cause to continue hearing a trial with 10 or 11 jurors should some of the empanelled jurors become incapacitated[2]; in all cases verdicts are delivered unanimously or by a simple majority.

EXCUSAL OF JURORS

16.02 Any person who is on the jury list but who desires to be excused from jury service must apply to be excused prior to the empanelling of the jury and the presiding judge may excuse that juror from jury service[3]. Excusal is at the discretion of the court and suitable grounds might include illness, work or urgent family commitments, holidays or other relevant circumstances[4].

THE BALLOT

16.03 The jury is chosen in open court in the presence of the judge and the parties[5]. The clerk of court will have already prepared the ballot slips[6] and he then draws them out one by one from the glass container or box in which

---

1 Court of Session Act 1988, s 13(1) derived from s 21 of the Jury Trials (Scotland) Act 1815. Section 21 was later repealed by the Statute Law Revision Act 1873 and from then until 1988 a jury of 12 merely "reflected the usual practice of the Court": Maclaren, pp 604–605.
2 See **16.12** below.
3 Rule 37.4.
4 See, for instance, the rather unusual circumstances in *M v HM Advocate* 1974 SLT (Notes) 25.
5 Thompson and Middleton, p 106.
6 See **15.03**.

they have been placed[7], calling out the name of each person who has been successfully balloted in turn. The person called then comes forward to take his or her place in the jury box unless challenged. The process then continues until all 12 jurors are in place. As each juror enters the jury box he or she is given a copy of the issue and, if there is one, the counter-issue.

CHALLENGE OF JURORS

16.04 Each party to the action may challenge the selection of any juror whose name has been drawn in the ballot and such challenges may be divided into (a) peremptory challenges, limited in number to four per party, and (b) challenges for which an assigned reason has to be given[8]. In this context "each party" means each individual set of pursuers and defenders[9] – "on any other principle it might happen, in the case of a number of defenders, that they would have it in their power to challenge the whole jurymen summoned"[10]. Care should be taken when the pool of potential jurors who have attended at the diet is less than about 20[11] since the exercise of challenges by all parties may result in there being an insufficient number of jurors left to be empanelled, with the consequence that a postponement of the diet and the wasted expenses that this would entail might then be inevitable. All discussions relating to the challenge of jurors are recorded[12].

Peremptory challenges

16.05 Peremptory or unassigned challenges are usually indicated by counsel saying "need not come" or similar words, and the clerk of court will then usually say to the person so challenged something akin to "Robert Jones, you need not come. Please remain in your seat." There is little agreement between practitioners as to the science or art of such challenges and, in the absence of jury vetting, any challenges are bound to be intuitive. The occupation of jurors is no longer given on the jury list so that peremptory challenges now tend to be made when counsel wish to strike a balance by way of age or sex of the jurors which the random nature of the ballot may not have achieved. An American writer has noted that "the peremptory challenge allows flexibility

---

7 Court of Session Act 1988, s 13(2).
8 Court of Session Act 1988, s 13(3). The right to peremptory challenges in criminal cases was abolished in Scotland by the Criminal Justice (Scotland) Act 1985, s 8.
9 *Dobbie v Johnston and Russell* (1861) 23 D 1139.
10 Macfarlane, p 121; *Wallace v Gray* (1836) 14 S 720.
11 In practice it is not uncommon for the pool of potential jurors to be severely depleted before the balloting takes place and rarely do the full 36 attend.
12 Rule 37.5A(2)(a)(i).

in striking jurors about whom you feel uncomfortable, but cannot show bias sufficient for a challenge for cause"[13], and he added that the institution of the peremptory challenge "has been criticised for causing resentment in the jurors so challenged".

Assigned challenges

16.06 Assigned challenges can be made for reasons such as a juror having a particular enmity towards a party[14], a close connection with a party or witness[15], an incapacity which would seriously affect his ability to be a juror[16], an interest in the subject-matter of the cause[17] or any other sufficient cause for challenge. An assigned challenge must be made on a ground personal to the prospective juror and not on any general ground[18], and if a party is aware that he would have a good ground for such challenge then he should make it then and there[19]. Jury vetting is not carried out in Scotland[20] and there is no equivalent to the American *voir dire* process. In practice assigned challenges are now rarely heard[21] and when they are made "seldom or ever is there occasion to raise discussion in reference to challenge for cause. When any doubt exists on the point the parties would not find it necessary to raise any discussion on it, as the objecting party would always have it in his power to reserve one of his peremptory challenges for any juryman so situated."[22]

ADMINISTRATION OF OATH OR AFFIRMATION TO JURORS

16.07 Once 12 jury members have been successfully balloted, the clerk of court will read out to them the issue and the counter-issue, including the full designation of the parties, and will ask them once again if any of them has any personal knowledge of the parties or any interest in the cause which would

---

13 Lynn, *Jury Trial Law and Practice* (New York, 1986), p 97.
14 A recent example of this in a criminal case is found in *McTeer v HM Advocate* 2003 JC 66.
15 In *Dickson v Scottish Borders Council*, Lady Paton, 9 July 2003* a juror was excused after the jury had been empanelled on the grounds that in a different case he had once acted as a skilled witness for the defender's agent. For the position in criminal cases see *Gray v HM Advocate* 2005 SLT 159.
16 Renton & Brown, *Criminal Procedure*, para 18–36.
17 Maclaren, pp 605–606; cf *Watson v North British Railway Co* (1901) 3 F 342.
18 *HM Advocate v Devine* (1962) 78 Sh Ct Rep 173.
19 *Hay v HM Advocate* 1995 SCCR 659.
20 *McDonald v HM Advocate* 1997 SLT 1237.
21 Maxwell, p 333.
22 Macfarlane, p 120.

prevent them from returning a true verdict in the cause. Should there be no such declaration of personal interest then matters will proceed accordingly but, in the event of there being such a declaration, then the juror concerned will require to step down and an alternative juror will have to be balloted. Once all 12 jurors have been balloted the administration of the oath or affirmation will then take place.

16.08 The clerk of court should make it clear to jurors that they have a choice between the oath or affirmation since it is often casually assumed that all jurors would have no objection to swearing the oath. The clerk of court will then administer the oath collectively[23] to all of the jurors who have not elected to affirm by asking them to stand and to raise their right hand. He will then ask them "Do you swear by Almighty God that you will well and truly try the issue and give a true verdict according to the evidence?" To this the jurors should reply "I do"[24]. Where it is not reasonably practicable to swear the juror in a manner appropriate to his religious belief without inconvenience or delay, he or she must affirm instead[25].

16.09 In the case of a juror who wishes to affirm, he is required to repeat after the clerk the words "I solemnly, sincerely and truly declare and affirm that I will well and truly try the issue and give a true verdict according to the evidence."[26]

ADJOURNMENT AFTER OATH

16.10 It is then usual for the court to allow the jury members to retire for a short period to make themselves comfortable and to make telephone calls and other necessary arrangements. The normal practice in civil trials is that the presiding judge will usually take the opportunity to thank those potential jurors who attended but were not balloted or who were challenged for their attendance, and he will direct them in relation to the payment of their expenses unless the clerk of court has already done so and then dismiss them. However, there is much to be said for the practice in criminal jury trials whereby those potential jurors who attended but were not balloted are asked to remain in court until such time as the first witness has been sworn to give evidence and thus obviating the problems caused by the not uncommon occurrence of jurors discovering during the adjournment that they do, in fact, have some knowledge of the case or parties which would render it inappropriate for them to continue sitting as

23 Rule 37.6(1).
24 Rules, Form 37.6-A.
25 Oaths Act 1978, s 6(1).
26 Rule 37.6(2) and Form 37.6-B.

jurors[27]; in a civil trial the appropriate moment for discharging the unballoted jurors would probably be at the point where the jury has returned to court to hear the opening speeches.

16.11   Once the jurors have left the court and any uncalled jurors have been sent out, all remaining incidental matters or motions which have not already been disposed of will normally then be heard.

SUBSEQUENT DEATH OR ILLNESS OF A JUROR

16.12   Where, in the course of a trial, the presiding judge is satisfied that any member of the jury is, by reason of illness[28], unable to continue to serve on the jury or, for any other reason[29], ought to be discharged from the jury, then he may discharge that juror. Should such a discharge take place, or should a juror die or become otherwise incapacitated from serving during the trial, then, provided that there are not less than 10 remaining jurors to try the cause, the trial will proceed and the remaining members of the jury are deemed to constitute the jury for the purpose of the trial, any verdict returned by them whether unanimous or by a majority "shall be of the like force and effect as a unanimous verdict or a verdict by majority of the whole number of the jury"[30].

27 In *Dickson v Scottish Borders Council*, Lady Paton, 9 July 2003★ an empanelled juror declared before the evidence was led that he had acted as a skilled witness for the defender's agents in a previous cause and was excused. The pool of potential jurors had already been discharged and thus no replacement juror could be empanelled. A juror subsequently fell ill and was discharged. Another juror then requested to be excused as her husband had been taken into hospital and this request was refused since, if granted, the remaining jurors would have to be discharged and a fresh trial diet with a new jury would require to be assigned.

28 Court of Session Act 1988, s 15. A recent example of illness was in *Dickson v Scottish Borders Council*, Lady Paton, 9 July 2003★, where a juror suffering from sciatica was discharged on the second day of the trial.

29 "For any other reason" is not defined but is generally thought to be similar to the construction of s 90(1)(b) of the Criminal Procedure (Scotland) Act 1995, i.e. "the court is satisfied that it is for any reason inappropriate for any juror to continue serving as a juror". Modern examples of this during a civil jury trial include *Dickson* (above) where a juror was discharged after he revealed that he had acted as a skilled witness in a previous action involving the defender's agents and *Honer v Wilson*, Lord Menzies, 25 Jan 2005★, where a juror was discharged after learning of the death of his father-in-law that morning. In *Horner* another juror intimated that she was feeling unwell because of the distressing nature of the evidence and an adjournment was granted; the case settled before the court sat again. In *Gillies v Lynch* Lady Clark of Calton, 21 March 2006★ a male juror was discharged after stating that he was suffering from deafness and could not follow the evidence being led. The case continued with the remaining jury of 10 women and one man.

30 1988 Act, s 15.

Chapter 17

The opening speeches

OPENING SPEECH FOR PURSUER[1]

17.01   The trial commences with a speech from counsel for the party upon whom the initial burden of proof rests. In most cases this will be the pursuer[2] and, where that party is represented by two counsel, the usual practice is that it is the junior who will make the opening speech[3]. He or she does this by leaving the bar and standing before the jury. The jurors will already have been supplied with copies of the issue and counter-issue by the clerk of court but they will not have copies of the pleadings or any productions before them. All speeches are recorded as part of the tape recording taken of the proceedings[4].

Identifying the parties

17.02   Unless the presiding judge has already done so, counsel will normally indicate who the parties to the action are and who represents them in court[5]. This is usually done by pointing out the pursuer and defender (if they are in court) and by identifying the junior and senior counsel for each party by name and by pointing them out to the jurors.

Purpose of opening speech

17.03   The purpose of the first opening speech is to explain to the jury, in

1 An example opening speech is found in Appendix II below.
2 However, in defamation cases where the onus of proving *veritas* is upon the defender, his junior will normally make the first speech: see **17.14** below.
3 Although in modern times this practice has been invariable, see e.g. Thompson and Middleton, p 108 and Maxwell, p 335; in the case of *Shaw v Russell*, Lord Carloway, 5 May 2004★ the practice was not followed and senior counsel for one of the parties delivered both the opening and closing speeches.
4 Rule 37.5A(2)(e). The previous practice whereby counsel's speeches were not normally recorded and a motion to have them recorded could be refused (e.g. as in *Gordon v Lang* (1916) 2 SLT 86) has now been superseded.
5 McEwan, *Pleading in Court*, para 06-41.

general terms, the nature of the case and to set the scene so that the evidence which the jury will hear will be in a meaningful context. Accordingly there are no rules laid down for defining the scope of the opening speech and it has been remarked that it would be neither necessary nor desirable to lay down any such rules[6]. It should, however, be borne in mind that the object of the speech is to enable the jury to understand how the question, which has been formulated in the issue, arises[7]. The question in dispute and the speech must be fairly related both to the record (which the jury does not have before it) and to the issue[8]. The speech need not be co-extensive with the pleadings and it has been said that "it offends against the standards of advocacy simply to read the record"[9]. It should always be borne in mind that the jury has had no previous involvement with the action and thus the opening speech is the first opportunity for counsel to bring their case before it at the stage when the intensity of juror attention is probably at its greatest – "this is the time to pique the jury's interest with the significant factors of your case"[10].

17.04   The facts of the case should be briefly stated and "the point on which the pursuer's counsel is most apt to go wrong relates to his mode of stating the evidence by which he undertakes to make out his case"[11]. The speech should therefore embrace a simple narrative of the facts averred on record and give an indication of the general line of evidence rather than rehearse the evidence at great length and it should be "clear and compelling listening" for the jury[12]. Counsel should say nothing which he is not prepared or able to prove, or which is irrelevant to the issues[13], and in particular no fact or document should be referred to if counsel does not fully believe that he will be able to prove it[14]. Counsel cannot give to the jury during his opening speech any document not already admitted in evidence[15].

17.05   When in an opening speech the pursuer's counsel deliberately omits to mention any particular averment on record because he or she is no longer relying upon it then, at the end of the speech, this should be made clear to the defender's counsel[16]. Care should be taken, for if counsel does not mention the

---

6 Maxwell, p 335.
7 Thompson and Middleton, p 108.
8 *Robertson v Federation of Icelandic Co-operative Societies* 1948 SC 565 at 569 per Lord Justice-Clerk Thomson.
9 *Greig v Sir William Arrol & Co Ltd* 1965 SLT 242 at 245 per Lord Wheatley.
10 Warsaw, *Masters of Trial Practice*, p 30.
11 Mackay, p 349.
12 Thompson and Middleton, p 108; see also Price, *Defamation Law, Procedure and Practice* (1997), para 27.04.
13 Macfarlane, p 123; *Greig v Edmonstone* (1819) 4 Mur 71; see also T Pyszcynski et al, *Opening Speeches in a Jury Trial: The Effect of Promising More than the Evidence Can Show* (1981) 11 Journal of Applied Social Psychology 434.
14 *Haddaway v Goddard* (1816) 1 Mur 152; *Whyte v Clarke* (1817) 1 Mur 233 at 239.
15 *Houldsworth v Walker* (1819) 2 Mur 80.
16 *Greig v Sir William Arrol & Co Ltd* 1965 SLT 242 at 246 per Lord Walker.

omission and then proceeds to lead evidence in support of the omitted aver-ment it is open to the defender to object to that evidence on the ground that it was not covered in the opening speech and, if such an objection is upheld, that evidence would be excluded. If such an objection is repelled then, and the evidence objected to is allowed, this might result in a successful motion for a new trial on the basis of undue admission of evidence[17]. If the omission to mention any particular averment is due to oversight then, providing that the defender has suffered no particular prejudice, objection should not be taken and, if taken, should be repelled; the test to be applied in these circumstances is that of fairness[18]. Objections on the grounds of relevance are not normally entertained during the opening speech unless they are "palpable"[19]. Where an opening speech has been vague, any of the other parties may ask for clarification of any matter[20].

17.06 Extraneous factors which might affect the verdict should be avoided and the fact that the defender may be insured in respect of the claim (even if this may be thought to be reasonably obvious to the average juror) should never be mentioned[21]. No mention should ever be made of any offers to settle, tenders or the lack of them[22]. The jury should not be referred to any authorities but should counsel wish to refer to any authorities, he should do so by addressing the judge at the end of his speech[23].

Personal injury actions

17.07 Counsel should refer to the grounds of fault averred and which are still being relied upon, although he does not have to explain the law at this stage. Where the issues specify "fault" there is probably no reason to mention in detail all of the statutory grounds relied upon provided that counsel has already covered the factual basis for such breaches.

DAMAGES

17.08 The jury may be directed to the various heads of damage contained within the issue but it should be told that the sum that appears in the issue is merely the maximum sum which it may award having heard all of the evidence. No specific sums, other than those which have already been agreed,

17 *Robertson v Federation of Icelandic Co-operative Societies* 1948 SC 565.
18 *Greig v Sir William Arrol & Co Ltd* 1965 SLT 242.
19 McEwan, para 06–43.
20 Macfarlane, p 123.
21 *Stewart v Duncan* 1921 SC 482.
22 *Reekie v McKinven* 1921 SC 733; *Avery v Cantilever Shoe Co* 1942 SC 469 at 470–471 per Lord President Normand.
23 McEwan, para 06–43.

should be suggested at this stage. Where the total damages are agreed but liability is still in dispute then the jury should be advised that, if it answers the question in the issue in the negative then, subject to any deduction in respect of contributory negligence if there is a counter-issue to that effect, it will award damages in the agreed sum.

AGREED FACTS

17.09   Counsel may refer to the existence of any joint minute or minutes of admission or notices to admit or to the fact that certain matters are no longer in dispute or are admitted on record, but the detailed contents of any minutes or notices (especially where they deal with monetary sums) are usually left until the end of the pursuer's case. Where liability is admitted counsel should still give a brief narration of the facts of the case so that the jury understands the context in which it is being asked to award damages and counsel should make it clear to the jury that it will be directed to answer the question in the issue in the affirmative and that its task will be to ascertain the amount of damages to be awarded to the pursuer.

17.10   Having concluded his or her opening speech, it is usual for counsel to thank the jury for its attention in listening to counsel and then to invite it to listen to the evidence for the pursuer[24]. It has, however, been suggested that it is somewhat condescending to thank a jury for listening to counsel when in practice it has no choice in the matter but an American writer has suggested that "a simple thank you to the jury is acceptable as a courtesy. But jurors are doing a job. So are you. Get on with it!"[25]

OPENING SPEECH FOR DEFENDER

17.11   At the conclusion of the pursuer's case and in the absence of any motion being made to withdraw the case from the jury[26] the defender's counsel may elect to make an opening speech and, where a defender is represented by two counsel, this speech is normally made by the junior. Where there are several defenders, counsel for each is entitled to make an opening speech before leading his or her evidence, provided that separate grounds of defence have been stated[27].

17.12   It is now highly unusual for there to be no opening speech for the de-

---

24 McEwan, para 06–42.
25 Lynn, *Jury Trial Law and Practice*, p 142.
26 See **18.39** et seq below.
27 Macfarlane, p 124; *Johnston v Pennycook* (1818) 1 Mur 291; *Whyte v Clarke* (1817) 1 Mur 233 at 237.

fender where he intends to lead evidence, and where there is a counter-issue it has been said that the absence of such a speech is highly undesirable since the counter-issue remains before the jury for its verdict thereon[28]. Formerly it was the practice that at the close of the pursuer's case the defender's counsel was entitled to ask the jury whether it required him to address it, and no speech was made if the jury indicated that it was prepared to find a verdict for the defender without hearing any further evidence[29], but this practice is now in desuetude and has, in effect, been superseded by the practice of making a motion to withdraw the case from the jury. It is uncommon, but not thought to be incompetent, for the opening speech of the defender to be made before the pursuer has closed his or her case, for example where an expert witness for the pursuer has been cited to appear at a time before which the pursuer has already led all the other witnesses that it is intended to call. In these circumstances the court may, for reasons of expediency, allow the defender to begin his case under reservation of the right to supplement his opening speech if necessary, but this practice is undesirable in that it may confuse the jury and, if opposed by the pursuer, should not in normal circumstances be followed.

Purpose of opening speech

17.13   The purpose of the opening speech for the defender is to explain the nature of the defender's case, i.e. the defence and any evidence which is to be adduced in support thereof[30], and reference is made to the pursuer's case only when it is necessary to do so to explain the defender's own case. Counsel should not make a reasoned attack on the pursuer's case at this stage[31]. As in the pursuer's opening speech, no reference should be made to the quantum of damages and incidental matters such as insurance or the incidence of expenses should not be mentioned. Where contributory negligence is being relied upon and there is a counter-issue, the defender's opening speech should make direct reference to this and, in the absence of any such reference, the pursuer's counsel is entitled to assume that the counter-issue (and thus the question of contributory negligence) is no longer being relied upon[32].

Defamation actions

17.14   Where the defender has been ordained to lead in the trial, for example where the defence is one of *veritas*, junior counsel for the defender will make

---

28 *Dellett v Winter* 1969 SLT (Notes) 27.
29 Macfarlane, p 124; Mackay, p 351.
30 Macfarlane, p 124.
31 Maclaren, p 607.
32 *Lawrie v Glasgow Corporation* 1952 SC 361 at 365–366 per Lord Justice-Clerk Thomson.

the opening speech for the defender at the outset of the trial. He or she should explain to the jury the nature of the defence, making the facts of the case (insofar as they are admitted) clear, and it may be necessary to set the scene so that the jury can understand the basis of both the case being brought and the defence which is being proffered.

Chapter 18

Leading the evidence

18.01 Subject to certain modifications and peculiarities dealt with below, the normal civil rules of evidence apply to jury trials[1]. After the opening speech for the pursuer the evidence is led in a similar way to that at a proof and when the pursuer has closed his case the defender, after his opening speech, may then lead such evidence as he wishes; the order is reversed if the defender has been ordained to lead; in defamation actions the pursuer may be allowed to reserve his evidence upon a counter-issue of *veritas* until the close of the defender's case[2].

WITNESSES

Attendance of witnesses

18.02 It is the duty of each party to cite their witnesses in the correct manner[3], and it is further their duty to ensure that during the diet the witnesses are in attendance in the vicinity of the courtroom and available to give evidence[4]. Each party is required, before his case begins, to give to the macer of the court a numbered list of any witnesses and the order in which it is proposed to call them[5], and it is good practice to inform the macer of any disabilities which a witness may be suffering from and the pronunciation of the name of the witness if it is difficult or unusual. No party, other than the party citing the witness, shall have access to that witness while he or she is in attendance at court[6] unless the party calling the witness allows such access for a specified purpose, for example to take a precognition or statement.

---

1 The normal rules of evidence are dealt with in Macphail, *Evidence*; Walker and Walker, *The Law of Evidence in Scotland* (2nd edn, 2000) and in Morrison, para 36.11.2.
2 *Kessack v Kessack* (1899) 1 F 398.
3 Rule 36.2 applied to jury trials by rule 37.4.
4 Rule 36.9(1) applied by rule 37.4.
5 Rule 36.9(2) applied by rule 37.4.
6 Rule 36.9(4) applied by rule 37.4.

Presence of witness in court

18.03   Jury trials are, like proofs, heard in open court[7] and the parties may be present throughout, whether they intend to give evidence or not[8]. With that exception, no witness shall, without the leave of the court, be present in the courtroom during the proceedings prior to the giving of their evidence or leave the courtroom after giving evidence[9]. The evidence of a witness who is in court before giving evidence may, however, be admissible if the presence of that witness was not due to culpable negligence or intent and the witness was not unduly instructed or influenced by what was heard[10]. A motion may be made to have a skilled witness present to hear the evidence of that party's or the opposing party's ordinary witnesses but will usually be refused if it seeks to have the skilled witness present during the evidence of the other party's skilled witnesses or is merely for the purpose of assisting counsel during the trial. The fact that a witness was present in court during the evidence of another can be a matter for comment to the jury in the closing speeches.

Oath and affirmation

18.04   Witnesses are required to take the oath or to affirm before giving evidence. In the case of the oath, the witness raises his or her right hand and repeats the words "I swear by Almighty God that I will tell the truth, the whole truth, and nothing but the truth"[11]. Where a person wishes to affirm they do not raise their right hand but repeat the words "I solemnly, sincerely and truly declare and affirm that I will tell the truth, the whole truth, and nothing but the truth"[12]. No comment should be passed as to why a witness chooses to affirm rather than take the oath. It is permissible to take the oath in another form appropriate to the religious belief of the witness but where this cannot be done without inconvenience or delay the witness must affirm[13]. The oath is not given to children under 12 or to persons with severe learning difficulties; in both cases the presiding judge will admonish them to tell the truth after being satisfied that they understand the difference between truth and lies. Children between the ages of 12 and 14 may be sworn or admonished at the discretion of the presiding judge. Children of 14 and over are normally expected to take the oath or affirmation.

---

7 Court of Session Act 1693.
8 If a party does testify after having heard earlier evidence in the case, the fact of this can be a matter of comment to the jury: *Perman v Binny's Trs* 1925 SC 123.
9 Rule 36.9(3) applied by rule 37.4.
10 Evidence (Scotland) Act 1840, s 3; *Gerrard v R W Sives Ltd* 2003 SC 475.
11 Rule 37.10 and Form 37.10-A applied by rule 37.4.
12 Rule 37.10 and Form 37.10-B applied by rule 37.4; Oaths Act 1978, s 5(1).
13 Oaths Act 1978, s 5(2).

RECORDING OF EVIDENCE

18.05   The entire proceedings at a jury trial are now recorded[14] and this is done either by a shorthand writer to whom the oath *de fideli administratione officii* had been administered on their appointment as a shorthand writer in the Court of Session or by means of a tape recorder or other mechanical means approved by the Lord President[15]. In practice the proceedings in all civil jury trials are recorded by mechanical means[16] and, in order to make sense of the tapes when they are played back, it has been suggested that counsel and the presiding judge use stage directions so as to make it clear who is speaking at any particular time[17]. Without prejudice to the generality, the proceedings to be recorded include not only the evidence but also discussions with respect to the challenge of a juror, any question arising during the course of a trial, the decision of the presiding judge in relation to these two matters, the charge to the jury, counsel's speeches, the verdict of the jury and any exceptions to the judge's charge[18].

Transcripts of recordings

18.06   A transcript of the record of proceedings will only be made on the direction of the court and the cost thereof shall, in the first instance, be shared equally by the agents for the parties[19]. Any such transcript is to be certified as a faithful record of the proceedings by either the shorthand writer or, in the case of a mechanical recording, the person who transcribed the tapes[20], and the presiding judge may make such authenticated alterations to the transcript as appear to him necessary after hearing the parties[21]. Where a transcript has been made for the use of the court, copies of it may be obtained from the transcriber on payment of a fee[22]. Except with the leave of the court, the transcript may be borrowed from process only for the purpose of enabling a party to consider whether to reclaim against the interlocutor of the court applying the verdict of the jury or whether to apply for a new trial[23]. Where a transcript is required for either of these purposes and has not already been made either party may request a transcript from the shorthand writer or person who might

---

14 Rule 37.5A introduced by SI 1998/890; prior to that time it was mandatory to record only the evidence and the judge's charge.

15 Rule 37.5A(1).

16 Notice (sic), 6 March 1997.

17 *Tape Recording of Evidence – Guidance for Judges, Advocates-Depute, Counsel and Solicitor-Advocates*, Scottish Courts Service, 1997.

18 Rule 37.5A(2).

19 Rule 37.5A(3).

20 Rule 37.5A(4).

21 Rule 37.5A(5).

22 Rule 37.5A(6).

23 Rule 37.5A(7).

have transcribed it had the court so directed, and the cost thereof is to be borne by the agent of the party seeking the transcript on the basis that it will be lodged in process and that all other parties may obtain a copy of it upon payment of the transcriber's fee[24].

18.07   The parties in a jury trial require to make their own arrangements with a contractor of their choice to have the recordings transcribed and this may involve sending the contractor a copy of the closed record, productions and other relevant documents[25]. The contractor should be requested to obtain the tapes for transcription directly from the Court of Session and, on receipt of such a request, the court will send the tapes to the contractor along with a covering letter; tapes are not given directly to the parties or their agents[26].

ORDER OF WITNESSES

18.08   The particular order in which witnesses are called "must, of course, depend very much on the nature of the case, and of the taste and tact of the counsel who conducts it"[27]. The initial witnesses may well have to set the scene for the jury so that they understand the evidence in its proper context and accordingly their evidence may take longer than those subsequently called. The testimony of eye-witnesses is of particular importance before a jury, and to engage the attention of the jury these witnesses should normally be called first[28]. So far as possible the evidence should be presented in a seamless thread without obvious gaps or an excessive movement between different chapters of evidence. It is usually accepted that the chronological or "story pattern" of leading evidence is the one which finds most favour with juries, being the way in which they can follow the unfolding picture which counsel is attempting to put before them, but it has also been stressed that the witnesses who gave the earliest evidence at the trial, particularly the parties themselves, make the most impact on a jury. If this is not confusing enough, there is a definite school of thought to suggest that a party should attempt to finish his evidence on a high point with the testimony of a particularly good witness who will remain in the jurors' minds and convince them of the strength of that party's case long after they have forgotten less compelling witnesses. Care should be taken to schedule witnesses in such a way as to avoid running out of them early so that the trial has to be adjourned to the next day but this is sometimes unavoidable and when it does occur a simple apology to the presiding judge and to the jurors should be tendered.

---

24 Rule 37.5A(8).
25 Notice (sic), 6 March 1997.
26 *Tape Recording of Evidence etc*, Scottish Courts Service, Jan 1997.
27 Macfarlane, p 127.
28 Warsaw, *Masters of Trial Practice*, p 40.

ORAL EVIDENCE

General

18.09 It is the duty of counsel to lead such evidence as they feel necessary to establish their own case before the jury and it is the role of the presiding judge to see that the cause is conducted fairly[29]. Thus, the judge should not unduly interrupt so as to frustrate a line of questioning and should only question witnesses with caution and after cross-examination to clear up an ambiguity or obscurity. The onus of proof will lie upon the pursuer unless another party has been ordained to lead, for example a defender in a defamation action where there is a defence of *veritas*. It should always be remembered that lay jurors may not be familiar with the court setting, legal language and, above all, the assimilation of large amounts of verbal evidence and, in consequence, "it may be difficult to make evidence interesting and compelling for the jury but an attempt should be made, otherwise some of it will be lost"[30]. Corroboration of evidence is no longer required and hearsay is admissible[31] although the weight that can be placed on such evidence is a matter for the jury, particularly where a crucial witness is not led to substantiate a party's position[32].

Style of advocacy

18.10 The style of advocacy in a civil jury trial is very much a matter for counsel and a sympathetic but sincere approach has much to recommend itself[33]. Questions should be kept simple and clear and precise in form and counsel should carefully listen to what a witness has to say and wait for him to answer. Unnecessary detail should be avoided and "curiosity about a meaningless fact or compulsive neatness about tying up every loose end does not improve your case in the eyes of the jury"[34]. Double questions, i.e. those which ask a witness two separate things in the one question, must be avoided and care should be taken to avoid questions so convoluted and prolix that when the witness eventually gives his answer, the original question has been long forgotten by the jurors. Two simple rules are (a) admit weak points but

---

29 *Thomson v Glasgow Corporation* 1962 SC (HL) 36 at 52 per Lord Justice-Clerk Thomson.

30 J Carruthers, "Influencing the Jury" (2001) 46 JLSS July/19.

31 Civil Evidence (Scotland) Act 1988, ss 1, 2.

32 *Rae v Chief Constable, Strathclyde Police* 1998 Rep LR 63.

33 There are numerous works on the subject including DuCann, *The Art of the Advocate* (1985); Napley, *The Technique of Persuasion* (1991); Munkman, *The Technique of Advocacy* (1991); Evans, *The Golden Rules of Advocacy* (1996); McEwan, *Pleading in Court* (1995) and two entertaining American works, Lynn (ed), *Jury Trial Law and Practice* (New York, 1987) and Warsaw (ed), *Masters of Trial Practice* (New York, 1988).

34 Lynn, p 132.

tone them down, and (b) keep the witnesses in hand and prevent them straying off the point.

Extraneous and prejudicial matters

18.11   One peculiarity of jury trials is that witnesses should be restrained from mentioning extraneous matters which might have a prejudicial effect on the minds of the jurors such as the visit of an insurance company representative to the locus of an accident, which would then alert the jury to the fact that the defender is insured in respect of the risk forming the subject-matter of the trial[35] or to the fact that there have been any negotiations between the parties or any attempts to settle the action. Witnesses should also not be asked questions which are directed towards matters not directly relevant to the matters in dispute but which are designed to provide the jury with extraneous information which might then be used by counsel in their closing speeches. Questions which might be thought to be irrelevant and improper would include (a) a line of questioning to the pursuer relating to average house prices in the locality where the pursuer lived which was apparently put with a view to forming part of the submissions on the quantum of solatium and was thus successfully objected to as having nothing to do with the substance of the action[36], (b) "Are you insured?" being asked of the defendant[37], and (c) "Did you say after the accident to the mother of the injured child that she should not be afraid to make a claim because your car was insured for claims of up to

---

35 *Stewart v Duncan* 1921 SC 482 and **19.04**, n 5 below. In *Bishop v Queensberry House Hospital*, Lord Milligan, 9 Dec 1992★, a witness in answer to a question said that he had inspected a machine involved in an accident "in the presence of the insurers' representatives". The defenders objected and then asked the presiding judge to direct the jury to ignore this answer. He declined on the basis that the question had not deliberately sought this answer and that to so direct the jury would merely draw its attention either to the fact that the employers were insured for that particular risk or, if unaware of the nature of such insurance, to a matter to which it had probably attached no significance. In *MacIntosh v Findlay*, Lord Kingarth, 16 Jan 2001★, where the personal representatives of a deceased driver were being sued as defenders, a newspaper report published during the trial made it quite obvious that it was the deceased's insurers who would, in fact, be meeting the claim. The defenders drew this matter to the presiding judge's attention outwith the presence of the jury who subsequently gave the jurors a direction that they were to decide the case solely on the evidence led at the trial and that they should ignore anything that they might have read in the newspapers. He then allowed the trial to continue.

36 *Shaw v Russell*, Lord Carloway, 10 May 2004★; the position would, of course, have been different if the claim had included a specific head of damage relating to the purchase of a new home.

37 *Wright v Hearson* [1916] WN 216 – in that case the defendant did not answer the question and the judge, after commenting that the matter was irrelevant, added that "nowadays every prudent and sensible man was insured".

£1,000?"[38] The cardinal rule applied in such cases is for the court to ask whether the question posed was part of a deliberate attempt to prejudice the minds of the jurors by the improper mention of the irrelevant matter such as insurance indemnity and, if this was so, then the question should be disallowed and the jurors instructed accordingly or, if the damage is already done, then it may form the basis of a motion for a new trial at a later date[39].

DOCUMENTARY EVIDENCE

18.12 Any documents which a party intends to put before the jury should already have been copied prior to the trial diet[40]. However, whether or not the jury is allowed to see a particular production, either during the leading of the evidence or afterwards, is a matter for the discretion of the presiding judge and, although he would usually be expected to accede to such a motion, he must nevertheless exercise that discretion in the interests of justice in the particular case[41]. The jury must not be shown documents which include matters not admitted on record or proved in evidence or which have been held inadmissible and should not be invited to speculate on matters such as in whose handwriting the document is or whether or not it is genuine since these questions are, properly, ones which should be addressed by expert or other evidence. An exception to this might be made in the case of a document which was difficult to decipher and the jurors could be invited to determine for themselves what was written on the document[42].

VIDEO EVIDENCE

18.13 Videotaped evidence can be led at any time during the trial provided that it is lodged as a production or agreed between the parties and arrangements should be made so that the jury has a clear view of it. A large screen placed before them is an effective way of ensuring this, with separate monitors for the judge and counsel. Live-link televised evidence should be presented in a similar fashion.

REAL EVIDENCE

18.14 Physical objects can be shown to the jury provided that these have

---

38 *Stewart v Duncan* 1921 SC 482. The question was allowed in that case on the basis that it had been asked to establish the defender's lack of credibility rather than to alert the jury to the existence of insurance.
39 See also A Hajducki, "Insurers, Indemnifiers and the Jury" 2005 SLT (News) 51.
40 See **14.15** above.
41 *Munro v HM Advocate* 2000 SLT 950.
42 *Megrahi v HM Advocate* 2002 JC 99 at 102.

been lodged as productions, but the jurors should not be invited to handle them or carry out their own experiments on them unless the presiding judge allows this[43]. The jury should not be allowed to draw inferences from its own examination of objects unless the party against whom the inference is drawn has had an opportunity to challenge that inference[44].

EXAMINATION-IN-CHIEF

18.15   It is for the pursuer to prove his case and, in particular, it is the duty of counsel to bring to the knowledge of the jury, before the pursuer's case has closed, the precise issue of fact between the parties and the nature of the defence which has been made to the action[45]. Leading questions should be avoided if they are anything other than of a formal nature and relate to the facts in issue as such questions tend to irritate the jury and, in any event, are of little evidential value[46]; they are, however, permitted of a hostile witness[47].

DEFENDER'S EVIDENCE

18.16   Following upon the opening speech of the defender's counsel, the defender may lead such evidence as he thinks fit but he is under no obligation whatsoever to lead any evidence and, should he choose not to do so, he is not precluded from seeking a verdict in his favour at the end of the day.

Skilled witnesses

18.17   One particular difficulty which is encountered at trial is the leading of expert evidence before a jury. A balance has to be struck between leading the evidence of the expert in such a manner as to encompass the party's case while at the same time not losing the attention of the jurors, and it is important that the language used by counsel and experts does not make it difficult for the jury to follow the evidence. This is particularly so when experts use technical expressions not generally understood by lay people, words of foreign origin, polysyllabic and uncommon words, everyday words in a specialised and precise sense, passives, conditional constructions and qualifiers, formal grammar and syntax, long and complex sentences, double negatives, two-word adjectival constructions and adjectives as nouns[48]. Reports are not nor-

---

43 *Sandells v HM Advocate* 1980 SLT (Notes) 45.
44 *McCann v Adair* 1951 JC 127; *Sandells v HM Advocate* 1980 SLT (Notes) 45.
45 *Wilson v Thomas Usher & Sons Ltd* 1934 SC 332 at 337; *Bryce v British Railways Board* 1996 SLT 1378.
46 *Bishop v Bryce* 1910 SC 426 at 435 per Lord President Dunedin.
47 *Avery v Cantilever Shoe Co* 1942 SC 469.
48 Freckleton, *The Trial of the Expert* (Melbourne, 1987), pp 141–142.

mally read out in whole and the usual practice is to put specific and relevant points from the report to the jury or to allow the skilled witness to explain in straightforward language the salient matters *de novo*, concentrating on whether the jury appears to be following the evidence.

CROSS-EXAMINATION

18.18   The principal aims of cross-examination are to destroy the credibility of an opponent's witness, to bring new evidence to light which might contradict the evidence-in-chief, or at least call it into question, and to break down the evidence-in-chief, which failing to weaken its impact. Leading questions can be used but it is important that counsel do not appear too aggressive even if the witness is acting in such a manner. Some basic rules might include (a) knowing the difference between treating the cross-examination of a witness as an argument and picking an argument with the witness, (b) avoiding repetition unless this is to emphasise a particular point, (c) avoiding asking a witness questions without knowing the answer thereto, and (d) avoiding asking the one question too many times which would allow a witness to retract or qualify what he has just said. "There is one basic rule of cross-examination – Don't! In addition to all the practical difficulties that can be caused by unnecessary cross-examination – repetition of unfavourable testimony, witnesses blurting out new, damaging information, etc – it bores the jury"[49]. Commonly used techniques of cross-examination include probing, insinuation, undermining, pinning down, obtaining detailed admissions, confrontation and taking a witness by surprise, but when and where to use any of these is a matter for counsel based upon the strength or otherwise of one's case, and the need to speculate about how a jury may react should be kept to a minimum.

18.19   Where credibility is in issue, a witness may be questioned about the truth of a statement made by him in examination-in-chief even if collateral to the crucial facts and even if there is no record for it[50], and a document used to test credibility may be produced at the bar without having been previously lodged[51], but if it is desired that the jury should see the document if it is so produced then additional copies of it should be produced in advance. A statement made by a witness otherwise than in the course of the trial is inadmissible unless it reflects on that person's credibility[52], with the exception of collateral statements, precognitions and certain other statements. It is not incumbent for counsel to cross-examine the pursuer and foreshadow every single point of the

---

49 Lynn, *Jury Trial Law and Practice*, p 133.
50 *Clinton v News Group Newspapers Ltd* 1999 SC 367.
51 *Paterson & Sons (Camp Coffee) v Kit Coffee Co Ltd* (1908) 16 SLT 180; *Robertson v Anderson* 2001 GWD 17-669.
52 Civil Evidence (Scotland) Act 1988, s 3.

pursuer's point as the jury is entitled to accept only part of the evidence of a witness[53].

Skilled witnesses

18.20   Skilled witnesses are notoriously difficult to cross-examine effectively before a jury and it may be better rather than try to labour a point to see if the difference in expert testimony is because different assumptions have been made, different information supplied or that the facts relied on by the other side's skilled witness are wrong. Jurors rarely understand complicated arguments about disputed methodology and "most juries are at a disadvantage understanding scientific or technical concepts"[54], so once again it is important that the evidence be presented in a form which can be relatively easily assimilated. In the case of a defender's medical witness the jury may be interested to know how many times he or she has examined the pursuer and may well favour the skilled witness who seems to have had a continuing involvement with the party rather than merely having examined them once some considerable time prior to the trial[55]. Expert witnesses should, even under intensive and hostile cross-examination, as an ideal remain polite and confident but not over-confident[56].

RE-EXAMINATION

18.21   Re-examination at a jury trial is restricted to matters which arise out of or relate to points raised in the cross-examination and should not be used to raise new matters or cover questions which counsel forgot to ask in examination-in-chief. The court may, however, allow re-examination to take place on a new matter, in which case the party or parties who conducted the cross-examination will have the opportunity to indulge in further cross-examination. Leading questions are not permitted in re-examination.

ADDITIONAL EVIDENCE

18.22   A witness may be recalled at the instance of a party or the presiding judge[57] where, *inter alia*, a party would be prejudiced by his opponent's case not being properly put in cross-examination[58], where an ambiguity was to be

---

53   *Tait v Campbell* 2003 Rep LR 35.
54   Lynn, *Jury Trial Law and Practice*, p 142.
55   Warsaw, *Masters of Trial Practice*, p 241.
56   Freckleton, *The Trial of the Expert*, p 145.
57   Evidence (Scotland) Act 1852, s 4.
58   *Wilson v Thomas Usher & Sons Ltd* 1934 SC 332 at 338–339 per Lord Justice-Clerk Aitchison.

cleared up[59], or where the maker of a statement is called to give evidence. There are few examples of such evidence being led at a jury trial (and indeed it might well be thought that jurors would be confused by this being done) but it is nevertheless competent to do so.

EVIDENCE OBTAINED ON COMMISSION

18.23 Any evidence which has been taken on commission will need to be put before the jury since the deposition containing it cannot be used until and unless it has been made part of the evidence at the trial[60]. Where that evidence is contained in a transcript the usual method adopted in these circumstances is for junior counsel for the party who led the witness to read the transcript out in its entirety, although one text suggests that each junior should only read the parts elicited by his or her own side[61]. Where the evidence is contained in a videotape or digital video recording then the video should be shown in its entirety without comment and counsel should have before them the transcript produced by the shorthand writer[62]. The appropriate time to read the deposition out or to show the video recording is usually at the end of the evidence being led on behalf of that party and before the close of their case, although there is no reason why this should not be done at any appropriate time during the trial. However, if the party who obtained the commission does not wish to use the evidence therein, then any of the other parties is entitled to use it but, if the witness whose evidence was taken on commission attends and gives parole evidence at the trial, then the deposition or video recording may no longer be used at the trial[63].

18.24 In order that the jury understands the purpose of the deposition or video recording the presiding judge should briefly address the jury and explain to it that, for example in the case of a deposition:

"Ladies and gentlemen, you are now about to hear the evidence of Dr X, who is a witness for the pursuer and whose evidence was taken on commission because he is unable to be present here today because of infirmity [or illness or commitments elsewhere, etc]. His evidence was led by Mr A, senior counsel for the pursuer, and was subject to cross-examination by Miss B, the defender's counsel, in the same way that the other witnesses who gave evidence for the pursuer were cross-examined. Mr A's junior counsel, Mr C, will now read out the transcript of that evidence and you should listen carefully as what is being read out will form part of the pursuer's evidence in the same way as if Dr X had today given his evidence in court."

59 Dickson, *Evidence*, para [1769].
60 *Cameron v Woolfson* 1918 SC 190.
61 McEwan, *Pleading in Court* (2nd edn, 1995), para 06-44.
62 As in e.g. *Dickson v Scottish Borders Council*, Lady Paton, 9 July 2003★.
63 *Forrest v Low's Trs* 1907 SC 1240.

Mr C should then read out the deposition, making it clear which statements are questions being asked and which are the answers that the witness gave. He should attempt to do this by using appropriate tones of voice but any attempt to over-dramatise the evidence should be avoided as should a dull monotone or repetition of the annoying formula of for example, "Question: What colour was the car? Answer: I think it was black. Question: Are you sure of that? Answer: Maybe it was dark blue." It is suggested that a video recording should be introduced in a similar way and that no extraneous commentary should accompany its showing.

AGREED OR ADMITTED FACTS

18.25   As at a diet of proof, any facts not in dispute between the parties can be agreed in a joint minute and, if otherwise admissible as evidence, can be used in evidence at the trial[64]. During the course of the trial counsel can indicate, verbally or by lodging a further joint minute, that additional facts have now been agreed. Certain written statements may be received without being spoken to if sanctioned by the court[65], and any matter admitted or deemed to have been admitted in term of the notice to admit procedure may also be treated as agreed evidence[66]. Admissions and statements not made by minute but contained in the pleadings may be put in as evidence to prove the facts stated or admitted[67] provided that any admission is express and not implied[68].

18.26   All agreed evidence, whether in a joint minute, answers to a minute to admit, in the pleadings or otherwise, needs to be formally placed before the jury and this is usually done by the pursuer's junior counsel reading out all such minutes or other documents before the pursuer's case has been closed, even if the contents thereof have already been mentioned in the opening speech.

SECOND TRIALS

18.27   At a second or subsequent trial (i.e. one that follows upon a successful motion for a new trial) the fact that a first trial has taken place may be mentioned but it is improper to enter into any details of the first trial or to found any argument upon its result for the purpose of influencing the jury in the second trial[69]. The principle to be applied is that "in conducting a second trial, the whole proceedings should be as little mixed up with or connected with

---

64 Rule 36.7 applied to jury trials by rule 37.4.
65 Rule 36.8 applied to jury trials by rule 37.4.
66 Rule 28A.1 and 28A.2 which replaced the former rule 36.6.
67 *Macfarlane & Co v Taylor & Co* (1867) 6 M (HL) 1 at 4.
68 *Lee v National Coal Board* 1955 SC 151.
69 *Leven v Young & Co* (1818) 1 Mur 380.

that of the first as possible"[70], and thus even the amount of damages awarded at the first trial may not be mentioned to the jury[71]. The witnesses at the second trial should be examined in the same manner as they would have been examined had the first trial not taken place[72], subject only to any questions which might arise in connection with credibility relating to any previous inconsistent statements or evidence given at the first trial.

OBJECTIONS TO EVIDENCE

18.28   It is always open to parties to object to the admission of a line of evidence or to specific questions on the basis that there is no record for it, that it was not covered in the opening speech, that it is a leading question, or on any other basis which would have formed a valid ground of objection at a proof. However, it should be recognised that:

> "[O]bjections taken in the course of a jury trial have a measure of importance which they do not possess in a proof before a judge sitting alone. Failure to take objections of any description, at the earliest possible opportunity, generally militates against the force of the objection, though not invariably excluding its later consideration. In a jury trial, however, there being no review in the ordinary sense of the term, appeal against a trial judge's ruling on objections is conditional on the objection being taken at the proper time and in the proper manner."[73]

18.29   The practice of allowing evidence for which there is no record has been severely criticised and it has been said that when an attempt is made to lead such evidence by a pursuer, the duty of counsel for the defender is to state, once and for all, that he objects to the question put and to all the questions on the same line of evidence. This having been done, the judge may either reject the evidence or admit it under reservation of all questions of competency and relevancy and it is then open to him to direct the jury to disregard such evidence which is inconsistent with the record on which the issue is founded[74]. However, the trial judge is not bound to refuse to admit evidence if facts, although not stated on the record in detail, were substantially in agreement with the pursuer's averments and in these circumstances the question of prejudice, if any, is one for the jury[75].

18.30   In a civil jury trial the presiding judge must accept responsibility for admitting or excluding evidence which is challenged as inadmissible because a jury is more likely than a judge to be influenced by incompetent or irrelevant

---

70 Macfarlane, p 281.
71 *Robertson v Allardyce* (1830) 5 Mur 327.
72 Macfarlane, pp 282–283.
73 *McCallum v Paterson (No 2)* 1969 SC 85 at 92 per Lord Guthrie.
74 *Littlejohn v Brown & Co* 1909 SC 169 at 176 per Lord Ardwall.
75 *Bain v Fife Coal Co* 1935 SC 681.

evidence[76] and thus the judge must direct the jury members to dismiss from their minds any such evidence[77]. Although a party wishing to object to a particular question or line of questioning should make his or her objection known before the witness has begun to answer (and, if the witness has begun to answer, he should be asked firmly but politely to desist from continuing), it may transpire that the question in itself was competent but the answer given was inadmissible; in these circumstances the proper remedy is for the presiding judge to tell the jury to disregard that evidence[78]. The trial judge should not on his own initiative improperly elicit evidence since this could influence the jury and, if counsel feel that he has done so, then that improperly elicited evidence must be objected to at the time[79]. He should refrain from saying anything to or about a witness which might suggest to the jury that he has formed a view about the credibility of that witness[80] and he should not be seen to unduly criticise counsel in front of the jury[81].

18.31   It is incompetent to make an application for a new trial based upon the grounds of undue admission or undue rejection of evidence unless objection was taken to the admission or rejection at the trial and that objection was recorded[82]. Thus, if no objection was taken to evidence being led and the case goes before the jury on the basis of that evidence, the defenders in a motion for a new jury trial may be unable to rely on the fact that such evidence was contrary to the averments on record[83]. Timing is all important here and "that which is not objected to at the time cannot afterwards be opened"[84]. All objections should therefore be made timeously and preferably outwith the presence of the jury and the witness in question.

18.32   It has been observed that objections relating to admissibility are undesirable in themselves and that they sometimes operate prejudicially against the party taking objection[85]. An American writer has commented that "the most resented request is that the jury be excused while the lawyers take up a matter with the court. The jurors are then prevented from hearing something interesting, as well as being inconvenienced."[86] A study of criminal jury trials in New Zealand concluded that in one-third of the trials they had studied when questions were objected to "at least some of the jurors formed the view

---

76 Adam, *Practical Treatise and Observations on Trial by Jury etc*, p 171.
77 *McDonald v Duncan* 1933 SC 737 at 744.
78 *Hamilton v Hope* (1827) 4 Mur 241; Macfarlane, p 129.
79 Thompson and Middleton, p 112; *McCallum v Paterson (No 2)* 1969 SC 85 at 92.
80 *Millar v Lees* 1992 SLT 725; *Hogg v Normand* 1992 SLT 736.
81 *Edwards v HM Advocate* 1991 GWD 24-1360.
82 Court of Session Act 1988, s 29(1)(b); rule 39.1(3). Note that since 1998 all objections are automatically recorded on tape: rule 37.5A(1), (2).
83 *Neil v James Muir & Son* 1954 SLT 49 at 50 per Lord Patrick.
84 *Brownlie v Tennant* (1855) 17 D 422 at 423; see also *McGlone v British Railways Board* 1966 SC (HL) 1 which deals with the situation at a proof.
85 *Boyle v Glasgow Corporation* 1949 SC 254 at 251 per Lord Justice-Clerk Thomson.
86 Lynn, *Jury Trial Law and Practice*, p 136.

that evidence was being deliberately withheld from them"[87]. Accordingly some caution should be exercised in the making of such objections.

> "Objections should only be taken where necessary and always in a measured manner. A voluble and outraged objection may only raise suspicions in the mind of the jury. There is also a danger that frequent interruptions may cause the evidence to become fragmented."[88]

18.33 Once an objection has been taken, the presiding judge is required to make a final ruling on the matter of admissibility (or, indeed, on any other objections to evidence) and he cannot reserve questions of competency and relevancy to the end of the trial in the way that he could at a proof diet. However, if there are questions of admissibility which may pose some difficulty then it is competent to adjourn the proceedings for a short period (such as overnight) in order to consider the objection and any further points that counsel may wish to raise[89].

18.34 One counsel for each party is usually heard in respect of the objection and a speech in reply may be allowed; in exceptional circumstances both senior and junior for each party may be heard[90]. Difficulties may arise when objectionable evidence of doubtful relevancy is led or elicited by the judge rather than by the parties but the principle is the same, i.e. the party taking objection should do so immediately; the normal procedure is then followed.

18.35 If any party is dissatisfied with the ruling of the presiding judge on the matter of an objection to evidence then his ruling may form the basis of a motion for a new trial and all objections are noted, but in the meantime and notwithstanding this, the trial proceeds on the basis of the given ruling.

AMENDMENT OF PLEADINGS

18.36 It is competent to seek to amend the record or issues during the course of the trial[91] although it may prove difficult to convince the court to allow this after the jury has been empanelled for anything other than formal amendments, and it has been said that motions to amend at this stage are practically unknown and that late amendments are usually refused[92].

---

87 NZ Law Commission, Preliminary Paper 37, vol 1, *Juries in Criminal Trials*, Pt 2, para 4.8.
88 J Carruthers, "Influencing the Jury" (2001) 46 JLSS July/19 at 21.
89 E.g. *Cameron v Lanarkshire Health Board* 1997 SLT 1040; *Clinton v News Group Newspapers Ltd* 1999 SC 367.
90 Thomson and Middleton, p 113, Maxwell, p 334.
91 Rule 24.1.
92 *Lawrie v Glasgow Corporation* 1952 SC 361 at 366; *Rafferty v Weir Housing Corporation Ltd* 1966 SLT (Notes) 23, although in that case one of the reasons that leave to amend was refused was because the motion was made too late in the day. For amendment prior to the empanelling of the jury, see **15.21** above.

18.37   The matter of whether or not to allow late amendments in a jury trial
must be based upon the principle of fairness to both parties and in practice has
sometimes been allowed[93], particularly where it can be shown that no real
prejudice has been caused to the other party and that the amendment is necessary for determining the real issue between the parties[94] and does not involve
so radical a change as to effectively substitute a new case for the existing one[95].
If an amendment is allowed then the party who opposed it can legitimately
comment upon the change in the pleadings in his closing speech[96].

18.38   The motion to amend the pleadings should come at the earliest
possible stage, i.e. once the difficulty which makes it necessary arises. Where a
party gets into difficulties as a result of the evidence given by a witness at the
trial and such evidence indicates that an amendment will be required, a motion
to amend should be made as soon as possible thereafter[97].

WITHDRAWAL OF CASE FROM JURY

18.39   At any point during the course of the trial a motion may be made to
the presiding judge to have the case withdrawn from the jury and the effect
of such a motion, if granted, is that the action will fail since the judge will be
required to direct the jury to return a verdict for the defender[98]. Such a
motion should not be made in the presence of the jury[99] and would usually be
made once the pursuer has closed his case[100], although it can be made after the
evidence for both sides has been led, but is incompetent to move for the case
to be withdrawn from the jury after the judge has charged the jury[101].
Although it is most unusual, the presiding judge may make such a motion *ex
proprio motu*[102]. One of two defenders cannot challenge the withdrawal of the
case against the other[103]. If a motion to withdraw the case from the jury is
made at the end of the pursuer's evidence, it is a matter for the discretion of the
presiding judge as to whether or not to grant the motion and a refusal to do

---

93 As in e.g. *McLean v Bell* 1930 SC 954.
94 E.g. *Cameron v Lanarkshire Health Board* 1997 SLT 1040. The defenders sought to
    challenge the ruling in a motion for a new trial which was dismissed by the Inner
    House on 31 Oct 1996.
95 Cf *McPhail v Lanarkshire County Council* 1951 SC 301; *Dryburgh v National Coal Board*
    1962 SC 485.
96 *Cameron v Lanarkshire Health Board* 1997 SLT 1040.
97 *Cameron v Lanarkshire Health Board* at 1043C–E.
98 Maclaren, p 610.
99 Thompson and Middleton, p 113.
100 Maclaren, p 610.
101 *Park v Wilsons and Clyde Coal Co* 1926 SC (HL) 38.
102 *Tully v North British Railway Co* (1907) 46 SLR 715; *Mitchell v Caledonian Railway Co*
    1910 SC 746.
103 *Robertson v Federation of Icelandic Co-operative Societies* 1948 SC 565.

so does not constitute a misdirection[104]. However, if the judge himself withdraws the case from the jury at this stage then this may be a misdirection which will entitle the pursuer to a new trial[105].

18.40 The three usual grounds[106] upon which a motion may be made to withdraw the case from the jury are:

(a) that the facts adduced by the pursuer set up an essentially different case from that stated on record and, on that basis, do not constitute a relevant case in relation to the pleadings or the issue;

(b) that the pursuer has failed to produce sufficient evidence to support the case on record, i.e. a similar submission to that of "no case to answer" in a criminal trial; or

(c) that the defender has not had fair notice on record of the pursuer's case and that in consequence he has been prejudiced by the surprise or change in direction and it would now be inequitable to allow the altered case to go to the jury.

18.41 Examples of the first type of case include a situation where the discrepancy between the record and the evidence was such that had the pursuer described the accident on record in the way in which it was proved to have occurred no issue would have been granted[107], and a defamation action where malice had not been averred and the case was taken from the jury after the judge found that on the evidence the statement complained of had been a privileged one[108]. The motion is liable to be refused if the discrepancy is a minor and immaterial one[109], and leave to amend the pleadings to bring them in line with the evidence may be refused if the judge has already indicated that he is intending to grant the motion to have the case withdrawn from the jury[110].

18.42 Examples of an insufficiency of evidence include where the evidence led only established that a pursuer caused the accident by his sole fault[111],

104 *Keeney v Stewart* 1909 SC 754.
105 *Gibson v Nimmo & Co* (1895) 22 R 491; *McDonald v Duncan* 1933 SC 737.
106 This list is not an exhaustive one: see Lord Murray in *McDonald v Duncan* 1933 SC 737 at 745.
107 *Tully v North British Railway Co* (1906) 46 SLR 715 at 718 per Lord President Dunedin; *Mitchell v Caledonian Railway Co* 1910 SC 746.
108 *Ritchie & Son v Barton* (1883) 10 R 813.
109 E.g. as in *McDonald v Duncan* 1933 SC 737.
110 *Grant v W Alexander & Sons* 1937 SLT 572; *Rafferty v Weir Housing Corporation Ltd* 1966 SLT (Notes) 23.
111 Cf *Mulligan v Caird (Dundee) Ltd* 1973 SLT 72 where the First Division granted a new trial on the basis that the evidence did not unequivocally show that the accident was caused by the pursuer's own actings and that there was no such direct and clear-cut contradiction in the evidence of the pursuer's witnesses as to entitle the judge to withdraw the case from the jury. It is understood that at the second trial the jury unanimously assoilzied the defenders.

where there was no evidence that a driver was not keeping a proper look-out or travelling at an excessive speed[112], and where there was no evidence to establish the reason why a person had fallen to the ground and no inference could be drawn that any person had been negligent[113]. In the past when corroboration was required and when a finding of contributory negligence precluded a verdict in the pursuer's favour, such motions were more common[114].

18.43   In the third category, that of a lack of fair notice on record, it is essential that prejudice has been caused to the party seeking the withdrawal[115], and if any discrepancy between the record and the evidence led was not material and admitted without objection then the motion may be refused. It is too early to say whether or not the simplified pleadings now required in Chapter 43 personal injury actions will result in an increase in motions made under this head.

18.44   A similar power exists to withdraw a defence (either partial or whole) from the jury if there is no evidence to support it so that, for example, where the defender had a counter-issue on the question of the pursuer's contributory negligence in his failure to wear a seat-belt, the counter-issue was withdrawn from the jury on the basis that there had been no evidence to the effect that the wearing of a seat-belt would have made any difference to the injuries sustained by the pursuer and that in any event the exact mechanism of the injury was unknown[116]. In a recent defamation action the pursuer sought to have a counter-issue of fair comment withdrawn from the jury on the basis that there was an insufficiency of evidence showing that the representations complained of were comment as opposed to representations of fact and that it was plain on the evidence that, if the representations were comment at all, they were based on misstated facts. The defenders contended that whether or not the article could be viewed as comment at all was a matter of law and thus could not be reopened at this stage, that it was a matter for the jury as to whether or not the words were comment[117], that no evidence was admissible as to whether the words complained of were comment and that whether or not the underlying facts were substantially true was a jury question. The judge refused the motion on the basis that this was not a question of sufficiency but an argument as to relevancy which was no longer open to the pursuer and that in any event the central questions – whether or not the words complained of were comment

---

112 *McCaffery v Lanarkshire Tramways Co* 1910 SC 797.

113 Cf *Ross v Fife Healthcare NHS Trust* 2000 SCLR 620 where although the motion to withdraw the case from the jury was refused a new trial was subsequently granted on the basis of a verdict contrary to the evidence.

114 E.g. *Cook v Paxton* (1910) 48 SLR 7; *Grant v W Alexander & Sons* 1937 SLT 572; *Mutch v Scott's Shipbuilding and Engineering Co* 1955 SLT 45; *Rafferty v Weir Housing Corporation* 1966 SLT (Notes) 23.

115 *McDonald v Duncan* 1933 SC 737 at 741 per Lord Justice-Clerk Alness.

116 *Walker v Moncur*, Lady Paton, 14 Feb 2001★.

117 *Jeyaretnam v Goh Chok Tong* [1989] 1 WLR 1109.

and, if so, whether they were based on the facts – were classically matters for the jury to decide[118].

18.45 Withdrawal of a case from the jury is, however, a course which is rarely adopted and, when it is, the factual basis upon which such a motion is made should be unequivocal and clear-cut[119]. Accordingly it is more usual to allow the trial to proceed to a verdict and thereafter the aggrieved party can, if so advised, apply for a new trial on the basis that the verdict was contrary to the evidence[120]. The effect of wrongfully withdrawing a case from the jury will be a successful motion for a new trial.

ADJOURNMENT OF TRIAL

18.46 Once the trial has begun it is continued on successive days (excluding Saturdays, Sundays and public holidays) until the jury has reached its verdict. Where, however, a diet in excess of four days was allocated, e.g. a six- or eight-day diet commencing on a Thursday or Tuesday, then the court will not normally sit on the intervening Monday. The presiding judge, however, has the power to adjourn a trial which has already begun where the circumstances of the case require it, but where it is possible to avoid such an adjournment a motion to adjourn will, in the usual course of events, not be granted[121]. Where it is sought to adjourn the trial to the next day (e.g. where a party has unexpectedly run out of witnesses, one of the participants in the trial is unwell, or where a legal matter has arisen and counsel or the court needs time to clarify it[122]) there are no particular procedural difficulties and the inconvenience to jurors will be slight, but where a longer adjournment is proposed the court will be less inclined to grant such a motion. Thus, for instance, where an essential witness falls ill once a trial has commenced, the court will be faced with the dilemma of considering whether the interests of justice are best served by adjourning the trial or by taking the evidence of that witness on commission[123]. An adjournment should only be granted if necessary and has been refused when a party sought it for the purpose of obtaining additional evidence which would be of assistance to him[124]. No adjournment is granted upon a party objecting to the opinion or direction of the presiding judge and the trial must continue until such time as the jury reaches a verdict or the case is withdrawn from it[125].

---

118 *McCormick v Scottish Daily Record & Sunday Mail*, Lord Menzies, 18 Jan 2006★: for the verdict of the jury see App III, 3 [4].
119 *Mulligan v Caird (Dundee) Ltd* 1973 SLT 72.
120 For a recent example of this see *Ross v Fife Healthcare NHS Trust* 2000 SCLR 620.
121 Macfarlane, p 245; Maclaren, p 611.
122 An example of this being found in *Cameron v Lanarkshire Health Board* 1997 SLT 1040.
123 As in e.g. *Forbes v Leys* (1820) 5 Mur 289.
124 *Clark v Thomson* (1816) 1 Mur 161.
125 Court of Session Act 1988, s 16.

18.47 When an adjournment is granted or the case is adjourned because of
the lateness of the hour it is usual for the presiding judge to caution the jurors
not to enter into any discussions or conversations about the subject of the
trial[126].

ABANDONMENT OR SETTLEMENT OF THE ACTION

18.48 The pursuer may at any time before the presiding judge has begun to
charge the jury, abandon the action under payment of the taxed expenses and a
failure to pay these will result in the defenders or other party to whom the
expenses are due being entitled to absolvitor[127]. The parties may also settle an
action at any stage prior to the retiral of the jury to consider its verdict and if
the action settles before the jury has been empanelled then the court will pronounce an interlocutor discharging the trial diet. If the case settles after the jury
has been sworn in and the evidence has commenced then the presiding judge
will discharge the jury without a verdict. It has been said that settlements during the course of a trial are "not viewed with favour by the court"[128] but,
however regrettable and inconvenient to both the court and the jurors, late
settlement has always been a feature of our system of civil litigation. It remains
to be seen whether the new Chapter 43 procedure in personal injury actions
will make any significant change to this state of affairs. It is usual for settlement
during the trial to be effected by a joint minute signed by counsel to which the
presiding judge will then interpone authority.

126 Macfarlane, p 246.
127 Rule 29.1.
128 Maxwell, p 343.

Chapter 19

The closing speeches

ORDER AND TIMING OF SPEECHES

19.01   At the conclusion of the evidence, counsel will address the jury in closing speeches, one for each party. The order of the speeches will usually be in the same order as the evidence was led and will thus start with a speech by the pursuer's counsel which, where the pursuer is represented by both junior and senior counsel, will be made by the senior[1]. It should, however, be noted that the order of the speeches is at the discretion of the presiding judge, and in a defamation action where the defender had been ordained to lead on his *veritas* plea and had therefore made the first opening speech, the pursuer will often be directed to make the first closing speech[2]. Where evidence in replication has been led by a pursuer after the defender has concluded his speech, a further speech may be allowed but such a speech would be confined merely to matters covered in that additional evidence[3] and it would be better practice to allow the additional evidence to be led prior to any closing speech being made.

CONTENT OF SPEECHES

19.02   There are no hard and fast rules as to what should be covered in the closing speeches but counsel should state fully the grounds upon which he or she contends that the party whom they represent is entitled to a verdict and these grounds should be based upon the evidence led in support of them[4]. The facts and any inferences which the jury might draw from them are referred to with particular emphasis upon what interpretation the jury is invited to place upon any potentially harmful or disputed evidence. The evidence and demeanour of individual witnesses can be commented upon and advice given

---

1 Formerly the pursuer was not entitled to make a closing speech if the defender had led no evidence: Macfarlane, p 125.
2 E.g. *Winter v News Scotland Ltd*, reported on another matter in the Inner House at 1991 SLT 828.
3 Macfarlane, p 125.
4 Mackay, p 351.

as to how the jury might reconcile the evidence of skilled witnesses who do not agree. Counsel can refer to any document, plan or other production which has been placed before the jury or covered in the evidence and can invite the jury to look again at that evidence.

19.03 No mention may be made of any matter which has not been proved except insofar as it might be relevant for the purposes of contrasting what was said by the other party in his opening speech. No extraneous factors should be mentioned, such as sympathy for a party or any irrelevant evidence or other matters which could prejudice the jury. It is thus improper to mention the presence of any indemnity insurance[5], the possibility of any alternative remedy[6], the presence of any tender or offer or the lack thereof[7] or the incidence of expenses[8], and all comments such as "you need not worry about making a high award because the insurers will be paying", or "if you award a high sum this will only make insurance premiums for the likes of all of us rise", must be avoided. Any amendment to the pleadings or departure from the party's case in evidence can be commented upon as a matter affecting the credibility or reliability of a party or their witnesses[9] but counsel should always be careful not to make any suggestions or invite the jury to speculate on any matter which is not justified by the evidence.

19.04 Usually counsel will explain the law insofar as it affects the issue and thus in a personal injury action the nature and extent of any common law and statutory duties will be set out and the relationship between an alleged breach of those duties and the evidence led will be explained. The concepts of the various heads of damages should be covered, with particular emphasis on explaining what is covered by solatium and heads which might not be readily understood by lay persons, such as loss of employability, necessary services from relatives, lost services and the various components of awards made under section 1(4) of the Damages (Scotland) Act 1976. In a defamation action counsel will explain to the jury the meaning of concepts such as publication, innuendo and *veritas*, where there is a counter-issue, the concepts raised therein, such as *volenti non fit injuria* and contributory negligence. In the case of the latter some suggestion will be made as to how the jury is to quantify this on the basis of a proportion or percentage allocation between the parties.

---

5 *Stewart v Duncan* 1921 SC 482; however, since Directive 2000/26/EC and the European Communities (Rights Against Insurers) Regulations 2002 (SI 2002/3061) relating to insurance against civil liability of motor vehicles now permit a direct right of action against the insurers after a road traffic accident, this fact may well become obvious to the jury from the instance in such a case. See also A Hajducki, "Insurers, Indemnifiers and the Jury" 2005 SLT (News) 49; see also *McFarlane v Thain* [2006] CSIH 3.

6 *Jamieson v W Brown & Sons* 1938 SC 456.

7 *Reekie v McKinven* 1921 SC 733; *Avery v Cantilever Shoe Co* 1942 SC 469 at 470–471 per Lord President Normand.

8 *Simpson v Liddle* (1821) 2 Mur 582.

9 E.g. *Cameron v Lanarkshire Health Board* 1997 SLT 1040 at 1043.

19.05   Patrimonial loss can be quantified by referring both to agreed figures which might cover the whole of one head of damages or a part of it, such as wage loss up to a particular point supported by the evidence, or to agreed multiplicands and multipliers which would enable the jury to make a calculation itself. Where there is no agreement, then figures can be suggested in respect of multiplicands based on the evidence, multipliers based on the evidence with or without reference to the appropriate actuarial tables, the value of services lost or provided and any other matter, bearing in mind only that there must be an evidential basis for all such suggestions unless some sort of general knowledge of reasonable sums on the part of the jury is being relied upon, i.e. that the daily rate for domestic help is likely to be in the order of a particular sum or that it might consider that the value of the services rendered by a mother to young children is likely to be X. It should be borne in mind, however, that such an approach may well be criticised in a motion for a new trial.

19.06   There can be no particular objection to each party placing before the jury a written schedule setting out that party's position and calculations in relation to particular aspects of patrimonial loss such as multiplicands for wage loss or services and suggested multipliers and this, indeed, may be a sensible method to adopt particularly where such calculations are detailed or complex or where alternative positions in relation to promotion prospects, job security or "back to work" dates are being suggested, provided that the content and purpose of such schedules are carefully explained to the jury[10]. A statement of valuation of claim prepared under the Chapter 43 procedure should not normally be placed before a jury since, although it would not be incompetent to do so[11], such statements can be varied or amended at any time up to trial and they will include information such as a party's valuation of solatium which should not be disclosed to the jury. The Ogden actuarial tables can be placed before the jury and the judge would then have to give the appropriate directions to the jury on their use. Where applicable, the jury must be told to apportion the sums it awards between the past and future or, for benefits

---

10 Such written schedules were put to the jury in *Leeder v Advocate General for Scotland* 2004 Rep LR 99 and in *Sneddon v Deutag Services*, Lord Carloway, 1 Nov 2004★ where, despite objection from the defenders, the pursuer was allowed to distribute copies of his three-page summary of his patrimonial loss calculations to the jury in order to save it from having to take detailed notes in relation thereto.

11 R Milligan, "Statements of Valuation of Claim" (2003) 53 Rep L Bul 4 at 6; **8.17** above. However, in *Sneddon v Deutag Services*, Lord Carloway, 1 Nov 2004★ the defenders, despite the pursuer's objection, were allowed to put to the pursuer in cross-examination questions relating to why a particular sum had been included for solatium in his statement of valuation of claim on the basis that the statement of valuation formed part of the pleadings, and thereby the jury was made aware of what the pursuer's advisers, at an early stage in the proceedings, thought that his claim for solatium was worth. The relevance of those questions is unclear – see further **20.15**.

purposes, to make an apportionment of a sum it awards to cover the relevant period covered in the issues.

19.07 Probably the most contentious part of the closing speech is that, unless the trial is in respect of liability or patrimonial loss only, it will be necessary for counsel to discuss the matter of compensation for non-patrimonial loss without giving any indication to the jury as to what a reasonable award would be. No reference can be made to any other awards made by juries in similar circumstances or by judges in other cases, and it can only be suggested to the jury that it should make such award as it thinks reasonable in all the circumstances. The sum sued for (which is set out in the issue) can be referred to by way of the maximum that the jury can award, i.e. that it can award this sum if it feels it is the appropriate sum, less if it feels that is appropriate but not more if it feels it insufficient, but the jury cannot be directed by counsel to award a named sum or sums. This is not to say that a hint cannot be given in the form of "if you accept the evidence of Mr X, then the injury that the pursuer sustained was a fairly minor one and therefore you would probably consider that the sum which you should award would reflect this", or "it is difficult to conceive of a more catastrophic injury than that which the pursuer has sustained and accordingly you may think that a very substantial award is called for", but no reference can be to comparisons such as "the price of a new car/house/equivalent of one year's wages" etc[12]. Expressions such as "you may think that a six figure sum is appropriate" have been used in closing speeches without comment[13] but it is suggested that this practice is regrettable and inevitably leads to the other party making counter-suggestions to a bemused jury.

19.08 Whether not being able to direct the jury as to a particular sum or comparison is a good thing has been a matter of controversy[14] although it is not current practice to do so, nor apparently ever has been. It is often better for

---

12 See n 36 to **18.11** above.
13 E.g. *Shaw v Russell*, Lord Carloway, 10 May 2004*, where the pursuer suggested a "six-figure sum" and the defenders a five. For the judge's charge, see **20.15** below, n 41. In *Carmichael v Isola Werke (UK) Ltd*, Lord Bracadale, 19 May 2005*, counsel for the pursuer suggested "a six figure sum" for solatium to the jury; counsel for the defenders contended that this would be far more than had ever been awarded for a comparable injury (the loss of four fingers on the dominant right hand) and that it would leave the award open to challenge on appeal and that an appropriate award might be "in the low to mid range of five figures" – in the event the jury awarded £85,000. In *Shaw v McKinlay*, Lord Hardie, 21 Oct 2005* counsel for the pursuer in her speech invited the jury to award "tens of thousands" for solatium while counsel for the defenders suggested that, on the pursuer's own evidence, the claim was worth "very low four figure sums" and, if the defender's experts were accepted, "hundreds of pounds". For the judge's charge see **20.15** below and for the actual award see Appendix III, 2 [29].
14 See e.g. the views of Lords Kirkwood and Abernethy in *Girvan v Inverness Farmers' Dairy (No 2)* 1996 SLT 631 at 636L–637A and 643B–C; Lord Hamilton in *Heasman v Taylor* 2002 SC 326 at 346C–347B and A Hajducki, "Civil Juries and Solatium" 2002 SLT (News) 271. For a further discussion see **20.14** below.

a defender's counsel to make little reference to what sum the jury should award for solatium unless it is contended that a nominal or minimal sum only might be appropriate and exhortations such as telling a jury not to be too generous with other people's money will often have the opposite effect from that intended. A direction that the jury must compensate the pursuer rather than punish the defender is usually as far as one should go, particularly if the jury seem well disposed to the pursuer.

19.09 When during a closing speech counsel says something which the opposing counsel thinks is erroneous and ought to be corrected, the point should be raised at the time[15] although whether this should be done by physically interrupting counsel or by waiting until the end of his speech is a matter which should be considered carefully.

19.10 It should always be borne in mind that the closing speech is the final contact that the counsel will have with the jury and it is important therefore that all of the relevant facts and law which a party wishes to bring to the jury's attention is contained within that speech. It is too late to refer to anything which was not brought out in evidence but not too late to ask the jurors to use their common sense provided that this is based upon the evidence adduced. It is also the last time in which the personal characteristics of the participants in the trial may influence the jurors and, as one American commentator put it:

> "Remember that jurors throughout the trial are looking for charisma, competence and credibility on the part of the advocate. During closing submissions these factors are still being assessed. Your charisma will prevail if you demonstrate competence in applying the facts to the law in a credible fashion. Admit the vulnerability of your case, but demonstrate how the law, in its compassion, still allows your client to prevail. Force your adversary to present an argument on the law and on the facts to rebut your conclusions by anticipating his or her defenses. Remind the jurors of their oath [and] if you have honed the presentation of proof to the law, your presentation of a sincere and credible closing argument will persuade them to be on your side."[16]

---

15 *Jamieson v W Brown & Sons* 1938 SC 456 at 459.
16 Warsaw (ed), *Masters of Trial Practice*, p 102.

Chapter 20

The judge's charge

GENERALLY

20.01 Following upon the closing speeches of counsel for the pursuer and defender, it is then the duty of the presiding judge to charge the jury and this he or she does by addressing them on a number of matters. The timing of the charge is a matter for the court and because it is desirable for the charge to be immediately followed by the retiral of the jury, it is not considered good practice for the judge to begin his charge late in the day, particularly after a long and difficult trial[1]. Once the charge has been commenced it is no longer open to the pursuer to abandon the action and the parties are precluded both from leading any further evidence or from further addressing the jury. The charge is recorded by the shorthand writer or on tape[2] in full so that it is available for the Inner House should there be a motion for a new trial[3]. Misdirection of the jury on the part of the judge in his or her charge gives the party dissatisfied the right to take exception to the charge and, in turn, this may form the basis for review of the action by the Inner House[4].

20.02 There are no particular rules for the regulation of the presiding judge in charging the jury[5] but, notwithstanding the desirability of the charge being relatively brief, there are a number of matters which should be brought to the attention of the jury in relation both to the facts and the law.

THE FACTS

20.03 The presiding judge should in the charge make it clear to the jury that

---

1 *Aitken v HM Advocate* 1984 SCCR 81 applied to a civil jury trial in *Shaw v Russell* 10 May 2004★, where Lord Carloway, after counsel's closing speeches, adjourned the trial at 4.30 pm on a Friday until 9 am on the following Monday.
2 Rule 37.5A(2)(d) and see further **18.05** above.
3 *Douglas v Cunningham* 1963 SC 654 at 670 per Lord Guthrie; *McArthur v Weir Housing Corporation Ltd* 1970 SC 135 at 138–139 per Lord Wheatley; rule 37.5A(7).
4 Court of Session Act 1988, s 29(1)(a).
5 Macfarlane, p 236.

it is the master of the facts and that it is a matter for the jurors, and them alone, to decide upon the credibility and reliability of individual witnesses, the weight and cogency of any evidence led and the inferences which are to be drawn from any circumstantial evidence[6]. The jury will normally be told that it is to have regard to its own recollections of the evidence or assessments of the witnesses and that it should prefer these recollections and assessments when they do not coincide with those of the judge or counsel. Unless the evidence has been in short compass, the judge will usually marshall in a convenient order the evidence which has been led so as to assist the jurors in applying their minds to it[7], and the modern tendency is to refer to the evidence in fairly general and brief terms unless there is cause to do otherwise.

20.04   The judge may direct the jury as to the various possible views which may be taken of the facts[8], indicate the relative importance of the facts proved on one side or the other[9] and recall to the jury the material arguments presented by each side in the speeches of counsel, generally ensuring, so far as possible, that the jury has before it the arguments put forward by each side[10]. Specific directions may be given in relation to the result of finding certain facts proved or not proved[11] or on the reliability of evidence with the lapse of time[12].

20.05   Should the presiding judge, while referring to the facts in the course of his or her charge, make any mistake in respect of them, counsel should notify the judge of this at the time, either by interruption of the charge or by the immediate passing of a note via the clerk of court for the attention of the judge[13]. Where the clerk has given an erroneous direction on a matter of fact and fails to correct it after counsel have brought it to his or her attention, this may amount to a ground for ordering a new trial, provided that this was essential for the justice of the cause[14].

THE LAW

20.06   The judge must, in clear and unambiguous terms, lay down to the

---

6 Maclaren, p 512; Thompson and Middleton, p 109; *Ferguson v Western SMT Co* 1969 SLT 213.
7 Thompson and Middleton, p 109.
8 *Gelot v Stewart* (1870) 9 M 957.
9 Thompson and Middleton, p 109.
10 Thompson and Middleton, p 109.
11 *Ferguson v Western SMT Co* 1969 SLT 213.
12 *Devine v Beardmore & Co* 1955 SC 311.
13 Macfarlane, p 237; Maclaren, p 612; *Leven v Young & Co* (1818) 1 Mur 366; *Davidson v Dunbar* (1826) 4 Mur 43.
14 *Woods v Caledonian Railway Co* (1886) 13 R 1118.

jury the principles of law which apply to the case and he must make it clear to it that it has to accept his legal directions[15], especially where these differ from those suggested by counsel. He should explain the particular principles of law which apply to the case, including any alleged breaches of statutory duty, and he should tell the jury what facts it will require to find established in order to support each case pled[16]. He must point out any parts of the case which, in law, have to be disregarded as not being supported by such evidence as the law requires and he should inform the jury of the result of its finding certain facts proved or not proved, as the case may be[17]. He must direct the jury in respect of the appropriate standard of proof required in any particular case[18] and it may be helpful to the jurors if he emphasises the difference between the civil standard of proof and the concept of the criminal standard of proof with which they are probably more familiar.

20.07 The presiding judge should make it quite clear to the jurors that they must dismiss from their minds any evidence given during the trial which was held to be irrelevant[19] and that they should decide the case solely on the basis of the evidence led and witnesses who were heard. He must make it clear as to where the burden of proof lies and upon which party it is incumbent to satisfy that burden by leading sufficient evidence, so that in a normal case he will inform the jury that it is not up to the defenders to exonerate themselves from culpability but that it is the duty of the pursuer to prove his own case on the balance of probabilities. The judge should explain to the jury that in relation to any counter-issue the burden of proof is upon that particular defender. When liability is admitted, the issue is still in the usual general form and the judge should, accordingly, formally direct the jury to answer the question in the issue in the affirmative.

20.08 Where there are specific defences which must be established by the defenders, the presiding judge should explain these to the jury and thus, for example, where *volenti non fit injuria* is pled in defence, he should explain that the defenders must first obtain from the jury a finding in fact that the pursuer freely and voluntarily, with full knowledge of the nature and extent of the risk that he ran, impliedly or expressly agreed to incur that risk[20]. In defamation actions the presiding judge should make it clear that the onus of establishing the facts on which the defences of *veritas*, fair comment and privilege are based

---

15 Maclaren, p 612; Thompson and Middleton, p 109.
16 Thompson and Middleton, p 109.
17 Thompson and Middleton, p 109.
18 *Hendry v Clan Line Steamers* 1949 SC 320.
19 *McDonald v Duncan* 1933 SC 737. A recent example is found in *MacIntosh v Findlay*, Lord Kingarth, 17 Jan 2001★: see **18.11** above.
20 *Letang v Ottawa Electric Railway* [1926] AC 725 at 731; *Reid v Mitchell* (1885) 12 R 1129; *Stewart's Exrx v Clyde Navigation Trs* 1946 SC 317; *Rowand v Saunders & Connor (Barrhead) Ltd* 1953 SC 292.

lies upon the defenders[21]. He should explain to the jury that where an innuendo is capable of being construed in a defamatory manner, it is up to it to decide whether or not the words should reasonably be construed in that sense[22] and whether they were so construed by those to whom they had been communicated[23]. In actions relating to false imprisonment and malicious prosecution, the concepts of "maliciously" and "without justification" should be explained[24]. Other matters which might require directions from the judge would include the standard of care necessary in cases involving professional negligence[25], the nature of a pursuer's claim where it involves difficult concepts such as the psychological effects of stillbirth[26] or of sexual abuse[27] or the consequences on the evidence led of a relevant criminal conviction following upon a guilty plea[28].

20.09 The fact that pleadings have been held or conceded to be suitable for jury trial does not mean that the presiding judge is bound to accept every statement of duty in the pleadings as being an accurate statement of the law applicable and to direct the jury that each such duty in the terms referred to in the pleadings is a duty in law, nor does he have to instruct the jury that its only function in that regard is to decide if, on the facts found, that duty as pled has been breached[29].

20.10 In relation to the wording of the issues themselves, any words which have a technical legal meaning should be explained to the jury. These words might include "fault", "solatium", "falsely and calumniously" and "necessary services". In the case of a relative's claim for damages following upon a death, the presiding judge should explain to the jury the various component parts of the claim that are being pursued under section 1(4) of the Damages (Scotland) Act 1976 and inform the jury that, for the purposes of the award, it is not required to state any apportionment between those component parts. Where words used in the issues have a technical, scientific or artistic meaning then the particular meaning relied upon must have been proved in evidence and the judge can direct the jury to that part of the evidence. Where words used have no special meaning and are to be construed in their normal everyday sense, no direction is necessary[30].

---

21 *Harper v Provincial Newspapers* 1937 SLT 462; *Andrew v Penny* 1964 SLT (Notes) 24; in relation to fair comment, see also the Hong Kong Court of Final Appeal case of *Tse Wai Chun Paul v Cheng* [2001] EMLR 31.
22 *Webster v Paterson & Sons* 1910 SC 459 at 469; *Fairbairn v Scottish National Party* 1980 SLT 149 at 152.
23 *Bernhardt v Abrahams* 1912 SC 748.
24 *Robb v Sutherland; Irvine v Sutherland* 1994 GWD 38-2251.
25 *Hunter v Hanley* 1955 SC 200.
26 *McMartin v Gindha* 1995 SLT 523.
27 *Livingstone v Fife Council* 2004 SLT 161.
28 *Shearer v Bevan's Exrs* 1985 SLT 226.
29 *Adamson v Roberts* 1951 SLT 355; *Ayre v Milne* 1989 SLT 659.
30 *Macfarlane & Co v Taylor & Co* (1867) 6 M (HL) 1 at 5.

CONTRIBUTORY NEGLIGENCE

20.11 Where there are counter-issues on the question of contributory negligence, Lord President Cooper[31] summed up the matter as to how the jury should be charged as follows:

> "The jury will be instructed by the presiding judge as to the onus of proof of fault, and of contributory negligence respectively. They should be instructed, as was held in *Smith v Petterson*[32], not to return a verdict 'for the pursuer' or 'for the defenders' but to give specific answers to the questions. Subject to such directions they can be told (if the evidence admits of it) that there are three possibilities with three results, viz (1) sole fault on the defenders, in which case they answer the issue 'Yes' and the counter-issue 'No'; (2) sole fault on the [pursuer] in which case they answer the issue 'No' and disregard the counter-issue and (3) fault on both sides, in which event they answer both issue and counter-issue 'Yes' and then add the appropriate fractions. In cases (1) and (3) they must be told to make the assessment of damages, actual or hypothetical, required by the Act of 1945."

20.12 Thus the jury must determine the total damages which would have been recoverable if the claimant had not been at fault and the extent to which those damages are to be reduced[33]. The judge should make it clear to the jury that it has a latitude to apportion fault so long as it does so in accordance with the evidence[34].

MULTIPLE DEFENDERS

20.13 Where there are several defenders the jury should be told to apportion the damages awarded as between the various defenders in such proportions as it finds from the evidence[35] and, if appropriate, the pursuer if there is a counter-issue on the question of contributory negligence. The jury may use either fractions, or as is more common in current practice, percentages.

QUANTUM OF DAMAGES

Solatium

20.14 Where the jury in an action with a conclusion for damages finds for the pursuer then it is for the jury to assess the amount of damages[36] and the

31 *Hayden v Glasgow Corporation* 1948 SC 143 at 146; this was the first case to reach the Inner House following upon the change in the law to permit apportionment between the parties where contributory negligence was found.
32 1940 SC 18.
33 Law Reform (Contributory Negligence) Act 1945, s 1(6).
34 *Ward v Upper Clyde Shipbuilders* 1973 SLT 182; *Kirkland v British Railways Board* 1978 SC 71.
35 Law Reform (Miscellaneous Provisions) (Scotland) Act 1940, s 3.
36 Court of Session Act 1988, s 17(4).

presiding judge should make it clear that, if the jury finds for the pursuer, the quantum of damages is a matter with which it must deal. The nature of the various heads of claim, including past and future wage loss and solatium, should be explained to the jury and it should be told that its total award cannot exceed the sum stated as the total sum in the issue, that sum being the upper ceiling level.

20.15   No direction is given to the jury as to what sum it should award as solatium[37] but "the jury should take a reasonable view of the case and give what they consider in the circumstances to be fair compensation"[38]. It is suggested that it is always better to say as little to a jury as possible on the subject of the value of the solatium and the position adopted in early cases where comments such as "I am persuaded that you will not in this case give anything like the sum claimed"[39] is not followed in modern practice[40]. Where counsel have, however, made general suggestions in their closing speeches, it may be that the presiding judge feels that a comment thereon is necessary but this should always be done with great caution since there is a danger that a judge in so doing will inadvertently influence the minds of the jurors and, for all practical purposes, usurp their function. A better direction might be to say simply that the jury has heard counsel's submissions but that it is up to it on the basis of the evidence led to consider those submissions and to award what it thinks is fair and reasonable in the light of the evidence and not to suggest any sum or range of sums which the judge might consider reasonable in the circumstances[41]. However, where the jury has been made aware of what sum

---

37 *Girvan v Inverness Farmers' Dairy (No 2)* 1998 SLT 21 at 34E–G per Lord Hope. However, see the views expressed by Lords Kirkwood and Abernethy in the Inner House at *Girvan (No 2)* 1996 SLT 631 at 636L–637A and 643B–C and Lord Hamilton in *Heasman v Taylor* 2002 SC 326 at 346C–347B and the commentary by A Hajducki in "Civil Juries and Solatium" 2002 SLT (News) 271.

38 *Casey v United Collieries* 1907 SC 609 at 693 per Lord Kinnear. He went on to add that "I do not think it advisable to lay down any more exact rule."

39 Lord Adam in *Hyslop v Miller* (1816) 1 Mur 43 at 54.

40 Although see R Milligan, "Jury Trial Awards: A Case Study" (2002) 48 Rep L Bul 2 where he reports that in *Mitchell v North Glasgow University Hospitals NHS Trust*, Lord Johnston, 1 Oct 2003★ the jury, after being told of the sum sued for, was cautioned its award "should not be remotely near that for this type of injury".

41 E.g. *Shaw v Russell*, Lord Carloway, 10 May 2004★ (see **19.07** above) where the presiding judge commented that the jury need not necessarily award a six-figure sum but should award what it thought was moderate and reasonable. The dangers of this are, however, illustrated in *Warnock v Clark Contracts*, Lord Wheatley, 18 Nov 2004★ when the pursuer's counsel suggested that a "six-figure sum" could be justified in respect of a family's Damages (Scotland) Act 1976, s 1(4) claims and the defenders' counsel merely said that the jury should award what it felt to be "fair, just and reasonable". The presiding judge in his charge commented on the pursuer's counsel's suggestion but said that for the widow the jury should think of a figure "in the tens of thousands, but in the moderate or modest end of this". For the three children he suggested that the jury "might think it appropriate" to award each child one-third or one-quarter of that which was awarded to the widow. The pursuers took exception to this and a supplementary charge was given to the jury that if the impression had been given to it that it was not

was being sought by the pursuer by way of solatium in either the evidence or submissions of counsel (for instance by having had its attention drawn to the statement of valuation) then it should be told to disregard any such sums in considering what it would consider to be a fair figure to award under this head[42]. The same would apply to any figures relating to the defender's valuation.

20.16   In one reported case, Lord Guthrie in an often quoted passage directed the jury

> "to make such award as you think is moderate and reasonable, but adequate, having in view the particular circumstances of this case, because the only rule of law which applies to an award of solatium is that it is dependent upon the particular circumstances – for example, upon such matters as the gravity of the injury, upon its permanent or temporary character, upon the amount of pain endured by the injured party, and by the duration of that pain. These are circumstances which you have to bear in mind and you have to make an award which is reasonable in relation to the particular circumstances. You will have regard to the present value of the pound."[43]

It is suggested that this type of charge is still most suitable in dealing with solatium and that to say any more may well open up a basis for a motion for a new trial.

20.17   In relation to past solatium and future solatium, the jury should be told to reach a figure for solatium as a whole and then apportion that sum by dividing it into past and future elements.

20.18   The presiding judge may usefully point out to the jury that it has heard all of the evidence, that it is aware of the value of money and that it is up to the jury to make what it feels, in all of the circumstances, is a fair award. It is probably advisable to suggest that the jury considers each head of damage separately and that it does not use the sum sued for (which appears in the issue)

---

free to make whatever awards it wished then this was not intended and that it should make fair and reasonable awards without any imposed ceiling. No further exception was taken. In the event the jury awarded £40,000 to the widow and £16,250 to each child – see Appendix III, I [1]. In *Shaw v McKinlay*, Lord Hardie, 21 Oct 2005*, after counsel had respectively made suggestions as to the ranges that a solatium award might fall into (see **19.07**, n 13 above), the presiding judge charged the jury that the claim was worth maybe hundreds of pounds *and no more than a few thousand in four figures*. A note of exceptions was taken by the pursuer's counsel and the judge then emphasised to the jury that the question of quantum was a matter for it and that his guidance was simply that: guidance on the area in which solatium was to be considered. The jury awarded £6,000, suggesting that they may well have been influenced by such "guidance".

42 This direction was given by Lord Carloway in *Sneddon v Deutag Services*, 1 Nov 2004* but the jury then proceeded to award the pursuer the same sum for solatium as had appeared in his statement of valuation, possibly showing how difficult it is to erase such information from the minds of the jurors once they have become aware of it.

43 *Traynor's Exrx v Bairds & Scottish Steel* 1957 SC 311 at 314.

as a starting-point and work backwards from there. Although a judge might say that if the jury is satisfied that the pursuer has suffered severe injuries for which the defenders are liable, then it might think that a substantial sum is appropriate and vice versa, this is about as far as he probably should go without risking making a misdirection. Where solatium is agreed then the judge should direct the jury to award the agreed sum under that head.

Patrimonial loss

20.19 In relation to patrimonial loss the judge should explain to the jury all technical terms such as loss of employability, necessary personal services etc. If there are recoverable benefits then the fact that these exist is not brought to the jurors' attention but the judge should explain that they will need to calculate particular losses to the dates specified in the issue for reasons which need not concern them and that they may have to attribute these to loss of mobility and care. In respect of sums agreed, the judge must direct the jury to return in its verdict these sums if it is satisfied that any award is justified by the evidence (unless it is agreed that these sums are to be awarded in any event), but he cannot direct the jury to a specific multiplier or multiplicand unless these have been agreed, although he may suggest how the jury approaches the matter on the basis of evidence before it which it may accept or reject. He may give it directions as to appropriate multipliers contained in actuarial tables if these actuarial tables form part of counsel's submissions and may give it copies of these tables and a calculator if appropriate.

EXCEPTIONS TO CHARGE

20.20 Where a party to an action disagrees with any part of the judge's charge in relation to a direction given on a point of law, or that party wishes to request the judge to give a different or supplementary direction from that which the judge has already given in the charge, then the person taking exception thereto must intimate his exception to the presiding judge immediately upon the conclusion of the charge[44]. Unless the correct procedure is followed and exception is taken, there can be no subsequent review of the matter by the Inner House[45] and a new trial on the basis of the judge's misdirection will not be competent[46]. Objection must not be taken during the course of the charge and it must relate solely to a direction in law given or omitted[47] and it is

44 Rule 37.7.
45 *McLean v Bell* 1930 SC 954.
46 Rule 39.1(3)(a); Court of Session Act 1988, s 29(1)(a).
47 *McDougall v Girdwood* (1867) 5 M 937 at 941; *Woods v Caledonian Railway Co* (1886) 13 R 1118.

incompetent to take exception to a matter of fact[48]. Exceptions must be un-ambiguous[49] and, if requesting a supplementary direction, both relevant and of the essence of the case[50]. In the absence of an exception being taken, it is presumed that the judge's charge has been made correctly and it cannot be challenged subsequently[51].

20.21   The party who is taking exception must formulate his or her objection in writing, stating either the exception which he is taking or the direction sought, and this written objection is recorded in a document known as a note of exceptions[52]. If exception is being taken to a particular direction, then the note should also contain the substance of the direction which counsel contends should have been given in its place[53]. A note of exceptions[54] is a contemporaneous record of what takes place, drawn up by counsel in the heat of the battle and, although important because misdirection is a ground for seeking a new trial, it is rarely a precise, meticulous exposition of the point at issue, but it should state shortly and explicitly what counsel is objecting to and what he seeks[55]. In order to be prepared it may be advantageous to have a blank note of exceptions ready for use in the event, however unlikely that might seem, that it may be required.

20.22   Once a party has intimated to the presiding judge his note of exceptions, a hearing on the note of exceptions will take place outwith the presence of the jury[56]. The judge, having heard counsel, has to rule on the note of exceptions and he must decide whether or not to make any further direction to the jury. His decision must be recorded on the note of exceptions and he must then certify it[57]. Once he has done so, the judge may give in open court such further or other directions to the jury as he thinks fit before it retires to consider its verdict[58]. Whatever his decision, however, the trial must continue and proceed to a verdict[59].

---

48 *Duncan v British Railways Board* 1964 SLT (Notes) 73.
49 *Fraser v Younger* (1867) 5 M 861.
50 *Keeney v Stewart* 1909 SC 754.
51 *McKibben v Glasgow Corporation* 1920 SC 590 at 596.
52 Rule 37.7(2).
53 *Baird v Bell* (1856) 18 D 734; *Wilson v Dick's Co-operative Institutions* 1916 SC 578; *Glacken v National Coal Board* 1951 SC 617.
54 For the style of a note of exceptions see Appendix I, Styles C1 and C2 below and *McArthur v Weir Housing Corporation Ltd* 1970 SC 135.
55 *Robertson v Federation of Icelandic Co-operative Societies* 1948 SC 565 at 572.
56 Rule 37.7(1). The hearing was originally held in the presence of the jury: Macfarlane, p 236.
57 Rule 37.7(2).
58 Rule 37.7(3).
59 Court of Session Act 1988, s 16.

FURTHER QUESTIONS FOR THE JURY

20.23 After the evidence has been led, the judge may submit to the jury in writing, along with the issue and counter-issue, such further questions as he thinks fit[60]. These should be questions which appear to the judge to be required by the circumstances of the case and are supplementary to the questions in the issue and counter-issue, for example "Was the pursuer (a) employed by the defenders as their servant, (b) employed by X as their servant, or (c) employed by an independent contractor who, not being a servant of the defenders, had undertaken work on their instructions?"[61] It is no longer competent to seek a special verdict, i.e. a verdict given when the jury was asked to answer specific questions of fact to which the judge then applied the law[62].

DIRECTIONS AS TO HOW TO REACH A VERDICT

20.24 At the end of his charge, the presiding judge will give the jury formal instructions as to the method by which it must reach its verdict and will direct it that its verdict must either be unanimous or by a simple majority of not less than seven or, should the number of jurors have fallen to 11 or 10, by a majority of six[63]. He will direct the jurors to choose one of their number to speak for them when returning their verdict[64], i.e. a chancellor (to use the correct Scots legal form) or, in the language of the statute, "a person to speak for you".

---

60 Rule 37.8.
61 *Park v Wilsons and Clyde Coal Co* 1928 SC 121 at 124.
62 Rules of the Court of Session 1965, rule 128 – this was not re-enacted in the 1994 Rules, by which time it was thought that the practice was obsolete.
63 Court of Session Act 1988, s 15. There is no equivalent to the provision of s 90(2)(a) of the Criminal Procedure (Scotland) Act 1995 whereby if the number of jurors has fallen below 15, a majority of eight for a guilty verdict is still required.
64 Court of Session Act 1988, s 17(1). Formerly the jurors were asked to choose their chancellor by casting votes when they were first sworn with the juror first empanelled having a casting vote in the event of a tie but a direction to this effect was "unknown in modern times" and disappeared with the repeal of the Jury Trials (Scotland) Act 1815, s 33.

Chapter 21

The verdict

ENCLOSURE OF JURY

21.01 Following upon the judge's charge, the jury will normally retire to the jury room to consider its verdict although it may reach a decision immediately without leaving the jury box – this, however, is uncommon in practice and juries usually retire, even if only for a few minutes. Once the jury has retired "they are segregated from the whole world while they conduct their deliberations"[1], and are prohibited from communicating with any person except the presiding judge with whom they communicate through the clerk of court[2].

FURTHER DIRECTIONS

21.02 The jury may return to court for the purpose of consulting the judge in relation to a matter of law and practice, i.e. to receive supplementary directions about any matter of which it is unsure[3], and may ask the judge to give a direction as to the party entitled to the verdict on the basis of the facts found by it[4], whether it was constrained by the sums claimed under a particular head[5] and for further directions as to the use of the Ogden actuarial tables when it was given advice as to the appropriate table to use together with the loan of a calculator[6].

Productions and real evidence

21.03 If the jury asks to see a production or wishes to take it in to the jury

1 *Pirie v Caledonian Railway Co* (1890) 17 R 1157 at 1160 per Lord President Inglis.
2 Thompson and Middleton, p 109.
3 *Pirie v Caledonian Railway Co* at 1161.
4 *Smith v Paton* 1913 SC 1203.
5 *Wells v Hay* 1999 Rep LR 44 (unreported on this point).
6 *MacIntosh v Findlay*, Lord Kingarth, 17 Jan 2001★. In *Warnock v Clark Contracts*, Lord Wheatley, 18 Nov 2004★, the jury was given two calculators, presumably so that a cross-check could be made on the calculations.

room while it deliberates, then the presiding judge will normally allow it to do so provided that he is of the view that this would be in the interests of justice[7], and the same discretion will be given to him in respect of real evidence[8]. If counsel wish to make any representations on the matter of whether or not the jury should be permitted to view productions or real evidence then the presiding judge should allow them to do so outwith the presence of the jury and before it is given the items in contention[9]. The jury may be permitted to see again a video recording played during the trial but only for the purpose of assessing the evidence of witnesses who interpreted what was on the tape and not for the purpose of carrying on its own detective work, for example to see whether it could identify a person whom a witness could not[10]. In criminal trials the video is normally played in open court in the presence of the judge, counsel and the parties[11] although by consent the jury can view the video in the jury room in the presence of the video operator and clerk of court[12]; in a civil trial it is submitted that even the presence of these individuals would be unnecessary provided that at least one of the jury members is capable of operating the machine himself.

RETURNING A VERDICT

21.04   The jury may at any time return a verdict which is either unanimous or by a simple majority, i.e. seven in favour and five against[13], and must return a verdict on each and every question posed in the issues and counter-issues and on each head of damages in the schedule. Where during the course of the trial the jury has been depleted for any reason (such as illness) and wishes to return a majority verdict then there must still be a majority of the remaining jurors.

21.05   In the event of the jury having been enclosed for three hours and being unable to either agree upon a verdict or return a verdict by a majority, then the presiding judge may discharge the jury and order that the action be tried before a different jury[14] and the proceedings must start again *de novo* at the stage of having a new diet for trial fixed. If, however, it appears that the jury might be capable of reaching a majority verdict within a short time (i.e. there is not an immovable six-six deadlock) or that with a further direction they may reach

 7 *Munro v HM Advocate* 2000 SLT 950.
 8 *Collins v HM Advocate* 1993 SLT 101.
 9 *Boyle v HM Advocate* 1992 SLT 681.
10 *Donnelly v HM Advocate* 2000 SCCR 861.
11 *Gray v HM Advocate* 1999 SCCR 24.
12 *Carroll v HM Advocate* 1999 SCCR 617.
13 Court of Session Act 1988, s 17(2); note, however, that where the jury has fallen to 10 or 11 in number the majority required will be 6-5 or 6-4 as appropriate: 1988 Act, s 15. Originally in all cases the verdict had to be unanimous but the Jury Trials (Amendment) Act 1854 permitted a majority verdict of nine-three after six hours of deliberations.
14 Court of Session Act 1988, s 17(2).

a verdict, then juries have in practice been given further reasonable time beyond the three-hour period at the discretion of the presiding judge.

CONFIDENTIALITY OF DELIBERATIONS

21.06 The deliberations of the jury are, and remain, confidential and it is a contempt of court to obtain, disclose or solicit any particulars of statements made, opinions expressed, arguments advanced or votes cast by members of a civil jury in the course of its deliberations[15]. The provision does not, however, apply to the disclosure in a trial of any particulars for the purpose of enabling the jury to arrive at its verdict or in connection with the delivery of that verdict or evidence in the course of any subsequent criminal trial for alleged offences in relation to the jurors or to the publication of any particulars so disclosed[16]. It is not permissible for any party or the court to make inquiry of the members of the jury as to the terms of its deliberations even when the verdict in the case in which it deliberated is under review.

"Whatever discrepancies there may have been . . . the utmost danger and uncertainty would be the consequence if questions were to be raised against the verdicts of jurors by examining jurors themselves after their verdict was delivered and the jurors discharged."[17]

Thus the principle of justice not only having been done but having been seen to have been done does not apply to what may or may not have happened in the jury room[18], and "it is very much better that injustice should happen . . . than that every verdict should be open to be challenged upon grounds involving questions as to what happened during the deliberations of the jury"[19].

21.07 The deliberations of the jury are, however, strictly restricted to what actually happened in the jury room[20]. Thus, misconduct of jurors during an adjournment[21] or view[22] may be examined, particularly where there is a clear suggestion of some form of bias on the part of a juror or jurors which may have affected the verdict reached[23].

15 Contempt of Court Act 1981, s 8(1).
16 1981 Act, s 8(2).
17 *Stewart v Fraser* (1830) 5 Mur 166 at 178–179 per Lord Chief Commissioner Adam.
18 *Russell v HM Advocate* 1992 SLT 25.
19 *Pirie v Caledonian Railway Co* (1890) 17 R 1157 at 1162 per Lord Shand.
20 *Scottish Criminal Cases Review Commission, Petrs* 2002 SLT 1198.
21 *McWhir v Maxwell* (1836) 15 S 299.
22 *Hoekstra v HM Advocate (No 5)* 2002 SLT 599.
23 *McCadden v HM Advocate* 1986 SLT 138 applied in *Gray v HM Advocate* 1994 SLT 1237 and *Swankie v HM Advocate* 1999 SLT 1225. See also *McTeer v HM Advocate* 2003 SCCR 282; *Russell v HM Advocate* 1991 SCCR 791; *R v Mirza* [2004] 1 AC 1118 and *Gray v HM Advocate* 2005 SLT 159 and P Ferguson, "Jury Secrecy and Criminal Appeals" 2004 SLT (News) 43.

DELIVERING THE VERDICT

21.08   When the jury is ready to return its verdict it will communicate this to the clerk of court who will reconvene the parties and judge. He will then, in open court, ask the jury to indicate the juror whom it has nominated to deliver the verdict using words such as "Ladies and gentlemen, who speaks for you?" Once this juror has been identified the clerk will then usually ask the following series of questions, the form of which will depend on the individual circumstances of the case[24]. "Have you reached a verdict?" will be followed by "How do you answer the issue, yes or no?" If liability has already been admitted, then the latter question will still be asked although it will be qualified by "I formally put it to you that, as directed by His Lordship, you [unanimously] answer the question in the affirmative", and where the case has been withdrawn from the jury the question will be qualified by the same statement with the substitution of the last word by "negative". Where the question of liability has been left with the jury then the clerk will follow up the verdict by asking the jury "Is your verdict unanimous or by a majority?" and, if by a majority, he will ask "What is your majority?"[25] Care should be taken when the answer to this latter question is given since if there appears to be confusion in the minds of the members of the jury as to what, in fact, constitutes a simple majority then the matter should be clarified by the presiding judge. For example, where a jury returned a verdict on the stated basis of "six, four, two", a new trial was granted when the judge erroneously instructed this verdict to be entered as a majority one[26].

21.09   If the issue is answered in the affirmative then the clerk will pose a series of questions, depending on the form of the issue[27]. He will need to ascertain from the jury how much it has awarded under each head set out in the schedule to the issue, including any heads where it has made a nil award, and the form of questions may be either "How do you assess damages in respect of Head 1 / Head 2 / (etc)?" or, perhaps less confusingly, "How do you assess damages in relation to solatium to date / future solatium / past wage loss / (etc)?" Whether or not any particular head of damages was awarded unanimously or by a majority is not normally asked of the jury[28]. Any apportionment necessary for the purposes of interest or the recovery of benefits will be

---

24 Court of Session Act 1988, s 17(3), (4).
25 In a somewhat unusual departure from practice, in the case of *Warnock v Clark Contracts*, Lord Wheatley, 18 Nov 2004*, the chancellor was asked by what majority the jury had returned a verdict of contributory negligence and, after he indicated that he was not sure, each juror in turn spoke as to whether or not they had supported the finding.
26 *McGuire v Brown* 1963 SC 107.
27 Court of Session Act 1988, s 17(3), (4).
28 The editor's note to *Wells v Hay* 1999 Rep LR 44 records that in that case the presiding judge asked the jury to indicate whether the sums it awarded were unanimous or by a majority.

ascertained since the heads of damages will have been framed to take these into account. Where the total amount of damages or amount of damages under any particular head or heads has been agreed then the clerk will say "I formally put to you that as directed by His Lordship you assess total damages [inclusive of interest] at £ . . .", or "damages for past wage loss at £ . . ." (etc).

21.10 Where there is a counter-issue, the jury should be asked "How do you apportion liability?" and the proportion attributable to the pursuer, defender (or defenders or third parties, as appropriate) should be ascertained along with the information as to whether the counter-issue was answered unanimously or by a majority and, if by a majority, what that majority was. Where a simple question is posed in the counter-issue which requires a simple yes/no answer, such as "was the pursuer fit to return to work on [a specified date]" or the question relates to *veritas* in a defamation action, the jury will be asked to answer the question in the affirmative or negative.

21.11 If the question in the issue is answered in the negative then the clerk of court will go on to record a negative verdict.

RECORDING THE VERDICTS

21.12 As the verdicts are being delivered by the person appointed to speak for the jury, the clerk of court is required to record them in writing on the principals of the issue and counter-issue[29]. The record of the verdict will start with the formal preamble:

> "At Edinburgh on the [*date*] before the [Right] Honourable Lord X compeared the pursuer[s] and defender[s] by their respective counsel and solicitors, and a jury having been empanelled and sworn [or having affirmed] to try the issue[s] in the cause the jury say . . .".

Thereafter the record will depend upon the individual circumstances of the case and the following words may be appropriate:

> "upon their oath [or affirmation] that in respect of the matters proved before them unanimously [by a majority of . . . to . . .] answer the issue for the pursuer in the affirmative [negative] and assess the damages claimed under head 1 [solatium to date] at £ . . . . . (etc) making a total of £ . . . . .".

Where there is a counter-issue the record will go on to state:

> "and unanimously [by a majority of . . . . to . . . .] answer the counter-issue for the defender in the negative [affirmative and that the proportion of blame attributable to the pursuer is . . . . per cent and to the defender . . . . per cent]."

29 Court of Session Act 1988, s 17(3). The verdict is also mechanically recorded on tape: rule 37.5A(2)(f).

Where liability has not been left to the jury then the record will state:

> "the jury say upon their oath [and affirmation] that in respect of the matters proved before them, they say, as directed by the presiding judge [unanimously] answer the issue for the pursuer in the negative [affirmative and assess the amount of damages claimed under Head 1 . . . (etc)]."

Where the amount of damages agreed between the parties has been approved then the wording will be:

> "the jury say upon their oath [or affirmation] that in respect of the matters proved before them they unanimously [by a majority of . . . . . to . . . . .] answer the issue for the pursuer in the affirmative and as directed by the presiding judge assess total damages [inclusive of interest] at £ . . . ."

And where certain heads only of damages have been agreed then the record will be adapted accordingly.

21.13   Once the verdicts have been recorded, the clerk reads back the record to the jury and asks it if those are its verdicts. Unless any juror objects (and, in this context, a lack of objection has been held to be equivalent to acquiescence in the verdict recorded)[30] the verdicts are then dated and signed by the clerk of court[31]. If, however, the record of the verdicts does not state what the jury, on the direction of the presiding judge, had meant to say then, in those limited circumstances only, it may be corrected[32]. Once the verdicts have been engrossed then it is incompetent for the court to entertain any challenge of them by any of the jurors, or by any other person, on any ground[33], for example on the basis that the verdict was reached by the jurors casting lots[34], or that the votes were incorrectly counted[35] and, insofar as relating to the facts found by the jury, the verdicts are final[36].

21.14   The verdict ought to exhaust all of the issues and counter-issues[37] but where there are several issues and counter-issues and, by answering one or more of them, the answers to the others become otiose because the result is either decree as craved or absolvitor, then the jury does not require to answer the remaining questions in the issues or counter-issues because they have in effect become superseded[38]. For example, if there is a counter-issue on contributory negligence and the jury answers the question in the issue in the negative then there is no point in considering the question in the counter-

---

30 *Pirie v Caledonian Railway Co* (1890) 17 R 1157 at 1163.
31 Rule 37.9.
32 *Marianski v Cairns* (1854) 1 Macq 766 at 770 per Lord Chancellor Cranworth.
33 Maclaren, p 616 but also see **21.06** above.
34 *Stewart v Fraser* (1830) 5 Mur 166.
35 *Pirie v Caledonian Railway Co* (1890) 17 R 1157 at 1163.
36 Court of Session Act 1988, s 17(5).
37 Macfarlane, p 239; *Clark v Spence* (1825) 3 Mur 472.
38 *Campbell v Scottish Educational News Co* (1906) 8 F 691.

issue. However, a verdict which is negative of the pursuer's case but not affirmative of the defender's will still result in the defender being assoilzied[39].

21.15 Should the jury return a verdict in ambiguous terms then the presiding judge may, when the verdict is being delivered, intervene and direct the jury as to how to express its finding in a clear and unambiguous form[40]. Where a jury is at a loss merely as to the forms and terms of its verdict, the judge may direct it as to the proper form of the verdict[41]. However, if a verdict is truly ambiguous then the preferable practice is to hear counsel before deciding whether to record that verdict as it stands, in which case the significance of the verdict will have to be decided at the stage of applying the verdict, or (a) to leave it to be elucidated by means of questioning by the presiding judge[42], or (b) to send the jury back to reconsider its verdict with directions to make a specific finding one way or the other[43]. The judge can direct the jury to return a verdict in accordance with the facts which it has found proved, for example where the issue was as to whether or not the defender had slandered the pursuer on or about 12 March and the jury found that the slander had been uttered in February, the jury was directed by the presiding judge to enter a verdict for the defender[44].

DISCHARGE OF JURY

21.16 Once the jury has returned its verdict, it is discharged by the presiding judge who will invariably thank the members of the jury for undertaking their duty as jurors. The verdict does not, however, take effect until it is applied. A motion for certification of expert witnesses may, if desired, be made at this stage or reserved until the motion for applying the verdict is heard.

PAYMENT OF JURORS

21.17 Jurors in a civil trial were formerly paid ten shillings per day and the unsuccessful party had to pay them individually before they left the jury box having returned a verdict[45]. Now any person who attends for jury service, whether or not he has been empanelled, is entitled to receive payment at the prescribed rates for travelling and subsistence expenses and also for financial

39 *Melrose v Hastie* (1854) 17 D (HL) 4.
40 Macfarlane, p 239; *Robertson v Barclay* (1828) 4 Mur 517; *Robertson v William Hamilton (Motors) Ltd* 1923 SC 838.
41 Macfarlane, p 239; *Harley v Lindsays* (1818) 1 Mur 301.
42 *McBurnie v Central SMT Co* 1939 SC 66 at 71.
43 *Morgan v Morris* (1858) 20 D (HL) 18.
44 *Smith v Paton* 1913 SC 1203.
45 Jury Trials (Scotland) Act 1815, s 30 as amended.

loss sustained as a consequence of his attendance, including any loss of income or benefits[46]. Payments are made by the cashier at the court and a claim form is issued as part of the citation to attend for jury service[47]. The clerk of court will normally give discharged jurors appropriate instructions in relation to such claims.

46 Juries Act 1949, ss 24 and 25 as amended by Law Reform (Miscellaneous Provisions) (Scotland) Act 1980, Schs 2 and 3; see also Jurors Allowances (Scotland) Regulations 1977 (SI 1977/445).
47 Form 37.2-B.

Chapter 22

Applying the verdict

NECESSITY FOR APPLYING VERDICT

22.01 Although the verdict of the jury is final and conclusive as regards the matters in dispute between the parties, it is in itself only a finding in fact and in order to give any effect to it, it is necessary to make a formal application to the court to have the verdict applied so that decree can be pronounced and an appropriate interlocutor can be framed[1].

MOTION TO APPLY VERDICT

22.02 After the expiry of seven days after the date upon which the verdict was written upon the issue and signed (i.e. the date upon which the verdict was given) any party to the cause may apply by motion to apply the verdict, grant decree in accordance with it and make any award in relation to expenses[2]. Such motions normally require the appearance of counsel and are, in the first instance, heard before the Lord Ordinary who presided at the trial[3].

22.03 Since all matters which would normally be dealt with at the conclusion of a proof are dealt with at the stage when the motion is heard, particular care should be taken if, in a personal injuries action, the pursuer has received any state benefits which are deemed to be repayable since an appropriate schedule of damages will have to be prepared and lodged in process prior to the hearing of the motion[4]. If the verdict results in an award of damages being made to a child under the age of 16 years, parties should give some thought as to how such an award might be administered on the child's behalf since the court has the power on applying the verdict to make such

1 *Flensburg Steam Shipping Co v Seligmann* (1871) 9 M 1011 at 1014.
2 Rule 37.10; if appropriate both parties may apply to have the verdict applied: *Kerr v Clark & Co* (1868) 7 M 51.
3 Maxwell, p 345, Maclaren *Expenses*, p 4.
4 Social Security (Recovery of Benefits) Act 1997; Court of Session Practice Note No 3 of 1997.

order in relation to the payment and management of the sum for the benefit of the child as it thinks fit[5].

Where verdict challenged

22.04 If a party against whom the verdict was granted applies for review of the decision by the Inner House, then the application of the verdict is postponed or, if granted, superseded, and where a motion for a new trial has already been enrolled, a motion to apply the verdict will not be competent until the matter of the new trial has finally been disposed of. Should the parties have decided to compromise the action (e.g. if the award of the jury is regarded by both parties as being excessive and they have agreed the matter of quantum of damages and expenses extra-judicially), then the party in whose favour the verdict was granted will not move to have the verdict applied and the action can then be disposed of at a later stage by way of a motion interposing authority to a joint minute.

Defective, bad or uncertain verdicts

22.05 When applying the verdict, the court has a limited power to correct an error in the entering of a verdict[6] but where the verdict has been correctly recorded but is apparently ambiguous or self-contradictory and cannot be applied for by either party then it must be set aside and a new trial granted[7]. The verdict must meet the issue[8], but any explanation[9], surplus words[10] or riders[11], insofar as they are not inconsistent with the verdict, can be ignored and the verdict applied. There is no power to amend the verdict or to substitute a new verdict for the one given by the jury, even when that verdict is uncertain[12] or "manifestly bad" for not being based upon the evidence[13], and the only remedy in these cases is for the aggrieved party to apply for a new trial. If, when attempting to apply the verdict, the court considers that it is ambiguous, imperfect or inconsistent and thus incapable of application, then it may *ex proprio motu* set the verdict aside and order a new trial[14]. The verdict

---

5 Children (Scotland) Act 1995, s 13.
6 Macfarlane, p 239; *Kirk v Guthrie* (1817) 1 Mur 279; *Marianski v Cairns* (1854) 1 Macq 766 at 770 per Cranworth LC. A recent English example of this is found in *Igwemna v Chief Constable of Greater Manchester Police* [2001] 4 All ER 751.
7 *Florence v Mann* (1890) 18 R 247.
8 Maclaren, p 617; *Broomfield v Greig* (1868) 6 M 992; *Smith v Paton* 1913 SC 1203.
9 *Balfour v Kerr* (1857) 19 D 789.
10 *Kane v Stephen & Sons* (1900) 2 F 739.
11 *Burns v Steel Co of Scotland* (1893) 21 R 39.
12 *Morgan v Morris* (1858) 20 D (HL) 18.
13 *Simpson v Glasgow Corporation* 1916 SC 345.
14 Adam, p 294; Macfarlane p 252.

of the jury has been described as "a single part" and thus it cannot be applied in part only so that where a jury returned a verdict in an action with two defenders against the first defenders only and the first defenders then applied for a new trial, it was held that the second defenders could not seek to have the original verdict applied *quoad* themselves only[15].

INTEREST

Time to apply for

22.06   The proper time to ask for interest on the sums awarded by the jury is at the stage of the application to apply the verdict and it is incompetent to ask for interest once the verdict has been applied[16].

General principles

22.07   Where the court applies the verdict, it has the power to make an award of interest on all of the sums awarded in accordance with the usual principles and having regard to the statutory provisions relating to interest[17]. Thus in applying the verdict after a jury trial there is a discretionary power to award interest, where appropriate[18], from the date of the event giving rise to the action until the date of citation[19] and from the date of citation until decree[20], the latter being the date upon which the verdict is applied rather than the date upon which the jury returned its verdict. At common law interest runs at the judicial rate from the date of decree (i.e. the date upon which the verdict was applied) until payment[21].

22.08   The calculation of interest in respect of solatium and patrimonial loss should prove relatively straightforward since the modern practice is to draft issues in such a way as to differentiate, where appropriate, between the past and future elements of all claims[22], but even where this has not been done, either in relation to one or all of the heads of claim, the court may still use its discretion to award interest[23]. Recoverable state benefits are now

---

15 *Richmond v Glasgow Corporation* 1950 SLT 301.
16 *Handren v Scottish Construction Co* 1967 SLT (Notes) 21.
17 See generally McEwan & Paton, ch 3.
18 *Macrae v Reed & Mallik* 1961 SC 68.
19 Interest on Damages (Scotland) Act 1971, s 1.
20 Interest on Damages (Scotland) Act 1958, s 1 as amended by the 1971 Act.
21 *Macrae v Reed & Mallik* 1961 SC 68.
22 *MacDonald v Glasgow Corporation* 1973 SLT 107.
23 *Ross v British Railways Board* 1972 SLT 174, where the court achieved "rough justice" by applying various rates of interest to a jury award.

no longer deducted from any past loss elements when calculating interest on those elements[24].

Interest following upon unsuccessful motion for new trial

22.09 Where the verdict is applied following upon an unsuccessful motion for a new trial interest is normally added to the award of the jury at the full judicial rate from the date upon which the verdict would have been applied but for the making of the motion for the new trial, irrespective of at whose instance the motion for a new trial was made, and it has been held that it is only in exceptional circumstances that a pursuer should suffer a lower rate of interest on his award as a result of the passage of time "arising out of the exercise of what was an undoubted right to seek a new trial"[25]. The former practice, whereby interest was only granted following upon an unsuccessful motion for a new trial if that motion could be said to be "groundless and absurd"[26] or abandoned[27], is no longer followed, its rationale having gone with the passing of the Interest on Damages (Scotland) Act 1971.

RECOVERABLE BENEFITS

22.10 Where decree is to be pronounced in terms of the verdict of the jury and there are recoverable state benefits, the court will be required to specify what part of the patrimonial loss is attributable to the statutory "relevant period" and which elements thereof are attributable to "care" and "loss of mobility"[28]. However, in practice few problems will be encountered at this stage since the schedule of damages appended to the issue will already have identified the separate items required and the jury will have identified the sums it has awarded when it gives its verdict in terms of that schedule.

EXPENSES

When to apply

22.11 Any award of expenses, insofar as not already dealt with prior to the verdict being applied, must be dealt with at the time when the motion to apply the verdict is being made[29], and any incidental motions relating to

---

24 *Wisely v John Fulton (Plumbers) Ltd* 2000 SC (HL) 95.
25 *Tait v Campbell* 2004 SLT 187 at 190K.
26 *Flensburg Steam Shipping Co v Seligmann* (1871) 9 M 1011.
27 *Killah v Aberdeen Milk Marketing Board* 1961 SLT 232.
28 Social Security (Recovery of Benefits) Act 1997, s 15(2) and Sch 2; *Mitchell v Laing* 1998 SC 342.
29 Rule 37.10.

expenses such as motions for the certification of expert witnesses (if not already made at the trial diet), motions for an additional fee and motions for any modification of expenses including those relating to parties in receipt of legal aid should all be made at the same time[30]. A motion for the allowance of an additional fee should be made at this stage but it is not incompetent to make a motion once the verdict has been applied, provided that this is done prior to taxation[31].

General principles

22.12   The normal rule that expenses follow success subject to the discretion of the court, modification and taxation applies to jury trials in much the same way as it does to proofs. The principle was summed up by Lord Meadowbank in the leading case of *Heriot v Thomson*[32] as one of "when a party gains his cause, he ought to get expenses as a matter of course, unless the losing party can show good reason for withholding them and the onus lies on him to show cause why he should not be found liable in them". The court, however, always has a discretion in jury trials, as in all other cases, to depart from this general rule should circumstances dictate otherwise[33]. Where there has been mixed or divided success

> "the question always is, whether the party asking for the expenses comes to the court with a fair and proper case and has substantially succeeded in the point at issue. Where that question can be answered in the affirmative, it is of little consequence, with reference to the matter of expenses, that he has not succeeded to the full extent of his claims."[34]

Success in this context is defined as "substantial success" so that if the pursuer is awarded a substantial sum by way of solatium but fails in establishing all of his patrimonial loss claims, or where he is found to be guilty of contributory negligence but nevertheless receives a substantial award of damages[35], then he will usually be entitled to recover the whole of his expenses. Where the pursuer has been successful at a second trial and expenses are awarded to him "so far as not already dealt with" these expenses will not include items used at the first trial (such as the expenses of copying documents) even though they were also used at the second trial[36].

---

30 These all being matters "in relation to expenses" in terms of rule 37.10.
31 Rule 42.14; *UCB Bank plc v Dundas & Wilson CS* 1991 SLT 90.
32 (1833) 12 S 145.
33 *Shepherd v Elliot* (1896) 23 R 695; cf *Campbell v Scottish Educational News Co* (1905) 13 SLT 925.
34 Macfarlane, p 287.
35 As in *Howitt v Alexander & Son* 1948 SC 154.
36 *Maltman v Tarmac Civil Engineering Ltd* 1967 SC 177.

Multiple pursuers or defenders

22.13 Where there are separate pursuers (irrespective of whether they are separately represented or not) and the jury awards damages to only one of them, then the successful pursuer will still be entitled to his expenses even if the other pursuers will not[37]. Where the jury returns a verdict against only one of several defenders then those found not liable will be entitled to seek their expenses either against the pursuer or, where appropriate, the other defenders. If the jury apportions liability between two or more defenders then the apportionment of the expenses *inter se* will be a matter for the discretion of the court and will not necessarily be awarded on the same basis as the jury has apportioned liability[38].

Modification

22.14 Where the Lord Ordinary does make an award of expenses, he has the power to direct that those expenses shall be subject to such modification as the court thinks fit[39]. Thus, modification of expenses is very much a matter for the presiding judge to consider in the light of the individual circumstances of each case and the fact that the pursuer received only a small amount of damages from the jury will not, *per se*, affect his entitlement to the full expenses of the action. This proposition is particularly true in actions of defamation or those involving the deprivation of liberty[40].

22.15 Examples of where the power of modification has been exercised after a jury trial include (a) a modification to three-quarters of the total where there was a minimal award of damages coupled with a finding of contributory negligence to the extent of 90 per cent[41], (b) a modification to one-half of the total where the defender was assoilzied in a defamation action but the Lord Ordinary held that he had provoked the action by persistently provoking the pursuer[42], and (c) a similar modification where the sum awarded as damages was substantially less than the expenses incurred and it was said that that was always likely to have been the case[43]. It has been held that the wish to have a jury trial merely to test the level of damages awarded by the courts is not, in itself, an adequate justification for selecting the Court of Session as a tribunal and, accordingly, when a low sum was awarded modification was made to

---

37 *McPhail v Caledonian Railway Co* (1903) 5 F 306.
38 *Shaw v Russell & Anor*, Lord Carloway, 2004 GWD 21-460.
39 Rule 42.5(1).
40 Macfarlane, p 287 and the cases cited therein.
41 *Bradie v National Coal Board* 1951 SC 576.
42 *Shepherd v Elliot* (1896) 22 R 695.
43 *Woods v British Steel Corporation* 1974 SLT (Notes) 24.

expenses on the sheriff court ordinary scale with sanction for counsel[44], although the position may now be different if the cause was a personal injuries action raised under the Chapter 43 procedure[45]. Where a pursuer received from a jury a sum which, had she raised the action in the sheriff court would have resulted in an award of expenses on the summary scale, an award of Court of Session expenses modified to one-third was made[46], and in a recent case where a pursuer was awarded damages of £1,000 by a jury, but with a finding of 80 per cent contributory negligence, the court modified the expenses to those of the sheriff court ordinary scale with no sanction for counsel[47].

22.16 Modification has been refused where the jury awarded one-third of the sum claimed subject to a finding of contributory negligence of 70 per cent; here the Lord Ordinary awarded the pursuer his expenses in full and commented on the lack of a tender, stating that the pursuer "had been forced to vindicate his rights"[48]. In a recent example a pursuer was awarded £3,830 subject to a finding of contributory negligence of 60 per cent, and thus received in her hand a sum slightly less than the privative jurisdiction limit of the sheriff court; here the judge, apparently influenced by the fact that all involved in the case thought that the award of the jury was on the low side and the contributory negligence finding on the high, refused the defender's motion for modification[49].

22.17 In addition to the above powers of modification, the court has the normal powers to modify the liability of an unsuccessful legally-aided party when the successful party so moves[50].

Tenders and offers

22.18 Provided that a tender is made in the correct form and subsequently rejected by the pursuer, then if the jury awards less than the sum tendered he will be liable to pay the whole expenses of the trial from the date of the tender[51] and the court may supercede extract of the decree until such expenses have been paid[52]. A tender must, to be in the correct form,

---

44 *Smillie v Lanarkshire Health Board* 1996 Rep LR 100; cf *Elliot v Abela* 1996 Rep LR 99.
45 *Wilson v Glasgow City Council* 2004 SLT 1189; *Benson v Edinburgh City Council* 2004 SLT 1227.
46 *McArthur v AEI Telecommunications Ltd* 1974 SLT (Notes) 39.
47 *Manton v Commissioners for Northern Lights*, Lord Carloway, 6 Feb 2003*.
48 *Chalmers v Atlas Steel Foundry & Engineering Ltd* 1964 SLT (Notes) 98; the jury awarded £250 which allowing for inflation the 2004 value is about £970.
49 *Mitchell v North Glasgow University Hospitals NHS Trust* reported in R Milligan, "Jury Trial Awards: A case study" (2002) 43 Rep L Bul 2.
50 Legal Aid (Scotland) Act 1986, s 18(2); see e.g. *McNeish v Advocate General for Scotland* Temporary Judge J G Reid QC, 2004 GWD 26-560.
51 *Heriot v Thomson* (1833) 12 S 145; *Ferguson v MacLennon Salmon Co* 1999 SLT 428.
52 *Fry v North Eastern Railway Co* (1882) 10 R 290.

include expenses[53] but unless the level of expenses is expressly referred to in the tender then it must be assumed that the expenses offered are the appropriate level of expenses in the exercise of the court's discretion and it is open for a defender to seek modification[54].

22.19   If the total amount of damages beats a tender only by reason of interest which has accrued since the date upon which it was lodged being added to the sum awarded by the jury, then the court may treat the tender as not having been beaten and award to the defender the expenses from the date of tender[55]. The jury is, of course, unaware of the existence of any tender or offer to settle and no reference to it or any offer may be made during the course of the trial.

22.20   In determining the effective date of the tender, the pursuer is always allowed a reasonable time in which he can consider it and take the advice of counsel, and it has been said that "defenders who delay making tenders until a late date do not deserve much sympathy, and are not to be allowed to hustle pursuers into what may be hurried and hasty decisions"[56]. This is particularly true where a pursuer's future depends to a great extent on the amount of damages which he might receive[57]. Thus, where tenders are received a few days prior to the trial diet[58] or after the commencement of the evidence[59], defenders may well find that they come too late to avoid a substantial part of the expenses of the trial.

22.21   A tender remains operative until it is expressly withdrawn or becomes no longer operative due to a material change of circumstances[60] and in a jury action a tender if still operative remains open for acceptance until the moment that the jury returns its verdict and gives its assessment of damages, at which point the tender is rendered inoperative[61] and cannot be accepted subsequently, even though the verdict may not yet have been applied[62]. It is perfectly competent in a jury action to have a series of tenders made on different dates which are all still operative and it has been said that, depending on the circumstances, it might be beneficial to a pursuer to accept a lower tender even though a larger one might seem *prima facie* attractive[63].

---

53 *McKenzie v H D Fraser & Sons* 1990 SLT 629; cf *Martin v Had-Fab Ltd* 2004 SLT 1192.
54 *Gillespie v Fitzpatrick* 2003 Rep LR 135.
55 Morrison, para 36.11(5).
56 *Wood v Miller* 1960 SC 86 at 98 per Lord Justice-Clerk Thomson.
57 Lord Carloway in *Pagan v Miller Group Ltd* 2002 SC 281.
58 *Wood v Miller* at 98.
59 *Pagan v Miller Group Ltd* 2002 SC 281.
60 *Macrae v Edinburgh Street Tramways Co* (1885) 13 R 265; *Bright v Low* 1940 SC 280.
61 *Tait v Campbell* 2004 SLT 187.
62 An example where the pursuer tried to do this and was held to be too late was *Buchanan v Mason*, Lord Bonomy, 11 March 2001★.
63 *Tait v Campbell* 2004 SLT 187 at 190E per Lady Paton.

22.22   There are no special peculiarities in relation to jury trials in respect of separate tenders where there is a plurality of parties or where Williamson or Houston tenders are concerned[64]. Where an action for the death of a relative is brought by several family members as pursuers and separate tenders are made to each of them, then those who receive a jury award in excess of their individual tender will be entitled to their full expenses subject to such modification as might be due to their association with the other pursuers, but any family member who fails to beat the tender will be liable to the defenders in expenses after the date of the tender so far as they were due directly to his or her presence in the case[65].

Offers

22.23   Informal offers made in writing by a defender to a pursuer which state that they will be founded upon in any question of expenses following a trial may be brought to the attention of the court at the time at which the verdict is to be applied and, although such offers will usually be considered and may be taken into account, there is no guarantee that the court will treat them in the same way as it would a tender.

Pursuer's tenders

22.24   Even though there is currently no longer any provision for pursuer's tenders in the Rules of Court, there would not appear to be any reason why they cannot still be used in the context of jury trials.

Certification of expert witnesses

22.25   Any party who wishes to have the additional remuneration of an expert witness who attended at the trial paid must have that witness certified as a skilled person who made investigations which qualified him or her to give evidence at the trial[66], and the Auditor has no power to allow any such re-

---

64 *Shaw v Russell & Anor*, Lord Carloway, 29 June 2004; see also C N McEachran, "The Gentle Art of Tendering" 1969 SLT (News) 53.

65 *Peggie v Keddie* 1932 SC 721 applied in *Warnock v Clarke Contracts*, Lord Wheatley, 13 Oct 2005* where the widow beat the tender but the children failed to do so even though the total of all the sums awarded was £50,000 in excess of the total sums tendered – here the Lord Ordinary found the children liable to the defender in the expenses after the date of tender but only insofar as they could be shown to be additional expenses directly and solely referable to the continuation of the children in the action after the date of the tender; the matter was determined to the Auditor to ascertain what those additional expenses might be.

66 Rule 42.13(2).

muneration for a skilled witness not so certified[67]. Formerly such a motion had to be made at the time that the verdict was applied, but now the motion may be made at any time up to the diet of taxation[68]. The general principle to be applied is that the pursuer is entitled to present his or her case in the most persuasive manner possible[69] but the matter of whether or not it was reasonable to have such an expert instructed is at the discretion of the presiding judge. The appropriate time to test whether or not the instruction of such a witness was necessary is at the time of his or her instruction and does not depend on whether or not the jury awarded the pursuer only a modest sum[70].

---

67 *Clark v Laddaws Ltd* 1994 SLT 792.
68 Rule 42.13(3).
69 *Magee v Glasgow City Council* 2003 GWD 13-423.
70 *Allison v Orr* 2004 SC 453.

Chapter 23

Appeals against interlocutors

23.01 In civil jury trial procedure there are several ways in which decisions taken before, at and after the diet can be challenged and this chapter deals with the first of these matters, i.e. the challenge of interlocutors which were pronounced by a Lord Ordinary prior to the hearing of the action by the jury.

INTERLOCUTORS WHICH MAY BE RECLAIMED

23.02 In the procedure prior to trial, there will be a number of separate interlocutors pronounced by the Lord Ordinary or Clerk of Session from the time that the summons was signetted up to the time when the jury was empanelled. In the majority of instances, these interlocutors are neither objectionable to any of the parties nor contentious, but where circumstances arise where either or both of the parties does not accept the ruling of the court on an interlocutory matter they may wish to invoke the appeal procedures contained in the Rules of Court and reclaim a particular decision. This chapter does not deal with the great number of motions which can be made to the Inner House in respect of personal injury actions, defamation actions or any other of the enumerated causes and which could arise irrespective of whether or not the action was to be heard by a jury or by way of proof but concentrates on the special motions which might be heard in relation to civil jury trials alone[1].

ALLOWANCE OR REFUSAL OF ISSUES

23.03 The interlocutor which allows or refuses issues, irrespective of whether pronounced after a procedure roll or motion roll hearing, can be reclaimed, without leave, within 14 days after the date upon which the interlocutor was pronounced[2] except for interlocutors which both refuse issues and also dispose of the whole merits of the cause (i.e. by dismissing the action) in which case

---

1 The general power to reclaim against Outer House interlocutors is contained in the Court of Session Act 1988. s 28 and Chapter 38 of the Rules and the reader is referred to Morison for a detailed treatment of such motions.
2 Rule 38.3(4)(b).

21 reclaiming days are allowed[3]. The party seeking to review the interlocutor allowing or refusing issues must mark a reclaiming motion in the prescribed form[4] before the expiry of the reclaiming days[5], although where due to mistake or inadvertence the motion is marked late then the court may still be prepared to hear the motion[6]. With all motions a copy of the reclaiming print should be lodged[7] and thereafter the party seeking to reclaim must seek an early disposal of the motion before the Inner House[8]. The motion itself will normally be heard on the summar roll.

23.04   The decision of the Lord Ordinary as to whether or not issues should be allowed is a discretionary one[9] but "if it appears that, although moved to exercise it, he has not done so, the Inner House must [be] slow to interfere and rarely (if ever) does so, except on some general ground which would apply to a class of similar cases"[10]. This does not, however, give a judge at first instance an unlimited power to find special cause.

> "The Lord Ordinary must . . . correctly identify the special cause and, in particular, he must find it established by reference to the circumstances of the case he is considering and not to some consideration of general character. There must be facts in the case that can reasonably bring it into the region of special cause. There must, in other words, be material before the Lord Ordinary to justify his determination that special cause has been established."[11]

23.05   The Lord Ordinary cannot be asked to review his own interlocutor granting or refusing issues so that where the pursuer's motion for the allowance of issues at a procedure roll diet at which the defenders had not appeared was granted, and where it subsequently transpired that the defenders had had a reasonable excuse for their non-appearance and moved to restore the case to the procedure roll and effectively recall the interlocutor allowing a jury trial, it was held that as there was no clerical or other error of expression in the interlocutor which would have permitted it to be corrected or altered[12] and the judge was not being asked to review the substance of his decision, the order for the allowance of issues had to stand[13].

23.06   The effect of marking a reclaiming motion is that the action is effec-

---

3 Rule 38.3(2), (4).
4 Form 38.6.
5 Rule 38.6(1).
6 Rule 38.7.
7 Rule 38.6, 38.18.
8 Rule 38.3(4)(b), 38.7A, 38.13.
9 *Graham v Associated Electrical Industries Ltd* 1968 SLT 81; *Robertson v Smith* 2000 SC 591 and see also **6.03** above.
10 *Walker v Pitlochry Motor Co* 1930 SC 565.
11 *Morris v Fife Council*, Extra Div, 2004 SLT 1139; see also *Graham v Paterson & Sons* 1938 SC 119 and *McKeown v Sir William Arrol & Co* 1974 SC 97.
12 Rule 4.15(6).
13 *Black v Somerfield Stores Ltd* 1998 SLT 1315.

tively brought to a halt pending the review of the interlocutor by the Inner House and the Lord Ordinary is thereby precluded from considering the terms of any issues or counter-issues lodged until the Inner House has considered whether the allowance or refusal of issues will be upheld.

ADJUSTING OF ISSUES

23.07 An interlocutor adjusting the issues in a jury trial can be reclaimed against, without leave, within 14 days of being pronounced[14] and thereby a party who desires to vary, add or substitute an issue or counter-issue in a way which was not allowed by the Lord Ordinary at the stage of the approval of the issues and counter-issues can bring the matter before the Inner House. The normal reclaiming procedure is followed with the addition that the party who seeks to reclaim must, on enrolling the motion to reclaim, lodge in process the issue or counter-issue proposed by him, showing the amendment to the issues, as adjusted, sought to be made and send a copy of that issue or counter-issue to every other party[15]. An early disposal of the reclaiming motion before the Inner House must be sought[16].

23.08 The adjustment of issues by the Lord Ordinary is at his discretion[17] and the same principles will apply in relation to review by the Inner House as in the case of the allowance or refusal of issues.

APPLICATION OF THE VERDICT

23.09 The interlocutor applying the verdict of the jury may be reclaimed against, for example in respect of the expenses or interest, although reclaiming against discretionary matters such as these is generally discouraged[18] and the appellant must clearly demonstrate the way in which the presiding judge has wrongly applied the verdict. The discretion in relation to interest "must be exercised on a selective and discriminating basis and the exercise of that discretion after a jury trial is open to review on the question of whether or not the circumstances of the case warranted the course taken"[19]. The court will only reconsider matters such as whether or not a motion to certify skilled witnesses was wrongly granted or refused *de novo* when it can be shown that, for instance, irrelevant matters were taken into account by the presiding judge[20].

14 Rule 38.3(4)(d).
15 Rule 38.12.
16 Rule 38.3(4)(d), 38.7A, 38.13.
17 *Taylor v National Coal Board* 1953 SC 349 at 350.
18 Maxwell, p 546.
19 *Macrae v Reid & Mallik Ltd* 1961 SC 68 at 72.
20 E.g. *Allison v Orr* 2004 SC 453.

Chapter 24

Review of the verdict

24.01   This chapter deals with the substantive grounds upon which a party can seek to challenge the verdict of the jury while the following chapter deals with procedural matters connected with the bringing of a motion for a new trial.

GROUNDS OF REVIEW

24.02   Any party who is dissatisfied with the verdict of the jury in a civil action may apply to the Inner House to have that verdict set aside and to have a new trial granted on one or more of the following statutory grounds:

(a)   a misdirection by the presiding judge;
(b)   the undue admission or rejection of evidence at the trial;
(c)   that the verdict is contrary to the evidence led at the trial;
(d)   that the jury awarded an excess or inadequacy of damages;
(e)   *res noviter veniens ad notitiam*

or on such other ground as is essential to the justice of the cause[1].

24.03   Each of these grounds is sufficient, in itself, to justify the making of a motion for a new trial but it is at least implied by the wording of the last ground that any of the other grounds will succeed only if it too is essential to the justice of the cause[2]. As a general principle, the grant or refusal of a new trial must always depend on the particular and peculiar circumstances of the

---

1 Court of Session Act 1988, s 29(1). In England and Wales, under the Civil Procedure Rules, r 52.11(3), an appeal will only be allowed where the jury's decision is "wrong" or "unjust because of a serious procedural or other irregularity in the proceedings". In *Hamilton v Al Fayed (No 4)* [2001] EMLR 15, Lord Phillips MR commented that "a new trial should be ordered where the interests of justice so demand. Where a party has behaved fraudulently or has been guilty of procedural impropriety or some other irregularity has affected the fairness of the trial, the vital question to be asked is whether there is a real danger that has influenced the outcome. If there is, a retrial should normally be ordered."
2 *Maltman v Tarmac Civil Engineering Ltd* 1967 SC 177 at 183 per Lord Guthrie, approved by Second Division in *Tate v Fischer* 1998 SLT 1419.

individual case being considered by the court[3]. However, it should be noted that where there are two or more defenders in an action, it is not competent to seek to set aside the verdict against one of them only and leave the verdict standing against the other for if the challenge to the verdict is successful on any one of the statutory grounds then a new trial will be ordered against all of the defenders[4]. Where there are interrelated and family claims it is incompetent to grant a new trial in respect of one of those claims only – the court should either grant a new trial in respect of all of the claims or none of them[5]. Each of the grounds of review is now examined in detail.

MISDIRECTION BY THE PRESIDING JUDGE

24.04   There is a presumption that everything at the original trial was rightly done and rightly laid down by the presiding judge and, unless exception was taken to something being misstated or omitted, this presumption will be applied when a subsequent challenge is made to any direction given or omitted by the judge at the trial[6]. Thus an application for a new trial on the basis of a misdirection cannot be made unless the correct procedure at the trial in relation to exceptions to the judge's charge was complied with, i.e. the application is incompetent unless a note of exceptions was tendered at the proper time[7]. In order to consider the matter the courts will also usually require an extended transcript of the whole of the judge's charge.

24.05   In considering the matter of misdirection, it is not necessary to show that the jury was actually misled by the direction complained of – indeed given the fact that the deliberations of the jury are confidential, that would be a virtually impossible matter to prove – and all that is required is to show that the jury might have been misled because the direction was calculated or likely to mislead[8].

24.06   Examples of misdirection held sufficient to merit a new trial include (a) a situation where the direction given to the jury that it should find for the defenders if satisfied that the deceased "ought not to have been in the mash-house" was ambiguous in that it was unclear as to whether this meant that it was the fault of the deceased for being in the mash-house or of the defenders

3 *Maltman v Tarmac Civil Engineering Ltd* at 184.
4 *Simpson v Glasgow Corporation* 1916 SC 345.
5 *Campbell v West of Scotland Shipbreaking Co* 1953 SC 173; *Leadbetter v National Coal Board* 1952 SC 19.
6 Maclaren, p 362; *Robertson v Fleming* (1861) 23 D (HL) 8; *Addie v Western Bank* (1865) 3 M 899; *Hogg v Campbell* (1865) 3 M 1018; *McKibben v Glasgow Corporation* 1920 SC 590.
7 Rule 39.1(3)(a); *Mitchell v McHarg & Son* 1923 SC 657.
8 *Cleland v Weir* (1847) 6 Bell's App 70 at 76 per Lord Cottenham LC.

directly or vicariously for having allowed her to go there in the first place[9], (b) where a direction was given that was contrary to the case pled in that the judge directed that if an item of safety equipment had been provided by employers the jury could consider whether it was suitable or not when the record was that no such equipment had ever been provided[10], and (c) where the judge directed that the case should be withdrawn from the jury in that the evidence established that an accident had occurred through the sole fault of the pursuer when, in fact, the evidence did not unequivocally show that[11].

24.07 Motions for a new trial on the basis of misdirection have been refused where the trial judge has refused to give a direction which would not have been sound in law and thus was not a misdirection. An example of this occurred in a case involving the collision between a motor-cycle and a van where the presiding judge refused to direct the jury that if it was satisfied that the collision occurred in the manner claimed by the defenders then no blame could attach to them and the House of Lords held that such a direction would have been wrong and that the judge was correct in not so directing the jury[12].

UNDUE ADMISSION OF EVIDENCE

24.08 Where the ground for a new trial is that evidence should not have been admitted by the presiding judge at the trial but was allowed, then the motion will be competent only if objection was taken during the trial at the time when the evidence objected to was admitted and the objection was recorded in the notes of evidence under the direction of the presiding judge[13].

24.09 If the court is of the opinion that the exclusion of the evidence objected to could not have led to a verdict different from that actually returned by the jury, then the motion for a new trial must fail[14]. The onus of showing that evidence which was adduced but should have been excluded was, in fact, immaterial and would not have affected the verdict lies upon the party who adduced that evidence[15] and it may prove difficult to persuade the court that the exclusion of such evidence could have led to a different verdict than that returned by the jury. A new trial may be allowed where the evidence

9 *Fraser v Younger & Sons* (1867) 5 M 861.
10 *Smith v The Anchor Line* 1961 SLT (Notes) 54; see also *Burns v Dixon's Iron Works* 1961 SC 102.
11 *Mulligan v Caird (Dundee) Ltd* 1973 SLT 72.
12 *Douglas v Cunningham* 1964 SC (HL) 112 reversing the Inner House at 1963 SC 564.
13 Rule 39.1(3)(b).
14 Court of Session Act 1988, s 30(1).
15 *Livingstone v Strachan, Crerar & Jones* 1923 SC 794.

admitted was incompetent[16] and where it was objectionable on the ground of surprise on the basis that the evidence complained of was foreshadowed neither in the pleadings nor in cross-examination[17].

UNDUE REJECTION OF EVIDENCE

24.10   As in the case of undue admission of evidence, a motion for a new trial based upon the undue rejection of evidence is competent only where objection thereto was taken at the trial and was recorded in the notes of evidence[18]. In relation to parole evidence, the party seeking a new trial must show not only that the evidence was wrongly rejected but also that its admission might have led the jury to a different verdict. If it can be shown that, whatever the evidence, no reasonable jury would have returned a verdict for the party taking objection, the application will fail[19]. Where the motion is made on the ground of the undue rejection of documentary evidence and it appears to the court from the documents themselves that these ought not to have affected the verdict which the jury has arrived at, a new trial may be refused[20]. Even where there are several separate issues before the jury and the evidence improperly rejected relates only to certain of those issues, the court will usually order a new trial on all of the issues rather than the one confined to only those issues or heads affected by the rejected evidence[21].

VERDICT CONTRARY TO THE EVIDENCE

24.11   Subject to the power of the court to order a new trial, the verdict of the jury is final so far as relating to the facts found by it[22] and it is not the function of the Inner House to review the verdict. In an early case it was said that "the verdict must not only be against the evidence, but in the face of it"[23], and the test to be applied when considering a motion under this head is now as follows:

> "It is the province of the jury to determine the issue of fact, and it is not the function of the court to review their verdict or to order a new trial, merely because, on consideration of the evidence, the court disagrees with their findings. But it is the duty of the court to apply their minds to the evidence before

16 *Gilmour v Hansen* 1920 SC 598 (where refused); cf *Livingstone v Strachan, Crerar & Jones* 1923 SC 794 (where allowed).
17 *Christie's Curator ad litem v Kirkwood* 1996 SLT 1299.
18 Rule 39.1(3)(b); all objections if taken during the trial will now be automatically recorded.
19 *Greig v Sir William Arrol & Co Ltd* 1965 SLT 242.
20 Court of Session Act 1988, s 30(2).
21 *Cameron v Cameron's Trs* (1850) 13 D 412.
22 Court of Session Act 1988, s 17(5).
23 *Baillie v Bryson* (1818) 1 Mur 341.

them as reasonable men of ordinary intelligence and in the term 'reasonable' I include fair-minded, and in the term 'ordinary intelligence' I include ordinary capacity to appreciate the manner in which cases are presented to a jury. If it can be said that the jury in their verdict have come to a conclusion to which reasonable men of ordinary intelligence would not have come, it is the duty of the court to quash their verdict. But it is frequently maintained that a verdict is contrary to or against the weight of the evidence. I consider that to be a mis-leading expression, as it may mean anything between a case where a jury have merely gone wrong in a conflict of evidence, in determining which scale tips the beam, and a case where the evidence against the evidence is so preponderat-ing that no reasonable man of ordinary intelligence would have come to their conclusion."[24]

24.12 A verdict will not be set aside lightly[25] since conclusions of fact em-bodied in the verdict of the jury cannot be subjected to the same degree of re-examination "for the course of reasoning by which the verdict has been reached is not disclosed – and consequently the verdict of a jury must stand if there was any evidence to support it and if the conclusion is one at which a reasonable jury when properly directed might reasonably arrive"[26]. However, it is not sufficient for a party who is supporting a jury's verdict to point to some piece of evidence, however unconvincing, and claim that the verdict should stand as it is supported by that evidence[27]. It is a legitimate exercise to question various individual parts of the evidence when moving for a new trial provided that the fundamental question[28] is, at the end of the day, addressed[29]. It is within the discretion of the court as to whether or not a new trial is to be granted, provided that it is satisfied that the verdict was returned either where there was no evidence to support it or where the verdict is flagrantly contrary to the evidence[30].

24.13 In order to succeed in setting the verdict aside on the basis that it was contrary to the evidence, the party seeking to do so must be able to show that there was no evidence upon which a jury, properly directed, could reasonably

---

24 *Keenan v Scottish Co-operative Wholesale Society* 1914 SC 959 at 961 per Lord Johnston, subsequently approved by Lord Guest in *Potec v Edinburgh Corporation* 1964 SC (HL) 1 at 7 and *Macarthur v Chief Constable, Strathclyde Police* 1989 SLT 517 at 518 per Lord Justice-Clerk Ross. See also *McWhinnie v Western SMT Co* 1949 SLT (Notes) 8 and Lord Osborne in *Currie v Kilmarnock and Loudon District Council* 1996 SC 55. A similar test applies in England and Wales, see e.g. *Grobelaar v News Group Newspapers* [2002] 1 WLR 3024, HL, per Lord Bingham at para [26] "the task of an appellate court . . . is to seek to interpret the jury's decision and not, because of justifiable dissatisfaction with the outcome, to take upon itself the determination of factual issues which lay within the exclusive province of the jury."

25 *Park v Wilsons and Clyde Coal Co Ltd* 1929 SC (HL) 38; *Robertson v John White & Son* 1963 SC (HL) 22 at 29 per Lord Guest.

26 *Thomas v Thomas* 1947 SC (HL) 48 per Viscount Simon.

27 *Potec v Edinburgh Corporation* 1964 SC (HL) 1.

28 I.e. that posed in *Keenan* at **24.14** below.

29 *Currie v Kilmarnock and Loudon District Council* 1996 SLT 481 at 491 per Lord Osbourne.

30 *Magistrates of Elgin v Robertson* (1862) 24 D 301 at 305 per Lord Wood.

have come to the conclusion that it did[31]. This is a high test and the court cannot merely interfere with the jury's assessment of evidence but must conclude
that, as a matter of law, "there is simply not enough evidence to justify any
reasonable jury, properly directed, in arriving at the verdict returned by the
jury"[32]. The test applies to all actions tried before a jury including defamation
actions[33], although it has been said that in defamation actions as a general rule
the court will not be disposed to interfere with the jury's verdict especially
where that verdict was in favour of the defender[34].

24.14   The jury must decide in any case as to the facts and any inference that
can be drawn therefrom and the court can set aside a verdict which is claimed
to be contrary to the evidence only if the jury has gone "flagrantly" wrong[35]
and the verdict is one which cannot from any point of view be reconciled
with the weight of the evidence[36]. The fact that the presiding judge[37] or the
Inner House might disagree with the jury and have found differently had they
been trying the case at first instance is not in itself enough[38] and, in particular,
it is difficult to successfully challenge the jury's assessment of credibility of a
party or a material witness[39].

24.15   Each case is to be decided on its merits[40] and the opinion of the trial
judge may carry some weight although it is not conclusive[41] but the mere fact
that a verdict was returned by a majority is not in itself a ground for a new
trial[42]. Examples of cases where a verdict has been overturned by reason of
being contrary to the evidence include (a) where "on a careful perusal of the
evidence" in a personal injuries action, no fault against the defenders could be
established by the Inner House and consequently the jury's verdict was
described as "manifestly perverse and stupid"[43], (b) where there was insufficient evidence to justify the jury drawing an inference that the pursuer had

---

31 *Robertson v John White & Son* 1963 SC (HL) 22 at 29 per Lord Guest; *Cleisham v British
    Transport Commission* 1964 SC (HL) 8.
32 *Ross v Fife Healthcare NHS Trust* 2000 SCLR 621 at 624C per Lord Caplan.
33 *Ross v McKittrick* (1886) 14 R 255.
34 *Campbell v Scottish Educational News Co* (1906) 8 F 691.
35 *Robertson v Ainslie's Trs* (1838) 16 S 1239 at 1240 per Lord Justice-Clerk Boyle; *Ross v
    McKittrick* (1886) 14 R 255 at 262 per Lord President Inglis; *Campbell v Scottish
    Educational News Co* (1906) 8 F 691.
36 *Kinnell v Peebles* (1890) 17 R 416 at 424; *Park v Wilsons and Clyde Coal Co* 1929 SC
    (HL) 38 at 40; *Robertson v John White & Son* 1963 SC (HL) 22 at 30; cf *Rankin v Waddell*
    1949 SC 555.
37 *McWhir v Maxwell* (1837) 15 S 873.
38 *Keenan v Scottish Wholesale Co-operative Society* 1914 SC 959 at 961.
39 *Byres v Forbes* (1866) 4 M 388 at 390–391.
40 Further examples are contained in Maclaren at p 622.
41 *Fraser v Edinburgh Street Tramways Co* (1882) 10 R 264 at 268.
42 *Beattie v Mackay & Paterson* (1863) 1 M 279 at 283; cf *Magistrates of Elgin v Robertson*
    (1862) 24 D 301 at 305.
43 *Madden v Glasgow Corporation* 1923 SC 102 at 107 per Lord Justice-Clerk Alness; see also
    Collum v A M Carmichael Ltd 1957 SC 349.

fallen to the ground as a result of the negligent actings of another and such an inference "could only be founded on unwarranted speculation"[44], (c) where the evidence upon an essential part of the pursuer's case was self-contradictory and not such as to justify the jury in arriving at the verdict which it did[45], (d) where the pursuer, by failing to cross-examine the defender's witnesses on an essential point, had, in substance, admitted that the evidence of his own witnesses had been discredited and had accordingly failed to prove the cardinal facts of his case[46], (e) where it was not established that the pursuer was in the employment of the defenders at the material time[47], and (f) in a defamation action where there was no evidence of malice and want of probable cause led before the jury even though these were essential elements for liability[48].

24.16 Examples of where a motion has been refused under this head include cases where, (a) when corroboration was necessary, there was only partial corroboration of a single witness in that the pursuer claimed to have boarded a bus at a recognised bus-stop and the only other witness said that she had seen her waiting there prior to the arrival of the bus[49], (b) where the pursuer's witnesses were self-contradictory as to the speed of a bus at the time that it collided with a motor cycle at a crossroads[50], (c) where a jury awarded future solatium but no future loss of earnings beyond the agreed sum attributable to the period immediately following upon the accident and where the court held that it could do so since the pursuer had worked for a period after the accident and the jury was accordingly sceptical of her claim for future loss[51], (d) where there was medical evidence to support the pursuer's contention that she had been assaulted by the police[52], and (e) where a jury verdict was set aside as being contrary to evidence and at a second trial on the same evidence the jury again returned the same verdict, the court refused to grant a third trial on the basis that the facts were a matter for the jury to determine and weigh and they had already done so twice[53].

Contributory negligence

24.17 The Inner House will be reluctant to interfere with the verdict of a

---

44 *Ross v Fife Healthcare NHS Trust* 2000 SCLR 620.
45 *McGhee v Glasgow Coal Co* 1923 SC 293.
46 *Keenan v Scottish Co-operative Wholesale Society* 1914 SC 959 although note that Lord Skerrington set the verdict aside on the ground that this was essential to the justice of the cause rather than contrary to the evidence.
47 *Littlejohn v Brown & Co* 1909 SC 169.
48 *West v Mackenzie* 1917 SC 513; *Mills v Kelvin and James White* 1913 SC 521 (wrongous information given to police and slander).
49 *Spindlow v Glasgow Corporation* 1933 SC 580.
50 *Lowe v Bristol Motor Omnibus Co* 1934 SC 1.
51 *Tait v Campbell* 2003 Rep LR 35.
52 *Macarthur v Chief Constable, Strathclyde Police* 1989 SLT 517.
53 *McQuilkin v Glasgow District Subways Co* (1902) 4 F 462.

jury in relation to contributory negligence if there is any evidence which the jury could have had regard to[54]. The approach that the court will take has been characterised as:

> "It is possible that if each of us had been trying the case without a jury, different apportionments might have been made. That however is not the question. Apportionment of fault for contributory negligence is essentially a question for the jury, who saw and heard the witnesses, who were entitled to give such weight as was thought proper to such evidence as was accepted and who were entitled to draw such inferences as they thought proper from the acceptable evidence. An appellate *court* would only interfere with the verdict of a jury, properly directed as this jury admittedly was, if it was so flagrantly wrong that no reasonable jury could have reached that verdict, either because there was no evidence to justify it or possibly because of other exceptional circumstances. It could only be in very rare and exceptional cases that an appellate court could say that a jury's verdict on apportionment, a matter on which opinions may well differ, could not stand where, as here, there was evidence to justify the apportionment."[55]

Thus where a trackman was struck by a train while examining some rails and the jury found him to be 20 per cent to blame for the accident when he was wearing high-visibility clothing but knew that the line was open to traffic and the train driver had sounded a whistle and where the defenders argued that "any jury acting reasonably and properly instructed would have found over 50 per cent contributory negligence", the Second Division refused to overturn that verdict[56].

Apportionment between defenders

24.18   Although there is a dearth of case law on the subject, it would appear that the same principle would apply in relation to apportionment between defenders as in findings of contributory negligence and that, providing that there was proper evidence to justify such an apportionment, then the Inner House would be reluctant to interfere with the jury's verdict.

EXCESS OF DAMAGES

24.19   The basic principle to be applied in relation to whether or not the

---

54 E.g. *Ward v Upper Clyde Shipbuilders Ltd* 1973 SLT 182; the report also sets out the form of issues then in use in the sheriff court.

55 *Kirkland v British Railways Board* 1978 SC 71 at 74 per Lord Kissen.

56 *Kirkland v British Railways Board* 1978 SC 71; see also *Lowe v Bristol Motor Omnibus Co* 1934 SC 1 where the Second Division could not agree *inter se* in relation to contributory negligence. For examples of jury findings of contributory negligence in Scotland, see **7.07** above.

damages awarded by a jury are excessive is that the assessment of damages to be awarded is the function of the jury and that the sole function of the judges is to review the award of the jury under the limited statutory jurisdiction which is given to the Inner House[57]. The Inner House thus has the sole limited power to grant a new trial, restricted to the quantum of damages only, where it is of the view that the sole ground for granting such a new trial is the excess or inadequacy of damages awarded and that a new trial is essential to the justice of the cause[58]. The rationale behind this is that "the pocket of the wealthy is not to be picked by the ungrounded prejudice of the jury but, on the other hand, the sacred function of the jury is not to be invaded because the judges, if they had been on the jury, would not have given the same amount of damages"[59]. Lord Migdale put it thus:

> "The function of a court of law is to administer justice with impartiality. The figure of justice is not only portrayed as blindfolded, she also holds in her hands a pair of scales to show that she weighs not only the claim of the pursuer, but also the rights of the defender. And it follows that although the assessment of damages is primarily the function of the jury, that body is not free to fix any figure which commends itself."[60]

Essential to the justice of the cause

24.20   Before considering the question of excess, it must be noted that the statutory provisions for a new trial make it clear that the phrase "essential to the justice of the cause" must be given effect[61]. The jury, in returning its verdict, only makes a single award of damages to each pursuer, albeit apportioning, if appropriate, that single award between the different heads set out in the schedule. Therefore the excess of damages awarded must be neither *de minimis* nor of only little consequence in the context of the overall award. Thus, in a case where it was said that an error on the part of the jury in calculating damages had amounted to a 1.5 per cent excess in an overall award of some £200,000, the court held that even if the defenders' contentions were correct, a new trial would not be required as a matter of doing justice between the parties[62]. However, it is competent to seek to review only part of a total award, for example solatium, provided that the remaining heads of damages are agreed between the parties in the sums found by the jury and the matter is presented to the jury at the second trial in the form of a joint minute.

57 *Girvan v Inverness Farmers' Dairy (No 2)* 1998 SC (HL) 1 per Lord Hope.
58 Court of Session Act 1988, s 30(2).
59 Adam, p 199.
60 *McCallum v Paterson (No 2)* 1969 SC 85 at 93. This infamous case was a direct sequel to the first motion for a new trial, reported at 1968 SC 280. Lord Stott, the presiding judge at the second trial, recorded his trenchant views in his *Judge's Diary 1967–1973* (1995) at p 82.
61 Court of Session Act 1988, s 30(2).
62 *Tate v Fischer* 1998 SLT 1419; *Sandison v Graham Begg Ltd* 2001 SC 821.

General principles

24.21 From the earliest days of the civil jury trial in Scotland it was apparent that excess of damages was a problematic area and it was immediately recognised that it was not enough to say that the Inner House might not have awarded so much by way of damages had it been sitting as a jury but that the test must be that the amount awarded was "out of bounds [and] excessive" before it could be interfered with[63]. An early textbook commented that "the court is very little disposed to entertain [this ground] for the obvious reason that it is peculiarly the duty and province of the jury to fix the amount of the damages"[64].

24.22 The starting-point in considering whether or not there has been an excess of damages such as to warrant the granting of a new trial is the opinion of the whole court expressed by a Full Bench in the leading case of *Landell v Landell*[65]:

> "It is evidently not enough, in order to bring the damages within the definition of excessive, that they are more, and even a great deal more, than the amount at which the injury sustained might have been estimated, in the opinion of the individual members of the court to whom the application is made. . . . It is clear that, in order to warrant the application of the term 'excessive', the damages must be held to exceed, not what the court might think enough, but even the latitude which, in a question of amount so very vague, any set of reasonable men could be permitted to indulge. The excess must be such as to raise on the part of the court the moral conviction that the jury, whether from wrong intention or incapacity or some mistake, have committed gross injustice, and have given higher damages than any jury of ordinary men, fairly and without gross mistake exercising their functions, could have avoided."[66]

Patrimonial loss

24.23 In practice the application of these principles has proved to be far from straightforward. Where it is clear that the jury has underestimated or overestimated the amount suitable to a particular head of claim to the extent that it shows that it cannot properly have appreciated the evidence before it, then this will be sufficient to warrant the granting of a new trial[67]. Thus in cases involving elements of patrimonial loss which, by its nature, should be reason-

---

63 *Christian v Lord Kennedy* (1818) 2 Mur 51.
64 Macfarlane, p 26.
65 (1841) 3 D 819 – the background to this case is discussed by Lord Hope in *Girvan v Inverness Farmers' Dairy (No 2)* 1998 SC (HL) 1 at 5.
66 (1841) 3 D 819 at 825.
67 *Aitken v Laidley* 1938 SC 303 at 307 per Lord Justice-Clerk Aitchison.

ably easy for the jury to compute, given proper directions, there should be little difficulty in applying these principles and it may be thought that the same criteria applied to judge-made awards would be applicable, i.e. that the court will interfere only if "the assessment has been reached through the use of wrong facts or the application of wrong principles or a manifestly unfair assessment has been reached"[68].

24.24 Since patrimonial loss

> "is capable of reasonably precise calculation, a relatively small departure from the judicial assessment may be enough to enable the court to say that there is a gross injustice or that the result was palpably wrong. It is clear that the working rule of 100 per cent permissible error can have no application to such a case. It would be manifestly unjust for a pursuer to receive twice as much as he ought to have done if the amount of his award can be reduced to arithmetic. The same may be true where the award depends on the application to known figures of a factor such as a multiplier which cannot vary widely from case to case."[69]

24.25 The phrase "reasonably precise calculation" must, however, be applied with caution, since not all elements of patrimonial loss may necessarily fall into this category. However, patrimonial loss awards can be attacked more easily than solatium since the breakdown of the award into its component parts by the jury when it gives the sums applicable to each head listed in the schedule enables a party to concentrate his or her attack on those grounds which are objectionable subject to consideration of the overall sum awarded[70]. Where past wage loss is concerned, it may be possible to lead evidence of a true comparitor, i.e someone who does the same job at the same level as the pursuer and who would have been expected to have earned the same wage as him. However, if the pursuer were, for example, a self-employed taxi driver then more latitude would be given to the jury which would, of necessity, have to formulate its award on a broad-based approach and make a reasonable estimate of how much it felt he would have earned but for his incapacity[71].

24.26 In practice other problems might arise in areas such as future wage loss and services, particularly if a jury were to make an award using an exceptionally high multiplier, for example by awarding damages for wage loss for a period of 12 years for a pursuer who, according to the evidence, would have retired in 10 years time – this would, however, also constitute a verdict contrary to the evidence.

---

68 *Blair v F J C Lilley (Marine) Ltd* 1981 SLT 90 at 92.
69 *Girvan v Inverness Farmers' Dairy (No 2)* 1998 SC (HL) 1 at 17 per Lord Hope.
70 *Tate v Fischer* 1998 SLT 1419 at 1421F–G; *Sandison v Graham Begg Ltd* 2001 SC 821 at 828C–E.
71 *Tate v Fischer* 1998 SLT 1419.

Solatium

24.27 In *Landell* Lord Cockburn, in a dissenting judgment, said that "the only question . . . always is, what shall be held such excess, or such injustice, as to warrant the court's interference?"[72] The majority view, however, was that no form of expression could be devised to cover what was meant by excessive and there was a natural reluctance to raise what would, in effect, be a secondary jury question to be decided by the court. Lord Cockburn elaborated on his earlier statement when he said that the only occasion when a jury award should be set aside as excessive was when the court could be "satisfied that a palpable hallucination had come over the jury, and that no other twelve men could be expected to come to the same conclusion"[73].

24.28 By the end of the nineteenth century the so-called "working rule" that an award could be regarded as excessive if it was twice or more what should have been awarded was in place[74]. In one leading case Lord President Inglis explained that "when solatium is awarded by a jury, it is a working rule that the court will not interfere unless the award is so excessive as to be in the region of twice what a reasonable jury might award"[75]. However, a few years later Lord President Cooper, after doubting whether such a rule was appropriate, said that "tolerance of a 100 per cent permissible error may be of little consequence when the error is measured in the sum of £100, but it becomes a serious matter when . . . the error is measured in thousands of pounds"[76], and he pointed out that, interestingly, in all of the reported cases except one the rule had been applied to awards for solatium for the death of a child.

24.29 The real problem, however, was not so much whether or not the "working rule" was still in place but what the criteria are in considerations of excess. In practice it might appear to be a question of what the appellate judges think in any particular case is a reasonable award[77], but as Lord President Hope pointed out:

> "this starting point . . . may tell us a good deal about awards made by judges. What it does not do is to tell us what a reasonable jury might award, which was taken to be the starting point when the working rule was first formulated. . . . There is a risk that, by adhering to the relatively narrow band within

---

72 (1841) 3 D 819 at 826.

73 *Adamson v Whitson* (1849) 11 D 680 at 682.

74 *Young v Glasgow Tramway and Omnibus Co* (1882) 10 R 242 at 245 per Lord President Inglis followed in *McKiernan v Glasgow Corporation* 1919 SC 407; *Elliot v Glasgow Corporation* 1922 SC 146 and *Duffy v Kinneil Cannel and Coking Coal Co* 1930 SC 596.

75 *Inglis v London Midland and Scottish Railway* 1941 SC 551.

76 *McGinley v Pacitti* 1950 SC 364 at 369; see also *Campbell v West of Scotland Shipbreaking Co* 1953 SC 173; cf *Hewitt v West's Gas Improvement Co* 1955 SC 162 and *McGregor v Webster's Exrs* 1976 SLT 29 disapproved of by the House of Lords in *Girvan v Inverness Farmers' Dairy (No 2)* 1998 SC (HL) 1.

77 *McCallum v Paterson (No 2)* 1969 SC 85 per Lord Migdale.

which judges operate, judges will become increasingly out of touch with awards made by juries in the proper exercise of their functions. They are not subjected to the same discipline and they may legitimately vary more widely in their awards from one case to another."[78]

He then agreed with an earlier expressed view by Lord Justice-Clerk Ross[79] that the court must adopt a fairly broad approach in its examination of awards of solatium made by juries "and that any previous awards, whether by a judge or by a jury, can be no more than a rough guide to what is or what is not excessive".

24.30 In what is now the leading case on this area of the law, *Girvan v Inverness Farmers' Dairy (No 2)*[80], the Inner House took the view that there was possibly some force in the argument that judges were out of touch with properly made jury awards[81], and the fact that a jury had already made a substantial award for solatium here could not be left out of account, particularly where, in the words of Lord McCluskey:

"Two juries have now expressed a view as to the severity of the loss . . . twelve jurors from different walks of life and with different incomes and needs might be thought to be better placed to understand the value of money than a judge such as myself; indeed, as all the authorities show, it is just because juries are deemed to be more fitted to make such a judgment that judges have been so reluctant to interfere with their assessments of incalculable elements of damages, such as solatium."[82]

24.31 In a dissenting judgment Lord Abernethy disagreed with these propositions and held that the proper starting-point was judge-made awards[83]. In addition there were a number of interesting observations, namely that it would now be in the best interests of justice if juries were given some guidance as to the appropriate levels of awards[84], that the 100 per cent rule was of doubtful validity, particularly where large awards were being considered, that it was in any event inappropriate to take jury-made awards into account in any calculation[85], and that it might be advisable if the court was given power to assess damages on a motion for a new trial and so save further procedure[86].

---

78 *Currie v Kilmarnock and Loudon District Council* 1996 SLT 481 at 482.
79 *Girvan v Inverness Farmers' Dairy (No 1)* 1995 SLT 735 at 738J.
80 1996 SLT 631.
81 At 634E–F, 635G–H, 636J–L and 638D; the original jury award was held to be excessive in *Girvan v Inverness Farmers' Dairy (No 1)* 1995 SLT 735.
82 At 635E–G. For similar comments by the Supreme Court of Canada, see *Hill v Church of Scientology, Toronto* [1995] 2 SCR 1130.
83 At 640–642.
84 At 636L–637A per Lord Kirkwood and at 634B–C per Lord Abernethy.
85 At 637E–H per Lord Kirkwood and at 641–642 per Lord Abernethy.
86 At 643C–D per Lord Abernethy, following Lord Guthrie in *McCallum v Paterson (No 2)* 1969 SC 85; Lord Hope commented on this in the House of Lords at 1998 SC (HL) 1.

24.32   In the House of Lords the majority view of the Inner House judges in *Girvan (No 2)* was upheld and in a very full judgment[87] Lord Hope, after reviewing the authorities, held that the proper approach to questions of excess of damages was that expressed in *Landell*[88] and that in applying it the court must adopt a two-stage process by which it should first consider what a proper judicial assessment of solatium would be and then go on to consider whether or not the actual award made by the jury is excessive against this background. In considering what the proper judicial assessment might be, regard must be had to previous awards of solatium made in similar cases, both by judges and by juries, although in the case of jury awards no greater weight should be attached to them than would be given to them by a judge when making his own assessment and that any jury award which was currently under challenge should be disregarded.

24.33   In dealing with the question of excess Lord Hope went on to comment that an award of solatium:

> "is not a figure which is capable of precise calculation. Reasonable and fair minded jurors may quite properly arrive at widely differing figures in making their assessment of the amount to be awarded for pain and suffering and general inconvenience. It has to be recognised that a reasonable jury, when asked to value in money a claim for damages which cannot be calculated, may arrive at a result which is different from that which a judge will reach when basing his decision on previous awards. We have come a long way from 1815 when it was regarded as perfectly proper, subject only to limited safeguards, to leave it entirely to a jury to assess damages. But if there is any justification for preserving the present system it lies in this fact: that judges may, because of the different nature of the exercise on which they are engaged and their background of experience, take a quite different view from 12 ordinary men and women on the jury as to the current money value of the pursuer's claim. In this context the so-called working rule must be regarded. It cannot be treated, and never was intended to be treated, as a precise formula. It is no more a rule of thumb, or check, which the court may use as a guide to the decision in each case. It is really no more than a convenient way of describing the test laid down in *Landell* in order to illustrate the width of the approach. The court can use it or depart from it as it thinks fit. Two particular points, however, should be made. The first is that, in order to make sense of the rule in the light of current practice, the starting point for its application must be the figure, or the upper end of any range of figures, resulting from the judicial assessment. . . . The second point is that, in a case such as the present, where the case has already gone before a second jury for a new trial and the question is whether it should be sent to a jury for a third time, it would, as Lord McCluskey said in the pre-

---

87 1998 SC (HL) 1; for commentaries on this decision see A Hajducki, "Girvan – a Verdict for the Future?" 1997 SLT (News) 315 and articles by G Moore at 1998 JLSS 61 and D Kinloch at (1998) 19 Rep L Bul 1.

88 (1841) 3 D 819. This was said to be consistent with the position in England and Wales set out in *Scott v Musial* [1959] 2 QB 429 at 437–438 per Morris LJ.

sent case, be wrong to ignore the figures which the two previous juries arrived at in their overall assessment of whether the second award was an excessive award. To take these figures into account at the second stage is not a departure from judicial responsibility. On the contrary, the question before the court is whether the case should be sent back to a jury for a third trial. As Lord Reid said in *Broome v Cassell & Co*[89], before the court can properly do this, it must be well satisfied that no other jury would award so large a sum. I do not see how the court can properly disregard what the two previous juries have done in forming a view as to what a third jury would be likely to do on hearing the same evidence. But the court has its own responsibility to discharge, and this is only one factor to be taken into account in reaching the overall view as to whether or not there should be a new trial."[90]

24.34 Lord Hope went on to observe that it was inappropriate for the House of Lords to recommend any changes in the practice followed by the Court of Session in the conduct of jury trials which would achieve a greater uniformity between the awards of solatium made by judges and by juries, however desirable that might be[91]. He noted that there would be considerable procedural difficulties if juries were to be given more guidance as to the level of damages which ought to be awarded, although these difficulties were not necessarily insurmountable[92]. The question of whether or not the appeal court ought to be given the power to assess damages in lieu of an award successfully challenged as excessive was said to be more appropriately a matter for the consideration of the Scottish Law Commission[93]. Lord Clyde observed that it was not possible to devise any formula when considering excess of damages and that the question had to remain one for the court to resolve in the light of the circumstances of each case[94], that a jury, through its numerical strength and its varied experience, might be able to provide a direct reflection of what, in the eyes of the ordinary individual, might be considered as reasonable compensation and that it was therefore relevant to take into account any awards of solatium made by juries; thus it was desirable that awards of juries should be collected and classified[95]. It would therefore seem that, at the highest level, the principle of the jury being seen as having a positive contribution to make has been finally recognised and it is a far cry from the remarks of Lord Birnam who, when concurring in the refusal to order a new trial, stated that he was doing so "because it is quite likely that if a new trial were allowed, an equally unintelligent jury might arrive at an equally unjust result"[96].

89 [1972] AC 1027 at 1090I.
90 1998 SC (HL) 1 at 18. The approach adopted by Lord President Clyde in *McCallum v Paterson (No 2)* 1969 SC 85 was rejected.
91 1998 SC (HL) 1 at 20.
92 1998 SC (HL) 1 at 21.
93 1998 SC (HL) 1 at 22.
94 1998 SC (HL) 1 at 23.
95 1998 SC (HL) 1 at 24.
96 *Neil v James Muir & Son Ltd* 1954 SLT 49 at 50.

24.35 In *Girvan (No 2)* the House of Lords also considered the problem of the multiplicity of trials following upon one or more successful motions for a new trial on the basis of excess of damages. As Lord Clyde observed, the fact that a third jury trial might take place was not, *per se*, a sufficient reason for refusing an appeal but it was a factor which might indicate that the justice of the cause would not benefit from a new trial being ordered[97]. Mention was also made of two possible alternatives to a new trial, namely where the parties consent to the requantification of the awards being determined by the court[98] and where the court puts a revised figure to the pursuer on the basis that, if he was willing to accept it, a new trial could be avoided[99].

24.36 In the subsequent case of *McLeod v British Railways Board*[100], which involved the upholding of what was at that time the largest ever award of solatium by a jury – £250,000 to a 12-year-old boy with extensive electrical burning injuries – the Inner House, in following *Girvan (No 2)*, stated that scrutiny of jury awards by reference to the appeal judge's own assessment of a proper level of damages would run counter to the intention of Parliament in passing the legislation dealing with an excess of damages and that, although jury awards might be unpredictable and vary significantly, it was not a reason for saying that the defenders' right to a fair trial had been infringed in any way and, accordingly, that in the circumstances the sum awarded by the jury, although very large, was not one which no reasonable jury could have made.

> "As judges, we have access to no infallible secret recipe for transmuting what the pursuer has suffered and will continue to suffer into a money award of a precisely ascertainable level. Nor, it should be remembered, do jurors find any such recipe lying for them, ready to consult, on the table in the jury room. We fully and expressly acknowledge that any judicial award of damages is likely to have been very much less than the sum awarded by the jury. But, like everyone else, jurors live in a world where huge sums are paid to professional footballers and are won by competitors in television quiz shows. This may well affect the value which jurors put on money in general and in particular in re-lation to injuries such as the pursuer has suffered. Against that background, and having regard to all the circumstances of the case, we find it impossible to say that no reasonable jury, having duly and conscientiously considered the pur-suer's injuries in the light of the evidence, could have made the same award as the jury in this case. In the language of *Landell*, the sum awarded, although very large, does not raise in us the moral conviction that, whether from some

---

97 1998 SC (HL) 1 at 18.

98 *Wallace v West Calder Co-operative Society Ltd* (1888) 15 R 307 – if the parties do not so consent then a new trial must be allowed: *Boal v Scottish Catholic Printing Co* 1908 SC 667.

99 *Johnston v Dilke* (1875) 2 R 836 – to some this would seem to involve an element of compulsion or blackmail!

100 2001 SC 534.

wrong intention or incapacity, or some mistake, the jury has committed gross injustice. Nor, again, are all our hands 'lifted in astonishment' at the sum which the jury has awarded."[101]

Defamation

24.37 In defamation cases the courts have tended to take a fairly broad view of whether or not damages are to be regarded as excessive and, following the *Landell* principles, have held that the Inner House should proceed on the assumption that the jury determined the relevant facts in a manner which strongly supported the view that the award was not excessive[102]. On appeal, the court should be even more reluctant to interfere with the jury awards in a defamation case than in one involving personal injuries and it is inappropriate to make a direct comparison, in the circumstances, between solatium for personal injuries and solatium for injury to feelings and reputation[103]. The court will not interfere with an award which is much larger than one which it would have made itself on the basis of the information before it, provided that it is one which, in all the circumstances, cannot be regarded as one which a reasonable jury could not make[104]. It is proper for the courts to take into account comparable awards in Scotland for defamation, but English awards should be ignored[105].

INADEQUACY OF DAMAGES

24.38 Inadequacy of damages awarded was formerly not one of the statutory grounds upon which a new trial could be sought[106] but from an early date it was seen by the courts as falling within the catch-all category of "such other cause as is essential to the justice of the case"[107]. The general principle followed is that "the court is entitled to set aside an award on the grounds of inadequacy in any case where it is clear that the jury has underestimated the

---

101 2001 SC 534 at 540.
102 *Winter v News Scotland Ltd* 1991 SLT 828 at 829F. This approach was consistent with that of the House of Lords in *Girvan*. In the English case of *Kiam v MGN* [2002] 3 WLR 1036, the Court of Appeal held that a defamation award would only be considered excessive if it was out of all proportion to what could sensibly have been thought appropriate to compensate the claimant and re-establish his reputation.
103 *Adamson v Whitson* (1849) 11 D 680 at 682 per Lord Jeffrey; *McGinley v Pacitti* 1950 SC 276 at 278; *Winter v News Scotland Ltd* 1991 SLT 828 at 831J.
104 *Winter v News Scotland Ltd* 1991 SLT 828 at 831J; *Baigent v British Broadcasting Corporation* 2001 SC 281.
105 *Winter v News Scotland Ltd* 1991 SLT 828 at 831E.
106 Jury Trials (Scotland) Act 1815, s 6.
107 *Black v Croall* (1854) 16 D 431; *Reid v Morton* (1902) 4 F 438; *Madden v Glasgow Corporation* 1923 SC 102.

amount that is suitable to the claim, to an extent that shows that they cannot properly have appreciated the evidence before them"[108]. It is suggested that the courts would, following upon *Girvan (No 2)*, adopt a similar approach to that now followed in excess cases and, in the case of solatium, the "working rule" would be applied so that the court would not interfere unless the award was so inadequate as to be one-half or less of that which a reasonable jury might award[109].

24.39 Examples of where verdicts have been set aside on the ground of inadequacy of damages are not numerous but in a case where a lorry driver lost a leg and in consequence was unlikely to work again and a jury awarded damages of £550, despite proved past wage loss and the £300 cost of an artificial leg, a new trial was ordered[110]. Other examples include a case where, notwithstanding the uncontradicted evidence that the pursuer was attached to his son who was killed in an accident, a jury awarded some patrimonial loss but no solatium[111] and a case where, despite the pursuer having suffered substantial injuries, the jury awarded one farthing in damages[112]. The motion for a new trial was refused where the pursuer was awarded less in total than the actual wage loss that he had sustained but where the court held that he had failed to prove that he would have been continuously employed throughout the relevant period[113]. Inadequacy of damages cases are rare and a recent example, involving an award for future solatium but limited future wage loss, appears to have been pled as an inadequacy but was, in fact, argued on the basis of a verdict contrary to the evidence[114].

RES NOVITER VENIANS AD NOTITIAM

24.40 *Res noviter venians ad notitiam*, meaning literally "information newly discovered", covers both new fact and new evidence (whether documentary or parole) but the new evidence must involve a fact bearing upon the ground of action and not merely consist of additional evidence relating to a fact averred and upon which the evidence was led at the trial.

> "If the accidental turning up of an unexpected witness whose parole evidence promises only to give additional corroboration of the evidence already given for one party, and to add something to the contradiction of evidence already given for the other, is to be regarded as sufficient materiality to justify a new

108 *Aitken v Laidlay* 1938 SC 303 at 308.
109 *McGinley v Pacitti* 1950 SC 364.
110 *Aitken v Laidlay* 1938 SC 303.
111 *Gibson v Kyle* 1933 SC 30; cf *Rankin v Waddell* 1949 SC 555; *Davidson v Chief Constable, Fife Police*, Appendix III, 1 [6].
112 *Madden v Glasgow Corporation* 1923 SC 102.
113 *Reid v Morton* (1902) 4 F 438.
114 *Tait v Campbell* 2003 Rep LR 35.

trial, there would be no end to the multiplicity of trials in which a conflict of testimony occurs."[115]

24.41 Whether new facts or evidence will amount to *res noviter* justifying a new trial is a question of the circumstances of each case[116]. The new fact or evidence must be information which at the time of the trial was unknown to the party putting it forward, owing to no fault or omission on his or her part[117]. In addition the information must be of such a nature as to be capable of being considered as relevant to the justice of the cause[118]. Information will be material for these purposes if it can be said that it might have affected the verdict[119], but it is not necessary for the court to be convinced that the new material would either certainly or probably have led to a different verdict had it been led at the trial[120].

24.42 Thus where a haver examined at a commission before the trial had a bundle of documents in his possession but by innocent mistake had failed to disclose them until after the trial, this and the fact that the documents were held to be material, justified the granting of a new trial[121]. In contrast, where persons who had witnessed an accident, but were unknown to the parties and thus not cited at the trial, came forward after reading of the verdict in a newspaper, a new trial was refused on the basis that the evidence of those witnesses would merely have corroborated existing witnesses and would not have disclosed any new facts[122]. Where, however, a witness stated that he had spilled oil one hour before the pursuer slipped on it and the defenders, not having anticipated that the witness would give evidence at the trial, subsequently ascertained that this evidence was false because the witness had in fact left their employment four days prior to the accident, a new trial was ordered, the new evidence being *res nova* irrespective of whether the witness was genuinely mistaken or had committed perjury[123]. A motion for a new trial has been refused where events subsequent to the trial but foreshadowed in the evidence have occurred, such as a material improvement in the pursuer's health when

---

115 *Miller v Mac Fisheries Ltd* 1922 SC 157 at 163.
116 *Miller v Mac Fisheries Ltd* at 190.
117 *Miller v Mac Fisheries Ltd* at 165 per Lord President Clyde; *Byres v Forbes* (1866) 4 M 388.
118 *Miller v Mac Fisheries Ltd* at 160 per Lord President Clyde; *Maltman v Tarmac Civil Engineering Ltd* 1967 SC 177 at 181.
119 *Miller v Mac Fisheries Ltd* 1922 SC 157 at 160.
120 *Bannerman v Scott* (1846) 9 D 163 at 165 per Lord President Boyle; *Maltman v Tarmac Civil Engineering Ltd* 1967 SC 177 at 182.
121 *Bannerman v Scott* (1846) 9 D 157.
122 *Miller v Mac Fisheries Ltd* 1922 SC 157.
123 *Maltman v Tarmac Civil Engineering Ltd* 1967 SC 177 at 181 per Lord President Clyde and Lord Guthrie at 183. The Lord President disapproved, as being too widely stated, the proposition in Maclaren at p 162 that it was not a good ground for allowing a new trial that the party asking for it undertakes to prove that witnesses have perjured themselves.

medical witnesses had given evidence relating to his current state and prognosis[124].

24.43 If the *res nova* consists of facts which require amendment of the pleadings a minute of amendment should be lodged as soon as possible[125]. If, however, no amendment of the pleadings is called for then a separate minute should be lodged and the minute should set out both what the new evidence is and how it is proposed that it should be proved[126]. Details should be given as to the manner in which the new evidence or document was discovered and of the circumstances which would have borne upon the possibility of its earlier discovery[127]. An opportunity to answer the minute should be given[128] and any documents to be founded upon should be produced.

OTHER GROUNDS ESSENTIAL TO THE JUSTICE OF THE CAUSE

24.44 This is the general "catch-all" ground which will encompass any other ground upon which the court will allow the verdict to be set aside provided that such a ground is essential to the justice of the cause. No inclusive list of circumstances upon which this ground will be sustained can therefore be drawn up[129] but examples of the application of this provision can be given under a number of specific headings.

Surprise

24.45 If a party is taken by surprise by the leading of evidence by the other party which is not foreshadowed in the pleadings or in cross-examination then this may amount to surprise sufficient to justify a motion for a new trial[130], but the surprise must be of such a character that the party taken by surprise could not reasonably have been expected to anticipate it[131]. It is not enough to show that a party had not properly apprehended the meaning and intention of the pleas and averments of his opponent in the pleadings[132]. Surprise cannot be claimed merely because all of the minute detailed particulars of a case are not

---

124 *Shields v North British Railway Co* (1874) 2 R 126.
125 *Miller v Mac Fisheries Ltd* 1922 SC 157 at 161.
126 *Miller v Mac Fisheries Ltd* at 161; *Maltman v Tarmac Civil Engineering Ltd* 1967 SLT 177 at 182.
127 *McCarroll v McKinstery* 1926 SC (HL) 1 at 7; *Ross v Ross* 1928 SC 600.
128 *Maltman v Tarmac Civil Engineering Ltd* 1967 SLT 177.
129 *Maltman v Tarmac Civil Engineering Ltd* at 184.
130 *Burns v Dixon's Iron Works Ltd* 1961 SC 102; *Smith v The Anchor Line Ltd* 1961 SLT (Notes) 54; cf *Hendrie v The Scottish Ministers* 2003 GWD 13-389.
131 *Christie's Curator ad litem v Kirkwood* 1996 SLT 1299 at 1300I.
132 *Meek v Meek* (1834) 12 S 603.

spelled out in the record[133] and it is not constituted "in respect of any circumstances that due vigilance and a proper knowledge of law and practice might have provided against"[134]. Where the element of surprise is not substantial, a new trial will be refused, particularly when no objection was taken to the line of evidence and no motion made to lead proof in replication[135].

24.46 Examples of new trials granted on the basis of surprise include a case where the pursuer pled that there were certain errors in business books but at the trial attempted to found upon completely different errors[136] and where an element of damages was brought to the attention of the jury notwithstanding the lack of any record for it[137]. Where, however, a party has sufficient notice in the pleadings of the case being brought and the evidence led at the trial then a new trial will not be granted[138] and this will be so even if certain matters are not directly put in cross-examination[139]. Where a reasonable line of investigation by one party would have disclosed certain facts and notice of these facts has been given in the pleadings, then a new trial will not be granted and, in particular, a "surprise witness" will not result in a new trial when both parties had failed to exchange a list of witnesses[140].

Evidence led at the trial

24.47 The discretionary allowance by the presiding judge of additional evidence[141] or a proof in replication[142] are matters which can be challenged under this ground. Where a material witness has committed perjury and this has resulted in a miscarriage of justice a new trial may be allowed but the evidence upon which the allegation of perjury is based must be something which was not, and could not have been by reasonable diligence, available at the trial itself[143]. Evidence known to be false, or suspected at the time it was given to be false, does not fall within this ground since it will or should have been dealt with by normal cross-examination of the relevant witnesses. Where a document relied upon at a trial appears to have been forged or inauthentic a new trial may be granted[144].

---

133 *Dalziel v Duke of Queensberry's Exrs* (1825) 4 Mur 14.
134 Macfarlane, p 270.
135 *Wilson v Thomas Usher & Sons* 1934 SC 332; *Brown v Ross* 1935 SN 9.
136 *Gye & Co v Hallam* (1832) 10 S 710.
137 *Snare v Earl of Fife's Trs* (1852) 4 Jur 539.
138 *Mackenzie v Magistrates of Fortrose* (1842) 4 D 911; *McAuslin v Glen* (1859) 21 D 511.
139 *Wilson v Thomas Usher & Sons* 1934 SC 332.
140 *Christie's Curator ad litem v Kirkwood* 1996 SLT 1299.
141 *Christie v Thompson* (1859) 21 D 337 at 351.
142 *Rankine v Roberts* (1873) 1 R 225 at 229.
143 *Maltman v Tarmac Civil Engineering Ltd* 1967 SC 177 at 184; cf *Snodgrass v Hunter* (1879) 2 F 76.
144 *Miller v Fraser* (1826) 4 Mur 112 at 118.

Conduct of the trial

24.48   When something occurs in the course of a trial which is inconsistent with the conditions of fair trial and displaces any reasonable confidence in the result arrived at, this may amount to a ground for a new trial[145].

24.49   The fact that counsel has not carried out the wishes of his or her client in the conduct of a trial is not, however, *per se* a good ground on which to seek a new trial[146]. A new trial has been refused (a) where it could be shown that the jury wrongly counted their votes[147], (b) where a juror was in the employment of the defenders[148], (c) where the verdict was returned with a rider not inconsistent with the verdict[149], or even (d) where the jury appeared to have been under a misapprehension as to the meaning of its verdict[150].

24.50   The following situations have been held to be sufficient to allow the motion for a new trial to be granted: (a) where the jury has taken extraneous evidence into account, for example where a juror carried out his own site inspection of the locus and then reported back to the jury what he had seen[151]; (b) where the verdict returned was ambiguous[152], (c) where the verdict was neither unanimous nor by a majority[153], (d) where the verdict contained two mutually excusive verdicts on the issues[154], (e) where the verdict was self-contradictory and irrational[155], (f) where it could be shown that the jury must have decided the case on grounds not stated on record[156], and (g) where the presiding judge wrongfully withdrew the case from the jury[157]. Where an erroneous direction on a matter of fact has been given this may amount to a ground for ordering a new trial, provided that the direction was essential to the justice of the cause[158]. Where there has been misconduct on the part of the

---

145   *Woods v Caledonian Railway Co* (1886) 13 R 1118; *Reekie v McKinven* 1921 SC 733; *Jamieson v W Brown & Sons (Hamilton) Ltd* 1938 SC 456.
146   *Mackintosh v Fraser* (1860) 22 D 421; *Currie v Glen* (1846) 9 D 308.
147   *Pirie v Caledonian Railway Co* (1890) 17 R 1157.
148   *Watson v North British Railway Co* (1901) 3 F 342 – the fact that the defenders were Scotland's largest private company at the time may be contrasted with the situation had the juror been employed by a relatively small concern and thus known the management or directors more intimately.
149   *Burns v Steel Co of Scotland* (1893) 21 R 39.
150   *Fullarton v Caledonian Railway Co* (1882) 10 R 70; *Dobbie v Johnston & Russell* (1861) 23 D 1139.
151   *Sutherland v Prestongrange Coal & Fire Brick Co* (1888) 15 R 494; cf *Hope v Gemmell* (1898) 1 F 74.
152   *Florence v Mann* (1890) 18 R 247.
153   *McGuire v Brown* 1963 SC 107.
154   *Spring v Martin's Trs* 1910 SC 1087.
155   *Stewart v Caledonian Railway Co* (1869) 42 J 38.
156   *Littlejohn v Brown & Co* 1909 SC 169; cf *Murray v County Road Trs of Middle Ward of Lanarkshire* (1888) 15 R 737.
157   *Gibson v Nimmo & Co* (1895) 22 R 491.
158   *Woods v Caledonian Railway Co* (1886) 13 R 1118.

jurors outwith the jury room then the court may be prepared to review the situation[159] but, in a case involving the alleged relationship between a juror and an essential witness the European Court of Human Rights observed that:

> "It does not necessarily follow from the fact that a member of the tribunal has some personal knowledge of one of the witnesses in a case that he will be prejudiced in favour of that person's testimony. In each individual case it must be decided whether the familiarity in question is of such a nature and degree as to indicate a lack of impartiality on the part of the tribunal."[160]

THIRD TRIALS

24.51 Although there is ample precedent for the granting of a third trial[161], they are normally discouraged by the Inner House particularly when a question of fact has been tried twice over and two separate juries have come to the same conclusion upon the facts where it has been said that "it is highly desirable that litigation should come to an end . . . unless the verdict must have proceeded on some direct disregard of a direction in law given to them, where the duty of the court is [then] to set aside two or three verdicts in order that justice be done"[162]. The same principle applies where two juries have both returned verdicts with substantial damages for a pursuer[163].

---

159 See **21.07** above.
160 *Pullar v UK* (1996) 22 EHRR 391 at para 38.
161 Maxwell, p 566.
162 *Grant v William Baird & Co* (1902) 5 F 459 commented on by Lord Justice-Clerk Aitchison in *McKnight v General Motor Carrying Co* 1936 SC 17 at 21.
163 *Girvan v Inverness Farmers' Dairy (No 2)* 1996 SLT 631 at 635E–G per Lord McCluskey.

Chapter 25

Motions for a new trial

ENROLLING A MOTION

25.01 An application for a new trial is made by way of a motion within seven days after the date upon which the verdict of the jury was written on the issue and signed[1], i.e. the date upon which the jury delivered its verdict. The motion must specify on the motion sheet the statutory ground of review upon which the application is being made[2] although the court may, under reservation of any questions relating to competency, allow a party to amend a motion for a new trial subsequently so as to add further grounds of review[3]. On enrolling a motion for a new trial the party enrolling it must lodge a print of the whole pleadings and interlocutors in the cause, incorporating the issues and the counter-issues, the verdict of the jury and any notes of exception and the determination thereon by the trial judge[4].

EFFECT OF ENROLLING FOR NEW TRIAL

25.02 The effect of enrolling for an application for a new trial is the same as the effect of reclaiming any interlocutor at a proof[5] and thus once an application has been made the verdict of the jury cannot be applied until such time as the motion has been disposed of. The party applying for a new trial cannot withdraw his motion without the consent of the other parties to the cause and, if the party no longer wishes to insist on his motion then any other party may insist upon the motion in the same way as if it had been enrolled by that party[6]. An unopposed motion to refuse the application for a new jury trial is treated as if all the parties to the cause had consented in the motion[7].

1 Rule 39.1(1).
2 Rule 39.1(2); Court of Session Act 1988, s 29(1).
3 *Maltman v Tarmac Civil Engineering Ltd* 1967 SC 177 at 178.
4 Rule 39.1(4).
5 Rule 38.8 applied to jury trials by rule 39.1(5).
6 Rule 38.8(3) applied by rule 39.1(5).
7 Rule 38.8(4) applied by rule 39.1(5).

Late applications

25.03   When an application for a new trial is made late, i.e. outwith the seven-day period specified above, the motion seeking the application should include a motion for the application to be received and for leave to proceed with it out of time[8]. The grounds upon which such an application can be made are not set out in the Rules of Court but would, presumably, follow the general dispensing power therein and would include mistake, oversight or such other excusable cause[9]. The motion for an application for a new trial which is out of time can only be made where the verdict of the jury has not yet been applied after which time it is clearly incompetent.

25.04   Where the court grants an out-of-time application for a new trial, the procedure will then follow the same procedure applicable to applications which were made timeously[10].

OBJECTIONS TO COMPETENCY OF APPLICATION

25.05   Where an application for a new trial is made by a party, any other party to the cause may oppose the motion on the ground that it is incompetent[11], because, for example, the application is made out of time or is not based upon one of the statutory grounds for review. The court may also take an objection *ex proprio motu* to the competency of an application and will not entertain an incompetent application even if no objection thereto has been taken by the respondent[12].

25.06   Where the application has been objected to as incompetent the cause will then be put out in the Single Bills (i.e. the motion roll of the Inner House) where the court may then:

(a)   dispose of the objection to competency and, where it repels the objection, appoint the cause to the summar roll for a hearing or, alternatively, deal with the matter in the Single Bills;

(b)   appoint the cause to the summar roll for a full hearing on the objection; or

(c)   reserve the objection for hearing alongside the merits of the application and appoint the cause to the summar roll for a hearing[13].

In practice the latter course is usually, but not invariably, followed.

---

8 Rule 39.2(1).
9 Rule 2.1.
10 Rule 39.2(2).
11 Rule 39.3.
12 *Governors of Strichen Endowments v Diverall* (1891) 19 R 79.
13 Rule 39.3(2).

PROCEDURE WHERE NO OBJECTION TO COMPETENCY

Allocation of diets

25.07   Where an application for a new trial is made timeously and is not opposed as being incompetent, the court will, without hearing the parties, appoint the cause to the summar roll or, alternatively, direct that it be put out in the Single Bills[14]; in practice most applications are heard on the summar roll. The party seeking to have the application heard on the summar roll must give an estimate of the likely duration of the hearing[15] (in practice one or two days usually being sufficient) and if any other party considers this estimate too low then he will record on the motion his own estimate[16]. The Keeper will then allocate a diet, the duration of which will depend on the higher of the estimates given by parties[17]. Not less than five weeks prior to the allocated diet on the summar roll the Keeper will put the matter out for a hearing on the Inner House by order roll at which hearing the parties will advise the court whether or not the summar roll hearing is to proceed and whether the duration of such a hearing has been reassessed[18].

Appendices

25.08   Where, in a motion for a new trial, the applicant wishes to submit a transcript of the evidence or exception or any other relevant documents for the consideration of the court, then he must lodge six copies of an appendix containing such matter within three months of the cause having been appointed to the summar roll[19], and where he fails to do so the other parties to the action may apply by way of motion to the Inner House to have the motion for a new trial refused[20]. Where the party seeking a new trial considers that an appendix is unnecessary he must, within that three-month period, give written intimation of this fact to the Deputy Principal Clerk of Session and a copy thereof must be sent to the other parties to the cause[21] who may then lodge their own appendix within one month after the receipt of such intimation[22]. Should the other parties to the cause wish to include any documents or transcripts which the applicant for a new trial does not intend to include in the appendix then they may lodge their own appendices containing such material

14 Rule 39.4.
15 Rule 6.3(2).
16 Rule 6.3(3).
17 Rule 6.3(4).
18 Rule 6.3(5), (6).
19 Rule 38.19(1) applied by rule 39.5; rule 4.7(1)(f).
20 Rule 38.19(4) applied by rule 39.5.
21 Rule 38.19(2) applied by rule 39.5.
22 Rule 38.19(3) applied by rule 39.5.

as they think relevant insofar as not already lodged by the party applying for the new trial[23] but it is good practice for parties to discuss with each other what documentation should be placed before the court and to attempt to lodge only a single appendix containing all the relevant material. Only those parts of the transcript of evidence as are relevant to the motion for a new trial need to be lodged in the appendix. If the motion for a new trial relates to a misdirection on the part of the trial judge then the misdirection must be found within the four corners of the notes of exceptions, aided, where necessary, by the relevant parts of the record and evidence[24] and the whole of the charge is not usually contained in the appendix[25].

Amendment of record

25.09 Parties may be allowed to amend the record during the period between the motion being made and the hearing of the application[26]. Once the hearing has begun the court will only allow an amendment where it considers that to do so would be fair and just[27].

HEARING OF APPLICATION

25.10 At the hearing of the application for a new trial it is the usual practice to have only one speech per party and, where a party is represented by two counsel, by the senior[28]. If the notes of the transcript of evidence are to be read in full or in part, this task is usually carried out by the junior counsel for the party challenging the verdict. The party successful at the trial must support the verdict of the jury and if he does not then the court will not sustain the verdict and that party may be found liable in the expenses of the application[29]. The hearing is conducted in a similar manner to a reclaiming motion.

---

23 Rule 38.19(3) applied by rule 39.5.
24 *Douglas v Cunningham* 1964 SC (HL) 112 at 116.
25 *Robertson v Federation of Icelandic Co-operative Societies* 1948 SC 562 at 572 approved in *Douglas v Cunningham;* cf *McArthur v Weir Housing Corporation Ltd* 1970 SC 135.
26 E.g. as in *Burns v Dixon's Iron Works* 1961 SC 102.
27 *Stodart v British Transport Commission* 1956 SLT 71.
28 Thompson and Middleton, p 316; the practice was confirmed by the Inner House in *Winter v News Scotland Ltd* (reported on other matters at 1991 SLT 828).
29 *McNair v Glasgow Corporation* 1923 SC 397 at 401.

DISPOSAL OF APPLICATION

General

25.11 Having heard the motion the court may either grant or refuse it[30] and the disposal of the motion is a matter for the discretion of the court having regard to the peculiar circumstances of the individual case before it[31]. An appeal from the decision of the Inner House lies to the House of Lords. No jury verdict can be discharged or set aside upon an application for a new trial unless it is done by the majority of the judges hearing the application and, in the case of there being an equal division of the court, then judgment is to be given in conformity with the verdict, i.e. the motion is to be refused[32]. If the motion is granted then a new trial diet will be assigned in due course; a third trial can competently be granted although the existence of concurring verdicts in the first two trials is of weight but not conclusive[33]. If the motion is refused then the verdict of the jury will stand and can be applied in the usual manner. Where, however, there are two or more defenders, a verdict cannot be set aside against one defender and allowed to stand against the others and accordingly a new trial will be granted against all the defenders[34].

Verdict contrary to evidence

25.12 If after hearing an application for a new trial on the ground that the verdict was contrary to the evidence, the court is unanimously of the view that it was contrary to the evidence and the court has before it all of the evidence which could reasonably be expected to be obtained relevant to the cause, then it may set aside the verdict and enter judgment for the party unsuccessful at the trial[35]. The party who was unsuccessful at the trial should give notice to the successful party that he intends to rely upon this provision and will move the court to do so but a motion need not be enrolled to that effect[36].

25.13 The court is not, however, bound to enter a verdict for the defenders and the purpose of the statutory provision is limited, i.e. "it is to cover the situation where the court is satisfied that, for all practical purposes, all the available evidence was before the jury and that, accordingly, no useful purpose

---

30 Court of Session Act 1988, s 29(2).
31 *Maltman v Tarmac Civil Engineering Ltd* 1967 SC 177 at 184.
32 1988 Act, s 30(4).
33 *McCallum v Paterson (No 2)* 1969 SC 85 at 88 and see observations of Lord Hope in *Girvan v Inverness Farmers' Dairy (No 2)* 1998 SC (HL) 1.
34 *Simpson v Glasgow Corporation* 1916 SC 345; *Richmond v Glasgow Corporation* 1950 SLT 301.
35 1988 Act, s 29(3).
36 *Potec v Edinburgh Corporation* 1964 SC (HL) 1 at 8.

is to be achieved by allowing a new trial"[37]. Thus where no further evidence is available, the court will not allow a party the chance to see if, at a subsequent trial, such evidence as there is can be better presented[38].

Excess or inadequacy of damages

25.14   Where the court is of the opinion that the only ground for granting a new trial is an excess or inadequacy of damages, and it would be in the interests of justice to do so, a new trial restricted to the quantum of damages only can be granted[39]. Subject to the lack of challenge of any individual heads of damage, the new trial can be restricted to, for example, solatium only if the parties agree. The parties may also, of consent, allow the court to requantify the damages in whole or in part and substitute these for the awards made by the jury[40] but the court cannot refuse to grant a new trial and assess the damages *de novo* without the express consent of both parties[41].

EXPENSES

Where motion for a new trial has been refused

25.15   In the event of the motion for the new trial being refused, expenses will be dealt with at that stage since, subject to the discretion of the court, the party who obtained the verdict at the original trial will usually be entitled to expenses both for that trial and for the unsuccessful attempt to challenge the verdict[42]. The expenses of the unsuccessful motion for a new trial will be dealt with by the Inner House but the expenses of the original trial will normally be dealt with by the Lord Ordinary who was the presiding judge at that trial and at the stage when the party in whose favour the verdict was granted applies to have the verdict applied[43].

Where motion for a new trial has been granted

25.16   Where the motion for a new trial has succeeded then the court will,

---

37 *Moyes v Burntisland Shipbuilding Co* 1952 SC 429 at 434 per Lord Justice-Clerk Thomson.
38 *Ross v Fife Healthcare NHS Trust* 2000 SCLR 620 at 624D.
39 1988 Act, s 30(3).
40 *Wallace v West Calder Co-operative Society Ltd* (1888) 15 R 307.
41 *Ritchie & Son v Barton* (1883) 10 R 813; *Boal v The Scottish Catholic Printing Co* 1908 SC 667.
42 *McQuilkin v Glasgow District Subways Co* (1902) 4 F 462 at 464–465. Where there have been two trials the party upholding the verdict of the second trial may not always be awarded the expenses of the first trial: *Grant v William Baird & Co* (1903) 5 F 469.
43 E.g. *Tait v Campbell* 2004 SLT 187.

in the absence of any special circumstances, deal with both the expenses of the first trial and the motion itself[44]. The reason for this is that:

> "[T]he second trial constitutes a quite severable chapter in the case, and it seems illogical that, when the Lord Ordinary deals with expenses of the second trial, he should be asked to deal with the expenses occasioned in an earlier and quite separate chapter of the case of which he would and probably does know nothing. It would be equally unreasonable to ask him to deal with the expenses of a motion for a new trial incurred in the Inner House, liability for which he is not in a position to evaluate."[45]

However, the court can, and sometimes does, reserve the question of expenses until such time as the second trial has taken place and it will then deal with the matter unless it has authorised the presiding judge to deal with it or the parties have agreed that he should do so[46].

ALTERATION OF MODE OF INQUIRY

25.17   It is always open to the court to alter the mode of inquiry on the basis that the motion for a new trial opens up all of the interlocutors previously allowed and accordingly the court may, in granting a motion for a new trial, substitute a proof or a proof before answer in its place[47]. Where, however, the Inner House has stipulated that a new trial should take place and there is a change of circumstances such as a supervening special cause[48] or an amendment to the pleadings[49] which would raise the question of the mode of inquiry, then the matter should be referred back to the Division of the Inner House that granted the motion for the new trial[50].

---

44 *McInnes v British Transport Commission* 1961 SC 156.
45 *McCallum v Paterson (No 2)* 1969 SC 85 at 97 per Lord Clyde; see also Morton, "Expenses in Jury Trials" 1969 SLT (News) 129.
46 *Wason v British Transport Commission* 1961 SC 152.
47 *Moyes v Burntisland Shipbuilding Co* 1952 SC 429 at 436 per Lord Justice-Clerk Thomson.
48 E.g. *Graham v Associated Electrical Industries Ltd* 1968 SLT 81, where one of the pursuers abandoned part of her case.
49 *Ewart v Ferguson* 1932 SC 277; *Kerr v John Brown & Co* 1965 SC 144.
50 *Milne v Glasgow Corporation* 1951 SC 340.

Chapter 26

Applications to enter verdicts on points reserved

VERDICT ON POINTS RESERVED

26.01 Where the presiding judge at a trial gives the jury a direction upon any matter of law, any party against whom the verdict is subsequently returned may apply to the Inner House to enter a verdict for him on the basis that the direction was erroneous and that he or she is truly entitled to have the verdict returned in his favour[1]. This provision can be contrasted with the old and now abolished "special verdict" where the jury found for neither party but instead made findings on certain factual matters put to it in the issues and to which the court had then to apply the law and enter up the verdict accordingly. In the procedure being dealt with here the jury makes a positive finding for one party subject to a reservation on a point of law, leaving the unsuccessful party with a right to challenge that verdict in the manner stated. Applications to enter verdicts on points reserved are now rare and there are no modern reported examples of the procedure being used[2].

PROCEDURE

26.02 The application is made by way of motion[3] and the party enrolling the motion must lodge in process four copies of the closed record incorporating (a) all interlocutors pronounced in the case and any amendments, (b) the issues and counter-issues, (c) any notes of exception and the determination thereon of the presiding judge, and (d) the verdict of the jury. He or she must send a copy to each of the other parties[4]. Unless the court directs otherwise, it is not necessary to have the notes of evidence available, but the notes of the presiding judge may be produced at any time if required[5].

1 Court of Session Act 1988, s 31(1).
2 Examples of the use of the procedure in the nineteenth century include *Forbes' Exrs v Western Bank of Scotland* (1854) 16 D 807; *Kerr v Clark & Co* (1868) 7 M 51 and *Murray v Arbuthnot* (1870) 9 M 198.
3 Rule 39.6(1).
4 Rule 39.6(2).
5 Rule 39.6(3).

HEARING OF APPLICATION

26.03   The application will usually be dealt with as a single bill but, in a case of complexity or difficulty, the court may appoint the application to the summar roll for a full hearing[6].

DISPOSAL OF APPLICATION

26.04   At a hearing the court may do one of three things, namely:

(a)   where it is of the opinion that the direction in law of the presiding judge was erroneous and that the party making the application was truly entitled to the verdict in whole or in part, direct the verdict to be entered for that party in whole or in part, either absolutely or in such terms as it may think fit;

(b)   where the court is of the opinion that it is necessary, set aside the verdict and order a new trial; or

(c)   refuse the application[7].

6 Rule 39.6(4).
7 Court of Session Act 1988, s 31(2).

Chapter 27

Appeals from the Inner House

27.01   It is competent for parties in a civil jury cause to mark an appeal from the Inner House of the Court of Session to the House of Lords[1] in respect of any interlocutors which have been reclaimed, and leave is not required where either the interlocutor itself disposed of the whole merits of the cause or where, in the case of an interlocutory judgment, it was revealed that there was a difference of opinion between the judges in the Inner House[2].

27.02   An interlocutor of the court granting or refusing a new trial is appeallable to the House of Lords without leave from the Inner House[3]. On the hearing of such an appeal the House of Lords has the same powers available to it as the Inner House has and these include the power to set aside a verdict contrary to the evidence or to grant a new trial restricted to quantum where the ground of the challenge was one of an excess or inadequacy of damages[4]. In practice it is rare for such appeals to be taken in the House of Lords and since 1972 only one such case has been heard there[5].

27.03   It is incompetent to seek to appeal to the House of Lords directly from the interlocutor of a Lord Ordinary or the verdict of the jury unless the matter has already been considered by the Inner House[6].

27.04   The effect of an appeal to the House of Lords is similar to that of an appeal to the Inner House in that it opens up all of the previously pronounced interlocutors in the cause[7]. The House of Lords, in hearing the appeal, may

---

1 At the time of writing (2006) Part 3 of the Constitutional Reform Act 2005 had not come into force. When (and if) it does then all references to the House of Lords should be read as referring to the Supreme Court of the UK and the procedure therein will be regulated by the Supreme Court Rules which will be made under s 45 of the 2005 Act.
2 Court of Session Act 1988, s 40(1).
3 Until 1972 it was thought that only certain interlocutors were thus appealable: see *Lyal v Henderson* 1916 SC (HL) 167 and Thompson and Middleton, p 391. The position is now regulated by s 40(2) of the 1988 Act.
4 1988 Act, s 40(2).
5 *Girvan v Inverness Farmers' Dairy (No 2)* 1998 SC (HL) 1.
6 1988 Act, s 40(3).
7 1988 Act, s 40(4).

make such orders with regard to the payment of interest on damages as it thinks fit[8] and expenses, insofar as not already awarded, are at their Lordships' discretion. Their Lordships may make such orders as to expenses and interest as they think fit when an appeal is dismissed for want of prosecution[9].

8 1988 Act, s 42.
9 1988 Act, s 43.

Appendix I

Styles for issues, counter-issues and notes of exception

The following is a series of styles for issues, counter-issues and notes of exception and in each category, for the sake of brevity, the instance is not repeated after the first example and the heads of damage given in selected examples are not exhaustive but merely representative.

ISSUES

A1   Reparation – accident – single pursuer – single defender

PROPOSED ISSUE

For the Pursuer

in the cause

[Name, designation, address]   Pursuer

against

[Name, designation, address]   Defender

WHETHER on or about *[date]* at *[place]* the pursuer sustained injury caused by the fault of the defender.

DAMAGES CLAIMED   £ *[sum in conclusion]*

Solatium to date
Future *solatium*
Loss of earnings to date
Future loss of earnings
Past services rendered by daughter Jane
Future services rendered by daughter Jane
Past loss of services
Future loss of services

TOTAL DAMAGES:

Note: This style of issue is based on that approved of in *Macdonald v Glasgow Corporation* 1973 SC 52. The defenders in this example have disputed in the pleadings the fact of whether or not the accident actually occurred: see **10.09** above. The person who rendered the services (e.g. daughter Jane) should be named in the issue: see **10.17** above.

A2   Reparation – disease – single pursuer – single defender

WHETHER on or about *[date]* the pursuer contracted *[disease or condition]* through the fault of the defender [to the loss, injury or damage of the pursuer].

A3   Reparation – accident – single pursuer – single defender – contributory negligence

WHETHER the accident to the pursuer on or about *[date]* at *[place]* was caused by any extent by the fault of the defender.

Note: In this example the defenders do not dispute that an accident occurred.

A4   Reparation – accident – single pursuer – two defenders

WHETHER the accident to the pursuer at *[place]* on or about *[date]* was caused by the fault of either of the defenders.

Note: This situation would cover a case where the defenders are sued on a joint and several basis; where liability is being pled on two separate grounds then a separate issue against each defender will be required.

A5   Reparation – accident – single pursuer – defender and third party – contributory negligence

WHETHER the accident to the pursuer at *[place]* on or about *[date]* was caused to any extent by the fault of the defender.

Note: In this example the third party has not been convened as a defender by the pursuer.

A6   Reparation – accident – single pursuer – insurer sued directly

WHETHER the accident to the pursuer at *[place]* on *[date]* was caused by the fault of the late *[X]* for which the defenders are liable.

A7   Reparation – accident – multiple pursuers – single defender

WHETHER the accident to the pursuers at *[place]* on or about *[date]* was caused by the fault of the defenders.

DAMAGES CLAIMED

By the First Pursuer   £ *[sum in conclusion for first pursuer]*
[heads of claim]

TOTAL DAMAGES

By the Second Pursuer
[heads of claim]   £ *[sum in conclusion for second pursuer]*

TOTAL DAMAGES

A8   Reparation – accident – fatal case – vicarious liability

WHETHER the death of *[name]* on or about *[date]* at *[place]* was caused to any extent by the fault of *[name]* in the course of his employment with the defenders.

A9   Reparation – accident – fatal case – transmitted and family claims – multiple pursuers – single defender – contributory negligence

WHETHER the accident to the deceased at *[place]* on or about *[date]* was caused to any extent by the fault of the defender.

DAMAGES CLAIMED

By the First Pursuer as executrix of the deceased   £ *[sum in conclusion]*
Solatium [for the deceased's pain and suffering]
Past services rendered by the first pursuer
Funeral and headstone expenses

TOTAL DAMAGES

By the First Pursuer as an individual   £ *[sum in conclusion]*
s 1(4) Damages (Scotland) Act award – to date
s 1(4) Damages (Scotland) Act award – future
Loss of support to date
Future loss of support
Loss of services to date
Future loss of services

TOTAL DAMAGES

By the First Pursuer as guardian of the child *[name]*   £ *[sum in conclusion]*
s 1(4) Damages (Scotland) Act award – to date
s 1(4) Damages (Scotland) Act award – future
Loss of support to date
Future loss of support

TOTAL DAMAGES

By the Second Pursuer   £ *[sum in conclusion]*
s 1(4) Damages (Scotland) Act award – to date
s 1(4) Damages (Scotland) Act award – future

TOTAL DAMAGES

A10   Reparation – accident – single pursuer and defender – recoverable benefits

WHETHER the accident to the pursuer on or about *[date]* at *[place]* was caused by the fault of the defender.

DAMAGES CLAIMED   £ *[sum in conclusion]*

Solatium to date
Future *solatium*
Disadvantage in labour market
Past services by stepmother Susan
   (cost of care component £   )
   (loss of mobility component £   )
Past cost of tradesmen
Past cost of medical care
Future cost of medical care
   (amount to *[date]* £   )
   Cost of cancellation of Africa trip

TOTAL DAMAGES

Note: This style is based on the actual issues approved in *Mitchell v Laing*, reported in the Inner House at 1998 SC 342. The apportionments required for the purposes of the Social Security (Recoverable Benefits) Act 1997 are contained in the sub-heads and in this example the relevant period is still running, i.e. the quinquennium has not yet expired; if it had expired then the apportionment would be in respect of elements of past loss only. For other examples of issues involving benefits see (1998) Rep L Bul 21–23.

A11   Defamation – written – innuendo

WHETHER the statements in the article published by the defenders in the *[name of publication]* on *[date]* falsely and calumniously said that the pursuer *[specify statements referred to on record]* meaning thereby that *[specify defamatory innuendo set out on record]* to the loss, injury and damage of the pursuer.

A12   Defamation – written – solatium and patrimonial loss

WHETHER the statements in the article set out in the schedule hereto published by the defenders in *[name of publication]* on *[date]* falsely and calumniously represented that the pursuer *[set out defamatory aspects averred on record]* to the loss, injury and damage of the pursuer.

Alternative form of issue:
WHETHER the statements in an article published by the defenders in the *[name of publication]* on *[date]* falsely and calumniously represented that the pursuer was *[specify the defamatory aspect set out on record]* to the loss, injury and damage of the pursuer.

DAMAGES CLAIMED: £ *[sum in conclusion]*

Solatium to date
Future *solatium*
Loss of profits to date
Future loss of profits

TOTAL DAMAGES

A13   Defamation – broadcast – innuendo

WHETHER the statements in a television programme broadcast by the defenders on *[date]* falsely and calumniously said that the pursuer *[specify statements referred to on record]* meaning thereby that *[specify defamatory innuendo set out on record]* to the loss, injury and damage of the pursuer.

A14   Reparation – assault

WHETHER on or about *[date]* at *[place]* the defender assaulted the pursuer to his loss, injury and damage.

A15　Reparation – police assault

WHETHER on or about *[date]* at *[place]* the pursuer was assaulted by police officers of the *[name police force]* acting in the course of their duties, to his loss, injury and damage.

A16　Reparation – sexual and physical abuse

WHETHER between *[date]* and *[date]* at the defender's residential children's home at *[place]* the defender's employee *[name]* sexually and physically assaulted the pursuer to his loss, injury and damage.

A17　Reparation – wrongful arrest and imprisonment

WHETHER on or about *[date]* *[name]* acting in the course of his employment with the defenders maliciously and without probable cause apprehended the pursuer at *[place]* where he was detained, to his loss, injury and damage.

A18　Reparation – wrongful detention

WHETHER on or about *[date]* *[names]* acting in the course of their employment with the defenders wrongfully and illegally detained the pursuer at *[place]* to his loss, injury and damage.

A19　Wrongful prosecution

WHETHER the prosecution by the Procurator-fiscal, *[place]*, of the pursuer on *[date]* arose in consequence of police officers of the *[name police force]* acting in the course of their duties, reporting falsely and maliciously that the pursuer had committed a crime.

A20　Reduction of deed – total incapacity of granter

WHETHER the pretended *[specify deed, e.g. trust disposition and settlement]* dated *[date]* No *[ ]* of process is not the deed of *[name of purported granter]*.

A21　Reduction of deed – essential error – misrepresentation

WHETHER the pursuer signed *[specify deed]* dated *[date]* No *[ ]* of process while under essential error as to a material part of the contract, induced by a misrepresentation of the defender.

A22   Reduction of deed – force and fear

WHETHER *[specify deed]* No *[ ]* of process was obtained by the defender from the pursuer by force and fear without his receiving any [or the proper] value therefor.

COUNTER-ISSUES

B1   Reparation – accident – single pursuer – single defender – contributory negligence

PROPOSED COUNTER-ISSUE

for the Defender

in the cause

[name, designation and address]   Pursuer

against

[name, designation and address]   Defender

WHETHER the accident was caused partly by the fault of the pursuer and partly by the fault of the defender and, if so, what proportion of the blame is attributable to each.

1. Proportion attributable to pursuer	*[amount]* %
2. Proportion attributable to defender	*[amount]* %
	100 %

Note: This is the appropriate counter-issue to use with style A.3.

B2   Reparation – accident – single pursuer – two defenders

IF the accident was caused partly by the fault of the first defender and partly by the fault of the second defender and, if so, what proportion of the blame is attributable to both.

1. Proportion attributable to the first defender	*[amount]* %
2. Proportion attributable to the second defender	*[amount]* %
	100 %

Note: This is the appropriate counter-issue to use with style A4.

B3   Reparation – accident – single pursuer – defender, third party and contributory negligence

IF the accident was caused partly by the fault of the pursuer and partly by the fault of the defender and partly by the fault of the third party, what proportion of the blame is attributable to each of them.

1. Proportion attributable to the pursuer	*[amount]* %
2. Proportion attributable to defender	*[amount]* %
3. Proportion attributable to third party	*[amount]* %
	100 %

Note: This is the appropriate counter-issue to use with style A5.

B4   Reparation – accident – *volenti non fit injuria*

WHETHER the pursuer willingly and knowingly undertook the risk of accident and consequent loss, injury and damage.

B5   Defamation – veritas

WHETHER on or about *[date]* at or about *[place]* the pursuer *[e.g. dishonestly appropriated to his own use the sum of £100,000, the property of his employers, XY Ltd.]*

Note: The substance of the alleged defamation should be set out so as to mirror, as closely as possible, the substance alleged in the issue.

B6   Defamation – fair comment

Upon the assumptions that the statements complained of by the pursuer (i) bore the meanings (or any of them) put on them by the issue and (ii) were defamatory of the pursuer.

WHETHER the statements complained of by the pursuer bearing the said meaning(s) were written and published in good faith as fair comment on matters of public interest?

(a) . . .
(b) . . .
(c) . . .
(d) . . .

Note: This counter-issue was approved in *McCormick v Scottish Daily Record & Sunday Mail Ltd* and the specific matters (a) to (d) in that case are as listed in the report of the jury's verdict in Appendix III, 3 [4] below.

NOTES OF EXCEPTION

C1   Misdirection

NOTE OF EXCEPTIONS

For the *[pursuer/defender]*

in the cause

[Name, designation and address]   Pursuer

against

[Name, designation and address]   Defender

WHEREAS at the trial of the issue [and the counter-issue] in this cause held at Edinburgh on the *[ ]* day of *[ ]* 2005 The [Right] Honourable Lord *[name]*, in charging the jury, directed *inter alia* as follows:

[take in the objectionable part of the charge so far as can be accurately recalled]

WHEREUPON the counsel for the *[pursuer/defender]* excepted to the direction and further requested his Lordship to give the following direction *[take in direction sought]* which direction his Lordship refused to give; counsel for the *[pursuer/defender]* excepts to that refusal.

C2   Failure to direct

WHEREAS at the trial of the issue [and counter-issue] in this cause held at Edinburgh on the *[ ]* day of *[ ]* 2005 counsel for the *[pursuer/defender]* requested his Lordship to give the following direction *[take in direction sought]* which direction his Lordship refused to give; the counsel for the *[pursuer/defender]* excepts to that refusal.

Appendix II

Example opening speech for pursuer

The following is an example of an opening speech which junior counsel for the pursuer might make in a typical personal injuries action. It was prepared by Lord McGhie for a Faculty of Advocates seminar on jury trials held in 1997 and is reproduced here by his kind permission.

"Ladies and gentlemen, you are here today to deal with a claim brought by Mr Brown against the Secretary of State for compensation for injuries sustained in a road accident. The Secretary of State was not personally involved in the accident but he is named because he is responsible in law for the actings of drivers employed on certain types of official business and the accident involved one of his drivers.

"I am the junior counsel acting for Mr Brown who is the pursuer, or claimant, in this action. Mr Jones [pointing] is the senior counsel for the pursuer. Mr Jones will be responsible for leading the evidence on behalf of the pursuer, Mr Brown, and he will address you after you have heard the evidence to explain why you should award damages to Mr Brown and to help you assess how much. The defender in the case is, as I have told you, the Secretary of State but he is sued simply because he is responsible for the driver. He is represented by senior counsel, Mrs Black, and by junior counsel, Mr Smith. Once the evidence has been led, it will be your job to reach a decision on which parts of the evidence you believe to be true and reliable and to answer certain questions which I will discuss with you later. His Lordship's job is to decide on any matters of law which may arise. However, this is a straightforward case arising out of a road accident and it will be for you to reach all the important decisions.

"There is no dispute that there was a road accident. It is admitted that Mr Brown was driving his car in Dalkeith Road in Edinburgh. It is admitted that there was a collision at a set of traffic lights. There was no dispute that Mr Brown sustained serious injuries, including a broken leg. It is admitted that the driver of the car which struck his car was a driver for whom the Secretary of State is responsible.

"What Mr Brown says happened is that he was driving in a perfectly normal way down Dalkeith Road and crossed into the junction when the lights were showing green in his favour. As he was halfway across, he was struck by the official car. He says that the driver went through a red light and that that was the cause of the accident.

"Damages cannot be recovered in an action such as this unless the pursuer is able to satisfy you that the accident was caused by the fault of the defender or, in this case, the defender's driver. You may think that if he went through on a red light then there is not much difficulty about fault. However, the pursuer's case, in other words the pursuer's claim, is that the driver was travelling too fast. His case is that the driver did not keep a good look out. His case is that the driver was at fault, not only because he went through a red light but because he ought to have seen his car in time to stop or avoid it. Your job will be to listen to the evidence and to decide whether you agree that the pursuer has established fault on any of these grounds.

"If you decide that fault has been established, you will have to consider what will be the appropriate award for compensation for the injuries and trouble which he has sustained. You will hear evidence that he had a broken leg and was confined to the house for many weeks. His wife had to nurse him. He was off work. There are certain other losses which you will hear about. Senior counsel will address you in more detail about what you will make of the question of loss once you have heard the evidence.

"To help you in reaching your decision, and to assist the court when it comes to make a formal order at the end of the case, the issues for you have been set out in a document. I think that you have been given copies. This is the document headed with the words 'Issue for the Pursuer' and you will see the pursuer's name set out there and also the formal name and address of the Secretary of State. I think I have explained why his name appears there. It is because he is responsible for the actings of the driver of the official car. The questions which you have to answer are set out there. As I have told you, there is no dispute that there was an accident at the place and at the time which is set out in the question. It will be obvious to you that the real question is whether the accident was caused by the fault of the defender's driver. If once you have heard all of the evidence, you think it was, you should answer the question 'yes'. That is what senior counsel will be inviting you to do at the end of the case. He will also take you through the schedule of damages and invite you to consider the evidence which has been led on each point. You will see that you will be asked to make an award under the various headings. Perhaps I might explain at this stage the word *solatium*. That is the old Scots law word which we use because it is convenient to describe the award for compensation for pain and suffering. The English word 'solace' may give you some idea of what is in mind. You have to decide what is an appropriate award for the general pain and suffering which Mr Brown sustained. You will see that this is quite different from the claim for his loss of earnings which is a separate head of claim and you will see the other heads which are more or less self–explanatory and which will become clearer once you have heard the evidence and heard the closing speeches.

"Ladies and gentlemen, as I have already told you, it is the jury's job to hear the evidence and to answer the questions [holding up issue] in the light of the view that you take about the evidence. In a claim for damages like the present, your job is to decide things on a balance of probabilities. In other words, if you think that it is more likely than not, for example, the defender's car went through on the red light, you will be able to answer the issue 'yes'. This will be explained to you in greater detail before you are actually asked to go and consider your decision in private in the jury room. I will now invite you to consider the evidence in the case which will be led by senior counsel for the pursuer."

Appendix III

Some recent jury awards

This Appendix contains details of non-patrimonial awards made by Scottish juries during the last fifteen years although it does not claim to be exhaustive. Where no citation is given, the date stated is that upon which the verdict was delivered. Awards are listed in descending order of value and to ascertain their present day values the appropriate inflation tables in McEwan & Paton should be consulted. Counsel and agents involved in jury trials are encouraged to submit details of awards to the author for publication on the website www.civiljurytrials.com *and in the Reparation Law Reports.*

1. DEATH CLAIMS BY RELATIVES UNDER DAMAGES (SCOTLAND) ACT 1976, S 1(4)

[1] Warnock v Clark Contracts
Lord Wheatley and jury, 18 November 2004
Male, 34, sustained massive head injuries after falling through skylight and died the following day. No s 1(4)(a) element pled. The deceased lived in family with wife (aged 32) and three children – two boys aged 9 and 6 and girl aged 3. Trial 4½ years after accident. Loss of support awarded to widow £247,000 (£64,000 to past), eldest son John £23,000, younger son Brian £23,000, daughter Kimberley £23,000. Loss of services £12,000 to widow, £750 (£500 to past) to each child.
s 1(4) award to widow: £40,000 (£10,000 to past); £16,250 (£13,750 to past) to eldest son John; £16,000 (£13,750 to past) to younger son Brian; £16,000 (£13,750 to past) to daughter Kimberley

[2] McIntosh v Findlay
2001 Rep LR 66
Male, 19, killed in road traffic accident. At time of death his girlfriend was pregnant and his son was born a few days posthumously. Evidence that deceased would have been good parent to child despite not cohabiting with girlfriend.
s 1(4) award to child: £37,500

[3] Wells v Hay

1999 Rep LR 44

Male, 19, seriously injured in road traffic accident with multiple injuries and extensive burns. Conscious while rescued and died in hospital 16 days later. Mother was single parent who was very distressed by the extent of his injuries and his death. The jury awarded funeral expenses of £2,853.63 and the remainder of the sum sued for as solatium.

s 1(4) award to mother; £37,146.37 (£25,000 to past)

[4] Kempton v British Railways Board

(1993) McEwan & Paton, 13/93-2, The Scotsman, 15 May 1993

Male railway work, 39, killed by train on Forth Bridge. Three sons (16, 12, 8) and one daughter (6); two of children's claims settled extra-judicially. The jury awarded the widow and two sons who had not settled the sums sued for.

s 1(4) (unamended) award to widow: £35,000; to 12-year-old child: £11,500; to 8-year-old child: £11,500

[5] Strang v LeBrusq

2001 Rep LR 52

Parents claim in respect of death of male, 21, killed in road traffic accident. At time of death he had been living at home with parents with whom he had close relationship.

s 1(4) award: £30,000 to each parent

[6] Davidson v Chief Constable, Fife Police

Lord Hamilton and jury, 18 May 1995

Young man with extensive criminal record hanged himself in police cells while awaiting court appearance. Previous threats and attempts to commit suicide. Not put on "suicide watch". 95% contributory negligence finding.

s 1(4) (unamended) award to mother £10,000 (all to past); to cohabiting girlfriend NIL, to posthumous child £15,000 (£5,000 to past)

[7] Gillies v Lynch

Lady Clark of Calton and jury, 24 March 2006

Female, 24, killed with boyfriend in road traffic accident in December 1995. Deceased's mother was single parent who kept in daily contact with her and had long history of mental health and physical problems including recurring depression; unusual degree of emotional dependence on deceased. Psychiatrist described "nightmare scenario" of mother having been informed of death by police at 11 pm and of having to identify body in mortuary. Mother now suffering pathological grief reaction by reason of circumstances, nature of relationship and prior vulnerability meaning that in effect she was stuck in second stage of grief reaction (an inability to function normally because of intrusive thoughts, etc) and could not accept death of daughter and unlikely to move on to acceptance stage; psychiatrist stating that average period for this stage usually 6–12 months. Prognosis poor, particularly in view of continuing mental health problems. Liability admitted and funeral expenses agreed at £3,406.

s 1(4) award to mother £80,000 (£50,000 to past)

2. SOLATIUM AWARDS

[1] Shaw v Russell & Anor
2004 Rep LR 99
Woman, 24, pillion passenger on motorbike which collided with van suffered multiple injuries. Left-sided facial paralysis for 6 months and permanent eye injury. Residual weakness in left leg. Right non-dominant arm rendered useless by nerve damage. Underwent operations on arm after accident and 3 months later and required above elbow amputation 4 years later. Considerable pain over whole period and still suffered pain (including phantom pain). Single mother with two children required additional help and services. Patrimonial loss and services agreed at £440,000.
Solatium: £300,000 (£150,000 to past)

[2] McLeod v British Railways Board
2001 SC 534
Boy, 12, sustained burns all over his body after touching power cable. In hospital for 9 months, undergoing at least 10 operations including skin grafts and plastic surgery to various areas, and in great pain. Unable to dress himself for 2 years. Permanent scarring to left side of face and neck, to back and to hand. Ability to write and to carry still affected. Might need further operations.
Solatium: £250,000 (£200,000 to past)
Award upheld by Inner House.

[3] Leeder v Advocate General for Scotland
2004 Rep LR 99
Lance corporal, 31, member of parachute display team, landed on concrete and sustained serious back injury with one vertebra crushed, another fractured and severed nerves; 4 fractures in left foot. Left with ongoing pain in back and leg which increased on exercise. Required walking stick and special appliance for leg. Incontinent and had to evacuate bowels manually every day. Sexual function adversely affected. Developing arthritis and risk of fusion operation in future. Unable to continue in Army. £40,000 past wage loss; £334,000 future wage loss awarded.
Solatium: £250,000 (£100,000 to past)

[4] Mill v British Railways Board
(1996), McEwan & Paton, CN17-00
Male, 37, had right leg amputated below knee as a result of accident and subsequent amputation of left foot. Fractured ribs and muscle damage resulting in

acute renal failure and need for dialysis. Continuing problems, depression, anger and agitation.
Solatium: £225,000 (£150,000 to past)

[5] Middleton v Smith
(1992) BPILS Bulletin 11
Right-handed draftsman, 37, suffered severe injury to right arm in motorcycle accident. Arm amputated at shoulder and left with cosmetically disfigured shoulder. No benefit from prosthesis. Returned to work 3 months after accident. Retrained as left-handed draftsman. Able to live independently and had learned to drive since accident.
Solatium: £127,000 (£27,000 to past)

[6] Girvan v Inverness Farmers' Dairy (No 1)
1995 SLT 735
Solatium: £120,000 (£70,000 to past)
Held excessive and new trial ordered: see [8] below.

[7] Adamson v Lothian Health Board
2000 Rep LR (Quantum) 44
Male, 26, born with one testicle had that testicle removed after wrongly diagnosed malignant testicular cancer. Now unable to father child (which he might previously have been able to); adverse emotional reactions and obsessive compulsive disorder. Would require deep vein hormone injections for rest of life.
Solatium: £100,000

[8] Girvan v Inverness Farmers' Dairy (No 2)
1996 SLT 631 (IH); 1998 SC (HL) 1
Male, 39, sustained lacerations to head and knee, fracture to right dominant elbow with permanent deficit affecting ability as clay pigeon shot of international standing; possibility of further deterioration.
Solatium: £95,000 (£35,000 to past)

[9] Currie v Kilmarnock and Loudon District Council
1996 SC 481
Male, 46, minor injuries to right foot and serious crushing injuries including multiple fractures, lacerations and degloving to left leg with serious continuing disabilities. Four operations including toe amputation and grafts. Likely to require below-knee amputation. Social life and domestic tasks affected and unable to continue with athletics.
Solatium: £91,000 (£30,000 to past)

[10] Carmichael v Isola Werke (UK) Ltd
Lord Bracadale and jury, 19 May 2005
Female process worker, 29, suffered traumatic amputation of 4 fingers on dominant right hand 5 years prior to trial. Continuing pain and discomfort at

stump sites, reduced grip and unable to carry out intricate tasks. Fitted with prosthetic fingers which required regular replacement. Conscious of disfigurement and suffered severe post-traumatic stress disorder which, by date of trial, had significantly improved. Past loss of earnings (agreed) £11,361, disadvantage in labour market £10,000, prescription costs (agreed) £24, travelling expenses (agreed) £1,093.60, clothing loss (agreed) £20, GP fees (agreed) £20, prosthetic costs – past (agreed) £2,148 future £31,450, fitting lotion costs (agreed) past £16.11 future £232, section 8 services past (agreed) £1,000, section 9 services, past £1,500, future nil.
Solatium: £85,000 (£68,000 to past)

[11] Tate v Fischer
1998 SLT 1419
Male taxi driver, 45, suffered bruising and whiplash injury in road traffic accident with fractured sternum and shattered right heel bone. Asthma attack immediately after accident. Continuing heel problems with permanent discomfort and disability. Suffered post-traumatic stress and generally adverse effect on his life. £1,000 services award.
Solatium: £75,000 (£25,000 to past)
Award of solatium not challenged in Inner House.

[12] Davis v Bryson
24 May 2002; 2004 Rep LR 99
Male, 54, self-employed forester, injured in road traffic accident with fracture dislocation of right hips, small bowel perforations, haematoma; developed renal failure, a chest infection and a hernia. Hospital in-patient for 4 weeks. Still suffered pain after 5 years, walked with limp and left with residual disabilities. Risk of hip degeneration. Unable to return to work he enjoyed or take part in country pursuits. Agreed wage loss, services and patrimonial loss.
Solatium: £71,000 (£35,000 to past)

[13] Gartley v R McCartney (Painters) Ltd
1997 Rep LR (Quantum) 18
Painter with crush fracture of first lumbar vertebra and fracture of both heel bones. Confined to wheelchair for 6 months after accident and suffered pain and residual disabilities thereafter. Depressed and anxious and unable to return to work. Died 3 years later from unconnected reasons.
Solatium: £70,000 (all to past)

[14] Towers v Jack
2004 Rep LR 100
Female psychotherapist, 35, sustained life-threatening injuries in road traffic accident involving 4 fractures of the pelvis and associated bones, severe rib fractures, collapsed lung and liver damage and multiple lacerations. In intensive care for 4 days, thereafter in traction. Underwent 2 stomach operations.

Unable to return to work for 21 months and permanent sequelae including left sacro ilial joint pain.
Solatium: £70,000 (£45,000 to past)

[15] Bryce v Adam Stark Ltd
Lord McEwan and jury, 20 June 2005
Male air conditioning engineer, 25, suffered serious leg injuries in road traffic accident 4 years before trial. Broken fibulas, femur requiring external fixation, nailing and other treatment. Left with residual pain and likelihood that osteo-arthritis would set in with increasing pain and disability within next 5 years and that consequently he would have to give up pre-accident employ-ment. Past wage loss (agreed) £15,000, future wage loss (agreed multiplicand, disputed multiplier) £145,000, section 8 services to each parent £500, miscel-laneous outlays £7,500.
Solatium: £60,000 (£50,000 to past)

[16] Marnoch v British Railways Board
(1993) McEwan & Paton, CN3-00D
Male, 65, sustained multiple fractures of ribs, left pneumothorax, injuries to hand with permanent deficit, fracture of scapula with loss of power to arm; previous hip replacement affected adversely causing further symptoms, pain and disturbed sleep.
Solatium: £55,000

[17] Wells v Hay
1999 Rep LR 44
Male, 19, injured in road traffic accident. Conscious, moving, moaning and screaming while trapped in car for 40 minutes. Suffered fractured skull, fractures of right femur and left fibula, chest injuries, partial lung collapse and 60% full thickness burns to face, neck, chest, back, abdomen, arms, hands, upper buttocks and left leg. Kept in intensive care and died after 16 days. Regained consciousness at least once and showed signs of pain and dis-comfort.
Solatium awarded to executrix: £50,000

[18] Masse v Lord Advocate
1999 Rep LR (Quantum) 75
Man, early 50s, involved in horrific boating accident in which colleague sus-tained serious injury and died. Pursuer had minimal physical injuries but thought he was going to drown. Forced to witness colleague's suffering and felt guilty about not being able to help him. Suffered moderate post-traumatic stress disorder, off work 3 months, nightmares, irritability, poor temper con-trol, sexual dysfunction, prone to breaking down in tears, continuing fear of boat and swimming out of his depth. Ongoing symptoms.
Solatium: £42,000 (£32,000 to past)

[19] Stuart v Lothian and Borders Fire Board
1997 Rep LR (Quantum) 17
Fireman, 49, injured when carrying out rope line rescue of drunk man from Edinburgh Castle rock. Bruising of rib-cage, whiplash, soft tissue injury to neck and traction injury to shoulder. Post-traumatic stress disorder, personality change, depression and suicidal tendencies. Poor prognosis and continuing emotional and psychological problems.
Solatium: £35,000 (£20,000 to past)

[20] Walker v Moncur
2001 Rep LR 67
Male, 16, injured in road traffic accident and sustained a scar to his face which extended from the level of his ear to under his jaw and of which he was very self-conscious.
Solatium: £25,000

[21] Graham v The Ubiquitous Chip
1999 Rep LR (Quantum) 75
Part-time waitress, 31, slipped and fell while carrying wine glass and suffered serious hand injury requiring operation to repair nerve and tendon damage. Off work several months. Left with difficulty holding pen, scarring and numbness to her fingers. Award of £750 for disadvantage on labour market (pursuer had returned to work as a teacher with little difficulty).
Solatium: £24,000

[22] Cameron v Lanarkshire Health Board
(1996), McEwan & Paton, CN4-00
Female nurse, 39, suffered prolapsed lumbar disc; two painful operations. Persistent low back pain over 7 years to trial and continuing. Had TENS machine to alleviate pain and unable to carry out heavy domestic chores or return to work.
Solatium: £22,500 (£15,000 to past)

[23] Buchanan v Mason
2001 Rep LR 67
Male, 50s, injured in road traffic accident. Whiplash with claimed continuing neck pain for 4 years, along with "dead arm", loss of muscle power and depression. Unable to return to work. No award for services.
Solatium: £ 21,000

[24] Macarthur v Chief Constable, Strathclyde Police
1989 SLT 517
Female placed forcibly into police Land Rover and sustained avulsion fracture and ligament damage in fibula with permanent restriction and disability in left leg. Post-traumatic arthritic degeneration expected.
Solatium: £15,000

[25] George v Bank of Scotland
1997 Rep LR (Quantum) 18

Female bank worker, 37, slipped and fell heavily to ground, injuring right hip and shoulder. Suffered bruising and rotator cuff lesion and impingement requiring cortisone injections. Underwent decompression surgery and left with frozen shoulder and persistent symptoms for a period thereafter.
Solatium: £15,000 (all to past)

[26] Harmer v West Lothian NHS Trust
(1998), McEwan & Paton, CN4-04A

Female nursing auxiliary, 42, injured back assisting a patient. Suffered sprain of lower thoracic spine. Offwork 6 months and permanently unable for pre-accident employment but fit for light duties. Back pain recurred after modest exertion.
Solatium: £12,500 (£8,500 to past)

[27] Malcolm v Lothian and Borders Fire Board
23 November 1990

Fireman, 40s, injured when answering alarm call and missed fireman's pole. Fell 20 feet sustaining severe leg fractures and bruising. Left with limp and residual discomfort. Unable to return to employment.
Solatium: £11,143

[28] Ross v Fife Healthcare NHS Trust
1999 Rep LR (Quantum) 75

Right-handed female nursing auxiliary, 41, fell onto outstretched left hand and patient and nurse fell on top of her. Minimally displaced left Colles fracture, manipulated under analgesia and immobilised in plaster and sling. Off work for 10 months. Some continuing aching, tingling and restriction of movement. Reduced grip. Limited ability to lift, carry or climb ladders. Unable to bowl. £19,000 award for disability on labour market.
Solatium: £8,500 (£4,500 to past)

New trial ordered on basis that verdict contrary to evidence; solatium not challenged.

[29] Shaw v McKinlay
Lord Hardie, 21 October 2005

Male refrigeration engineer, 38, involved in accident in 1997 in which he sustained soft tissue injury with continuing pain and loss of a lateral incisor tooth requiring extensive root canal treatment and the fitting of a tooth implant. Awarded £50 for s 9 services, £3,150 for past dental costs, £1,500 for future dental costs.
Solatium: £6,000 (£5,000 to past)

[30] Baillie v Leafield Nursing Home
Lord Kirkwood, 31 March 1994

Care assistant, 33, slipped on wet floor and injured knee. Continuing pain and reduced movement in knee joint with residual restrictions. £40,000 award for disadvantage on labour market.

Solatium: £6,950 (£2,750 to past)

Action compromised after motion for new trial on basis of *res noviter* and verdict contrary to evidence intimated.

[31] Tait v Campbell

2004 Rep LR 100

Middle-aged female sustained injuries including extensive bruising and broken arm when thrown to floor of a bus which braked violently. Agreed wage loss: £500; agreed miscellaneous losses of £750.

Solatium: £5,000 (£3,000 to past)

Reported in relation to tender and expenses at 2004 SLT 187.

[32] Sneddon v Deutag Services

Lord Carloway and jury, 1 November 2004

Pursuer, while unscrewing drill pipe on oil platform, was hit in eye by hydraulic fluid escaping from high pressure pipe. Suffered eye injury and ongoing eye irritation and declared medically unfit to work offshore. Returned to onshore work 26 months after accident. Past wage loss (agreed) £38,278, future wage loss £50,000, loss of pension contributions £11,000.

Solatium: £5,000 (£4,000 to past)

[33] Campbell v Secretary of State for Scotland

7 October 1989, Scotsman

Male prisoner, 36, attacked in cell with weapons by prison officers. Sustained serious bruising and tear in bowel requiring hospital treatment. Said to have been in great pain for a period.

Solatium: £4,000

[34] Robb v Sutherland

Lord Osborne and jury, 30 January 1996

Male labourer, 20s, sustained lacerations to upper lip and wrists and bruising to head, face and body as a result of being thrown to the ground and repeatedly kicked and punched by police officers.

Solatium: £3,000

[35] Mitchell v North Glasgow University Hospitals NHS Trust

(2002) 48 Rep L Bul 2; 2004 Rep LR 100

Nurse, 45, slipped and sustained displaced Colles fracture of right wrist requiring manipulation under anaesthetic and subsequent surgery for carpal tunnel syndrome. Returned to work after 6 months but permanent sequelae including permanent reduction of grip and difficulties with fine manipulation. Past services award of £750.

Solatium: £2,750 (£2,500 to past)

[36] Jamieson v Higgins
1998 Rep LR (Quantum) 23

Female car passenger, 35, sustained whiplash injury, with emotional reaction resulting in sleeping difficulties, nightmares and car phobia lasting 1 year. Some physiotherapy and claimed to still be suffering from pain.

Solatium: £2,500 (all to past)

[37] Manton v Commissioners for Northern Lights
(2003) 43 JLSS Nov/55, 2004 Rep LR 100

Female, 59, slipped and sustained sore knee and minor tissue injury with muscular strain of shoulder exacerbating underlying condition and cut finger. Some pain and discomfort for about one year. No services award.

Solatium: £1,000 (all to past)

[38] Kirkpatrick v Secretary of State for Scotland
24 April 1997

Male prisoner, 25, assaulted by police officers. Subjected to restraining technique and sustained bruising injuries particularly to wrist which developed into carpal tunnel syndrome. Medical evidence complicated by onset of arthritis.

Solatium: £500

[39] Craig v Whitbread plc
Lord Turnbull and jury, 27 April 2006

Male service engineer, 31 at date of accident, 36 at trial, suffered severe gash to left non-dominant hand, severing ulnar nerve. Wound failed to heal, causing marked functional deficit and significant continuing pain to date. Psychological sequelae after accident triggered adjustment disorder with anxiety and depression. Agreed deduction for contributory negligence 15%. Past wage loss £9,500, future loss of employability £45,000, services £2,000.

Solatium: £16,000 (£8,000 to past)

3. DEFAMATION AWARDS

[1] Clinton v News Group Newspapers Ltd
Lord Nimmo Smith and jury, 18 December 1999

Series of newspaper articles describing "close six year relationship" and "bizarre cloak and dagger meetings" between pursuer, 50-year-old female teacher, and a 42-year-old priest, Fr Barry. A jury found that articles implied that pursuer and Fr Barry were having a sexual relationship. Unwanted publicity, damaged reputation, hurt feelings and harassment from journalists, photographers and members of public.

Award: £120,000

[2] Winter v News Scotland Ltd
1991 SLT 828

Female prison officer said to have had sex with prison inmate and thereafter continued affair with him. Adverse publicity and disciplinary proceedings. Associated depression and change in personality.

Award: £50,000

[3] Barry v News Group Newspapers Ltd
Lord Nimmo Smith and jury, 18 December 1999

Circumstances similar to conjoined action in *Clinton* above but there was evidence that the pursuer had had a previous sexual relationship with another woman.

Award: £45,000

[4] McCormick v Scottish Daily Record & Sunday Mail Ltd
Lord Menzies and jury, 19 January 2006

The pursuer was a solicitor who had acted on behalf of a religious order implicated in historical child abuse at a residential school in the 1960s and 1970s. He raised an action in respect of an article published in a newspaper following on the conviction of three men for sexual and physical abuse at the school. The jury rejected the newspapers' defence of fair comment and accepted that the article had defamed the solicitor by representing:

(a) that he had engaged in or was implicated in a "cover-up";
(b) that he had smeared witnesses who gave evidence at the criminal trial;
(c) that he had engaged in or was implicated in the said cover-up and smeared the witnesses because he was the son of a former governor at the school; and
(d) that he, in his capacity as a solicitor, had acted in a discreditable and dishonourable manner.

Award: £45,000 (all to past)

Index